JOHN TOLAND'S

Christianity not Mysterious

Johannes Toland
Hibernus

JOHN TOLAND'S
Christianity not Mysterious

text, associated works and critical essays

PHILIP MCGUINNESS
ALAN HARRISON
RICHARD KEARNEY
editors

THE LILLIPUT PRESS
MCMXCVII

First published in 1997 by
THE LILLIPUT PRESS LTD
62–63 Sitric Road, Arbour Hill,
Dublin 7, Ireland.

A CIP record for this
title is available from
The British Library.

ISBN 1 874675 97 X (cased)
ISBN 1 874675 95 3 (paper)

*The Lilliput Press receives financial assistance from
An Chomhairle Ealaíon/The Arts Council of Ireland.*

Set in 10 on 13.5 Goudy
with Univers display titles
Book design by mermaid turbulence
Cover design by djeribi + lucey
Printed in Dublin by ßetaprint of Clonshaugh

Contents

Preface

As Yugoslavia began its short spiral down to savagery in the early 1990s, the Yugoslav state media agency summarized the situation thus: 'The Balkans produce more history than they can consume.' Substitute Ireland for Balkans and the statement would still have the ring of truth about it. Perhaps, though, one can suggest that it is myth rather than history that is consumable. Simplifications and distortions of history are essential requisites of the belief systems of any nation, in Ireland and Britain as much as elsewhere. The need to believe untruths about one's neighbour is a sad yet significant part of political life on both islands. Thus personalities whose lives illuminate the complexity of the past are often relegated to obscurity. One such person is John Toland, who was at different times – perhaps even at the same time! – of his life a Catholic, Protestant, Dissenter, Freethinker, Republican, Monarchist, Irish and British.

This volume contains John Toland's most famous book, *Christianity not Mysterious*. It is a scintillating deconstruction of mystery in religion and a stylish pæan to reason. However, the book's appearance caused an anti-intellectual conflagration in both islands. In Britain and mainland Europe it was seen as religiously subversive, being the first major shot in the Deist controversy. In Ireland, this aspect of the book's infamy was eclipsed by its political implications. In the Preface Toland states that 'A wise and good Man ... knows no Difference between Popish Infallibility, and being oblig'd blindly to acquiesce in the Decisions of fallible Protestants.' To impute fallibility to the post-1690 Protestant élite was to destroy the moral foundation for Penal Law rule over both Catholics and Presbyterians. Thus did Toland, the zealous Protestant convert, become regarded as a Jesuit in disguise. When he put his name to the second edition he was forced to leave Ireland on pain of arrest, with his book being burned by the common hangman on the order of the Irish House of Commons. Perhaps as a result of this furious response, Toland abandoned plans for two additional volumes on Christianity and mystery, to which he refers several times in *Christianity not Mysterious* and in the apologias.

A flurry of books and pamphlets was directed against *Christianity not Mysterious*, and Toland replied to these. The second edition of *Christianity not Mysterious* included several changes to the first edition text. (We have added these here as footnotes to enable both editions to be read together; thanks are due to Gunter Gawlick, whose work on the differences between the two forms the basis of our notes.) In 1697 Toland published *An Apology for Mr. Toland*, which was a direct narrative of and reply to the book-burning episode. *A Defence of Mr. Toland* also appeared in 1697. This unsigned pamphlet is traditionally attributed to Toland. In 1702 Toland published *Vindicius Liberius* in order to defend himself and *Christianity not Mysterious* against the lower house of Convocation (synod of Anglican clergy). *Vindicius Liberius* is no mere ego-ridden *apologia*. It is a clear and vibrant illumination of Toland's support for the Glorious Revolution of 1688. We as editors felt that *Christianity not Mysterious* needed to be republished along with the three justificatory books. We believe that this is the first time that any of John Toland's books has been reprinted in total in his native Ireland.[1]

Textual changes have been minimal. The 'long s' has been replaced by its more familiar modern equivalent. All italicization and use of upper-case type has been preserved here. Words—such as 'knowlege/ knowledg' or 'shou'd/should'—are sometimes spelt differently *within* the texts; no attempt has been made to standardize spelling. Any glaring spelling errors have been 'corrected' to the spelling of the time: for example 'jndgment' is changed in our text to 'judgment'. Toland uses quotations in two different ways. Some quotations are in italics and were not indented in the original text: they have been reproduced faithfully. For non-italicized quotations in the original books, a single quotation mark appears at the start of each line of the quotation. We have indented such quotations in our volume. When Toland uses dialogue (Section 3, paragraph 35 of *Christianity not Mysterious*), it is treated as a normal piece of text by him, with, typically, one speaker's words beginning mid-line. We have added indentations for ease of reading.

Original notes on the text were in two forms: sidenotes and footnotes. The vast majority of such notes are either the Biblical source for a particular quotation (sidenotes), the original Greek version of a word (sidenotes), or the original Greek or Latin version of a quotation (footnotes). It was felt that having these as footnotes in this volume would be of limited elucidatory value today. In consequence we have placed them in endnotes. Our heartfelt thanks go to Prof. Fred Williams of Queen's University, Belfast, for his superb work on the Greek passages quoted by Toland.

We have added endnotes to explain many of the references to people, places, Christian doctrines and events in Toland's texts. In *Christianity not Mysterious*, the vast majority of these endnotes relate to the early Christian era. By contrast, the later three apologias were much more concerned with justifying Toland's writings against leading churchmen of the day. We hope that our endnotes help to explain both the nature and context of early Christianity and contemporary events and personalities in the political and religious world of the Williamite Settlement. These endnotes are enclosed in square brackets to distinguish them from both Toland's own footnotes and endnotes and from the footnotes giving the variants from the second edition of *Christianity not Mysterious*.

The editors and contributors believe strongly that John Toland has been sadly neglected, owing to the ravages of time and ideology in both Ireland and Britain. In mainland Europe his reputation is more secure, especially in France and Italy. Toland was the first 'Freethinker', and arguably the first 'Brit' (in all likelihood he invented the terms 'West, North and South Britain' for Ireland, Scotland and England, respectively, and was one of those who carried the Act of Succession to the House of Hanover). The essays in this volume explore various hues of the brightly coloured tapestry of Toland's life and *oeuvre*. Richard Kearney and David Berman offer biographical accounts of Toland. Philip McGuinness's first essay situates *Christianity not Mysterious* in the context of the early Enlightenment and evaluates Toland's influence on that great journey of the intellect. Alan Harrison charts the influence of Toland on Celtic Studies. John Toland is frequently secular radical and sectarian conservative at the same time and Philip McGuinness examines these paradoxical aspects of his legacy to Irish politics. Much of Toland's writing touches on the difficulty in believing something that one's reason cannot accept; Desmond Clarke's essay illustrates the continuing relevance of John Toland to such questions today. Toland invented the word 'pantheist' (though not 'pantheism'); Stephen Daniel looks at hitherto neglected aspects of Toland's pantheistic ideas. Finally,

Philip McGuinness's third essay interrogates the influence of Toland's pantheism on Isaac Newton's scientific achievements, and on the political views of Newton's followers.

It is hoped that this book will find an audience, not just among those interested in religious doctrinal controversy, but on people who are interested in the complex tangle of religion and politics both yesterday and today. John Toland had a rare capacity to draw out controversy by his style of writing and conversation. As an Irish-born Catholic who reinvented himself as a loyal Protestant and propagandist for the creation of Britain-as-political-entity, Toland crossed many political, religious and cultural barriers in his lifetime. Today, many of the long-cherished mainstays of our mental maps are being irrevocably altered. In the UK, the status of the Protestant Monarchy is keenly debated, and even the breakup of the UK is conceivable in the foreseeable future. In Ireland, irridentist Catholicism is slowly but surely being uncoupled from the southern body politic. These developments will ultimately transform the sectarian abyss in Northern Ireland. Depending on one's viewpoint, Europe promises or threatens to play a significantly greater role in our sense of identity. A deeper understanding of past religious and political tensions must surely help us to avoid future follies. The legacy of John Toland, philosopher of change, is that his life and times shed a welcome light on the origins and nature of many of our treasured identities on these islands. We need all the help we can get.

1   In 1737 Francis Hutcheson and Wiliam Bruce republished – in Dublin – Toland's 1700 edition of James Harrington's political writings, which included Harrington's *Oceana*. The *History of the Druids* appeared with a Dublin imprint on the title-page in 1815, but it seems that this is just an edition of the 1814 Edinburgh imprint prepared for the Irish market. *The Field Day Anthology of Irish Writing* (1991) has some extracts from *Christianity not Mysterious*, and from the *History of the Druids* (1726 [posthumously]). Since 1995 *The Humanist* – magazine of the Ulster Humanist Association – has published extracts from Toland's *Letters to Serena*.

Acknowledgments

ALAN HARRISON wishes to thank his colleagues, friends and family for their help and support during the preparation of this book.

RICHARD KEARNEY wishes to thank Professor Luke Gibbons (Dublin City University) and Dr Andrew Carpenter (Dept of English, University College Dublin) for their help.

PHILIP MCGUINNESS is deeply indebted to the following persons for their help, insights and enthusiasm while this volume was coming together. Professor Fred Williams (Dept of Greek, Queen's University, Belfast) did magnificent work on the *Christianity not Mysterious* footnotes in Greek and Latin. Dr Tommy Graham, Rod Eley and Dr Hiram Morgan at *History Ireland* published a shortened version of the last essay in this volume, on Toland and Newton; their advice was gratefully received. Rogelio Alonso drove me out to Ballycarry Graveyard, and his comments over the duration of this project were a great help. Thanks to the following who freely gave me information about the Irish Franciscan College at Prague: the Irish Franciscan headquarters at Killiney, Co. Dublin; Hiram Morgan; Jana Vejdovská (Prazská Informancní Sluzba); Claudia Carrington (Ceské Centrum, London); and Karel Melzmuf (British Council, Prague). As well as minding my two children, Aranka Komurkova translated much of the information sent to me by the above. I am doubly indebted to her. My thanks are also due to Paddy Close of the John Hewitt International Summer School committee, and to the Community Relations Group for a bursary enabling me to attend the 1996 summer school. Dr Ian Williams and Dr Ian Hughes (Dept of Pure and Applied Physics, QUB) made valuable comments about my essay on Toland and Newton. Professor Rhoda Rappaport (Dept of History, Vassar College) kindly lent me a sneak preview of an essay on

ACKNOWLEDGMENTS

Toland that appeared in the *Journal of the History of Ideas*, April 1997. Dr
Dele Layiwola (Queen's University at Armagh) went way beyond the call of
duty in advising me about a paper I gave on John Toland at the 'Beyond the
Margins: Ireland and Post-Colonialism' conference in Armagh in September
1996. I am grateful to the following who supplied information about
Inishowen and the Tolands still resident on the peninsula: Mary
McLoughlin (*Derry Journal*); Paddy Harte, TD; Dr Jim McDaid, TD; Jim
Harkin (Clonmany); Jim Toland (Manchester); and Maura Craig (Central
Library, Londonderry). Lydia Ferguson and Vincent Kinane of the Early
Printed Books section of Trinity College Library, Dublin, were helpful to me.
Darryl Smith (Ernest Larner and Sons), Rev. Dr Jonathan Draper (St Mary's
with All Saints, Putney), the Greater London Records Office and Linda
Bowyer (Co-Op Retail [Funeral] Services, Kingston-on-Thames) all con-
tributed information about John Toland's final resting place in Putney. My
thanks are also due to the following for help great and small: Mr Michael
Mann (School of Oriental and African Studies, London); Dr Gilbert Ansre
(University of Leiden); Dr John Lewis (Dept of French, QUB); Professor
David Hayton and Gloria Rickard (Dept of Modern History, QUB);
Catherine Donnelly and Ruth Walmsley; Mirentxu Cayuela and Mara
Ianelli; Andreas Platzer; and Nicholas Whyte.

At this point, it is normal – and perhaps obligatory – to mention 'the support of my wife, without whom ...'. However, the four works by Toland in
this volume would not have been retyped had Noeleen, Hugh and Ailsa not
been out of Ireland! Having said that, the support and encouragement that
Noeleen gave me—whether on the phone or at weekends in Ayrshire—cannot be adequately gauged. Quite simply, this book belongs to Noeleen as
much as to the three co-editors. It is dedicated to her.

Christianity not Mysterious :

OR, A

TREATISE

Shewing,

That there is nothing in the

GOSPEL

Contrary to

REASON,

Nor ABOVE it :

And that no Christian Doctrine
can be properly call'd

A MYSTERY.

---

*We need not desire a better Evidence that any Man is in the
wrong, than to hear him declare against Reason, and thereby
acknowledg that Reason is against him.* ABp Tillotson.

London, Printed in the Year 1696

Contents

The Preface

I Believe all Men will readily allow that none should speak with more Freedom and Assurance than he that defends or illustrates the Truth. But if we credit the History of former Time, or duly consider what passes in the present, we shall find none more backward to speak their Minds in publick than such as have Right on their side. Indeed the Goodness of their Cause and Design should fortify 'em, one would think, against all the Attacks of their Enemies: Nor are there wanting frequent Examples of Persons, who with unshaken Constancy suffer'd the most disgraceful and violent things for love of the Truth. Yet if we make a just Computation, and take in the Primitive Martyrs with the Prophets and Apostles themselves, the profess'd Defenders of Truth, only for Truth's sake, will be found to be a small handful with respect to the numerous Partizans of Error.

And such is the deplorable Condition of our Age, that a Man dares not openly and directly own what he thinks of Divine Matters, tho it be never so true and beneficial, if it but very slightly differs from what is receiv'd by any Party, or that is establish'd by Law; but he is either forc'd to keep perpetual Silence, or to propose his Sentiments to the World by way of Paradox under a borrow'd or fictitious Name. To mention the least part of the Inconveniences they expose themselves to, who have the Courage to act more above-board, is too melancholy a Theme, and visible enough to be lamented by all that are truly generous and vertuous.

The Pravity of most Mens Dispositions, and the Ambition of particular Persons makes this Matter seem less strange in Politick and Secular Affairs; and yet a Man may not only make new Discoveries and

Improvements in Law or Physick, and in the other Arts and Sciences impunibly, but also for so doing be deservedly encourag'd and rewarded. But wonderful! That the sacred Name of Religion which sounds nothing but Sanctity, Peace and Integrity, should be so universally abus'd to patronize Ambition, Impiety and Contention! And that what is our highest Interest perfectly to understand, should (for Reasons afterwards to be laid open) both be maintain'd to be obscure, and very industriously made so! Nay, it is come to this, that Truth meets no where with stronger Opposition, than from many of those that raise the loudest Cry about it, and would be taken for no less than the only Dispensers of the Favours and Oracles of Heaven. If any has the Firmness to touch the minutest thing that brings them Gain or Credit, he's presently pursu'd with the Hue and Cry of Heresy: And, if he values their Censures, compell'd to make honourable Amends; or if he proves contumacious, he falls a Sacrifice, at least in his Reputation, to their implacable Hatred.

Nor is he like, we may be sure, to receive fairer Quarter from the declar'd Antagonists of Religion, whose Principles, as they trample upon all Equity and Truth, so they oblige 'em to bate and molest the strenuous Assertors of these and all other Vertues. But of such depressing Considerations enough! Notwithstanding which, I have ventur'd to publish this Discourse, designing thereby to rectify, as much as I'm able, the narrow bigotted Tenets of the One, and the most impious Maxims of the Other.

No Athiest or Infidel of any kind can justly be angry with me for measuring Swords with them, and attacking them only with the Weapons they prescribe me. The true Christian can no more be offended when he finds me imploy Reason, not to enervate or perplex, but to confirm and elucidate Revelation; unless he is apprehensive I should render it too clear to my self, or too familiar to others, which are Absurdities no Body will own. I hope to make it appear, that the Use of Reason is not so dangerous in Religion as it is commonly represented, and that too by such as mightily extol it when it seems to favour 'em, yet vouchsafe it not a hearing when it makes against them, but oppose its own Authority to it self. These are high Privileges indeed, and the surest Means of having always the better of the Dispute that could possibly be devis'd.

That the mistaken Unbeliever may not say I serve a Hypothesis in the Defense of my Faith, like some who first imagine or receive an Opinion,

6

and then study Proofs to establish it, I solemnly declare the thing is much otherwise; and that I hold nothing as an Article of my Religion, but what the highest Evidence forc'd me to embrace. For being educated, from my Cradle, in the grossest Superstition and Idolatry, God was pleas'd to make my own Reason, and such as made use of theirs, the happy Instruments of my Conversion. Thus I have been very early accustom'd to Examination and Enquiry, and taught not to captivate my Understanding no more than my Senses to any Man or Society whatsoever. Now the best Method, I think, of communicating to others the Truth, is that by which a Man has learnt it himself.

That the well-meaning Christian may not suspect, as it falls out very ordinarily, that I aim at more than I declare, and cunningly disguise some bad Principles under the fair Pretence of defending the true Religion; I assure him that I write with all the Sincerity and Simplicity imaginable, being as thoroughly convinc'd of what I maintain, as I can be of any thing. If any good Man should after this Protestation persist to think hard of me, it must needs proceed from violent Prepossesions: for very few can be found that are not deeply engag'd in some of one sort or another, for which a due Allowance must be made. How fond are we all apt to be of what we learn'd in our Youth, as the Sight or Remembrance of the Places where we past that agreeable Time, does strangely affect us! A Mother is more charm'd with the lisping half-form'd Words of her pratling Infant, than with the best Language and most solid Discourses. That any Upstart, but of Yesterday, should pretend to overthrow what cost the Antients so much Time and Breath to establish, and themselves so great Pains and Charges to learn, is of hard Digestion to some. And when others are but pray'd to explain their Terms, which commonly signify nothing, or what they must be asham'd to own that would never be thought in an Error, they are uneasy, as an extravagant Merchant to examine his Accompts; and 'tis well if they can restrain their Passions. Not only a few Men, but oftentimes whole Societies, whilst they consider Things but very superficially, set such a Value upon certain Sounds, as if they were the real Essence of all Religion. To question or reject any of these, tho never so false and inconvenient, is dangerous Heterodoxy: And yet, as I hinted now, they either signify nothing, or have been invented by some leading Men to make plain things obscure, and not seldom to cover their own Ignorance. What is *unpardonable, the holy Scripture is put to the Torture to countenance this Scholastick Jargon, and all the metaphysical Chimeras of its Authors. But the Weakness of the greatest part of these Prejudices is so notorious, that to mention them is sufficient Confutation: Nor shall I be otherwise mov'd with any thing of this Nature, than a prudent Man would be at the Declamations of such as have Recourse to Railing when Reason fails them.*

As for those Gentlemen who suggest that the Credulity of Popery has frighted me to an unwarrantable Distance from it; I have nothing to say for their Satisfaction, but that I don't envy them the cheap and commodious Mean they boast of, while I think Truth and Error to be the two Extreams. Religion is not to be modell'd according to our Fancies, nor to be judg'd of as it relates to our private Designs; else there would be full as many Creeds as Persons: But how little soever our Notions agree, and let our worldly Conveniences be what they will, Religion is always the same, like God its Author, with whom there is no Variableness, nor Shadow of changing.

If any should ask me whether I have so good an Opinion of my own Abilities as to imagine that I can prove a rational Account may be given of all those jarring Doctrines, ambiguous Terms, and puzling Distinctions which have for so many Centuries sufficiently exercis'd the Learned of all sorts: I answer, that I don't pretend (as the Title-Page can testify) that we are able to explain the Terms or Doctrines of this or that Age, Council or Nation (most of which are impervious Mysteries with a witness), but the Terms and Doctrines of the Gospel. They are not the Articles of the East or West, Orthodox or Arian[1], Protestant or Papist, consider'd as such, that I trouble my self about, but those of Jesus Christ and his Apostles. And in managing this Argument with every other good Action, I don't merely rely upon my own poor Attainments, but also upon the Grace of God, who, I hope, will enable me to vindicate his reveal'd Will from the most unjust Imputations of Contradiction and Obscurity.

I may probably differ in many things from Persons deservedly eminent for their Learning and Piety; but that ought to be no Advantage against me if Truth is evidently for me. Since Religion is calculated for reasonable Creatures, 'tis Conviction and not Authority that should bear Weight with them. A wise and good Man will judg of the Merits of a Cause consider'd only in it self, without any regard to Times, Places or Persons. No Numbers, no Examples, no Interests can ever bias his solid Judgment, or corrupt his Integrity. He knows no Difference between Popish Infallibility, and being oblig'd blindly to acquiesce in the Decisions of fallible Protestants. And for my own part, as I would have none by false or unfair Consequences make me say what I never thought of; so I would not be told I contradict any thing but Scripture or Reason, which, I'm sure, agree very well together. Nor can it appear strange that I should insist upon these Terms, since I most readily submit my self to them, and give all the World the same Right over me. I am not therefore to be put out of Countenance by venerable Names, and pompous Citations, that have no Value but such as an ugly Rust and Colour give antient Coins. God alone, and such as are inspir'd by him, can prescribe Injunctions relating to the World to come, whilst humane Powers regulate the Affairs of this. Now, to speak more particularly concerning the following Performance, I don't expect any Deference should be paid me by the World, that spares no body; much less am I desirous of Abettors out of Singularity: but rather if the Reasons I offer be not cogent, I shall take in good part a modest and pertinent Animadversion. And if I am not so happy in rendring things perspicuous to others, as they seem to my self, yet I have fairly aim'd at it, and spoke what I think to be Truth without Fear or Favour; wherefore my good Intentions will need no other Apology.

Some Passages in the first Section, or preliminary Dissertation of Reason,* may prove somewhat obscure to ordinary Readers. They were not indeed intended for them, nor are they of necessary Consequence to any that will reason fairly; but they were inserted, to prevent the foreseen Wranglings of certain Men, who study more to protract and perplex than to terminate a Controversy: and a little Application of Thought will render them as familiar as the rest. Every where else I have endeavour'd** to

---

*   [This paragraph begins as follows in the second edition:]
      Some Passages in the first Section or preliminary Dissertation of Reason, which, in
      the former Edition, I suspected would prove a little obscure to ordinary Readers,
      are now render'd more familiar. And tho I then declar'd that the understanding of
      those Passages was of no Consequence to any that would reason fairly, being only
      interested to prevent the foreseen Wranglings of certain Men, who study rather to
      protract and perplex than to terminate a Controversy; yet I could not but readily
      comply at this time with the Desires of those, who wish'd 'em more clearly
      express'd, tho it should cost me a few Words more, whereof I shall always be as
      sparing as I can. I have likewise endeavour'd ...
**   [End of amendment to the second edition.]

speak very intelligibly, and am not without Hope that my Assertions do carry their own Light along with them. I have in many Places made explanatory Repetitions of difficult Words, by synonymous Terms of more general and known Use. This Labour, I grant, is of no benefit to Philosophers, but it is of considerable Advantage to the Vulgar, which I'm far from neglecting, like those who in every Preface tell us they neither court nor care for them. I wonder how any can speak at this rate, especially of those whose very Business it is to serve the Vulgar, and spare them the Labour of long and painful Study, which their ordinary Occupations will not allow them. Lay-men pay for the Books and Maintenance of Church-men for this very end: but I'm afraid some of the latter will no more believe this, than that Magistrates too are made for the People.

Nor can any from this Office of the Clergy infer, that the Vulgar are implicitly to receive their Arbitrary Dictates, no more than I am to make over my Reason to him I employ to read, transcribe, or collect for me. The Learned will not, contrary to the Experience of their own Taste, take the Brewer's or the Baker's Word for the Goodness of Bread or Drink, tho ignorant of their Craft. And why may not the Vulgar likewise be Judges of the true Sense of Things, tho they understand nothing of the Tongues from whence they are translated for their Use? Truth is always and every where the same; And an unintelligible or absurd Proposition is to be never the more respected for being antient or strange, for being originally written in Latin, Greek or Hebrew. Besides, a Divinity only intelligible to such as live by it, is, in humane Language, a Trade; and I see not how they can be angry at the Name, that are so passionately in love with the Thing. But of this in due Place.

The Poor, who are not suppos'd to understand Philosophical Systems, soon apprehended the Difference between the plain convincing Instructions of Christ, and the intricate ineffectual Declamations of the Scribes. For the Jewish Rabbies, divided at that time into Stoik, Platonick, and Pythagorean Sects, &c. did, by a mad Liberty of Allegory, accomodate the Scriptures to the wild Speculations of their several Masters. They made the People, who comprehended nothing of their Cabalistick Observations, believe 'em to be all profound Mysteries: and so taught 'em Subjection to Heathenish Rites, whilst they set the Law of God at nought by their Traditions. No wonder then if the disinterested common sort, and the more ingenuous among the Rulers, did reject these nonsensical Superstitions, tho impudently father'd upon Moses, for a Religion suted to the Capacities of all, delineated, and foretold by their own Prophets.

I wish no Application of this could be made, in the following Discourse, to the Case of any Christians; much less to the purer and better sort. Whoever considers with what Eagerness and Rigour some Men press Obedience to their own Constitutions and Discipline (conniving in the mean while at all Nonconformity to the Divine Law), how strictly they enjoin the Observation of unreasonable unscriptural Ceremonies, and the Belief of those unfathomable Explanations of what they stifly hold themselves to be incomprehensible; I say, who considers all this, is vehemently tempted to suspect they drive a more selfish Design than that of instructing the Ignorant, or converting the Sinner. That any should be hated, despis'd, and molested; nay, sometimes be charitably burn'd and damn'd, for rejecting those Fooleries superadded, and in many Cases substituted to the most blessed, pure and practicable Religion that Men could wish or enjoy, is Matter of Astonishment and Grief to such as prefer the Precepts of God to the Inventions of Men, the plain Paths of Reason to the insuperable Labyrinths of the Fathers, and true Christian Liberty to Diabolical and Antichristian Tyranny.

But the common Method of teaching and supporting this Mystery of Iniquity is still more intolerable. How many voluminous Systems, infinitely more difficult than the Scripture, must be read with great Attention by him that would be Master of the present Theology? What a prodigous Number of barbarous Words (mysterious no doubt), what tedious and immethodical Directions, what ridiculous and discrepant Interpretations must you patiently learn and observe, before you can begin to understand a Professor of that Faculty? The last and easiest part of your Labour will be, to find his Sentiments in the Bible, tho the holy Pen-Men never thought of them, and you never read that sacred Book since you were a School-Boy. But a Distrust of your own Reason, a blind Veneration for those that liv'd before you, and a firm Resolution of adhering to all the Expositions of your Party, will do any thing. Believe only, as a sure Foundation for all your Allegories, that the Words of Scripture, tho never so equivocal and ambiguous without the Context, may signify every where whatever they can signify: And, if this be not enough, believe that every

Truth is a true Sense of every Passage of Scripture; that is, that any thing may be made of every thing: And you'll not only find all the New Testament in the Old, and all the Old in the New; but, I promise you, there's no Explication, tho never so violent, tho never so contradictory or perplex'd, but you may as easily establish as admit.

But I will not repeat what I have expressly written of this Matter in an Epistolary Dissertation, now lying by me, entitul'd, Systems of Divinity exploded. *In the following Discourse, which is the first of three, and wherein I prove my Subject in general, the Divinity of the New Testament is taken for granted; so that it regards only Christians immediately, and others but remotely, who are pray'd to weigh my Arguments by the said Supposition. In the next Discourse, equally concerning Christians and others, I attempt a particular and rational Explanation of the reputed Mysteries of the Gospel. And in the third, I demonstrate the Verity of Divine Revelation against Atheists and all Enemies of reveal'd Religion.*

This seems to me to be the best Method; for the Order of Nature is in your Systems of Divinity quite inverted. They prove the Authority and Perfection, before they teach the Contents of Scripture; whereas the first is in great measure known by the last. How can any be sure that the Scripture contains all things necessary to Salvation, till he first reads it over? Nay, how can he conclude it to be Scripture, or the Word of God, till he exactly studies it, to speak now of no other Means he must use? This Confusion then I have carefully avoided; for I prove first, that the true Religion must necessarily be reasonable and intelligible. Next I shew, that these requisite Conditions are found in Christianity. But seeing a Man of good Parts and Knowledg may easily frame a clear and coherent System, I demonstrate, Thirdly, that the Christian Religion was not form'd after such a manner, but was divinely reveal'd from Heaven. These three Subjects I handle in as many Books; whereof, as I said before, the following Discourse *is the first.*

Before I finish, I must take notice of those Gentlemen who love to call Names in Religion: for what are all Party-Distinctions, but, according to them, so many sorts of Hereticks, or Schismaticks, or worse? But I assure them, that I am neither of Paul, *nor of* Cephas[2], *nor of* Apollos[3], *but of the Lord Jesus Christ, who alone is the Author and Finisher of my Faith. I have as much Right to have others call'd after my Name, as they* *to give me a Denomination, and that is no Right at all. I say not this to prevent being invidiously represented, according to a very common Artifice, under the Notion of any Sect in the World that is justly or unjustly hated by others. This would be a poor Consideration indeed! but it is my settl'd Judgment, that the thing is unlawful in it self to a good Christian. Leaving others nevertheless their Liberty in this Point, it must, at least, be granted inconvenient: for if you go under the Name of a Lutheran, for instance, tho you agree with those of your Communion but in the main Articles, yet their Adversaries will not fail upon occasion to charge you with those other Matters wherein you dissent: And should you then declare your Judgment, the rest of the Lutherans will not only be much offended, but be apt also to call your Sincerity in question about every thing besides. The only religious Title therefore that I shall ever own, for my part, is that most glorious one of being a* Christian.*

---

*   [The following is added to the Preface in the second edition:]

A Word or two more I must add in answer to the Malice or Mistake of some, who will needs have it that I'm a declar'd Enemy to all Church-men, and consequently (say they) to all Religion, because I make 'em the sole Contrivers of those inconceivable or mysterious Doctrines, which I also maintain are as advantageous to themselves, as they are prejudicial to the Laity. Indeed there are those, who, easily overlooking all Contempt to the true Religion, are very ready to treat 'em as pernicious Heretics, or unsufferable Atheists, that shew the least Dislike of what are acknowledg'd Additions to Christianity, whatever Convenience or Necessity may be pretended for their Establishment. If any such understand by Religion the mysterious Part of it, then truly it will be no hard matter to prove me as little favourable to this Religion, as I'm far from making any Apologies for my self to the Professors of it.

As for charging Church-men with being the Authors and Introducers of the Christian Mysteries, they must be my Enemies for telling the Truth, who are displeas'd at it: for there is no matter of Fact more evident from every Page both of the Civil, and Ecclesiastick Histories. Nor had the Laity ever any hand in that Business, otherwise than as confirming by Legal Sanctions what they were first perswaded to by the preaching of their Priests; as they do now sometimes, at their Sollicitation, imprison excommunicated, and prosecute erroneous Persons, after the Excommunication is first pronounc'd, and the Heresy decreed or declar'd by the Clergy. Now as all Church-men are not in their Opinions for these Practices, so I see no better Reason they have to be angry with any Body for writing against them that are, than a good Prince can pretend for punishing the Historian of a Tyrant's Vices, only because the Tyrant had been likewise a Prince.

To all corrupt Clergy-men therefore, who make a meer Trade of Religion, and build an unjust Authority upon the abus'd Consciences of the Laity, I'm a profest Adversary; as I hope every good and wise Man already is, or will be. But as I shall always remain a hearty Friend to pure and genuine Religion, so I shall preserve the highest Veneration for the sincere Teachers thereof, than whom there is not a more useful Order of Men and without whom there could not be any happy Society or well constituted Government in this World, to speak nothing of their Relation to the World to come, nor of the double Esteem they deserve for keeping Proof against the general Infection of their Profession. But I have no Apprehensions from the sincere; and if the designing Party discover their Concern by their Displeasure, it may well serve for a Mark to distinguish them, but will not be thought an Injury by me.

The State of the Question

There is nothing that Men make a greater Noise about, in our Time [1] especially, than what they generally profess least of all to understand. It may be easily concluded, I mean *the Mysteries of the Christian Religion*. The *Divines*, whose peculiar Province it is to explain them to others, almost unanimously own their Ignorance concerning them. They gravely tell us *we must adore what we cannot comprehend*: And yet some of 'em press their dubious Comments upon the Rest of Mankind with more Assurance and Heat, than could be tolerably justify'd, tho' we should grant them to be absolutely infallible. The worst on't is, they are not all of a Mind. If you be *Orthodox* to those, you are a *Heretick* to these. He that sides with a Party is adjudg'd to Hell by the Rest; and if he declares for none, he receives no milder Sentence from all.

Some of 'em say the *Mysteries of the Gospel* are to be understood only [2] in the Sense of the *Antient Fathers*. But that is so multifarious, and inconsistent with it self, as to make it impossible for any Body to believe so many Contradictions at once. They themselves did caution their Readers from leaning upon their Authority, without the Evidence of *Reason*: And thought as little of becoming a Rule of Faith to their Posterity, as we do to ours. Moreover, as all the *Fathers* were not Authors, so we cannot properly be said to have their genuine Sense. The Works of those that have written are wonderfully corrupted and adulterated, or not entirely extant: And if they were, their Meaning is much more obscure, and subject to Controversy, than that of the *Scripture*.

15

[3]   Others tell us we must be of the Mind of some *particular* Doctors[4], pronounc'd Orthodox by the Authority of the *Church*. But as we are not a whit satisfy'd with any Authority of that Nature, so we see these same *particular Doctors* could no more agree than the whole Herd of the *Fathers*; but tragically declaim'd against one another's Practices and Errors: That they were as injudicious, violent, and factious as other Men: That they were for the greatest part very credulous and superstitious in Religion, as well as pitifully ignorant and superficial in the minutest Punctilios of Literature. In a word, that they were of the same Nature and Make with our selves; and that we know of no Privilege above us bestow'd upon them by Heaven, except Priority of Birth, if that be one, as it's likely few will allow.

[4]   Some give a decisive Voice in the Unravelling of *Mysteries*, and the Interpretation of *Scripture*, to a *General Council*; and others to one Man whom they hold to be the Head of the *Church* universal upon Earth, and the infallible Judg of all Controversies. But we do not think such *Councils* possible, nor (if they were) to be of more Weight than the *Fathers*; for they consist of such, and others as obnoxious altogether to Mistakes and Passions: And besides, we cannot have Recourse, as to a standing Rule, for the Solution of our Difficulties, to a wonder by God's Mercy now more rarely seen than the secular Games of old. As for the *one Judg of all Controversies*, we suppose none but such as are strongly prepossess'd by Interest or Education can in good earnest digest those chimerical supreme Headships and Monsters of Infallibility. We read no where in the *Bible* of such delegate Judges appointed by *Christ* to supply his Office: And *Reason* manifestly proclaims them frontless Usurpers. Nor is their Power finally distinguish'd from that of *Councils* to this Hour, by the miserable Admirers of both.

[5]   They come nearest the thing who affirm, that we are to keep to what the *Scriptures* determine about these Matters: and there is nothing more true, if rightly understood. But ordinarily 'tis an equivocal Way of speaking, and nothing less than the proper Meaning of it is intended by many of those that use it: For they make the *Scriptures* speak either according to some spurious *Philosophy*, or they conform them right or wrong to the bulky Systems and Formularies of their several Communions.

16

Some will have us always believe *what the literal Sense imports*, with [6] little or no Consideration for *Reason*, which they reject as not fit to be employ'd about the reveal'd Part of Religion. Others assert, that we may use *Reason* as the Instrument, but not the Rule of our Belief. The first contend, some *Mysteries* may be, or at least seem to be *contrary to Reason*, and yet be receiv'd by Faith. The second, that no *Mystery* is contrary to *Reason*, but that all are *above* it. Both of 'em from different Principles agree, that several Doctrines of the *New Testament* belong no farther to the Enquiries of *Reason*, than to prove 'em divinely reveal'd, and that they are properly *Mysteries* still.

On the contrary, we hold that *Reason* is the only Foundation of all [7] Certitude; and that nothing reveal'd, whether as to its *Manner* or *Existence*, is more exempted from its Disquisitions, than the ordinary Phenomena of Nature. Wherefore, we likewise maintain, according to the Title of this Discourse, that *there is nothing in the Gospel contrary to Reason, nor above it; and that no Christian Doctrine can be properly called a Mystery.*

SECTION ONE

Of Reason

The State of the Question being thus fairly laid, our next business is [1]
to proceed to the proof thereof. But as the distinct and brief Explanation of the Terms is of indispensable use in discussing all Controversies; so an easy and natural Method is no less pleasing than profitable. It happily falls out that the Terms of the present Question are
dispos'd according to the Order I design to observe; which is, First, to
shew what is meant by *Reason*, and its Properties: Then to prove
there's no Doctrine of the Gospel contrary to *Reason*: After that, to
evince that neither is there any of them above *Reason*; and by consequence, that none is a *Mystery*.

- 1 -

What Reason is not

To begin with the first. It appears to me very odd, that Men should [2] need Definitions and Explanations of that whereby they define and explain all other things: Or that they cannot agree about what they all pretend, in some measure at least, to possess; and is the only Privilege they claim over Brutes and Inanimates. But we find by Experience, that the word *Reason* is become as equivocal and ambiguous as any other; though all that are not tickl'd with the Vanity of Singularity, or Itch of Dispute, are at bottom agreed about the Thing. I'll handle it here with what Brevity I can.

They are mistaken who take the *Soul, abstractedly consider'd,* for [3] *Reason*: For as the general Idea of Gold is not a Guinea, but a piece determin'd to a particular Stamp and Value; so the Soul acting in a certain and peculiar Manner, is *Reason*. They err likewise, who affirm *Reason* to be *that Order and Report which is naturally between all things*: For not this, but the Thoughts which the Soul forms of things according to it, may properly claim that Title. They speed no better, who call *their own Inclinations*, or the *Authority of others*, by that name. But it will better appear what it is from the following Considerations.

Everyone experiences in himself a Power or Faculty of forming [4] various Ideas or Perceptions of Things: Of affirming or denying, according as he sees them to agree or disagree: And so of loving and desiring what seems good unto him; and of hating and avoiding what he thinks evil. The right Use of all these Faculties is what we call

21

JOHN TOLAND

Common Sense, or *Reason* in general. But the bare Act of receiving Ideas into the Mind, whether *by the Intromission of the Senses*, as Colours, Figures, Sounds, Smells, *&c.* or by *the Soul's considering its own Operations about what it thus gets from without*, as Knowing, Doubting, Affirming, Denying, &c. this bare Act, I say, of receiving such Ideas into the Mind, is not strictly *Reason*, because the Soul herein is purely passive. When a proper Object is conveniently presented to the Eye, Ear, or any other Sense rightly dispos'd, it necessarily makes those Impressions which the Mind cannot refuse to lodg,* nor refrain from being conscious of what it does; and so forms the Operations of *Perceiving, Willing, Denying, Suspending the Judgment*, and the like.

---

* [Chapter 1 ends as follows in the second edition:]

... refuse to lodg. And we can find it can as little forbear being conscious of its own Thoughts or Operations concerning this Object: Thus when my Eyes are sound and open, as at this time, I have not only an Idea of the Picture that is before me, but I likewise know, I perceive, and affirm that I see it, I consider it, it pleases me, I wish it were mine. And thus I form, or rather after this manner I have first form'd, the Ideas of *Knowing, Perceiving, Affirming, Denying, Considering, Willing, Desiring*, and the Ideas of all the other Operations of the Mind, which are thus occasion'd by the Antecedent Impressions of sensible Objects.

By the word IDEA which I make so much use of here, and shall more frequently in the following Discourse, I understand *the immediate Object of the Mind when it thinks, or my Thought that the Mind imploys about any thing*, whether such a Thought be the Image or Representation of a Body, as is the Idea of a *Tree*; or whether it be some *Sensation* occasion'd by any Body, such as are the Ideas of *Cold* and *Heat*, of *Smells* and *Tastes*; or whether, lastly, it be a *meerly intellectual or abstracted Thought*, such as are the Ideas of *God* and *created Spirits*, of *Arguing*, of *Suspension*, of *Thinking* in general, or the like.

- 2 -

Wherein Reason consists

But these simple and distinct Ideas, thus laid up in the great Reposi- [5]
tory of the Understanding, are the Sole Matter and Foundation of
all our *Reasoning*: For the Soul does upon occasion compare them
together, compound them into complex Ideas, enlarge, contract, or
separate them, as it discovers their Circumstances capable or not. So
that all our Knowledg is, in effect, nothing else but *the Perception of
the Agreement or Disagreement of our Ideas in a greater or lesser Number, whereinsoever this Agreement or Disagreement may consist.* And
because this Perception is immediate or mediate, our Knowledg is
twofold.

First, *When the Mind, without the Assistance of any other Idea, imme-* [6]
*diately perceives the Agreement or Disagreement of two or more Ideas, as
that Two and Two is Four, that Red is not Blew; it cannot be call'd Reason, though it be the highest Degree of Evidence:* For here's no need of
Discourse or Probation, *Self-evidence* excluding all manner of Doubt
and Darkness. These Propositions so clear of themselves, their Terms
being once understood, are commonly known by the Names of
Axioms and *Maxims*. And it is visible that their Number is indefinite,
and not confin'd only to two or three abstracted Propositions made
from the Observation of particular Instances.*

---

* [In the second edition, the end of this sentence is as follows:]
 … and not confin'd only to two or three abstracted Propositions made (as all
 Axioms are) from the Observation of particular Instances; as, that *the Whole is
 greater than any Part*, that *Nothing can have no Properties.*

[7]　　But, Secondly, *when the Mind cannot immediately perceive the Agreement or Disagreement of any Ideas, because they cannot be brought near enough together, and so compar'd, it applies one or more intermediate Ideas to discover it*: as, when by the successive Application of a Line to two distant Houses, I find how far they agree or disagree in Length, which I could not effect with my Eye. Thus from the Force of the Air, and the Room it takes up, I know it has Solidity and Extension; and that therefore it is as much a Body (though I cannot see it) as Wood, or Stone, with which it agrees in the said Properties.* This Method of Knowledg is properly call'd *Reason* or *Demonstration* (as the former *Self-evidence* or *Intuition*); and it may be defin'd, *That Faculty of the Soul which discovers the Certainty of any thing dubious or obscure, by comparing it with something evidently known.*

[8]　　From this Definition it is plain, that *the intermediate Idea can be no Proof where its Agreement with both the Ideas of the Question is not evident; and that if more than one be necessary to make it appear, the same Evidence is requir'd in each of them.* For if the Connection of all the Parts of a *Demonstration* were not indubitable, we could never be certain of the Inference or Conclusion whereby we join the two Extreams: So that though *Self-evidence* excludes *Reason*, yet all *Demonstration* becomes at length *self-evident*. It is yet plainer, that *when we have no Notions or Ideas of a thing, we cannot reason about it at all; and where we have Ideas, if intermediate ones, to shew their constant and necessary Agreement or Disagreement, fail us, we can never go beyond* Probability.** But besides these Properties of *Reason*, we are

---

*　[This extra text is in the second edition:]
　Here Solidity and Extension are the Line by which I find Air and Body are equal; because Solidity and Extension agree to both. We prove the least imaginable Particle of Matter divisible, by shewing all Bodies to be divisible; because every Particle of Matter is likewise a Body; and after the like manner, is the *Mortality* of all living Bodies inferr'd from their *Divisibility*.

**　[In the second edition, the following text replaces that text in the first edition which follows 'Probability':]
　Tho we have an Idea of inhabited, and an Idea of the *Moon*, yet we have no intermediate Idea to shew such a necessary Connection between them, as to make us certainly conclude that *this Planet is inhabited*, however likely it may seem. Now, *since PROBABILITY is not KNOWLEDG, I banish all HYPOTHESES from my PHILOSOPHY*; because if I admit never so many, yet my Knowledg is not a jot increas'd: for no evident Connection appearing between my Ideas, I may possibly

yet most carefully to distinguish in it the *Means of Information*, from *the Ground of Perswasion*: for the Neglect of this easy Distinction has thrown Men into infinite Mistakes, as I shall prove before I have done.

---

take the wrong side of the Question to be the right, which is equal to knowing nothing of the Matter. When I have arriv'd at *Knowledg*, I enjoy all the Satisfaction that attends it; where I have only *Probability*, there I suspend my Judgment, or, if it be worth the Pains, I search after Certainty.

- 3 -

Of the Means of Information

[9] *The Means of Information* I call *those Ways whereby any thing comes barely to our Knowledg, without necessarily commanding our Assent. By the Ground of Perswasion,* I understand *that Rule by which we judg of all Truth, and which irresistibly convinces the Mind. The Means of Information* are *Experience* and *Authority: Experience* (as you may see N° 4) is either external, which furnishes us with the Ideas of sensible Objects; or internal, which helps us to the Ideas of the Operations of our own Minds. This is the common Stock of all our Knowledg; nor can we possibly have Ideas any other way without new Organs or Faculties.

[10]   *Authority,* abusively so call'd, as if all its Informations were to be receiv'd without Examen, is either *Humane* or *Divine: Humane Authority* is call'd also *Moral Certitude*; as when I believe an intelligible Relation made by my Friend, because I have no Reason to suspect his Veracity, nor he any Interest to deceive me. *Thus all possible Matters of Fact, duly attested by coevous Persons as known to them, and successively related by others of different Times, Nations, or Interests, who could neither be impos'd upon themselves, nor be justly suspected of combining together to deceive others, ought to be receiv'd by us for as certain and indubitable as if we had seen them with our own Eyes, or heard them with our own Ears.* By this means it is, I believe there was such a City as *Carthage,* such a Reformer as *Luther,* and that there is such a Kingdom as *Poland.**

---

*   [The following is added to the second edition:]
    When all these Rules concur in any Matter of Fact, I take it then for *Demonstration,*

The *Authority of God*, or *Divine Revelation*, is the Manifestation of [*11*] Truth by Truth it self, to whom it is impossible to lie: Whereof at large in *Ch.* 2 of the following Section. Nothing in Nature can come to our Knowledg but by some of these four means, *viz. The Experience of the Senses, the Experience of the Mind, Humane* and *Divine Revelation.*

---

which is nothing else but *Irresistible Evidence from proper Proofs*: But when any of these Conditions are wanting, the thing is *uncertain*, or, at best, but *probable*, which, with me, are not very different.

- 4 -

Of the Ground of Perswasion

---

[12] Now, as we are extreamly subject to Deception, we may, without some infallible Rule, often take a questionable Proposition for an *Axiom*, Old Wives Fables for *Moral Certitude*, and Humane Impostures for *Divine Revelation*. This infallible Rule, or Ground of all right Perswasion, is *Evidence*; and it consists in *the exact Conformity of our Ideas or Thoughts with their Objects, or the Things we think upon*. For as we have only Ideas in us, and not the Things themselves, 'tis by those we must form a Judgment of these.

[13]   Ideas therefore being representative Beings, their Evidence naturally consists in the Property they have of truly representing their Objects. Not that I think every Idea has a perfect Pattern to represent, as the Length and Motion in my Mind are like those of the Pen I handle; for some Ideas are but the Result of certain Powers in the Particles of Bodies, to *occasion* particular Sensations in us; as the Sweetness of Sugar and the Cold of Ice, are no more inherent in them than Pain in the Knife that cuts me, or Sickness in the Fruit that surfeits me. But though they have no Existence out of our Imagination, yet the Pleasure, Pain, and other Qualities they excite, shew us the Good or Harm their Subjects may do us; which renders the Knowledg of them as useful as that of the Properties which really exist in the Things themselves. Without the Heat and Light of Fire, what should its Figure and Quantity serve for? And what sets a Price upon Ambergreece, but the Perfume? The Reason then why I believe the Idea of a Rose to be evident, is the true Representation it gives me of that

28

Flower. I know it is true, because the Rose must contain all the Properties which its Idea exhibits, either *really*, as the Bulk and Form, or *occasionally*, as the Colour, Taste, and Smell. And I cannot doubt of this, because the Properties must belong to the exemplary Cause, or to Nothing, or be the Figments of my own Brain: But Nothing can have no Properties; and I cannot make one single Idea at my Pleasure, nor avoid receiving some when Objects work on my Senses: Therefore I conclude the Properties of the Rose are not the Creatures of my Fancy, but belong to the exemplary Cause, that is, the Object.

The Evidence of *the Ideas of the Operations of the Mind*, is infallible [14] as that of our own Being; and if by an Impossibility we should call the latter in question, 'twould but serve to give us the greater Assurance of it: For besides the unavoidable Supposition of our Existence in this very Proposition, *I doubt if I am*; it is clear, that whatever doubts must needs be as much something as what affirms, and this something I call *my self*. Let us now but strictly require this *Evidence* in all the Agreements and Disagreements of our Ideas in things meerly speculative, and as far as we can in Matters of common Practice (for these must of necessity sometimes admit *Probability* to supply the Defect of *Demonstration*); and we may without a lazy Reliance upon *Authority*, or a sceptical *Progress to Infinity*, successfully trace the Truth, and bring it to view the Light from those subterraneous Caverns where it is suppos'd to lie conceal'd. It is impossible for us to err as long as we take *Evidence* for our Guide; and we never mistake, but when we wander from it by abusing our *Liberty*, in denying that of any thing which belongs to it, or attributing to it what we do not see in its Idea. This is the primary and universal Origin of all our *Errors*.

But *God* the wise Creator of all (ever to be nam'd and thought [15] upon with Reverence), who has enabled us to perceive Things, and form Judgments of them, has also endu'd us with the Power *of suspending our Judgments about whatever is uncertain, and of never assenting but to clear Perceptions*. He is so far from putting us upon any Necessity of erring, that as he has thus privileg'd us on the one hand with a Faculty of guarding our selves against Prepossesion or Precipitation, by *placing our Liberty only in what is indifferent, or dubious and obscure*; so he provides on the other hand, that we should discern and embrace the Truth, *by taking it out of our Power to dissent from an evident Proposition*. We must necessarily believe, that *it is impossible the same thing should be and not be at once*: Nor can all the World perswade us to doubt of it. But we need not admit that there's no *Void* in Nature, or that the Earth absolves an annual Course about the Sun, till we get *Demonstrations* to that Effect.

[16]   *Wherefore let us attribute all our false Notions to our own Anticipation and Inattention: Let us confess our *Destruction to be of our selves;*[5] and cheerfully thank our kind Disposer, who has put us under a Law of bowing before the Light and Majesty of *Evidence*. And truly if we might doubt of any thing that is clear, or be deceiv'd by distinct Conceptions, there could be nothing certain: Neither Conscience, nor God himself, should be regarded: No Society or Government could subsist.**

[17]   If it should be asked, why Assent is deny'd to true Propositions, since *Evidence* necessarily requires it? I answer, 'tis *because they are not made evident*: For Perspicuity and Obscurity are relative Terms, and what is either to me may be the quite contrary to another. If Things be deliver'd in Words not understood by the Hearer, nor demonstrated to agree with other Truths already very clear, or now so made to him, he cannot conceive 'em. Likewise if the Order of Nature and due Simplicity be not observ'd, he cannot see them evidently true or false; and so suspends his Judgment (if no Affection sways him) where another, it may be, receives perfect Satisfaction. Hence it is that we frequently, with Indignation and Wonder, attribute that to the Stupidity and Obstinacy of others, which is the fruit of our own confus'd Ratiocination for want of having thoroughly digested our Thoughts; or by affecting ambiguous Expressions, and using such as the other has no Ideas to at all, or different ones from ours.

---

*   [The following is added to the beginning of this paragraph in the second edition:]
   If People precipitate their Assent, either because they find the Search of Truth attended with more Difficulties than they are willing to run through, or because they would not seem to be ignorant of any thing, this is their fault.
   2 Pet. 2.1.

**   [The following is added at the end of the paragraph in the second edition:]
   But it is as true, that if we could not suspend our Assent to dubious or obscure Propositions, Almighty Goodness (which is impossible) should be the real Cause of all our Errors.

SECTION TWO

That the Doctrines of the Gospel are not contrary to Reason

After having said so much of *Reason*, I need not operosely shew what [1]
it is to be contrary to it; for I take it to be very intelligible from the
precedent Section, that *what is evidently repugnant to clear and distinct
Ideas, or to our common Notions, is contrary to Reason*: I go on therefore to prove, that *the Doctrines of the Gospel*, if it be the Word of
God, *cannot be so*. But if it be objected, that very few maintain they
are: I reply, that no *Christian* I know of now (for we shall not disturb
the Ashes of the Dead) expressly says *Reason* and the *Gospel* are contrary to one another. But, which returns to the same, very many
affirm, that though the Doctrines of the latter cannot in themselves
be contradictory to the Principles of the former, as proceeding both
from God; yet, that according to our Conceptions of them, *they may
seem directly to clash*: And that though we cannot reconcile them by
reason of our corrupt and limited Understandings; yet that from the
Authority of *Divine Revelation*, we are bound to believe and acquiesce
in them; or, as the *Fathers* taught 'em to speak, *to adore what we cannot comprehend*.

31

- 1 -

The Absurdities and Effects of admitting any real or seeming Contradictions in Religion

This famous and admirable Doctrine is the undoubted Source of all [2] the *Absurdities* that ever were seriously vented among *Christians*. Without the Pretence of it, we should never hear of the *Transubstantiation*, and other ridiculous Fables of the Church of *Rome*; nor of any of the *Eastern Ordures*, almost all receiv'd into this *Western Sink*: Nor should we be ever banter'd with the *Lutheran Impanation*, or the *Ubiquity* it has produced, as one Monster ordinarily begets another. And tho the *Socinians*[6] disown this Practice, I am mistaken if either they or the *Arians* can make their Notions of a *dignifi'd and Creature-God capable of Divine Worship*, appear more reasonable than the Extravagancies of other Sects touching the Article of the *Trinity*.

In short, this Doctrine is the known Refuge of some Men, when [3] they are at a loss in explaining any Passage of the Word of God. Lest they should appear to others less knowing than they would be thought, they make nothing of fathering that upon the secret Counsels of the Almighty, or the Nature of the Thing, which is indeed the Effect of Inaccurate Reasoning, Unskilfulness in the Tongues, or Ignorance of History. But more commonly it is the Consequence of *early Impressions*, which they dare seldom afterwards correct by more free and riper Thoughts: So *desiring to be Teachers of the Law, and understanding neither what they say, not those things which they affirm,*[7] they obtrude upon us *for Doctrines the Commandments of Men.*[8] And truly well they may; for if we once admit this Principle, I know not what we can deny that is told us in the Name of the Lord. This Doctrine, I must remark it too, does highly concern us of the *Laity*; for however it came to be first establish'd, the *Clergy* (always excepting such as deserve it) have not been since wanting to themselves, but improv'd it so far as not only to make the plainest, but the most trifling things in the World *mysterious*, that we might constantly depend upon them for the Explication. And, nevertheless they must not, if they could, explain them to us without ruining their own Design, let them never so fairly pretend it. But, overlooking all Observations proper for this Place, let us enter upon the immediate Examen of the Opinion it self.

[4]   The first thing I shall insist upon is, that if any Doctrine of the *New Testament* be contrary to Reason, we have no manner of Idea of it. To say, for instance, that *a Ball is white and black at once*, is to say just nothing; for these Colours are so incompatible in the same Subject, as to exclude all Possibility of a real positive Idea or Conception. So to say, as the *Papists,* that *Children dying before Baptism are damn'd without Pain,* signifies nothing at all: For if they be intelligent Creatures in the other World, to be eternally excluded God's Presence, and the Society of the Blessed, must prove ineffable Torment to them: But if they think they have no Understanding, then they are not capable of Damnation in their Sense; and so they should not say they are in *Limbo*-Dungeon; but that either they had no Souls, or were annihilated; which (had it been true, as they can never shew) would be reasonable enough, and easily conceiv'd. Now if we have no Ideas of a thing, it is certainly but lost Labour for us to trouble our selves about it: For what I don't conceive, can no more give me right Notions of God, or influence my Actions, than a Prayer deliver'd in an unknown Tongue can excite my Devotion: *If the Trumpet gives an uncertain Sound, who shall prepare himself to the Battel? And except Words easy to be understood be utter'd, how shall it be known what is spoken?*[9] Syllables, though never so well put together, if they have not Ideas fix'd to them, are but *Words spoken in the Air;*[10] and cannot be the Ground of a *reasonable Service,*[11] or Worship.

[5]   If any should think to evade the Difficulty by saying, that the Ideas of certain Doctrines may be contrary indeed to common Notions, yet consistent with themselves, and I know not what supra-

intellectual Truths, he's but just where he was. But supposing a little that the thing were so; it still follows, that none can understand these Doctrines except their Perceptions be communicated to him in an extraordinary manner, as by new Powers and Organs. And then too, others cannot be edifi'd by what is discours'd of 'em, unless they enjoy the same Favour. So that if I would go preach the Gospel to the *Wild Indians, I must expect the* Ideas of my Words should be, I know not how, infus'd into their Souls in order to apprehend me: And according to this Hypothesis, they could no more, without a Miracle, understand my Speech than the chirping of Birds; and *if they knew not the Meaning of my Voice, I should even to them be a Barbarian,*[12] notwithstanding *I spoke Mysteries in the Spirit.*[13] But what do they mean by consisting with themselves, yet not with our common Notions? *Four* may be call'd *Five* in Heaven; but so the Name only is chang'd, the Thing remains still the same. And since we cannot in this World know any thing but by our common Notions, how shall we be sure of this pretended Consistency between our present seeming Contradictions, and the Theology of the World to come? For as 'tis by *Reason* we arrive at the Certainty of God's own Existence, so we cannot otherwise discern his *Revelations* but by their Conformity with our natural Notices of him, which is in so many words, to agree with our common Notions.

The next thing I shall remark is, That those, who stick not to say [6] *they could believe a downright Contradiction to Reason, did they find it contain'd in the Scripture*, do justify all Absurdities whatsoever; and by opposing one Light to another, undeniably make God the Author of all Incertitude. The very Supposition, that Reason might authorize one thing, and the Spirit of God another, throws us into inevitable *Scepticism*; for we shall be at a perpetual Uncertainty which to obey; Nay, we can never be sure which is which. For the Proof of the Divinity of *Scripture* depending upon Reason, if the clear Light of the one might be any way contradicted, how shall we be convinc'd of the Infallibility of the other? Reason may err in this Point as well as in any thing else; and we have no particular Promise it shall not, no more than the *Papists* that their Senses may not deceive them in every thing as well as in *Transubstantiation.* To say it bears witness to it self, is equally to establish the *Alcoran* or the *Poran*. And 'twere a notable Argument to tell a *Heathen*, that the *Church* has declared it, when all Societies will say as much for themselves, if we take their word for it. Besides, it may be, he would ask whence the *Church* had Authority to decide this Matter? And if it should be answer'd from the *Scripture*, a thousand to one but he would divert himself with this Circle. You must believe that the *Scripture* is Divine, because the *Church* has so determined it, and the *Church* has this deciding Authority from the *Scripture*. 'Tis doubted if this Power of the *Church* can be prov'd from the Passages alledged to that Purpose; but the *Church* it self (a Party concern'd) affirms it. Hey-dey! are not these eternal Rounds very exquisite Inventions to giddy and entangle the Unthinking and the Weak?

[7]   But if we believe the *Scripture* to be Divine, not upon its own bare Assertion, but from a real Testimony consisting in the Evidence of the things contain'd therein; from undoubted Effects, and not from Words and Letters; what is this but to prove it by *Reason?* It has in it self, I grant, the brightest Characters of *Divinity*: But 'tis Reason finds them out, examines them, and by its Principles approves and pronounces them sufficient; which orderly begets in us an Acquiescence of *Faith* or Perswasion. Now if Particulars be thus severly sifted; if not only the Doctrine of *Christ* and his *Apostles* be consider'd, but also their Lives, Predictions, Miracles, and Deaths; surely all this Labour would be in vain, might we upon any account dispense with Contradictions. O! blessed and commodious System, that dischargest at one stroak those troublesome Remarks about History, Language, figurative and literal Senses, Scope of the Writer, Circumstances, and other Helps of Interpretation! We judg of a Man's Wisdom and Learning by his Actions, and his Discourses; but God, who we are assur'd *has not left himself without a Witness*,[14] must have no Privileges above the maddest Enthusiast, or the *Devil* himself, at this rate.

[8]   But a Veneration for the very Words of God will be pretended: This we are pleas'd with; for we know *that God is not a Man that he should lie*.[15] But the Question is not about the Words, but their Sense, which must be always worthy of their Author, and therefore according to the Genius of all Speech, figuratively interpreted, when occa-

36

sion requires it. Otherwise, under pretence of *Faith in the Word of God*, the highest Follies and Blasphemies may be deduc'd from the Letter of *Scripture*; as, that God is subject to Passions, is the Author of Sin, that *Christ* is a Rock, was actually guilty of and defil'd with our Transgressions, that we are Worms or Sheep, and no Men. And if a Figure be admitted in these Passages, why not, I pray, in all Expressions of the like Nature, when there appears an equal Necessity for it?

It may be demanded why I have so long insisted upon this Article, [9] since that none expresly makes *Scripture* and *Reason* contradictory, was acknowledg'd before. But in the same place mention is made of some who hold, *that they may seem directly to clash*; and that though we cannot reconcile them together, yet that we are bound to acquiesce in the Decisions of the former. A seeming Contradiction is to us as good as a real one; and our Respect for the *Scripture* does not require us to grant any such in it, but rather to conclude, that we are ignorant of the right Meaning when a Difficulty occurs; and so to suspend our Judgments concerning it, till with suitable Helps and Industry we discover the Truth. As for acquiescing in what a Man understands not, or cannot reconcile to his Reason, they know the best fruits of it that practise it. For my part, I'm a Stranger to it, and cannot reconcile my self to such a Principle. On the contrary, I am pretty sure he pretends in vain to convince the Judgment, who explains not the Nature of the Thing. A Man may give his verbal Assent to he knows not what, out of Fear, Superstition, Indifference, Interest, and the like feeble and unfair Motives: but as long as he conceives not what he believes, he cannot sincerely acquiesce in it, and remains depriv'd of all solid Satisfaction. He is constantly perplex'd with Scruples not to be remov'd by his *implicite Faith*; and so is ready to be shaken, and *carried away with every wind of Doctrine*.[16] I will believe because I will believe, that is, *because I'm in the Humour so to do*, is the top of his Apology. Such are unreasonable Men, *walking after the Vanity of their Minds, having their Understandings darkned, being Strangers to the Life of God through the Ignorance that is in them, because of the Hardness of their Hearts*.[17] But he that comprehends a thing, is as sure of it as if he were himself the Author. He can never

37

be brought to suspect his Profession; and, if he be honest, will always render a pertinent account of it to others.

[10]   The natural Result of what has been said is, That to believe the Divinity of *Scripture*, or the Sense of any Passage thereof, without rational Proofs, and an evident Consistency, is a blameable Credulity, and a temerarious Opinion, ordinarily grounded upon an ignorant and wilful Disposition; but more generally maintain'd out of a gainful Prospect. For we frequently embrace certain Doctrines not from any convincing Evidence in them, but because they serve our Designs better than the Truth; and because other Contradictions we are not willing to quit, are better defended by their means.

- 2 -

Of the Authority of Revelation,
as it regards this Controversy

Against all that we have been establishing in this Section, *the* [11]
Authority of Revelation will be alledg'd with great shew, as if without a
Right of silencing or extinguishing *Reason*, it were altogether useless
and impertinent. But if the Distinction I made in the precedent Section, N°9, be well consider'd, the Weakness of the present Objection
will quickly appear, and this Controversy be better understood hereafter. There I said *Revelation* was not a necessitating Motive of
Assent, but a *Mean of Information*. We should not confound the Way
whereby we come to the Knowledg of a thing, with the Grounds we
have to believe it. A Man may inform me concerning a thousand
Matters I never heard of before, and of which I should not as much as
think if I were not told; yet I believe nothing purely upon his word
without *Evidence* in the things themselves. Not the bare Authority of
him that speaks, but the clear Conception I form of what he says, is
the *Ground of my Perswasion*.

If the sincerest Person on Earth should assure me he saw a Cane [12]
without two ends, I neither should nor could believe him; because
this Relation plainly contradicts the Idea of a Cane. But if he told me
he saw a Staff that, being by chance laid in the Earth, did after some
time put forth Sprigs and Branches, I could easily rely upon his
Veracity; because this no way contradicts the Idea of a Staff, nor
transcends Possibility.

I say *Possibility*; for *Omnipotency* it self can do no more. They [13]
impose upon themselves and others, who require Assent to things

contradictory, because *God*, say they, *can do all things, and it were lim-iting of his Power to affirm the contrary.* Very good! we heartily believe God can do all things: But that meer *Nothing* should be the Object of his Power, the very *Omnipotency* alledg'd, will not permit us to con-ceive. And that every *Contradiction*, which is a Synonym for *Impossi-bility*, is *pure nothing*, we have already sufficiently demonstrated. To say, for example, that *a thing is extended and not extended, is round and square at once*, is to say *nothing*; for these Ideas destroy one another, and cannot subsist together in the same Subject. But when we clearly perceive a perfect Agreement and Connection between the Terms of any Proposition, we then conclude it possible because intelligible: So I understand God may render immediately solid, what has been hith-erto fluid; make present Beings cease to exist; and *call those things things that are not, as tho they were.*[18] When we say then, *that nothing is impossible with God*, or that he can do all things, we mean whatever is possible in it self, however far above the Power of Creatures to effect.

[*14*]   Now, such is the Nature of a Matter of Fact, that though it may be conceiv'd possible enough, yet he only can with Assurance assert its Existence who is himself the Author, or by some *Means of Infor-mation* comes first to the certain Knowledg of it. That there was such an Island as *Jamaica*, no *European* could ever reasonably deny: And yet that it was precisely situated in such a Latitude, was water'd with those Rivers, cloth'd with these Woods, bore this Grain, produc'd that Plant, no *English-man* before the Discovery of *America*, could positively affirm.

[*15*]   Thus God is pleas'd to reveal to us in *Scripture* several wonderful Matters of Fact, as *the Creation of the World, the last Judgment*, and many other important Truths, which no Man left to himself could ever imagine, no more than any of my fellow-Creatures can be sure of my private Thoughts: *For who knoweth the things of a Man save the Spirit of a Man that is in him? even so the things of God knoweth none but the Spirit of God.*[19] But as *secret things belong unto the Lord; so those things which are reveal'd, belong unto us and to our Children.*[20] Yet, as we discours'd before, we do not receive them only because they are reveal'd: For besides the infallible Testimony of the Revelation from all requisite Circumstances, we must see in its Subject the indis-

putable Characters of *Divine Wisdom* and *Sound Reason*; which are the only Marks we have to distinguish the Oracles and Will of God, from the Impostures and Traditions of Men.

Whoever reveals any thing, that is, whoever tells us something we [16] did not know before, *his Words must be intelligible, and the Matter possible*. This Rule holds good, let *God* or *Man* be the Revealer. If we count that Person a Fool who requires our Assent to what is manifestly incredible, how dare we blasphemously attribute to *the most perfect Being*, what is an acknowledg'd Defect in one of our selves? As for unintelligible Relations, we can no more believe them from the Revelation of God, than from that of Man; for the conceiv'd Ideas of things are the only Subjects of Believing, Denying, Approving, and every other Act of the Understanding: Therefore all Matters reveal'd by God or Man, must be *equally intelligible and possible*; so far both Revelations agree. But in this they differ, that though the Revelation of Man should be thus qualifi'd, yet *he may impose upon me as to the Truth of the thing*: whereas what God is pleas'd to discover to me is not only clear to my Reason, (without which his Revelation could make me no wiser) but likewise *it is always true*. A Man, for example, acquaints me that he has found a Treasure: This is plain and possible, but he may easily deceive me. God assures me, that he has form'd Man of Earth: This is not only possible to God, and to me very intelligible; but the thing is also most certain, *God not being capable to deceive me, as Man is*. We are then to expect the same degree of *Perspicuity* from God as from Man, tho' more of *Certitude* from the first than the last.

This Reason perswades, and the Scriptures expresly speak it. [17] Those *Prophets* or *Dreamers*[21] were to be ston'd to Death that should go about to seduce the People from the Worship of One God to *Polytheism*,[22] though they should confirm their Doctrine *by Signs and Wonders*. And *though a Prophet spoke in the Name of the Lord, yet if the thing prophesied did not come to pass*, it was to be a rational Sign *he spoke presumptuously of himself, and not of God*.[23] It was reveal'd to the Prophet *Jeremy* in Prison, that his Uncle's Son would sell his Field to him, *but he did not conclude it to be the Word of the Lord till his Kinsman actually came to strike the Bargain with him*.[24] The Virgin *Mary*, tho of

JOHN TOLAND

that Sex that's least Proof against Flattery and Superstition, did not implicitely believe *she should bear a Child that was to be called the Son of the most High, and of whose Kingdom there should be no end,*[25] till the *Angel* gave her a satisfactory Answer to the strongest Objection that could be made: Nor did she then conclude (so unlike was she to her present Worshippers) it should unavoidably come to pass; but humbly acknowledging the Possibility,[26] and her own Unworthiness, she quietly wish'd and expected the event.

[18]   In how many places are we exhorted *to beware of false Prophets* and *Teachers, Seducers* and *Deceivers?*[27] We are not only *to prove or try all things, and to hold fast that which is the best,*[28] but also *to try the Spirits whether they be of God.*[29] But how shall we try? how shall we discern? Not *as the Horse and Mule which have no Understanding,*[30] but *as circumspect and wise Men,*[31] *judging what is said.*[32] In a word, it was from clear and weighty Reasons, both as to Fact and Matter, and not by a blind Obedience, that the Men of God of old embrac'd his Revelations, which upon the like Account we receive of their hands. I am not ignorant how some boast they are strongly perswaded *by the illuminating and efficacious Operation of the Holy Spirit,* and that they neither have nor approve other Reasons of their *Faith:* But we shall endeavour in its proper place to undeceive them; for no Adversary, how absurd or trifling soever, ought to be superciliously disregarded by an unfeigned Lover of Men and Truth. So far of Revelation; only in making it a *Mean of Information,* I follow *Paul* himself, who tells the *Corinthians,* that *he cannot profit them except he speaks to them by Revelation, or by Knowledg, or by Prophesying, or by Doctrine.*[33]

- 3 -

That by Christianity was intended a Rational and Intelligible Religion: prov'd from the Miracles, Method and Stile of the New Testament

What we discours'd of *Reason* before, and *Revelation* now, being duly   [*19*]
weigh'd, all the Doctrines and Precepts of the New Testament (if it
be indeed Divine) must consequently agree with *Natural Reason*, and
our own ordinary Ideas. This every considerate and well-dispos'd Person will find by the careful Perusal of it: And whoever undertakes
this Task, will confess the Gospel *not to be hidden from us, nor afar of,
but very nigh us, in our Mouths, and in our Hearts.*[34] It affords the most
illustrious Examples of close and perspicuous Ratiocination conceivable; which is incumbent on me in the Explication of its *Mysteries*, to
demonstrate. And tho the Evidence of *Christ's* Doctrine might claim
the Approbation of the *Gentiles*, and its Conformity with the Types
and Prophesies of the *Old Testament*, with all the Marks of the *Messiah*
concurring in his Person, might justly challenge the Assent of his
Countrymen; yet to leave no room for doubt, he proves his Authority
and Gospel by such Works and Miracles as the stiff-necked *Jews*
themselves could not deny to be Divine. *Nicodemus* says to him, *No
Man can do these Miracles which thou dost, except God be with him.*[35]
Some of the Pharisees acknowledg'd no *Sinner could do such things.*[36]
And others, *that they exceeded the Power of the Devils.*[37]

Jesus himself appeals to his very Enemies, ready to stone him for   [*20*]
pretended Blasphemy, saying; *If I do not the Works of my Father,
believe me not: But if I do, believe not me, believe the Works; that you
may know, and believe that the Father is in me, and I in him*[38]: That is,
believe not rashly on me, and so give a Testimony to my Works; but

43

search the *Scriptures*, which testify of the *Messiah*; consider the Works I do, whether they become such as become God, and are attributed to him: If they be, then conclude and believe that I am he, &c. In effect, several of the People said, *that Christ when he should come could do no greater Wonders*;[39] and *many of the Jews believ'd when they saw the Miracles which he did.*[40]

[21]   *How shall we escape*, says the Apostle, *if we neglect so great a Salvation which at the first began to be spoken by the Lord, and was confirm'd unto us by them that heard him; God also bearing them witness with divers Miracles, and Gifts of the Holy Spirit, according to his own Will?*[41] Those who heard *Christ*, the Author of our Religion, speak, and saw the Wonders which he wrought, *renounce all the hidden things of Dishonesty, all Craftiness and deceitful handling of the Word of God:* And *that they manifest nothing but Truth they commend themselves to every Man's Conscience*, that is, they appeal to every Man's Reason, *in the Sight of God.*[42] Peter exhorts Christians *to be ready always to give an Answer to every one that asks them a Reason of their Hope.*[43] Now to what Purpose serv'd all these Miracles, all these Appeals, if no Regard was to be had of Mens Understandings? if the Doctrines of Christ were incomprehensible? or were we oblig'd to believe reveal'd Nonsense?*

[22]   But to insist no longer upon such Passages, all Men will own the Verity I defend if they read the sacred Writings with that Equity and Attention that is due to meer Humane Works: Nor is there any different Rule to be follow'd in the Interpretation of *Scripture* from what is common to all other Books. Whatever unprejudic'd Person shall use those Means, will find them notorious Deceivers, or much deceiv'd themselves, who maintain the *New Testament* is written without any Order or certain Scope, but just as Matters came into the *Apostles* Heads, whether transported with Enthusiastick Fits (as some will have it), or, according to others, for lack of good Sense and a liberal Education. I think I may justly say, that they are Strangers

---

*   [In the second edition the following is added on to this paragraph:]
Now if these Miracles be true, *Christianity* must consequently be intelligible; and if false (which our Adversaries will not grant), they can be then no Arguments against us.

to true Method, who complain of this Confusion and Disorder. But the Proof of the Case depends not upon Generalities.*

The Facility of the *Gospel* is not confin'd only to Method; for the [23] Stile is also most easy, most natural, and in the common Dialect of those to whom it was immediately consign'd. Should any preach in *Xenophon's*[44] strain to the present *Greeks,* or in correct *English to the* Country-People in *Scotland,* 'twould cost them much more Time and Pains to learn the very Words, than the Knowledg of the things denoted by them. Of old, as well as in our time, the *Jews* understood *Hebrew* worse than the Tongues of those Regions where they dwelt. No Pretences therefore can be drawn from the Obscurity of the Language in favour of the *irrational Hypothesis*: for all Men are supposed to understand the daily Use of their Mother-Tongue; whereas the Stile of the Learned is unintelligible to the Vulgar. And the plainest Authors that write as they speak, without the Disguise of pompous Elegance, have ever been accounted the best by all good Judges. It is a visible Effect of Providence that we have in our Hands the Monuments of the *Old Testament*, which in the *New* are always suppos'd, quoted, or alluded to. Nor is that all, for the *Jewish* Service and Customs continue to this day. If this had been true of the *Greeks* and *Romans*, we should be furnish'd with those Helps to understand aright many unknown Particulars of their Religion, which make us Rulers and Teachers in *Israel*. Besides, we have the *Talmud*,[45] and other works of the *Rabbins*, which, however otherwise useless, give us no small Light into the antient Rites and Language. And if after all we should be at a loss about the Meaning of any Expression, we ought rather to charge it upon Distance of Time, and the want of more Books in the same Tongue, than to attribute it to the Nature of the thing, or the Ignorance of the Author, who might be easily understood by his Country-men and Contemporaries. But no Truth is to be establish'd, nor Falshood confuted from such Passages, no more than any can certainly divine his Fortune from the Sound of *Bow-bell*.

---

* [The second edition has the following addition:]

… Generalities; Tho, whenever it is prov'd, I will not promise that every one shall find a Justification of the *particular Method* he was taught, or he has chosen, to follow. *To defend any PARTY is not my business, but to discover the TRUTH.*

[24]   If any object, that the *Gospel* is penn'd with little or no Orna-ment, that there are no choice of Words, nor studied Expressions in it; the Accusation is true, and the Apostles themselves acknowledg it: nor is there a more palpable Demonstration of their having design'd to be understood by all. *I came not to you,* says *Paul,*[46] *with Excellency of Speech, or Wisdom, declaring unto you the Testimony of God. My Speech and my Preaching was not with enticing Words of humane Wisdom, but in Demonstration,* or Conviction *of the Spirit*[47] or Mind, *and in Power* or Efficacy. This he speaks in reference to the *Philosophers* and *Orators* of those Times, whose Elocution, 'tis con-fess'd, was curious, and Periods elaborate, apt to excite the Admira-tion of the Hearers, but not to satisfy their Reasons; charming indeed their Senses whilest in the *Theatre,* or the *Temple,* but making them neither the better at home, nor the wiser abroad.

[25]   These Men, as well as many of their *modern Successors,* were fond enough of their own ridiculous Systems, *to count the things of God Foolishness,*[48] because they did not agree with their precarious and sensual Notions; because every Sentence was not wrapp'd up in Mys-*tery,* and garnish'd with a Figure: not considering that only false or trivial Matters need the Assistance of alluring Harangues to perplex or amuse. But they were Enemies and Strangers to the Simplicity of Truth. All their Study, as we took notice, lay in tickling the Passions of the People at their Pleasure with bombast Eloquence and apish Gesticulations. They boasted their Talent of perswading for or against any thing. And as he was esteemed the best *Orator* that made the worst Cause appear the most equitable before the Judges, so he was the best *Philosopher* that could get the wildest Paradox to pass for Demonstration. They were only concern'd about their own Glory and Gain, which they could not otherwise support, but (according to an Artifice that never fails, and therefore ever practis'd) by imposing upon the People with their *Authority* and *Sophistry,* and *under pretence of instructing, dexterously detaining them in the grossest Ignorance.*

[26]   But the Scope of the *Apostles* was very different: Piety towards God, and the Peace of Mankind, was their Gain, and *Christ* and his *Gospel* their Glory. They came not magnifying nor exalting them-selves, not imposing but declaring their Doctrine. They did not con-

found and mislead, but convince the Mind. They were employ'd to dispel Ignorance, to eradicate Superstition, to propagate Truth and Reformation of Manners; *to preach Deliverance to Captives*,[49] (i.e.) the Enjoyment of Christian Liberty to the Slaves of the Levitical and Pagan Priesthoods, and to declare Salvation to repenting Sinners.

I shall add here some of the Characters which *David* gives of the [27] Law and Word of God, that we may admit nothing as the Will of Heaven but what is aggreeable to them: *The Law of the Lord*, says he, *is perfect, converting the Soul. The Testimony of the Lord is sure, making wise the Simple. The Statutes of the Lord are right, rejoicing the Heart. The Commandment of the Lord is pure, enlightening the Eyes. The Fear of the Lord is clean, enduring for ever. The Judgments of the Lord are true and righteous altogether. I have more Understanding than all my Teachers, for thy Testimonies are my Meditation. I understand more than the Antients, because I keep thy Precepts. Thy Word is a Lamp unto my Feet, and a Light unto my Path.* The *New Testament* is so full of this Language, and the Contents of it are every where so conformable to it, that I shall refer the Reader to the particular Discussion of the Whole in the second Discourse.*

---

* [Toland's projected second and third discourses never appeared. The following is added in the second edition:]

But I must remark in the mean time that not a Syllable of this Language is true, if any Contradictions *seeming* or *real* be admitted in Scripture. As much may be said of *Mysteries*; but we shall talk of that by and by.

Objections answer'd, drawn from the Pravity of Humane Reason

[28] There remains one Objection yet, upon which some lay a mighty Stress, tho it's like to do them little Service. Granting, say they, the *Gospel* to be as reasonable as you pretend, *yet corrupt and deprav'd Reason can neither discern nor receive Divine Verities.* Ay, but that proves not Divine Verities to be contrary to *sound Reason.* But they maintain that *no Man's Reason is sound.* Wherefore I hope so to state this Question, as to cut off all Occasion of Dispute from judicious and peaceable Men. *Reason* taken for the Principle of Discourse in us, or more particularly for *that Faculty every one has of judging of his Ideas according to their Agreement or Disagreement, and so of loving what seems good unto him, and hating what he thinks evil: Reason,* I say, in this Sense is whole and entire in every one whose Organs are not accidentally indisposed. 'Tis from it that we are accounted Men; and we could neither inform others, nor receive Improvement our selves any more than *Brutes* without it.

[29] But if by *Reason* be understood a constant right Use of these Faculties, *viz. If a Man never judges but according to clear Perceptions, desires nothing but what is truly good for him, nor avoids but what is certainly evil:* Then, I confess, it is extremely *corrupt.* We are too prone to frame wrong Conceptions, and as erroneous Judgments of things. We generally covet what flatters our Senses, without distinguishing noxious from innocent Pleasures; and our Hatred is as partial. We gratify our Bodies so much as to meditate little, and think very grosly of spiritual or abstracted Matters. We are apt to indulge our Inclina-

48

tions, which we term *to follow Nature*[50]: so that the *natural Man,*[51] that is, he that gives the swing to his Appetites, counts Divine Things mere Folly, calls *Religion* a feverish Dream of superstitious Heads, or a politick Trick invented by States-men to awe the credulous Vulgar. For as *they that walk after the Flesh mind the things thereof, so their carnal Wisdom is Enmity against God.*[52] *Sin easily besets us.*[53] *There is a Law in our Members* or Body, *warring against the Law of our Minds*[54] or Reason. And *when we would do Good Evil is present with us.*[55] If thus we become stupid and unfit for earthly Speculations, *how shall we believe when we are told of heavenly things?*[56]

But these Disorders are so far from being *Reason*, that nothing can [30] be more directly contrary to it. We lie under no necessary Fate of sinning. There is no Defect in our Understandings but those of our own Creation, that is to say, *vicious Habits easily contracted, but difficultly reformed.* 'Tis just with us as with the Drunkard, whose *I cannot give over Drinking* is a deliberate *I will not.* For upon a Wager, or for a Reward, he can forbear his Cups a Day, a Month, a Year, according as the Consideration of the Value or Certainty of the expected Gain does influence him. *Let no Man therefore say when he is tempted, I am tempted of God: For as God cannot be tempted to Evil, so neither tempteth he any Man: But every Man is tempted when he is drawn away, and entic'd of his own Lust.*[57]

Supposing a natural Impotency to reason well, we could no more [31] be liable to Condemnation for not keeping the Commands of God than those to whom *the Gospel* was never revealed for not believing on *Christ: For how shall they call on him in whom they have not believed? and how shall they believe in him of whom they have not heard?*[58] Were our reasoning Faculties imperfect, or we not capable to employ them rightly, there could be no Possibility of our understanding one another in Millions of things, where the stock of our Ideas should prove unavoidably unequal, or our Capacities different. But 'tis the Perfection of our *Reason* and *Liberty* that makes us deserve Rewards and Punishments. We are perswaded that all our Thoughts are entirely free, we can expend the Force of Words, compare Ideas, distinguish clear from obscure Conceptions, suspend our Judgments about Uncertainties, and yield only to Evidence. In a word, the Deliberations we use about our Designs, and the Choice to which we determine our selves at last, do prove us the free Disposers of all our Actions. Now what is *sound Reason* except this be it? Doubtless it is. And no *Evangelical* or other knowable Truth can prove insuperable or monstrous to him that uses it after this manner. But when we abuse it against it self, and enslave it to our debauch'd Imaginations, it is averse from all Good. We are so habituated, I confess, to precarious and hasty Conclusions, that without great Constancy and Exercise we cannot recover our innate Freedom, *nor do well, having accustom'd our selves so much to Evil.*[59] But tho 'tis said in *Scripture*, that *we will neither know nor understand*; 'tis there also said, that we may *amend our Ways, turn from our Iniquity, and choose Life.* Encouragements are proposed to such as do so. We can, upon serious Reflection, see our Faults, and find that what we held most unreasonable, did only appear so from *superficial Disquisitions*, or *want of necessary Helps*; from *Deference to Authority*, and *Principles taken upon Trust*; from *irregular Inclinations* and *Self-interest*, or *the Hatred of a Party*.

[32]   But notwithstanding all this, some are at a world of Pains to rob themselves (if they could) of their *Liberty* or *Freewill*, the noblest and most useful of all our Faculties, the only thing we can properly call ours, and the only thing that neither Power nor Fortune can take from us. Under whatever Vail these Men endeavour to hide their Folly, yet they are engag'd in it by extreme *Pride* and *Self-love*: For, *not willing to own their Ignorance and Miscarriages (which proceed from Passion, Sloth or Inconsideration), they would remove all the Blame from their Will, and charge it upon a natural Impotency not in their Power to cure.* Thus they ingeniously cheat themselves, and chuse rather to be rank'd in the same Condition with Brutes or Machines, than be oblig'd to acknowledg their humane Frailties, and to mend.

[33]   Since therefore the Perfection or Soundness of our Reason is so evident to our selves, and so plainly contained in *Scripture*, however wrested by some ignorant Persons, *we should labour to acquire Knowledg with more confident Hopes of Success.* Why should we entertain such mean and unbecoming Thoughts, as if Truth, like the Almighty, dwelt in Light inaccessible, and not to be discover'd by the Sons of Men? Things are always the same, how different soever the Concep-

tions of Men about them may be; and what another did not, I may happily find out. That nothing escap'd the Sight of former Ages is a Tale to be told where one Person only speaks, and no Body present must contradict him. The Slips and Errors which are taken notice of in the World every Day, serve only to put us in mind that many able Men did not examine the Truth with that Order and Application they should or might have done. There are a thousand things in our Power to know, of which, through Prejudice or Neglect, we may be, and frequently remain ignorant all our Life; and innumerable Difficulties may be made by imagining *Mysteries* where there are none, or by conceiving too discouraging and unjust an Opinion of our own Abilities: whereas, by a Parity of Reason, we may hope to outdo all that outdid others before us, as Posterity may exceed both. *'Tis no Presumption* therefore *for us to endeavour setting things in a better Light*; as to know what we are able to perform is not *Pride*, but foolishly to presume none else can equal us, when we are all upon the same Level: *For who maketh thee to differ from another? And what hast thou that thou didst not receive? Now if thou didst receive it, why dost thou glory as if thou hadst not received it?*[60] Have we not all the same sure and certain Promises of Light and Assistance from above, as well as the Privilege of Reason in common? *If any lack Wisdom let him ask it of God, who gives to all Men liberally, and upbraideth not, and it shall be given him.*[61]

To conclude, let no Body think to be excused by this imaginary [34] *Corruption*, but learn from the *Scripture*, our infallible Oracle, that the *Gospel*, if it be the Word of God, is only contrary to the Opinions and Wishes of lewd Men, *that love to walk after their own Lusts*;[62] *of those that speak Evil of the things which they understand not, and debauch themselves in what they know in common with Brutes.*[63] *It is hid to them whose Minds are blinded by the God of this World*;[64] and to those who live by the Ignorance and simple Credulity of their Brethren. To be brief, It is contrary to the false Reasoning of all that will not know what it is to reflect or consider; but it is not above the Possibility of their *Reason* when they shall better improve their Faculties. The Creation of the World was against the System of *Aristotle*, the Immortality of the Soul against the Hypothesis of *Epicurus*,[65] and the

51

Liberty* of the Will was impugn'd by many antient *Philosophers*. But is this to be *contrary to Reason?* Have not these Men been quite baffled by as very *Heathens* as themselves? And are not their other Errors since detected and exploded by most of the Learned? Besides, they wanted a principal *mean of Information*, viz. *Revelation*.

---

* *How the absolute Liberty we experience in our selves, is consistent with God's Omnipotency and our Dependance on him, shall in due place be consider'd.*

SECTION THREE

That there is nothing Mysterious, or above Reason in the Gospel

We come at length to enquire *whether any Doctrine of the Gospel be* [1] *above, tho not contrary to Reason.* This Expression is taken in a two-fold Signification. First, It denotes a thing intelligible of it self, but so cover'd by figurative Words, Types and Ceremonies, that *Reason* cannot penetrate the Vail, nor see what is under it till it be remov'd. Secondly, It is made to signify a thing of its own Nature inconceivable, and not to be judg'd of by our ordinary Faculties and Ideas, tho it be never so clearly reveal'd. In both these Senses *to be above Reason* is the same thing with *Mystery,* and, in effect, they are controvertible Terms in *Divinity.*

The History and Signification of Mystery in the Writings of the Gentiles

What is meant by *Reason* we have already largely discours'd; but to [2] understand aright what the word *Mystery* imports, we must trace the Original of it as far back as the Theology of the antient *Gentiles*, whereof it was a considerable Term. *Those Nations, who* (as *Paul* elegantly describes them) *professing themselves wise, became Fools; who chang'd the Glory of the incorruptible God into the Image and Likeness of corruptible Man, of Birds, of Beasts, and creeping things; who turned the Truth of God into a Lie, and worshipped the Creature as well as* (and sometimes more than) *the Creator*: Those Nations, I say, asham'd or afraid to exhibit their *Religion* naked to the view of all indifferently, disguis'd it with various Ceremonies, Sacrifices, Plays, &c. making the superstitious People believe that admirable things were adumbrated by these Externals. The *Priests*, but very rarely, and then obscurely, taught in publick, pretending the Injunctions of their *Divinities* to the contrary, lest their Secrets, forsooth, should be expos'd to the Profanation of the Ignorant, or Violation of the Impious. They perform'd the highest Acts of their Worship, consisting of ridiculous, obscene, or inhumane Rites, in the inmost Recesses of *Temples* or *Groves* consecrated for that purpose: And it was inexpiable Sacrilege for any to[66] enter these but such as had a special Mark and Privilege, or as much as to ask Questions about what passed in them. All the Excluded were for that Reason stil'd *the Profane*, as those not in Orders with us the *Laity*.

But the cunning *Priests*, who knew how to turn every thing to [3] their own Advantage, thought fit to *initiate* or instruct certain Persons in the Meaning of their Rites. They gave out that such as died *uninitiated*[67] wallow'd in infernal Mire, whilst the Purified and *Initiated* dwelt with the Gods; which as well increas'd their Veneration for, as a Desire of enjoying so great a Happiness. The *Initiated,* after some Years Preparation to make them value what cost so much Time and Patience, were devoutly sworn[68] never to discover what they saw or heard, tho they might discourse of them amongst themselves, lest too great a Constraint should tempt them to blab the Secret. And so religiously they kept this Oath, that some of them, after their Conversion to *Christianity,* could hardly be brought to declare what passed at their *Initiation* in *Gentilism.* The Athenians thought no Torments exquisite enough to punish *Diagoras* the Philosopher,[69] for divulging their *Mysteries*; and not content to brand him with *Atheism* for laughing at their Weakness, they promis'd a Talent as a Reward to any that should kill him. 'Twas Death to say *Adonis*[70] was a Man; some suffer'd upon that Account: And many were torn in pieces at the *Orgies of Bacchus,*[71] for their unadvis'd Curiosity.

[4]   Credible Authors report, that the *Priests* confess'd to the *Initiated* how these Mystick Representations were instituted at first in Commemoration of some remarkable Accidents, or to the Honour of some great Persons that oblig'd the World by their Vertues and useful Inventions to pay them such Acknowledgments. But let this be as it will, *Myein*[72] in their Systems signify'd *to initiate: Myesis,*[73] *Initiation: Mystes,* a Name afterwards given the *Priests,* denoted the Person *to be initiated,* who was call'd an *Epopt*[74] when admitted; and *Mystery*[75] the *Doctrine in which he was initiated.* As there were several[76] Degrees, so there were different sorts of Mysteries. The most famous were the *Samothracian,*[77] the *Eleusinian,*[78] the *Egyptian,* and those of *Bacchus,* commonly known by the Name of *Orgies*; tho the[79] word is sometimes put for any of the former.

[5]   From what has been said it is clear, that they understood by *Mystery* in those Days *a thing intelligible of it self, but so vail'd by others, that it could not be known without special Revelation.* I need not add, that in all the *Greek* and *Roman* Authors it is constantly put, as a very vulgar Expression, for any thing sacred or profane that is designedly kept secret or accidently obscure. And this is the common Acceptation of

it still: for when we cannot see clearly into a Business, we say it is a *Mystery* to us; and that an obscure or perplex'd Discourse is very *mysterious*. *Mysteries* of State, Sciences and Trades, run all in the same Notion.

But many not denying what is so plain, yet being strongly inclin'd [6] out of Ignorance or Passion to maintain what was first introduc'd by the Craft or Superstition of their Forefathers, will have some *Christian Doctrines* to be still *mysterious* in the second Sense of the Word, that is, *inconceivable in themselves however clearly reveal'd*. They think a long Prescription will argue it Folly in any to appear against them, and indeed Custom has made it dangerous. But, slighting so mean Considerations, if I can demonstrate that in the New Testament *Mystery* is always us'd in the first Sense of the Word, or that of the *Gentiles*, viz. *for things naturally very intelligible, but so cover'd by figurative Words or Rites, that Reason could not discover them without special Revelation*; and that the Vail is actually taken away; then it will manifestly follow that the Doctrines so reveal'd cannot now be properly called *Mysteries*.

This is what I hope to perform in the Sequel of this Section, to [7] the entire Satisfaction of those sincere Christians more concern'd for the Truth than the old or gainful Opinion. Yet I must first remove out of my way certain common Places of cavilling, with which, not only the raw Beginners of the most implicite Constitution raise a great Dust upon all Occasions, tho not able to speak of any thing pertinently when jostl'd out of the beaten Road; but truly their venerable Teachers are not asham'd sometimes to play at this small Game, which, they know, rather amuses the Prejudic'd of their own side, than edifies the Adversaries of any sort. I wish there were more even of a well-meaning Zeal without Knowledg, than of Art or Cunning in this Conduct.

That nothing ought to be call'd a Mystery, because we have not an adequate Idea of all its Properties, nor any at all of its Essence

---

[8] I shall discuss this Point with all the Perspicuity I am able. And, first, I affirm, *That nothing can be said to be a Mystery, because we have not an adequate Idea of it, or a distinct View of all its Properties at once; for then every thing would be a Mystery.* The Knowledg of finite Creatures is gradually progressive, as Objects are presented to the Understanding. *Adam* did not know so much in the twentieth as in the hundredth Year of his Age; and *Jesus Christ* is expresly recorded to have encreas'd *in Wisdom as well as in Stature.*[80] We are said to know a thousand things, nor can we doubt of it; yet we never have a full Conception of whatever belongs to them. I understand nothing better than this *Table* upon which I am now writing: I conceive it divisible into Parts beyond all Imagination; but shall I say it is *above my Reason* because I cannot count these Parts, nor distinctly perceive their Quantity and Figures? I am convinc'd that *Plants* have a regular Contexture, and a Multitude of Vessels, many of them equivalent or analogous to those of *Animals*, whereby they receive a Juice from the Earth, and prepare it, changing some into their own Substance, and evacuating the excrementitious Parts. But I do not clearly comprehend how all these Operations are perform'd, though I know very well what is meant by a *Tree*.

[9] The Reason is, because *knowing nothing of Bodies but their Properties, God has wisely provided we should understand no more of these than are useful and necessary for us;* which is all our present Condition needs. Thus our Eyes are not given us to see all Quantities, nor per-

haps any thing as it is in it self, but as it bears some Relation to us. What is too minute, as it escapes our Sight, so it can neither harm nor benefit us: and we have a better View of Bodies the nearer we approach them, because then they become more convenient or inconvenient; but as we remove farther off we lose their Sight with their Influence. I'm perswaded there's no Motion which does not excite some Sound in Ears dispos'd to be affected with proportionable Degrees of Force from the Air; and, it may be, the small Animals concern'd can hear the Steps of the *Spider*, as we do those of Men and Cattel. From these and Millions of other Instances it is manifest, that we have little Certainty of any thing but as it is noxious or beneficial to us.

Rightly speaking then, we are accounted to *comprehend* any thing [10] when its chief Properties and their several Uses are known to us: for[81] to *comprehend* in all correct Authors is nothing else but *to know*; and as of what is not knowable we can have no Idea, so it is nothing to us. It is improper therefore to say a thing is above our Reason, because we know no more of it than concerns us, and ridiculous to supercede our Disquisitions about it upon that score. What should we think of a Man that would stifly maintain *Water* to be above his Reason, and that he would never enquire into its Nature, nor employ it in his House or Grounds, because he knows not how many Particles go to a Drop; whether the Air passes through it, is incorporated with it, or neither? This is for all the World as if I would not go because I cannot fly. Now, seeing *the Denominations of things are borrow'd from their known Properties, and that no Properties are knowable but what concern us, or serve to discover such as do*, we cannot be accountable for comprehending no other, nor justly requir'd more by reasonable Men, much less by the all-wise *DEITY*.

The most compendious Method therefore to acquire sure and use- [11] ful Knowledg, *is neither to trouble our selves nor others with what is useless, were it known; or what is impossible to be known at all.* Since I easily perceive the good or bad Effects of Rain upon the Earth, what should I be the better did I comprehend its Generation in the Clouds? for after all I could make no Rain at my Pleasure, nor prevent its falling at any time. A probable Hypothesis will not give Satisfaction in such Cases: The Hands, for Example, of two Dials may have the same Motion, tho the Disposition of the latent Springs which produce it should be very different. And to affirm this or that to be the Way, will not do, unless you can demonstrate that no other possible Way remains. Nay, should you hit upon the real Manner, you can never be sure of it, because the Evidence of Matters of Fact solely depends upon Testimony: And it follows not that such a thing is so, because it may be so.

[12]   The Application of this Discourse to my Subject admits of no Difficulty; and it is, first, *That no Christian Doctrine, no more than any ordinary Piece of Nature, can be reputed a Mystery, because we have not an adequate or compleat Idea of whatever belongs to it.* Secondly, *That what is reveal'd in Religion, as it is most useful and necessary, so it must and may be as easily comprehended, and found as consistent with our common Notions, as what we know of Wood or Stone, of Air, of Water, or the like.* And, Thirdly, *That when we do as familiarly explain such Doctrines, as what is known of natural things* (which I pretend we can), *we may then be as properly said to comprehend the one as the other.*

[13]   They trifle then exceedingly, and discover a mighty Scarcity of better Arguments, who defend their *Mysteries* by this pitiful Shift of drawing Inferences from what is unknown to what is known, or of insisting upon adequate Ideas; except they will agree, as some do, to call every Spire of Grass, Sitting and Standing, Fish or Flesh, profound *Mysteries*. And if out of a pertinacious or worse Humour they will be still fooling, and call these things *Mysteries*, I'm willing to admit as many as they please in *Religion*, if they will allow me likewise to make mine as intelligible to others as these are to me.

[14]   But to finish this Point, I conclude, that neither God himself, nor any of his Attributes, are *Mysteries* to us for want of an adequate Idea: No, not *Eternity*. The *mysterious Wits* do never more expose themselves than when they treat of *Eternity* in particular. Then they think themselves in their impregnable Fortress, and strangely insult over those dull Creatures that cannot find a thing where it is not. For if any Bounds (as Beginning or End) could be assign'd to *Eternity*, it ceases immediately to be what it should; and you frame only a finite, or rather *a negative Idea*, which is the Nature of all

Limitation. Nor can it be said, that therefore *Eternity is above Reason* in this Respect, or that it is any Defect in us not to exhaust its Idea; for what greater Perfection can be ascrib'd to *Reason* than to know precisely the Nature of things? And does not all its Errors lie in attributing those Properties to a thing which it has not, or taking any away that it contains? *Eternity* therefore is no more above Reason, *because it cannot be imagin'd*, than a Circle, *because it may*; for in both Cases *Reason* performs its Part according to the different Natures of the Objects, whereof the one is essentially imaginable, the other not.

Now it appears that the pretended *Mysteriousness* of *Eternity* do's [15] not consist in the want of an adequate Notion, which is all that we consider in it at present. The Difficulties rais'd from its Duration, as, that *Succession seems to make it finite*, and that *all things must exist together if it be instantaneous*, I despair not of solving very easily; and rendring *Infinity* also (which is inseparable from it, or rather a different Consideration of the same thing) as little *mysterious* as that *three and two make five*. But this falls naturally into my *second Discourse*, where I give a particular Explication of the *Christian* Tenets, according to the general Principles I am establishing in this.

As we know not all the Properties of things, so we can never con- [16] ceive the *Essence* of any Substance in the World. To avoid Ambiguity, I distinguish, after an excellent modern Philosopher, the *Nominal* from the *Real Essence* of a thing. *The nominal Essence is a Collection of those Properties or Modes which we principally observe in any thing, and to which we give one common Denomination or Name.* Thus the nominal Essence of the *Sun* is a bright, hot, and round Body, at a certain Distance from us, and that has a constant regular Motion. Whoever hears the word *Sun* pronounc'd, this is the Idea he has of it. He may conceive more of its Properties, or not all these; but it is still a Collection of Modes or Properties that makes his Idea. So the *Nominal Essence* of *Honey* consists in its Colour, Taste, and other known Attributes.

But *the real Essence is that intrinsick Constitution of a thing which is* [17] *the Ground or Support of all its Properties, and from which they naturally flow or result.* Now tho we are perswaded that the Modes of things

61

must have such a Subject to exist in (for they cannot subsist alone), yet we are absolutely ignorant of what it is. We conceive nothing more distinctly than the mention'd Properties of the Sun, and those whereby Plants, Fruits, Metals, &c. are known to us; but we have no manner of Notion of the several Foundations of these Properties, tho we are very sure in the mean time, that some such thing must necessarily be. The observable Qualities therefore of things is all that we understand by their Names, for which Reason they are call'd their *Nominal Essence*.

[18]   It follows now very plainly, that *nothing can be said to be a Mystery, because we are ignorant of its real Essence, since it is not more knowable in one thing than in another, and is never conceiv'd or included in the Ideas we have of things, or the Names we give 'em*. I had not much insisted upon this Point, were it not for the so often repeated Sophistry of some that rather merit the Encomiums of great Readers than great Reasoners. When they would have the most palpable Absurdities and Contradictions go down with others, or make them place Religion in Words that signify nothing, or what they are not able to explain, then they wisely tell them, that they are ignorant of many things, especially the *Essence* of their own Souls; and that therefore they must not always deny what they cannot conceive. But this is not all; for when they would (instead of confuting them) make those pass for ridiculous or arrogant Pretenders, who maintain that *only intelligible and possible things are the Subject of Belief*, they industriously represent them as presuming to define the *Essence* of God with that of created Spirits. And after they have sufficiently aggravated this Presumption of their own coining, they conclude, that if the Contexture of the smallest Pebble is not to be accounted for, then they should not insist upon such rigorous Terms of Believing, but sometimes be content to submit their Reason to their Teachers, and the Determinations of the Church.

[19]   Who perceives not the Weakness and Slight of this Reasoning? We certainly know as much of the SOUL as we do of any thing else, if not more. We form the clearest Conceptions of Thinking, Knowing, Imagining, Willing, Hoping, Loving, and the like Operations of

the Mind. But we are Strangers to the *Subject* wherein these Operations exist. So are we to that upon which the Roundness, Softness, Colour, and Taste of a Grape depend. There is nothing more evident than the Modes or Properties of *BODY*, as to be extended, solid, divisible, smooth, rough, soft, hard, &c. But we know as little of the internal Constitution, which is the Support of these sensible Qualities, as we do of that wherein the Operations of the *SOUL* reside. And, as the great Man I just now mention'd observes, *we may as well deny the Existence of* Body, *because we have not an Idea of its real Essence, as call the Being of the* Soul *in question for the same Reason.* The Idea of the *Soul* then is every whit as clear and distinct as that of the *Body*; and had there been (as there is not) any Difference, the *Soul* must have carried the Advantage, because its Properties are more immediately known to us, and are the Light whereby we discover all things besides.

As for *GOD*, we comprehend nothing better than his Attributes. [20] We know not, it's true, the Nature of that eternal *Subject* or *Essence* wherein Infinite Goodness, Love, Knowledg, Power and Wisdom coexist; but we are not better acquainted with the *real Essence* of any of his Creatures. As by the Idea and Name of *GOD* we understand his known Attributes and Properties, so we understand those of all things else by theirs; and we conceive the one as clearly as we do the other. I remark'd in the Beginning of this Chapter, that we knew nothing of things but such of their Properties as were *necessary* and *useful*. We may say the same of *God*; for every Act of our Religion is directed by the Consideration of some of his Attributes, without ever thinking of his *Essence*. Our Love to him is kindled by his Goodness, and our Thankfulness by his Mercy; our Obedience is regulated by his Justice; and our Hopes are confirm'd by his Wisdom and Power.

I think I may now warrantably conclude, that nothing is a [21] Mystery, because we know not its *Essence*, since it appears that it is neither knowable in it self, nor ever thought of by us: So that the *Divine Being* himself cannot with more Reason be accounted *mysterious* in this Respect, than the most contemptible of his Creatures. Nor am I very much concern'd that these Essences escape my Knowledg: for I am fix'd in the Opinion, that *what Infinite Goodness has not been pleas'd to reveal to us, we are either sufficiently capable to discover our selves, or need not understand it at all.**

---

* [In the second edition the following is added:]
I hope now it is very manifest that *Mysteries in religion* are but ill argu'd from the pretended *Mysteries of Nature*; and that such as endeavour to support the former by the latter, have either a design to impose upon others, or that they have never themselves duely consider'd of this Matter.

- 3 -

The Signification of the word Mystery in the New Testament, and the Writings of the most antient Christians

---

Having so dispatch'd these *adequate Ideas*, and, I know not what, *real* [22] *Essences*, we come now to the main Point upon which the whole Controversy chiefly depends. For the Question being, *whether or no Christianity is mysterious*, it ought to be naturally decided by the *New Testament*, wherein the *Christian Faith* is originally contain'd. I heartily desire to put the Case upon this Issue, I appeal to this Tribunal: For did I not infinitely prefer the Truth I learn from these sacred Records to all other Considerations, I should never assert that *there are no Mysteries in Christianity*. The Scriptures have engag'd me in this Error, if it be one; and I will sooner be reputed Heterodox with these only on my side, than to pass for Orthodox, with the whole World, and have them against me.

Now by searching the *Scriptures* I find some of the Evangelick [23] Doctrines call'd *Mysteries*, in a more general, or in a more particular Sense. They are more generally so call'd with respect to all Mankind: for being certain Matters of Fact only known to God and lodg'd in his Decree, or such Events as were quite lost and forgot in the World, it was impossible for any Person, tho never so wise or learned, to discover them; for *the things of God knoweth none but the Spirit of God,*[82] as none can find out the secret Thoughts of Man till he tells them himself. Such Revelations then of God in the *New Testament* are call'd *Mysteries*, not from any present Inconceivableness or Obscurity, but with respect to what they were before this *Revelation*, as that is call'd our Task which we long since perform'd.

65

[24]   If any should question this, let him hear the Apostle *Paul* declare for himself and his Fellow-Labourers in the Gospel: *We speak*, says he, *the Wisdom of God hid in a Mystery, which God ordain'd before the world for our Glory, which none of the Princes of the world knew,*[83] *&c.* And, to shew that this Divine Wisdom was a *Mystery* for want of revealing Information, he presently subjoins, *Eye hath not seen, nor Ear heard, neither have entred into the Heart of Man the things which God hath prepar'd for them that love him; but God hath reveal'd them to us by his Spirit.*[84] The most perspicacious *Philosophers* were not able to foretel the Coming of *Christ*, to discover the *Resurrection* of the Body, nor any other Matter of Fact that is deliver'd in the Gospel: And if they happen'd now and then to say something like the Truth, they did but divine at best, and could never be certain of their Opinion. It is a most delightful thing to consider what Pains the enquiring *Heathens* were often at to give a Reason for what depended not in the least upon any Principles in their *Philosophy*, but was an historical Fact communicable by God alone, or such as had undoubted Memoirs concerning it. Of this I think it not amiss to add the following Example.

[25]   The same Experience that taught the *Gentiles* their mortal Condition, acquainted them also with the Frailty of their Natures, and the numberless Calamities constantly attending them. They could not perswade themselves that the Species of Man came in such deplorable Circumstances out of the Hands of an infinitely good and merciful Deity; and so were inclin'd to impute all to the Wickedness of adult Persons, till they perceiv'd that Death and Misfortune did not spare innocent Children more than Robbers and Pirates. At last they imagin'd a *pre-existent State*, wherein the Soul acting separately like Angels, might have contracted some extraordinary Guilt, and so for Punishment be thrust into the Body, which they sometimes compar'd to a Prison, but oftner to a Grave.[85] This was likewise the Origin of *Transmigration*, tho in Process of Time the Sins of this World became as much concern'd in that Opinion as those of the other. But nothing is more ingenious than the Account which *Cebes* the *Theban*[86] gives us of the Matter in his most excellent *Portraiture of humane Life*. He feigns[87] *Imposture* sitting in a Throne at the Gate of Life, in the Shape of a most beautiful Lady, holding a Cup in her Hand: She obligingly

presents it to all that are on their Journey to this World, and these as civilly accept it; but the Draught proves *Ignorance* and *Error*, whence proceed all the Disorders and Misery of their Lives.

This Point was a great *Mystery* to these honest Philosophers, who [26] had only Fancy to guide them, and could not pretend to Instructions from the *Mind of God*; but the thing is now no *Mystery* to us *that have the Mind of Christ.*[88] We know that *Adam* the first Man became also the first Sinner and Mortal; and that so the whole Race propagated from him could be naturally no better than he was: *By one Man Sin enter'd into the World, and Death by Sin.*[89]

But some Doctrines of the Gospel are more particularly call'd [27] *Mysteries*, because they were hid from God's peculiar People under the *Mosaick* Oeconomy; not that they knew nothing concerning them, for *the Law had a Shadow of good things to come;*[90] but they were not clearly and fully revealed till the *New Testament* Times, being vail'd before by various Typical Representations, Ceremonies, and figurative Expressions. *Christ* tells his Disciples, *Many Prophets and Kings have desir'd to see those things which you see, and have not seen them, and to hear those things which you hear, and have not heard them.*[91] Paul says, *we use great Plainness of Speech, and not as* Moses *who put a Vail over his Face:*[92] And then expresly adds, that *this VAIL is taken away in Christ,*[93] which could not be truly affirm'd, were the things reveal'd still inconceivable: for I know no Difference between not hearing of a thing at all, and not comprehending it when you do. In another Place *Paul* has these remarkable Words; *The Preaching of Jesus Christ according to the Revelation of the Mystery which was kept secret since the World began, but now is made manifest; and by the Scriptures of the Prophets, according to the Commandment of the everlasting God, made known to all Nations for the Obedience of Faith.*[94]

These Passages alone sufficiently prove the Assertions contain'd [28] in N°6 and 7 of this Section, *viz.* First, that *the Mysteries of the Gospel were certain things in their own Nature intelligible enough, but call'd* Mysteries *by reason of the Vail under which they were formerly hid.* Secondly, that *under the Gospel this Vail is wholly remov'd.* From which, Thirdly, follows the promis'd Conclusion, that *such Doctrines cannot now properly deserve the Name of* Mysteries.

[29]   It is observable, that the hottest Sticklers for the *Fathers* do cite
their Authority only where they think it makes for them, and slight
or suppress it when not favourable to their Cause. Lest it should be
malitiously insinuated, that I serve the *holy Scriptures* after the same
manner, I shall here transcribe all the Passages of the *New Testament*
where the word *Mystery* occurs, that a Man running may read with
Conviction what I defend. The whole may be commodiously reduc'd
to these Heads. First, *Mystery* is read for the *Gospel* or the *Christian*
Religion in general, as it was a future Dispensation totally hid from
the *Gentiles*, and but very imperfectly known to the *Jews*: Secondly,
Some particular Doctrines occasionally reveal'd by the *Apostles* are
said to be *manifested Mysteries*, that is, unfolded Secrets. And, Thirdly, *Mystery* is put for any thing vail'd under Parables or Enigmatical
Forms of Speech. Of all these in Order.

[30]   *Mystery* is read for the *Gospel* or Christianity in general in the following Passages: *Rom.16.25,26. The Preaching of Jesus Christ according
to the Revelation of the MYSTERY which was kept secret since the World
began; but now is made manifest, and by the Writings of the Prophets,
according to the Commandment of the everlasting God, made known to all
Nations for the Obedience of Faith.* Now, in what Sense could this
Mystery be said to be reveal'd, this Secret to be made manifest, to be
made known to all Nations by the Preaching of the *Apostles*, if it
remain'd still incomprehensible? A mighty Favour indeed! to bless
the World with a parcel of unintelligible Notions or Expressions,
when it was already overstock'd with the *Acroatick*[95] Discourses of
Aristotle, with the *Esoterick* Doctrines of *Pythagoras*,[96] and the *Mysterious* Jargon of the other Sects of Philosophers; for they all made high
Pretences to some rare and wonderful Secrets not communicable to
every one of the Learned, and never to any of the Vulgar. By this
means the obsequious Disciples apologiz'd for all that was found contradictory, incoherent, dubious or incomprehensible in the Works of
their several Masters. To any that complain'd of Inconsistency or
Obscurity, they presently answer'd, O, Sir, the *Philosopher* said it, and
you ought therefore to believe it: He knew his own Meaning well
enough, tho he car'd not, it may be, that all others should do it too.
So the Occasions of your Scruples, Sir, are only seeming, and not

real. But the *Christian Religion* has no need of such miserable Shifts and Artifices, there being nothing in it *above* or *contrary* to the strictest *Reason*: And such as are of another Mind may as well justify the idle Dreams of the *Philosophers*, the Impieties and Fables of the *Alcoran*, or any thing as well as *Christianity*. The second Passage is in 1 *Cor*.2.7 the Words were but just now read, and need not here be repeated. The third Passage is in 1 *Cor*.4.1 *Let a Man so account of us as the Ministers of Christ, and the Stewards* or Dispensers *of the MYS-TERIES of God*; that is, the Preachers of those Doctrines which God was pleas'd to reveal. The fourth Passage is in *Ephes*.6.9 *Praying—— for me, that Utterance may be given unto me that I may open my Mouth boldly, to make known the MYSTERY of the Gospel*. Parallel to this is the fifth Passage in *Col*.4.3,4 *Praying also for us, that God would open unto us a Door of Utterance to speak the MYSTERY of Christ——that I may make it manifest as I ought to speak*. The Clearness of these Words admits of no Comment. The sixth Passage is in *Col*.2.2 *That their Hearts might be comforted being knit together in Love, and unto all the Riches of the full Assurance of Understanding, to the Knowledg of the MYSTERY of God, and of the Father, and of Christ*. Here is evidently meant the Revelation of the Gospel-State: for whatever right Conceptions the *Jews* might have of the *Father*, they had not that full Knowledg of *Christ* and his Doctrines, which are the inestimable Privileges we now enjoy. The seventh Passage is in 1 *Tim*.3.8,9 *Likewise must the Deacons be grave, not double-tongu'd, not given to much Wine, not greedy of filthy Lucre, holding the MYSTERY of the Faith in a pure Conscience*; that is, living to what they believe. The eighth and last Passage relating to this Head is in 1 *Tim*.3.16 *And without Controversy great is the MYSTERY of Godliness: God was manifest in the Flesh, justify'd in the Spirit, seen of Angels, preach'd unto the Gentiles, believ'd on in the World, receiv'd up into Glory*. I will not now insist upon the various Readings of these Words, nor critically determine which is spurious or genuine. All Parties (how much soever they differ about their Sense) agree that the Gradations of the Verse are Gospel-Revelations; so that the *Mystery of Godliness* cannot be restrain'd to any one, but is common to them all: It refers not to the Nature of any of them in particular, but to the Revelation of them all in general. And it must be granted, without any Dispute, that the gracious Manifestation of *Christ* and his *Gospel* is not only to us wonderfully stupendous and surprizing, but that it was likewise a very great *Mystery* to all preceding the *New Testament-Dispensation*. From these Passages it appears, that the *Gospel* and the following Expressions are synonymous, viz. *The Mystery of the Faith, the Mystery of God and Christ, the Mystery of Godliness*, and the *Mystery of the Gospel*. No Doctrine then of the *Gospel* is still a *Mystery* (for *the Apostles conceal'd nothing from us that was useful, and have acquainted us with the whole Counsel of God*[97]:) but 'tis the *Gospel* it felt that was heretofore indeed a *Mystery*, and cannot now after it is fully reveal'd, properly deserve that Appellation.

[31] We design in the second place to shew, that *certain Matters occasionally reveal'd by the Apostles, were only Mysterious before that Revelation*. The *Jews*, who scarce allow'd other Nations to be Men, thought of nothing less than that the time should ever come wherein those Nations might be *reconcil'd to God*,[98] and be made *Cohiers* and *Partakers* with them of the same Privileges. This was nevertheless resolv'd upon in the Divine Decree, and to the *Jews* was a *Mystery*, but ceases so to continue after the Revelation of it to *Paul*, who, in his Epistles, has openly declar'd it to all the World. The first Passage we shall alledg to that purpose is in *Eph.3.1—6.9 If you have heard of the Dispensation of the Grace of God which is given me to youward, how that by Revelation he made known unto me the MYSTERY (as I wrote before in few Words, whereby, when you read, you may understand my Knowledg in the MYSTERY of Christ) which in other Ages was not made known unto the Sons of Men, as it is now reveal'd unto us, his holy Apostles and Prophets, by the Spirit; that the Gentiles should be Fellow-heirs, and of the same Body, and Partakers of his Promise in Christ by the Gospel—and to make all Men see what is the Fellowship of the MYSTERY, which from the Beginning of the World hath been hid in God.* The second Passage is in *Rom.11.25. For I would not, Brethren, that you should be ignorant of this MYSTERY, that Blindness in part is happen'd to Israel until the Fulness of the Gentiles be come in.* The third Passage is in *Col.1.25,26,27— The Church, whereof I am made a Minister according to the Dispensation of God which is given to me for you, to fulfil the Word*

of God, *even the* MYSTERY *which hath been hid from Ages and Generations, but now is made manifest to his Saints: to whom God would make
known what are the Riches of the Glory of this* MYSTERY *among the
Gentiles.* The fourth Passage is in *Eph.*1.9,10. *Having made known
unto us the* MYSTERY *of his Will, according to his good Pleasure which
he hath purpos'd in himself, that in the Dispensation of the Fulness of
times, he might gather together into one all things in Christ.* These Places
require no Explication, for the Sense of them all is, that *the Secret of
the Vocation of the Gentiles is in the Gospel made known, manifested and
declar'd; and therefore remains no longer a Mystery.* The next thing
under the Designation of a *Mystery* in the above-mention'd Sense is
one Circumstance of the *Resurrection.* The *Apostle* having no less
clearly and solidly than largely reason'd upon this Subject (1
*Cor.*15), obviates an Objection or Scruple that might be rais'd about
the State of such as should be found alive on the Earth at the last
day. *Behold,* says he, *ver.*51,52. *I shew you a* MYSTERY, I impart a
Secret to you; *we shall not all sleep,* or die, *but we shall all be chang'd in
a Moment, in the twinkling of an Eye; —the Dead shall rise, and we shall
be chang'd.* It is not the Doctrine of the *Resurrection* then, you see,
that is here call'd a *Mystery,* but only this particular Circumstance of
it, *viz.* that the Living shall at the Sound of the last Trumpet put off
their Flesh and Blood, or their Mortality, without Dying, and be in
an Instant rendred incorruptable and immortal as well as those that
shall revive. In the fifth Chapter to the Ephesians, *ver.*31,32, we
learn that the mutual Love and Conjunction of *Man* and *Wife* is a
Type of that indissoluble Union which is between *Christ* and his
Church. This was questionless a *great Mystery* before we were told it,
but now there is nothing more intelligible than the Foundation of
that Resemblance or Figure. The Kingdom of *Antichrist* in opposition
to the *Gospel* or Kingdom of *Christ* is also call'd a *Mystery,* because it
was a secret Design carry'd on insensibly and by degrees: but at
length, all Obstacles being remov'd or surmounted, it appears bare-
fac'd to the Light, and (as it was divinely foretold) ceases to continue
a *Mystery. Let no Man deceive you by any means,* says *Paul* to the *Thes-
salonians,* (2 Thess.2.3,4,5,6,7,8.) *for that Day shall not come except
there come a falling away or Apostacy first; and that Man of Sin be*

71

reveal'd, the Son of Perdition, &c. And now you know what withholdeth, that he might not be reveal'd in his time; for the MYSTERY *of Iniquity doth already work, only he who now hindreth, will hinder till he be taken out of the way, and then shall that wicked one be reveal'd.* These are all the Passages relating to the second Head.

[32]   Mystery is, Thirdly, put for any thing vail'd under Parables or Enigmatical Expressions in these parallel Places following. The first is in Mat.13.10,11. *The Disciples came and said unto him, Why speakest thou unto them in Parables? He answer'd and said unto them, Because it is given unto you to know the* MYSTERIES *of the Kingdom of Heaven, but to them it is not given.* The second Passage is in Mark 4.11. *And Jesus said to his Disciples, Unto you is given to know the* MYSTERY *of the Kingdom of God; but unto them that are without, all these things are done in Parables.* The same Words are repeated in *Luke* 8.10. And it is most evident from all of 'em, that those things which *Christ* spoke in Parables were not in themselves incomprehensible, but *mysterious* to them only to whom they were not unfolded, *that* (as it is there said) *hearing they might not understand.* It is now the most ordinary Practice in the World for such as would not be understood by every one, to agree upon a way of speaking peculiar to themselves. Nor is there any thing more easy, than the Explication which *Christ* gave of these Parables at the Request of his Disciples.

[32a]   [99]Having so particularly alleg'd all the Passages where there is mention made of *Mysteries* in the *New Testament,* if any should wonder why I have omitted those in the *Revelation,* to such I reply, that the *Revelation* cannot be properly look'd upon as a Part of the *Gospel;* for there are no new Doctrines deliver'd in it. Far from being a Rule of Faith or Manners, it is not as much an Explanation of any Point in our Religion. The true Subject of that Book or *Vision* is a Prophetical History of the External State of the Church in its various and interchangeable Periods of Prosperity or Adversity. But that I may not fall under the least Suspicion of dealing unfairly, I shall subjoin the few Texts of the *Revelation* wherein the word *Mystery* is contain'd. The first is in *Rev.*1.20. *The* MYSTERY *of the seven Stars which thou sawest in my right Hand, and the seven Golden Candlesticks:* Well, what is the *Mystery* or Secret of these Stars and Candlesticks? *The seven Stars are*

the Angels of the seven Churches; and the seven Candlesticks, which thou sawest, are the seven Churches, namely, of *Asia.* Another Passage is in *chap.*17.5,7. *And upon her Forehead was a Name written, MYSTERY, BABYLON THE GREAT, &c. And the Angel said,— I will tell thee the MYSTERY of the Woman.* This he performs too in the following Verses, which you may consult. The only remaining Text is in *chap.*10.5,6,7. *And the Angel which I saw stand upon the Sea and upon the Earth, lifted up his Hand to Heaven, and swore by him that liveth for ever and ever, who created Heaven and the things that therein are, and the Earth and the things that therein are, and the Sea and the things which are therein, that there should be time no longer; but that in the Days of the Voice of the seventh Angel, when he shall begin to sound, the MYSTERY of God should be finish'd:* that is, that all the things figuratively deliver'd in this Prophecy concerning the *Gospel* (which was shewn above to signify the same with *the Mystery of God*) should have their final Accomplishment, and so end with this Globe and all therein contain'd.

There are but two Passages only left, and *Mystery* in them has no [33] reference to any thing in particular, but it is put for all secret things in its utmost Latitude or Acceptation. The first Place is in 1 *Cor.*13.2. *And tho I have the Gift of Prophecy, and understand all MYSTERIES, and all Knowledg; and tho I have all Faith so that I could remove Mountains, and have no Charity, I am nothing.* The second, parallel to this, is in 1 *Cor.*14.2. *He that speaketh in an unknown tongue, speaketh not unto Men but unto God; for no Man understandeth him, however in the Spirit he speaketh MYSTERIES;* that is, what is intelligible enough to him, are Secrets to such as understand not his Language.

I appeal now to all equitable Persons, whether it be not evident to [34] any that can read, that *Mystery* in the whole *New Testament* is never put for *any thing inconceivable in it self, or not to be judg'd of by our ordinary Notions and Faculties, however clearly reveal'd:* And whether, on the contrary, it do's not always signify *some things naturally intelligible enough; but either so vail'd by figurative Words and Rites, or so lodg'd in God's sole Knowledg and Decree, that they could not be discover'd without special Revelation.* Whoever retains any real Veneration for the *Scripture,* and sincerely believes it to be the Word of God, must be ever concluded by its Authority, and render himself, in spight of all

Prejudices, to its Evidence. He that says the *Gospel* is his only Rule of Faith, and yet believes any thing not warranted by it, he is an arrant Hypocrite, and do's but slily banter all the World.

[35]   [100]Nor can a more favourable Opinion be harbour'd of those, who, instead of Submission to the Dictates of *Scripture* and *Reason*, straight have Recourse to such Persons as they specially follow or admire, and are ready to receive or refuse an Opinion, as these shall please to direct them.

> Pray, Doctor, says one of his Parishioners, what think you of such a Book? it seems to make things plain.
>
> Ah! dear Sir, answers the Doctor, it is a very bad Book; he's a dangerous Man that wrote it; he's for believing nothing but what agrees with his own purblind, proud and carnal *Reason*.
>
> P. Say you so, Doctor? then I'm resolv'd to read no more of it, for I heard you often *preach against humane Reason*; I'm sorry, truly, it should unhappily fall into my Hands, but I'll take care that none of our Family set their Eyes upon't.
>
> D. You'll do very well, Sir; besides, this Book is still worse than I told you, for it destroys a great many Points which we teach; and should this Doctrine take (which God forbid), most of the good Books you have at home, and which cost you no less Pains to read than Money to purchase, would signify not a Straw, and serve only for Waste-Paper to put under Pies, or for other mean Uses.
>
> P. Bless me, good Doctor, I pray God forgive me reading in such a vile Treatise; he's an abominable Man that could write it; but what? my Books worth nothing, say you? Dr. H's Sermons, and Mr. C's Discourses Waste-Paper?[101] I'll never believe it, let who will say the contrary; Lord, why don't you excommunicate the Author, and seize upon his Books?
>
> D. Ay, Sir, Time was,—but now it seems a Man may *believe according to his own Sense*, and not *as the Church directs*; there's a *Toleration* establish'd, you know.
>
> P. That *Toleration*, Doctor, will—
>
> D. Whist, Sir, say no more of it; I am as much concern'd as you can be; but it is not safe nor expedient at this time of day to find Faults.

[36]   There are others far from this Simplicity, but as firmly resolv'd to stand fast by their old Systems. When they tell us of *Mysteries*, we must believe them, and there's no Remedy for it. It is not the Force of Reasoning that makes these for *Mysteries*, but some by-Interest; and they'll be sure to applaud and defend any Author that writes in favour of their Cause, whether he supports it with *Reason* or not. But I'm not half so angry with these Men as with a sort of People that will not be at the Pains of examining any thing, lest they should become more clear-sighted or better inform'd, and so be tempted to take up a new Road. Such Persons must needs be very indifferent indeed, or they make Religion come into their Scutcheons.

The mention of Scutcheons naturally puts me in mind of those [37]
who are little mov'd with any Reasons, when *the Judgment of the
Primitive Church* comes in competition. The *Fathers* (as they love to
speak) are to them the best Interpreters of the Words of *Scripture*;

And what those honest Men, says a very ingenious[102] Person, could not make good
themselves by sufficient Reasons, is now prov'd by their sole Authority. If the Fathers
foresaw this, adds the same author, they were not to be blam'd for sparing themselves
the Labour of reasoning more exactly than we find they commonly did.

That Truth and Falshood should be determin'd by a Majority of
Voices, or certain Periods of Time, seems to me to be the most
ridiculous of all Follies.

But if *Antiquity* can in good earnest add any worth to an Opinion, [38]
I think I need not fear to stand its Decision:

For if we consider the Duration of the World, (says another celebrated[103] Writer) as
we do that of a Man's Life, consisting of Infancy, Youth, Manhood, and old Age; then
certainly such as liv'd before us were the Children or the Youth, and we are the true
Antients of the World. And if Experience (continues he) be the most considerable
Advantage which grown Persons have over the younger sort, then, questionless, the
Experience of such as come last into the World must be incomparably greater than of
those that were born long before them: for the last Comers enjoy not only all the
Stock of their Predecessors, but to it have likewise added their own Observations.

These Thoughts are no less ingenious than they are just and solid.
But if *Antiquity* be understood in the vulgar Sense, I have no Reason
to despair however; for my Hypothesis too will become antient to
Posterity, and so be in a Condition to support it self by this commodious Privilege of Prescription.

Yet seeing I am not likely to live till that time, it cannot be amiss [39]
to make it appear that these same *Fathers*, who have the good luck to
be at once both the Young and the Old of the World, are on my side.
'Tis not out of any Deference to their Judgments, I confess, that I
take these Pains. I have freely declar'd what Value I set upon their
Authority in the Beginning of this Book: but my Design is to shew
the Disingenuity of those, who pretending the highest Veneration for
the Writings of the *Fathers*, never fail to decline their Sentence when
it sutes not with their Humour or Interest.

Clemens Alexandrinus[104] has every where the same Notion of *Mys-* [40]
tery that I have, that the *Gentiles* had, and which I have prov'd to be

that of the *Gospel*. In the 5th Book of his *Stromates*, which merits the Perusal of all that are curious to understand the Nature of the *Jewish* and *Heathen Mysteries*; in that Book, I say, he puts the Matter out of all doubt, and quotes several of those Texts of Scripture, which I have already alleg'd to this purpose. Nay, he tells us, that the *Christian Discipline was call'd*[105] *Illumination, because it brought hidden things to light, the Master (CHRIST) alone removing the Cover of the Ark; that is, the Mosaick Vail.**

[41] Every one knows how the Primitive *Christians*, in imitation of the *Jews*, turn'd all the *Scripture* into Allegory; accomodating the Properties of those Animals mention'd in the *Old Testament* to Events that happen'd under the *New*. They took the same Liberty principally with Men, where they could discover the least Resemblance between their Names, Actions, or State of Life; and carry'd this Fancy at length to Numbers, Letters, Places, and what not. That which in the *Old Testament* therefore did, according to them, represent any thing in the *New*, they call'd the *Type* or *Mystery* of it. Thus TYPE, SYMBOL, PARABLE, SHADOW, FIGURE, SIGN and MYSTERY, signify all the same thing in *Justin Martyr*.[106] This Father affirms in his Dialogue with *Tryphon* the *Jew*,[107] that the Name of *Joshua* was a *Mystery* representing the Name *Jesus*; and that the holding up of *Moses's* Hands during the Battel with the *Amalekites* in *Rephidim*,[108] was a *Type* or *Mystery* of *Christ's Cross*, whereby he overcame Death, as the *Israelites* there did their Enemies: and then adds the following Remark *This is to be consider'd,* says he, *concerning those two holy Men and Prophets of God, that neither of them was able in his single Person to carry both MYSTERIES, I mean the Type of his Cross, and that of being call'd by his Name.*[109] In the same Dialogue he calls the Predictions of the Prophets.[110] *SYMBOLS, PARABLES and MYSTERIES.***

---

* [Toland added the following to the second edition:]
  He adds in express Words, that those things which were mysterious and obscure in the Old Testament are made plain in the New.

** [In the second edition, this sentence ends as follows:]
  ... *MYSTERIES* explain'd by the succeeding Prophets.

CHRISTIANITY NOT MYSTERIOUS

When *Tertullian*[111] in his Apology justifies the Christians from [42] those inhumane Practices whereof their Enemies most unjustly accus'd 'em, he cries,[112]

We are beset, we are discover'd every day; —But if we keep always hid, how are those things known which we are said to commit? Nay, who could make them known? Such as are guilty! Not so, surely: for all *Mysteries* are of Course under an Oath of Secrecy. The *Samothracian*, the *Eleusinian Mysteries* are conceal'd; how much rather such as being discover'd would now provoke the Justice of Men, and might expect to meet with that of God hereafter.

They are secret Practices, you see, and not incomprehensible Doctrines which this Father counted *Mysteries*.

Origen[113] makes the Encampments of the *Israelites* in their Journey [43] to the Promised Land to be[114] *Symbols* or *Mysteries* describing the way to such as shall travel towards Heaven, or heavenly things. I need not add what he says of the Writings of the *Prophets*, of the Vision of *Ezekiel*, or the *Apocalypse* in particular: for he is universally confess'd to have brought this Mystick or Allegorical Method of interpreting Scripture to its Perfection, and to have furnish'd Matter to all that trod the same Path after him. But he was so far from thinking any Doctrine of our Religion *a Mystery* in the present Sense of the Word, that he expressely affirms them[115] *to agree all with* COMMON NOTIONS, *and to commend themselves to the Assent of every well-dispos'd Hearer.*

The other *Fathers* of the three first Centuries have exactly the [44] same Notions of *Mystery*: And should they in this Matter happen to contradict in one Place what they establish'd in another (as they ordinarily do in most things), it would only serve *to exclude them from being a true Rule to others, that were none to themselves.* But what is no small Prejudice in our Favour, seeing we have to do with Men so apt to forget, they keep very constant to this Point: so that I may justly hope by this time the Cause of *Incomprehensible and Inconceivable Mysteries in Religion* should be readily given up by all that sincerely respect *FATHERS, SCRIPTURE* or *REASON.*

77

Objections brought from particular Texts of Scripture,
from the Nature of Faith, and Miracles, answer'd

---

[45]   Some Men are so fond of *Mysteries*, and it seems they find their
Account in it, that they are ready to hazard any thing sooner than
Part with them. In the mean time, whether they know it or not, they
lay nothing less than their Religion at stake by this Conduct; for it is
an ugly Sign when People profess that what they believe is above the
Examination of Reason, and will suffer it by no means to come into
question: *It argues in themselves a Distrust of their Cause; and others*
conclude, that what dares not abide the Trial of Reason, must needs it self
be unreasonable at bottom.

[46]   Notwithstanding these Consequences are so obvious, they harden
themselves against them, and are not asham'd to bring even *Scripture*
to countenance their Assertion. You shall hear nothing more frequently in their Mouths than these Words of the Apostle, *Beware lest*
any Man spoil you by PHILOSOPHY *and vain Deceit, after the Tradi-*
tion of Men, after the Rudiments of the World, and not after Christ.[116]
Ridiculous! as if Reason and Truth were Vanity and Craft! By *Philos-*
ophy is not here understood *sound Reason* (as all Interpreters agree),
but the Systems of *Plato*, of *Aristotle*, of *Epicurus*, of the *Academicks*,
&c. many of whose Principles are directly repugnant to common
Sense and good Morals. *Sophistry* was never more in vogue than in
the Days of *Paul*; and several out of these Sects imbracing
Christianity, found the way to mix it with their old Opinions, which
they were loth to quit for good and all. The Apostle therefore had
weighty grounds to warn his Converts not to confound the Inven-

78

tions of Men with the Doctrine of God. It appears nevertheless that
this good Advice was to little purpose, for you'll find the grossest
Mistakes and Whimsies of the *Fathers* to have been occasion'd by the
several Systems of *Philosophy* they read before their Conversion, and
which they afterwards foolishly endeavour'd to reconcile with *Christianity*, to the entire Ruine almost of the latter, as we shall shew in
the following Chapter.

But as no particular *Hypothesis* whatsoever has a Right to set up   [47]
for a Standard of Reason to all Mankind, much less may *vain Philosophy* or *Sophistry* claim this Privilege: and so far am I from aiming at
any such thing, that it is the very Practice I oppose in this Book.
When some have advanc'd the Metaphysical Nonsense of doting
Philosophers into Articles of Faith, they raise a loud Clamour against
Reason, before whose Evidence and Light their empty Shadows must
disappear. For as in *Philosophy* so in *Religion* every Sect has its peculiar Extravagancies, and the INCOMPREHENSIBLE MYSTERIES
of the latter do perfectly answer the OCCULT QUALITIES of the
former. They were both calculated at first for the same Ends, viz. *to
stop the Mouths of such as demand a Reason where none can be given,
and to keep as many in Ignorance as Interest shall think convenient.* But
God forbid that I should impute the like nefarious Designs to all that
contend for *Mysteries* now, Thousands whereof I know to be the best
meaning Men in the Universe. This *sophistical* or *corrupt Philosophy* is
elsewhere in the *New Testament* stil'd the *Wisdom of this World*,[117] to
which the Greeks were as much bigotted, as the *Jews* were infatuated
with a Fancy that nothing could be true but what was miraculously
prov'd so: *The Jews require a Sign, and the Greeks seek after Wisdom.*[118]
But this boasted Wisdom was then *Foolishness with God*, and so it is
now with considering Men.

A Passage out of the Epistle to the *Romans* is cited likewise to   [48]
prove Humane *Reason* not a capable Judg of what is divinely reveal'd.
The Words are, *The carnal Mind is Enmity against God; for it is not
subject to the Law of God, neither indeed can be.*[119] But if these Words
be spoken of *Reason*, there can be nothing more false; because *Reason*
do's and ought to subject it self to the Divine Law: yet this Submission argues no Imperfection in *Reason*, as our Obedience to just Laws

cannot be said to destroy our Liberty. *Reason* must first understand the Law of God, and then comply with it; for a Man can no more deserve Punishment for not observing such Laws as are unintelligible, than for not performing what was never enjoin'd him. The *carnal Mind* then in this Place is not *Reason*, but the carnal Desires of lewd and wicked Men; whose Practices, as they are contrary to the reveal'd Law of God, so they are to that of sound *Reason* too.

[49]   What has been discours'd of pretended Wisdom and sensual Minds may be easily appli'd to another Passage where it is said, that *the Weapons of our Warfare are not carnal, but mighty through God to the pulling down of strong Holds, casting down Imaginations, and every high thing that exalteth it self against the Knowledg of God, and bringing into Captivity every Thought to the Obedience of Christ.*[120] It is plain from the Words as well as the Scope of the whole, that these are the Thoughts and Imaginations of foolish and profane Men, and should be captivated or reform'd by *Reason* as well as *Scripture*; as, in effect, they often are: for such Persons not ordinarily allowing of Argument from *Scripture*, are first perswaded by *Reason*, and after that they receive the *Scripture*. But can *Reason* cast down or destroy it self? No; it reduces those vain and impious Sophisms which borrow its Name to cover or authorize the Disorders they occasion.

[50]   It would be extremely tedious to go one by one over all the Texts which ignorant or perverse Men alledg against that Use of Reason in Religion which I particularly establish. Any single Passage to my purpose should, one would think, give sufficient Satisfaction to all *Christian* Lovers of Truth: for the Word of God must be every where uniform and self-consistent. But I have quoted several in the 2*d* Chapter of the second Section, to speak nothing of what I perform'd in the foregoing Chapter of the present Section. Yet because this reasoning might be retorted, and to leave no plausible Pretences to Cavillers or Deceivers, I have punctually answer'd the strongest Objections I have observ'd in the most celebrated Pieces of *Divinity*; I say *which I have observ'd*, for I should read the *Gospel* a Million of Times over before the Vulgar Notion of *Mystery* could ever enter into my Head, or any Passage in that Book could suggest to me that the Sense of it was above Reason or Enquiry. Nor do I find my self yet inclin'd to

envy those who entertain other Thoughts of it, when all the while they openly acknowledg it to be a Divine Revelation. But seeing the most material Difficulty made to me by a Friend, is, that my Opinion destroys the Nature of *Faith*, I shall with all the Brevity I can deliver my Sentiments concerning this Subject.

I will spend no time upon the ordinary Divisions of *Faith* into His- [51] torical, Temporary or Justifying, Lively or Dead, Weak or Strong, because most of these are not so much *Faith* it self, as different Effects thereof. The word imports *Belief* or *Perswasion*, as when we give Credit to any thing which is told us by God or Man; whence *Faith* is properly divided into *Humane* and *Divine*. Again, *Divine Faith* is either when God speaks to us immediately himself, or when we acquiesce in the Words or Writings of those to whom we believe he has spoken. All *Faith* now in the World is of this last sort, and by consequence entirely built upon *Ratiocination*. For we must first be convinc'd that those Writings are theirs whose Names they bear, we then examine the outward State and Actions of those Persons, and lastly understand what is contain'd in their Works; otherwise we cannot determine whether they be worthy of God or not, much less firmly believe them.

To be confident of any thing without conceiving it, is no real [52] *Faith* or Perswasion, but a rash Presumption and an obstinate Preju- dice, rather becoming Enthusiasts or Impostors than the taught of God, who has no Interest to delude his Creatures, nor wants Ability to inform them rightly. I prov'd before (*Sect. 2 Chap. 2*) that the Dif- ference between *Humane* and *Divine Revelations* did not consist in degrees of Perspicuity, but in Certitude. So many Circumstances fre- quently concur in History as render it equal to Intuition: Thus I can as soon deny my own Being as the Murder of *Cicero*, or the Story of *William the Conqueror*; yet this happens only sometimes: But God speaks always Truth and Certainty.

Now since by *Revelation* Men are not endu'd with any new Facul- [53] ties, it follows that God should lose his end in speaking to them, if what he said did not agree with their common Notions. Could that Person justly value himself upon being wiser than his Neighbours, who having infallible Assurance that something call'd *Blictri*[121] had a

Being in Nature, in the mean time knew not what this *Blictri* was? And seeing the Case stands really thus, all *Faith* or Perswasion must necessarily consist of two Parts, *Knowledg* and *Assent*. 'Tis the last indeed that continues the formal Act of *Faith*, but not without the Evidence of the first: And this is the true Account we have of it all over the *New Testament*. There we read that *without Faith it is impossible to please God; but he that cometh to God must believe that he is, and that he is a Rewarder of them that diligently seek him.*[122] So the firm Perswasion of a pious Man that his Requests will be granted, is grounded upon his knowledg of the Being, Goodness, and Power of God. It was reckon'd no Crime not to believe in *Christ* before he was reveal'd; *for how could they believe in him of whom they had not heard?*[123] But with what better Reason could any be condemn'd for not believing what he said, if they might not understand it? for as far as I can see these Cases are parallel. *Faith* is likewise said *to come by hearing;*[124] but without Understanding 'tis plain this Hearing would signify nothing, Words and their Ideas being reciprocal in all Languages.

[54]　　The Author of the Epistle to the *Hebrews* do's not define *Faith* a Prejudice, Opinion or Conjecture, but Conviction or Demonstration: *Faith*, says he, *is the confident Expectation of things hop'd for, and the Demonstration of things not seen.*[125] These last Words, *things not seen*, signify not (as some would have it) things incomprehensible or unintelligible, but past or future Matters of Fact, as the Creation of the World, and the Resurrection of the Dead, or the Belief of some things invisible to our corporeal Eyes, tho intelligible enough to the Eyes of our Understanding. This appears by all the Examples subjoin'd to that Definition. Besides, there can be properly no *Faith* of things seen or present, for then 'tis Self-evidence and not Ratiocination: *Hope that is seen is not Hope, for what a Man sees why doth he yet hope for? But if we hope for what we see not, then do we with Patience wait for it.*[126] So the Patriarchs *receiv'd not the Promises, but saw them afar off, and were perswaded of them.*[127]

[55]　　Without conceiving Faith after this manner, how could *Christ* be term'd *the Light of the World,*[128] *the Light of the Gentiles?*[129] How could Believers be said *to have the Spirit of Wisdom,*[130] and to have *the Eyes of their Hearts enlightn'd?*[131] For the Light of the Heart or Understand-

ing is the Knowledg of things; and as this Knowledg is more or less, so the Mind is proportionably illuminated. *Be not unwise*, says the Apostle, *but understanding what the Will of the Lord is.*[132] And in another place he exhorts Men never to act in dubious Matters till they are *fully perswaded in their own Minds.*[133]

But to all this will be objected that remarkable Instance of *Abra-* [56] *ham's* Faith, who was ready to sacrifice his only Son, notwithstanding God had promis'd that Kings should descend of him, and his Seed be numerous as the Stars of Heaven, or the Sand upon the Seashore. Did *Abraham* blindly obey then, without reconciling the apparent Contradiction between God's present Command and his former Promises? Far from it: for 'tis expresly recorded, that *he that had receiv'd the Promises offer'd up his only begotten, of whom it was said, that in* Isaac *shall thy Seed be blessed;*[134] *Reasoning that God was able to raise him again from the Dead, from whence also he had receiv'd him in a Figure.*[135] He rightly concluded that God was able to revive *Isaac* by a Miracle, as he was miraculously born, according to another Promise, after his Parents were past having Children, and *so as good as dead:*[136] therefore it is elsewhere written of *Abraham*, that *being not weak in Faith, he consider'd not his own Body now dead, when he was about an hundred Years old, neither yet the Deadness of* Sarah's *Womb; nor stagger'd at God's Promise through Unbelief; but being strong in Faith he gave Glory to God, and was fully perswaded that what he had promis'd he was able also to perform.*[137]

Now what is there in all this, but very strict Reasoning from Expe- [57] rience, from the Possibility of the thing, and from the Power, Justice and Immutability of him that promis'd it? Nor can any Man shew me in all the *New Testament* another Signification of *Faith*, but a most firm Perswasion built upon substantial Reasons. In this Sense all *Christianity* is not seldom stil'd *the Faith*; as now we usually say that we are of this or that Perswasion, meaning the Profession of some Religion. But surely nothing can better *root* and *establish* our Perswasion than a thorow Examination and Trial of what we believe; whereas the Weakness and Instability of our *Faith* proceed from want of sufficient Reasons for it, whereupon Incredulity always follows; then fails Obedience, which is the constant Sign and Fruit of genuine *Faith*; and hence spring all the Irregularities of Mens Lives. *He that saith I know him, and keepeth not his Commandments, is a Liar*—For *he that saith he abideth in him, ought himself also to walk as he walked.*[138] Nor can it possibly fall out otherwise, but that he who believes without Understanding must *be tost and carri'd about with every Wind of Doctrine, by the Slight and Cunning of Men ready to deceive.*[139]

[58]   Tho the Authority of the New Testament be so clear in this Matter, yet I shall further confirm it by the following Observations. First, *if Faith were not a Perswasion resulting from the previous Knowledg and Comprehension of the thing believ'd, there could be no Degrees nor Differences in it*; for these are evident Tokens that Men know more or less of a thing, as they have Desires or Opportunities to learn it. But that there are such Degrees appears by the *Scripture*, where those that have only an imperfect and perfunctory Knowledg of Religion are compar'd to *Infants* who feed only upon Milk;[140] but they who arrive at a more full and accurate Certainty are liken'd to *grown Men* that can digest stronger Food.[141]

[59]   My next Observation is, that *the Subject of Faith must be intelligible to all, since the Belief thereof is commanded under no less a Penalty than Damnation*: He that believeth not shall be damned.[142] But shall any be damn'd for the Non-performance of Impossibilities? Obligations to believe do therefore suppose a Possibility to understand. I shew'd before that *Contradiction* and *Nothing* were convertible Terms; and I may now say as much of *Mystery* in the Theological Sense: for, to speak freely, *Contradiction* and *Mystery* are but two emphatick ways of saying Nothing. *Contradiction* expresses Nothing by a couple of Ideas that destroy one another, and *Mystery* expresses Nothing by Words that have no Ideas at all.

[60]   The third Observation shall be, that *if any part of Scripture were unintelligible, it could never be rightly translated*, except the Sound of the Words, and not their Sense, be look'd upon as the Revelation of God. Terms can by no means be understood, unless the things they denote be understood also. I may well understand Things without their Names, but never Names without knowing their Subjects. And, in good earnest, to what sort of Assurance can any Man pretend, that he has made a good Version of what he openly professes not to con-

ceive? It cannot be imagin'd how much the Notion of *Mystery* contributes to the Obscurity of *Scripture* in most Translations. When an able Linguist meets with a difficult Passage, he presently takes it for a *Mystery*, and concludes it is to no purpose to be at more Pains about what is in it self inexplicable. But an uncapable Translator lays his own blundring Nonsense, and all the *mysterious* Fruits of his Ignorance to God Almighty's Charge. These are the Wretches who plentifully furnish the *Atheistical* and *Profane* with all the Matter of their Objections against *Scripture*. But I hope in Time we may see a Remedy to these Disorders.

The fourth Observation is, that *except Faith signifies an intelligible* [61] *Perswasion, we cannot give others a Reason of our Hope,* as *Peter* directs us.[143] To say that what we believe is the Word of God, will be to no end, except we prove it to be so by Reason; and I need not add, that if we may not examine and understand our *Faith*, every Man will be oblig'd implicitely to continue of that Religion wherein he is first educated. Suppose a *Siamese* Talapoin[144] should tell a *Christian* Preacher that *Sommonocodom*[145] forbad the Goodness of his Religion to be tri'd by the Light of Reason; how could the *Christian* confute him, if he likewise should maintain that certain Points of Christianity were above Reason? The Question would not be then, whether *Mysteries* might be allow'd in the true Religion, but who had more Right to institute them, *Christ* or *Sommonocodom*?

My last Observation shall be, that *either the Apostles could not write* [62] *more intelligibly of the reputed Mysteries, or they would not.* If they would not, then 'tis no longer our Fault if we neither understand nor believe them: And if they could not write more clearly themselves, they were so much less to expect Credit from others.

But 'tis affirm'd, that God *has a Right to require the Assent of his* [63] *Creatures to what they cannot comprehend*; and, questionless, he may command whatever is just and reasonable, for to act Tyrannically do's only become the *Devil*. But I demand to what end should God require us to believe what we cannot understand? To exercise, some say, our Diligence. But this at first sight looks ridiculous, as if the plain Duties of the *Gospel* and our necessary Occupations were not sufficient to employ all our time. But how exercise our Diligence? Is it possible for us to understand those *Mysteries* at last, or not? If it be, then all I contend for is gain'd; for I never pretended that the *Gospel* could be understood without due Pains and Application, no more than any other Book. But if it be impossible after all to understand them, this is such a piece of Folly and Impertinence as no sober Man would be guilty of, to puzzle Peoples Heads with what they could never conceive, to exhort to and command the Study of them; and all this to keep 'em from Idleness, when they can scarce find leisure enough for what is on all hands granted to be intelligible.

[64] Others say that God has enjoin'd the Belief of *Mysteries* to make us more humble. But how? By letting us see the small Extent of our Knowledg. But this extraordinary Method is quite needless, for Experience acquaints us with that very day; and I have spent a whole Chapter in the second Section of this Book, to prove that we have not an adequate Idea of all the Properties, and no Idea of the real Essence of any Substance in the World. It had been a much better Answer, that God would thus abridg our Speculations, to gain us the more time for the practice of what we understand. But many cover a *Multitude of Sins* by their Noise and Heat on the behalf of such foolish and unprofitable Speculations.

[65] From all these Observations, and what went before, it evidently follows that *Faith* is so far from being an implicite Assent to any thing above Reason, that this Notion directly contradicts the Ends of Religion, the Nature of Man, and the Goodness and Wisdom of God. But at this rate, some will be apt to say, *Faith* is no longer *Faith* but *Knowledg*. I answer, that if *Knowledg* be taken for a present and immediate View of things, I have no where affirm'd any thing like it, but the contrary in many Places. But if by *Knowledg* be meant understanding what is believ'd, then I stand by it that *Faith* is *Knowledg*: I have all along maintain'd it, and the very Words are promiscuously us'd for one another in the *Gospel. We know, i.e.* we believe, *that this is indeed the Christ, the Saviour of the World.*[146] *I know and am perswaded by the Lord Jesus that there is nothing unclean of it self.*[147] *You know that your Labour is not in vain in the Lord.*[148]

[66] Others will say that this Notion of *Faith* makes *Revelation* useless. But, pray, how so? for the Question is not, whether we could discover

all the Objects of our *Faith* by Ratiocination: I have prov'd on the contrary, that no Matter of Fact can be known without *Revelation.* But I assert, that what is once reveal'd we must as well understand as any other Matter in the World, *Revelation being only of use to* enform us, whilst the Evidence of its Subject perswades us. Then, reply they, *Reason* is of more Dignity than *Revelation.* I answer, Just as much as a *Greek Grammar* is superior to the *New Testament*; for we make use of *Grammar* to understand the Language, and of *Reason* to comprehend the Sense of that Book. But, in a word, I see no need of Comparisons in this Case, for *Reason* is not less from God than *Revelation*: 'tis the Candle, the Guide, the Judg he has lodg'd within every Man that cometh into this World.

Lastly, It may be objected, that the Poor and Illiterate cannot [67] have such a *Faith* as I maintain. Truly if this can be made out, it may pass for a greater *Mystery* than any system of *Divinity* in *Christendom* can afford: for what can seem more strange and wonderful, than that the common People will sooner believe what is unintelligible, incomprehensible, and above their Reasons, than what is easy, plain, and suted to their Capacities? But the Vulgar are more oblig'd to *Christ*, who had a better Opinion of them than these Men; for he preach'd his *Gospel* to them in a special manner; and they, on the other hand, *heard him gladly;*[149] because, no doubt, they understood his Instructions better than the *mysterious* Lectures of their *Priests* and *Scribes.* The uncorrupted Doctrines of *Christianity* are not above their Reach or Comprehension, but the Gibberish of your *Divinity Schools* they understand not. It is to them the Language of the Beast, and is inconsistent with their Condition in this World, when their very Teachers must serve above an Apprenticeship to master it, before they begin the Study of the *Bible.* How slowly must the *Gospel* have mov'd at the Beginning, if such as were call'd to preach it had been oblig'd to qualify themselves after this manner! And no wonder that it has such little Effects now upon Mens Lives, after it is so miserably deform'd and almost ruin'd by those unintelligible and extravagant Terms, Notions, and Rites of *Pagan* or *Jewish* Original.

Thus I have distinctly answer'd the several Objections made to [68] me, and I shall add no more on this Subject of *Faith*, when I have consider'd a Passage in the first Epistle to *Peter*, where it is written, that *the Angels* desire to see into certain things; yet those things are not inconceivable *Mysteries*, but the Coming of *Christ* and the *Gospel-State of Salvation*, which were divinely foretold to the *Jews*, and concerning which they carefully reason'd then, tho, now those things are fulfill'd, we are not permitted that Liberty. *Receiving the end of your Faith*, says Peter, *the Salvation of your Souls; of which Salvation the Prophets have enquir'd and diligently search'd, who prophesi'd of the Grace that should come unto you; searching what or what manner of time the Spirit of Christ which was in them did signify, when it testify'd before-hand the Sufferings of Christ and the Glory that should follow: Unto whom it was reveal'd, that not unto themselves, but unto us they did minister the things which are now reported unto you by them that have preach'd unto you by the Holy Ghost sent down from Heaven, which things the Angels desire to look into.*[150] Now here's no great *Mystery* in all this, that the *Angels*, who being finite Creatures, can know nothing but by Experience, Ratiocination or Revelation, should be as curious as the *Jews* to penetrate into those future Events of such Importance, and so very obscurely reveal'd.

[69]   *When all other shifts prove ineffectual, the Partizans of *Mystery* fly to *Miracles* as their last Refuge; but this is too weak a Place to make any long Resistance, and we doubt not of beating 'em quickly thence with Ease and Safety. But seeing, for the most part, the State of this Controversy is never distinctly laid, I shall first endeavour to give a clear Notion of the Nature of *Miracles*, and then leave it to be consider'd whether I have much Reason to apprehend any Danger from this Objection. *A Miracle then is some Action exceeding all humane Power, and which the Laws of Nature cannot perform by their ordinary Operations.*

[70]   Now whatever is contrary to *Reason* can be no *Miracle*, for it has been sufficiently prov'd already, that *Contradiction* is only another word for *Impossible* or *Nothing*. The *miraculous* Action therefore must be something in it self intelligible and possible, tho the manner

---

*   [In the second edition, this paragraph marks the beginning of a new Chapter (V), called *Objections, drawn from the Consideration of MIRACLES, answer'd.* Chapter V of the first edition becomes Chapter VI in the second edition.]

of doing it be extraordinary. So for a Man to walk safe in the midst of Fire is conceivable, and possible too, should any thing capable of repelling the Heat and Flames surround him: but when such a Security is not provided by Art or Chance, but is the immediate Effect of supernatural Power, then it makes a *Miracle*. An able *Physician* do's sometimes restore Sight to the Blind, and a Hand or Foot must dry up, when the Circulation of the Blood and Humours is too much excluded from it: but if without the ordinary Time and Applications those Members be cur'd in an Instant, at the Command or Desire of any Person, such an Action is truly *miraculous*, as well as the sudden Restoration of a sick Body to Health, which Art or Nature must spend a great deal of Time and Pains upon.

No *Miracle* then is contrary to Reason, for the Action must be [71] intelligible, and the Performance of it appear most easy to the Author of *Nature*, who may command all its Principles at his Pleasure. Therefore all those *Miracles* are fictitious, wherein there occur any Contradictions, as that *Christ* was born without opening any Passage out of the *Virgin's* Body; that a Head spoke some Days after it was sever'd from the Body, and the Tongue cut out; with Multitudes of this kind that may be met with among the *Papists*, the *Jews*, the *Bramins*, the *Mahometans*, and in all Places where the Credulity of the People makes 'em a Merchandize to their Priests.

Let us next consider, that God is not so prodigal of *Miracles*, as to [72] work any at random. The Order of Nature is not alter'd, stopp'd or forwarded, unless for some weighty Design becoming the Divine Wisdom and Majesty. And, indeed, we learn from *Scripture* and *Reason*, that no *Miracle* is ever wrought without some special and important End, which is either appointed by those for whom the Miracle is made, or intended and declar'd by him that works it. If the *Apostles* had barely cur'd the blind, the deaf, the lame, the diseas'd, this would certainly procure 'em an extraordinary Esteem; and in some Places too Divine Worship, as it hapned to *Paul* and *Barnabas* at *Lystra*,[151] when they had cur'd a born Cripple without any farther Circumstance; but this was only a Means to gain the Attention of these Idolaters to the Doctrine they were about to preach in their City. Nor is there any *Miracle* mention'd in the *New Testament*, but what serv'd to confirm the Authority of those that wrought it, to procure Attention to the Doctrines of the *Gospel*, or for the like wise and reasonable Purposes.

[73]   By this Rule the celebrated Feats of *Goblins* and *Fairies*, of *Witches*, of *Conjurers*, and all the *Heathen Prodigies*, must be accounted idle and superstitious Fables; for in all these there appears no End deserving a Change in *Nature*. Besides, they evidently contradict our Idea of God, and quite subvert his Providence. Diabolical Delusions would hereby receive equal Confirmation with Divine Revelation, *Miracles* being perform'd in favour of both. Nay, the Wonders of the *Devil* and his Agents would infinitely exceed in Number and Quality those of God and his Servants: which Assertion must hold true, were no Stories believ'd but the best attested in every County of *England*, to speak nothing of more credulous Nations; for it is very observable, that the more ignorant and barbarous any People remain, you shall find 'em most abound with Tales of this nature, and stand in far greater Awe of *Satan* than *Jehovah*. In a word, the *Heathens*, after this rate, would be rivetted in their *Idolatry*, and the ugliest Hag or most beggarly Astrologer equalize the Prophets and Apostles. But why should good Reasons be spent in confutation of mere Fictions? for I challenge any Person whatsoever to produce one Instance of these lying Wonders that contains all the true Characters of Historical Evidence; and withal I dare engage as soon to prove the Goodness of the *Alcoran* as of the *Gospel*, if the Belief of any *Miracles*, except Divine ones, be granted me.*

[74]   After what has been already observ'd, I need not add, that all *Miracles* secretly perform'd, or among that Party only to whose Profit and Advantage the Belief of them turns, must be rejected as counterfeit and false; for as such cannot bear the Test of moral Certitude, so they contradict the very Design of Miracles, which are always wrought in favour of the Unbelieving. But the *Papists* alone must be the Witnesses of their own *Miracles*, and never the *Hereticks* they would convert by them: nor is their Practice less ridiculous in confirming one

---

*   [The second edition contains the following additional text:]
    But they must draw some Advantage from the superstitious Fear of the People, who so industriously cherish it.

Miracle by another, as that of *Transubstantiation*, for instance, by Millions of other Prodigies which may be read in their Legends.*

From all this laid together, it follows, that nothing contrary to [75] Reason, whether you consider the Action or Design, is *miraculous*. But there's a good old Distinction that serves all turns: Tho *Miracles* are not contrary to Reason, says one, yet they are surely above it. In what Sense pray? Which is above Reason, the Thing or the Manner of it? If it be answer'd, the last, I suppose the Objector thinks I mean by *Miracle* some Philosophical Experiment, or some *Phenomenon* that surprizes only by its Rarity. Could I tell how a *Miracle* was wrought, I believe I might do as much my self; but what may be said to have been this or that way perform'd, is no *Miracle* at all. It suffices therefore, that the Truth of the Action be demonstrated, and the Possibility of it, to any Being able to govern Nature by instantaneously extracting, mollifying, mixing, infusing, consolidating, &c. and this, it may be, by the Ministry of thousands at once; for Miracles are produc'd according to the Laws of Nature, tho above its ordinary Operations, which are therefore supernaturally assisted.

But finally, it will be said, that in *the State of the Question*, at the [76] beginning of my Book, I maintain'd the Manner as well as the Thing was explicable. But of what? of *Miracles*? No; but of those *Doctrines* in Confirmation whereof the *Miracles* are wrought. This I stand by still, and may add, I hope, that I have clearly prov'd it too: But to say as much of *Miracles* would be to make 'em no *Miracles*, which shews the Impertinence of this Objection**; tho People in Distress are generally allow'd to do any thing.

---

* [In the second edition, this sentence ends as follows:]
  ... as that of Transubstantiation, by several more.
** [In the second edition this sentence ends here.]

- 5 -

When, why, and by whom were Mysteries brought into Christianity

[77]   *The End of the LAW being Righteousness,*[152] *JESUS CHRIST came not to destroy, but to fulfil it:*[153] for he fully and clearly preach'd the purest Morals, he taught that reasonable Worship, and those just Conceptions of Heaven and Heavenly Things, which were more obscurely signifi'd or design'd by the Legal Observations. So having stripp'd the Truth of all those external Types and Ceremonies which made it difficult before, he rendred it easy and obvious to the meanest Capacities. His Disciples and Followers kept to this Simplicity for some considerable time, tho very early divers Abuses began to get footing amongst them. The converted *Jews*, who continu'd mighty fond of their *Levitical*[154] Rites and Feasts, would willingly retain them and be Christians too. Thus what at the Beginning was but only tolerated in weaker Brethren, became afterwards a part of *Christianity* it self, under the Pretence of *Apostolick* Prescription or Tradition.

[78]   But this was nothing compar'd to the Injury done to Religion by the *Gentiles*; who, as they were proselyted in greater Numbers than the *Jews*, so the Abuses they introduc'd were of more dangerous and universal Influence. They were not a little scandaliz'd at the plain Dress of the *Gospel*, with the wonderful Facility of the Doctrines it contain'd, having been accustom'd all their Lives to the pompous Worship and secret *Mysteries* of Deities without Number. The *Christians* on the other hand were careful to remove all Obstacles lying in the way of the *Gentiles*. They thought the most effectual way of gaining them over to their side was by compounding the Matter, which

led them to unwarrantable Compliances, till at length they likewise set up for *Mysteries*. Yet not having the least Precedent for any Ceremonies from the *Gospel*, excepting *Baptism* and the *Supper*, they strangely disguiz'd and transform'd these by adding to them the Pagan Mystick Rites: They administred them with the strictest Secrecy; and, to be inferiour to their Adversaries in no Circumstance, they permitted none to assist at them, but such as were antecedently prepar'd or *initiated*. And to inspire their *Catechumens* with most ardent Desires of Participation, they gave out that what was so industriously hid were[155] *tremendous and unutterable Mysteries.*

Thus lest *Simplicity*, the noblest Ornament of the Truth, should [79] expose it to the Contempt of Unbelievers, *Christianity* was put upon an equal Level with the *Mysteries* of *Ceres*,[156] or the *Orgies* of *Bacchus*. Foolish and mistaken Care! as if the most impious Superstitions could be sanctifi'd by the Name of *Christ*. But such is always the Fruit of prudential and condescending Terms of Conversion in Religion, whereby the Number and not the Sincerity of Professors is mainly intended.

When once the *Philosophers* thought it their Interest to turn *Christians*, [80] Matters grew every Day worse and worse: for they not only retain'd the Air, the Genius, and sometimes the Garb of their several Sects, but most of their erroneous Opinions too. And while they pretended to imploy their *Philosophy* in Defence of *Christianity*, they so confounded them together, that what before was plain to every one, did now become intelligible only to the Learned, who made it still less evident by their Litigious Disputes and vain Subtilties. We must not forget that the *Philosophers* were for making no meaner a Figure among the *Christians* than they did formerly among the Heathens; but this was what they could not possibly effect, without rendring every thing abstruse by Terms or otherwise, and so making themselves sole Masters of the Interpretation.

These Abuses became almost incurable, when the supreme Magistrate [81] did openly countenance the *Christian* Religion. Multitudes then profess'd themselves of the Emperor's Perswasion, only to make their Court and mend their Fortunes by it, or to preserve those Places and Preferments whereof they were possess'd. These continu'd *Pagans* in

93

their Hearts; and it may be easily imagin'd that they carri'd all their old Prejudices along with them into a Religion which they purely embrac'd out of Politick Considerations: And so it constantly happens, when the Conscience is forc'd and not perswaded, which was a while after the Case of these *Heathens*.

[82]   The zealous Emperors erected stately Churches, and converted the Heathen Temples, Sanctuaries, Fanes or Chappels, to the Use of *Christians*, after a previous Expiation, and placing the Sign of the *Cross* in them to assure their Possession to *Christ*. All their *Endowments*, with the Benefices of the *Priests*, *Flamens*, *Augurs*, and the whole sacred Tribe, were appropriated to the *Christian Clergy*. Nay their very Habits, as *white Linen Stoles*, *Mitres*, and the like, were retain'd, to bring those, as was pretended, to an imperceptible Change, who could not be reconcil'd to the *Christian* Simplicity and Poverty. But indeed the Design at bottom was to introduce the Riches, Pomp and Dignities of the *Clergy* which immediately succeeded.

[83]   Things being in this Condition, and the Rites of *Baptism* and the *Supper* being very sensibly augmented, it will not be amiss before I pass further to lay down a short Parallel of the antient Heathen and new-coin'd Christian *Mysteries*. And I shall endeavour so to do it, as to make it evident they were one in Nature, however different in their Subjects.

[84]   *First*, Their Terms were exactly the same without any Alteration: They both made use of the words *initiating*[157] and *perfecting*.[158] They both call'd their MYSTERIES *Myeseis*,[159] *Teleioseis*,[160] *Teleiotika*,[161] *Epopteiai*,[162] &c. They both look'd upon *Initiation* as a kind of *deifying*.[163] And they both stil'd their Priests *Mystagogues*, *Mystes*, *Hierotelestes*,[164] &c.

[85]   *Secondly*, The Preparatives to their Initiations were the same. The *Gentiles* us'd several[165] Washings and *Lustrations*;[166] they[167] fasted, and[168] abstain'd from Women before *Initiation*; tho the wiser sort did laugh at those who thought such Actions could[169] expiate Sin or appease Heaven. But the *Fathers*, the admir'd *Fathers*, imitated them in all these things; and this was the Origin of Abstinence from certain kinds of Meat, of your mock anniversary Fasts, and the Clerical Celibacy.

Thirdly, The *Christians* kept their *Mysteries* as secret as the *Hea-* [86]
thens did theirs. *Chrysostom*[170] says, *We shut the Doors when we cele-*
brate our Mysteries, and exclude the uninitiated. Basil of Cesarea[171]
assures us, *that the Esteem of Mysteries is preserv'd only by Silence.* And
Synesius[172] says, that the *Gentile Mysteries were perform'd by Night,*
because their Veneration proceeds from Mens Ignorance about them. But
why should that deserve Blame in others, good *Synesius*, which you
allow in your own Party? or is it that the *Christians* have a better
Right to *Mysteries* than the *Gentiles*?

Fourthly, The *Fathers* were extremely cautious not to speak intelli- [87]
gibly of their *Mysteries* before Unbelievers or the Catechumens;
whence you frequently meet in their Writings with these or the like
Expressions, [173]*The Initiated know, the Initiated understand what I say.*
And as the *Heathens* did by Proclamation[174] drive away all the *Pro-*
fane from their *Mysteries*, so the Deacons of the Primitive Church
cri'd aloud before the Celebration of *Baptism*, but chiefly of the *Sup-*
per, [175]*Go out all you Catechumens, walk out all that are not initiated*, or
something to this Effect*.[176]

Fifthly, The Steps and Degrees in both their Initiations are the [88]
same. The Heathens had [177]five Degrees necessary to Perfection.
First, *common Purgation*; Secondly, *more private Purgation*; Thirdly, *a*

---

* [In the second edition extra text is as follows:]
     . . . to this Effect, for they often vari'd the Form. Cyril of Jerusalem has a
very singular Passage to our purpose, Now when catechising is rehears'd, if a Cate-
chumen should ask you what the Teachers said, tell it by no means to any that is
not initiated: for we entrust you with a Mystery, and the hope of a Life to come.
Keep this Mystery then to him that rewardeth: and if any should say unto you,
What harm is it, if I also learn? Answer him, that so sick Persons desire Wine: But
if it be given to any unseasonably, it makes him frantick, and so two Evils happen;
both the sick Man is destroy'd and the Physician is disparag'd. Thus if a Catechu-
men hears those things from any of the Faithful, he grows likewise frantick; for not
understanding what he heard, he argues against the thing, and laughs at what is
said: so the Believer that told him is condemn'd as a Betrayer of Secrets. Now you
being one of us, see that you blab out nothing: not that what we say are not worthy
to be spoken, but that others are not worthy to hear them. When you were a Cate-
chumen your self, we never told you what was propos'd. But when you have learnt
by experience the Sublimity of those things which are taught, you will then be
convinc'd that the Catechumens are unworthy to hear them.

liberty of standing amongst the Initiated; Fourthly, *Initiation*; and, Lastly, *the Right of seeing every thing*, or being *Epopts*. Among the *Christians* likewise there were five Steps by which their Penitents were re-admitted to Communion. First they were oblig'd to remain some Years separate from the Congregation lamenting their Sins, whence this Step was call'd *Proclausis*.[178] Secondly, they were remov'd nearer the People, where during three Years they might hear the Priests tho not see them: this Step was therefore call'd *Acroasis*.[179] Thirdly, for three Years more they might hear and see, but not mix with the Congregation: this Period was call'd *Hypoptosis*.[180] Fourthly, they might stand with the People, but not receive the Sacraments: this was their *Systasis*.[181] And, Fifthly, they were admitted to Communion, which was call'd *Methexis*.[182] The new Converts likewise, under Preparation to participate of the Mysteries, were stil'd *Catechumens*; then *competent*; and, lastly, *Epopts, perfect*, or *Believers*: which are the very Degrees in Name and Quality, to which Pythagoras oblig'd his Disciples.

[89]   I could draw out this Parallel much larger, but here's enough to shew *how Christianity became mysterious*, and how so divine an Institution did, through the Craft and Ambition of *Priests* and *Philosophers*, degenerate into mere *Paganism*.

[90]   Mystery prevail'd very little in the first Hundred or Century of Years after *Christ*; but in the second and third, it began to establish it self by *Ceremonies*. To *Baptism* were then added the tasting of Milk and Honey, *the Sign of the Cross, a white Garment, &c. There was quickly after a farther Accession of Questions and Answers, of antecedent Fastings and Watchings, anointing, kissing, and set times of Administration. Next were added Injection of Salt and Wine into the Mouths of the Baptiz'd, and a second Unction, with Imposition of Hands: But in later times there was no end of Lights, Exorcisms, Exsufflations, and many other Extravagancies of Heathen Original. From this Source sprang not only the Belief of *Omens, Presages, Apparitions*, and other vulgar Observations among Christians; but also *Images, Altars, Musick*, Dedications of Churches, and in them

---

*   [In the second edition, the argument in this chapter is backed up with citations from Tertullian, Aristophanes, Cicero, Horace, Ovid and Lucian.]

distinct Places for the Laity (as they speak), and the Clergy: for there is nothing like these in the Writings of the Apostles, but they are all plainly contain'd in the Books of the Gentiles, and was the Substance of their Worship.

All the Rites of the *Supper*, too tedious to particularize, were [91] introduc'd by degrees after the same manner. So by indeavouring to make the plainest things in the World appear *mysterious*, their very Nature and Use were absolutely perverted and destroyed, and are not yet fully restor'd by the purest Reformations in *Christendom.**

Now their own Advantage being the Motive that put the Primi- [92] tive *Clergy* upon reviving *Mystery*, they quickly erected themselves by its Assistance into a separate and politick Body, tho not so soon into their various Orders and Degrees. For in the two first Centuries we meet with no *sub-Deacons, Readers*, or the like; much less with the Names or Dignities of *Popes, Cardinals, Patriarchs, Metropolitans, Archbishops, Primates, Suffragans, Archdeacons, Deans, Chancellors, Vicars*, or their numerous Dependants and Retinue. But in small time *Mystery* made way for those and several other Usurpations upon Mankind, under pretence of *Labourers in the Lord's Vineyard*.

The Decrees or Constitutions concerning *Ceremonies* and *Disci-* [93] *pline*, to increase the Splendor of this new State, did strangely affect or stupify the Minds of the ignorant People; and made them believe they were in good earnest Mediators between God and Men, that could fix Sanctity to certain Times, Places, Persons or Actions. By this Means the *Clergy* were able to do any thing; they engross'd at length the sole Right of interpreting *Scripture*, and with it claim'd *Infallibility*, to their Body.

This is the true Origin and Progress of the *Christian Mysteries*; and [94] we may observe how great a share of their Establishment is owing to *Ceremonies*. These never fail to take off the Mind from the Substance of *Religion*, and lead Men into dangerous Mistakes: for *Ceremonies*

---

*   [The second edition has extra text as follows:]
    But we must not forget how Tertullian himself has acknowledg'd that for their frequent *Crossings* and other *Baptismal* Rites, for their scrupling to let any of the *Bread* and *Wine* fall to the Ground, or to receive them from any hand but the *Priest's*, with the like Ceremonies, they had no Colour of Authority from the Scriptures, but only from *Custom* and *Tradition*.

being easily observ'd, every one thinks himself religious enough that exactly performs them. But there is nothing so naturally opposite as *Ceremony* and *Christianity*. The latter discovers Religion naked to all the World, and the former delivers it under mystical Representations of a merely arbitrary Signification.

[95]   It is visible then that Ceremonies perplex instead of explaining; but supposing they made things easier, then that would be the best Religion which had most of them, for they are generally, and may all be made, equally significative. A Candle put into the Hand of the *Baptiz'd*, to denote the Light of the Gospel, is every whit as good a *Ceremony* as to make the Sign of the Cross in token of owning Christ for their Master and Saviour. Wine, Milk and Honey signify spiritual Nourishment, Strength and Gladness, as well as standing at the *Gospel* betokens our Readiness to hear or profess it.

[96]   In short, there's no degree of *Enthusiasm* higher than placing Religion in such Fooleries; nor any thing so base as by these fraudulent Arts to make the *Gospel* of no effect, unless as far as it serves a Party. But I shall have a better Occasion of exhausting the Subject of *Ceremonies* elsewhere. I treat of 'em here only as they made up the *Gentile Mysteries*, and were afterwards brought in to constitute those of the *Christians*. But as the vast Multitudes of the latter rendred all secret Rites almost impossible, so to preserve the *Mystery*, things were purposely made downright unintelligible. In this Point our pretended *Christians* outdid all the *Mysteries* of the *Heathens*; for the Honour of these might be destroy'd by Discovery, or the babbling Tongue of any initiated Person: But the new *Mysteries* were securely plac'd above the Reach of all Sense and Reason.*

---

*   [The following is added to the second edition:]
    Nay, so jealous were the CLERGY of their own Order, lest any of 'em should irreligiously unfold those sublime Mysteries to the profanely inquisitive LAITY, that they thought fit to put it as much out of the Power of the Holy Tribe itself, as of ours, to understand them; and so it continues, in a great measure, to this day.

The Conclusion

Thus I have endeavour'd to shew others, what I'm fully convinc'd of my self, that there is no MYSTERY in CHRISTIANITY, or the most perfect *Religion*; and that by Consequence nothing *contradictory* or *inconceivable*, however made an *Article of Faith*, can be contain'd in the *Gospel*, if it be really the Word of God: for I have hitherto argu'd only upon this Supposition, for the Reasons to be seen towards the End of the Preface.* My next Task therefore is (God willing) to prove the Doctrines of the *New Testament* perspicuous, possible, and most worthy of God, as well as all calculated for the highest Benefits of Man. Some will not thank me, it's probable, for so useful an

---

*   [In the second edition, Toland inserted the following new paragraph:]

Notwithstanding all Pretences that may be made to the contrary, it is evident that no particular *Instances* or *Doctrines* of any sort can serve for a proper Answer to this DISCOURSE; for, as long as the Reasons of it hold good, whatever *Instance* can be alleg'd must either be found not *mysterious*, or if it prove a MYSTERY, not divinely *reveal'd*. There is no middle way, that I can see. When those Passages of *Scripture* I have cited for my Assertion, are either reconcil'd to such as any would bring against me; when my Arguments against all *inconceivable Mysteries*, and the absurdity of God's *revealing* any such Mysteries, are confuted, 'tis time enough then for others to produce Examples, or for me to consider 'em. And tho by convincing People that *all the Parts of their RELIGION must not only be in themselves, but to them also must appear sound and intelligible*, I might justly leave every one to discover to himself the Reasonableness or Unreasonableness of his Religion (which is no difficult Business, when once Men are perswaded that they have a right to do it); yet the duties I owe GOD and the World oblige me to procede further according as I enjoy Health or Leisure, without limiting myself as to any time, that being a thing in no Man's Power to command at his Pleasure.

Undertaking; and others will make me a *Heretick* in grain for what I have perform'd already. But as it is Duty and no Body's Applause which is the Rule of my Actions, so, God knows, I no more value this cheap and ridiculous Nickname of a *Heretick* than *Paul*[183] did before me: for I acknowledg no ORTHODOXY but the *TRUTH*; and, I'm sure, where-ever the *TRUTH* is there must be also the CHURCH, of God I mean, and not any Humane Faction or Policy. Besides, the Imputation of *Heterodoxy* being now as liberal upon the slightest Occasions, out of Ignorance, Passion or Malice, as in the Days of *Irenaeus* and *Epiphanius*, so it is many times instead of a Reproach the greatest Honour imaginable.

Some good Men may be apt to say, that supposing my Opinion never so true, it may notwithstanding occasion much harm; because when People find themselves impos'd upon in any part of *Religion*, they are ready to call the whole in question. This Offence is plainly taken, not given; and my Design is nothing the less good, if ill-dispos'd Persons abuse it, as they frequently do *Learning, Reason, Scripture*, and the best things in the World. But it is visible to every one that they are the *Contradictions* and *Mysteries* unjustly charg'd upon *Religion*, which occasion so many to become *Deists* and *Atheists*. And it should be consider'd likewise, that when any, not acquainted with it, are dazl'd by the sudden Splendour of the *Truth*, their Number is not comparable to theirs who see clearly by its Light. Because several turn'd *Libertines* and *Atheists* when PRIESTCRAFT was laid so open at the *Reformation*, were *Luther, Calvin* or *Zwinglius*[184] to be blam'd for it? or which should weigh most with them, these few prejudic'd *Scepticks*, or those thousands they converted from the Superstitions of *Rome*? I'm therefore for giving no Quarter to *Error* under any pretence; and will be sure, where-ever I have Ability or Opportunity, to expose it in its true Colours, without rendring my Labour ineffectual by weakly mincing or softning of any thing.

FINIS

Notes

1   [Arianism is a Christian heresy named for Arius (c.250-c.336), who was a priest in Alexandria. He denied the full deity of Jesus Christ. Arius said of the Son of God: 'There was a time when he was not.' Arianism caused such disunity in the Christian church that the emperor Constantine convoked a church council at Nicaea in 325. Led by Athanasius, Bishop of Alexandria, the council condemned Arianism and decreed that the Son was consubstantial with the Father; of *one* substance against the Arian position of *like* substance. Although much of the dispute about Arianism appears as a battle over words, a fundamental issue involving the integrity of the Gospel was at stake: whether God was really in Christ.]

2   [Jesus gave St Peter the Aramaic name *Cephas*.]

3   [Apollos (*fl.* first century AD): born in Alexandria; early Christian missionary, converted from Judaism; he had a following in Corinth which Paul rebuked in Corinthians (I Corinthians 1:10-12, 3:4-6, 16:12). He combined his Jewish heritage with faith in Christ.]

4   [The phrase 'Doctors of the Church' has been used since the Middle Ages to denote outstanding Christian theologians on the basis of both their doctrinal orthodoxy and their holiness. 'Fathers of the Church' refers to such holy and learned men from the early centuries of Christian Church history.]

5   2 Pet. 2.1.

6   [Socinianism is the name given to the form of anti-trinitarianism proposed by the Italian theologian Fausto Paolo Sozzini (1539-1604, a.k.a. Socinus) and developed during the early seventeenth century, particularly in Poland. Socinus doubted the divinity of Christ. This conflicted with the teachings of both Roman Catholicism and the Reformation. Socinus proposed a form of unitarianism which stated that Christ was a man who received divine power because of his blameless life and resurrection. John Biddle – who founded English unitarianism – was influenced by Socinianism.]

7   1 Tim.1.7.

8   Mat.15.9.

9   1 Cor.14.8,9.

10 Ver.9.

11 Rom.12.1.

12 1 Cor.14.11.

13 Ver.2.
14 Acts 14.17.
15 Num.23.19.
16 Ephes.4.14.
17 Ephes.4.17,18.
18 Rom.4.17.
19 1 Cor.2.11.
20 Deut.29.29.
21 Deut.13.1,2,3.
22 The Service of Many Gods.
23 Deut.18.21,22.
24 Jer.32.7,8.
25 Luke 1.34,35.
26 Ver.38.
27 Mat.7.14; 2 Tim.3.13; Tit.1.10.
28 1 Thess.5.21.
29 1 Joh.4.1.
30 Psal.32.9.
31 Eph.5.15.
32 1 Cor.10.15.
33 1 Cor.14.6.
34 Deut.30.11,14.
35 Joh.3.2.
36 Joh.9.16.
37 Joh.10.21.
38 Joh.10.37,38.
39 Joh.7.31.
40 Joh.2.23.
41 Heb.2.3,4.
42 2 Cor.4.2.
43 1 Pet.3.15.
44 [Xenophon (c.430-c.354 BC) was one of the greatest ancient Greek historians.]
45 [*Talmud* is Hebrew for 'teaching'. It is a huge collection of Jewish law and lore: the foundation-stone of Jewish religious life.]
46 1 Cor.2.1.
47 Ver.4.
48 1 Cor.2.14.
49 Luk.4.18.
50 1 Cor.2.14.
51 Ψυχικὸς *constantly signifies the* animal, *and never the* natural *State of Man. It should be in this Place translated* sensual, *as it is very rightly,* Jam. 3.15. *and* Jude, v.19.
52 Rom.8.5-7.
53 Heb.12.1.
54 Rom.7.23.
55 Ver.21.
56 Joh.3.12.
57 Jam.1.13,14.

58 Rom.10.14.

59 Jer.13.23.

60 1 Cor.4.7.

61 Jam.1.5.

62 2 Pet.3.3.

63 Jude v.10.

64 2 Cor.4.3,4.

65 [Epicurus (341-270 BC) was a Greek philosopher. Epicureans believed that the human soul is composed of atomic bodies and that there was nothing immortal about it.]

66 _____ Procul, O procul este Profani!
Conclamat vates, totoq[ue]; absistite luco.
Virg.
Callimach[us] in Hymn. [2.2] ἑκὰς ἑκὰς ὅστις ἀλιτρός.

67 Ὅς ἀμύητος καὶ ἀτέλεστος εἰς ᾅδον ἀφίκηται, ἐν βορβόρῳ κείσεται· ὁ δὲ κεκαθαρμένος τε καὶ τετελεσμένος ἐκεῖσε ἀφικόμενος μετὰ θεῶν οἰκήσει.
Plat[o, *Phaedo* 69c4].

68 Quis Cereris ritus audet vulgare Profanis?
Magnaque Threïcio sacra reperta Samo?
Ovid.
Ὦ κακῶς ἐξοργιασάμενοι τὰ μυστήρια, ὦ τὰ ἄξαντα ςήναντες.
Aristid[es].

69 [Diagoras (*fl.* fifth century BC): Greek poet and sophist, known as 'The Atheist'; pupil of Democritus; rubbished the Eleusinian mysteries (see note 77) and was condemned to death for impiety as a result; fled to Corinth where he died.]

70 [In Greek mythology, Adonis was a handsome young shepherd loved by Aphrodite. Adonis became revered as a god who could rise from the dead. There was a midsummer festival in Athens representing his death and resurrection.]

71 [Bacchus was the Roman god of wine. The Bacchanalia was an annual festival in his honour. Drunken orgies eventually caused its prohibition in 186 BC.]

72 Μυεῖν.

73 Μύησις.

74 Μύστης.

75 Μυστήριον.

76 ἔστι τὰ μικρὰ ὥσπερ προκάθαρσιη καὶ προάγνευσιη τῶν μεγάλων.
Schol[ia] in Plut[um] Aristophan[is].

77 [Samothracia is an island in the north-eastern Aegean Sea. It was an important religious centre for the Pelasgian cult of the Cabiri (or Cabeiri). On the island there are ruins of 'the sancutary of the great Gods'.]

78 [The Eleusinian mysteries were conducted at the temple of Demeter near Athens. The rites were based on the idea of death and rebirth. All initiates kept the secrets of the religion and believed that they would enjoy a life after death because of their initiation into these mysteries.]

79 Pars obscura cavis celebrabant Orgia cistis,
Orgia quæ frustra cupiunt audire Profani.
Cat.

80 Luk.2.52.

81 Ἐγὼ δ' οὔτ' ἄλλο τι καταλεπτὸν ἡγοῦμαι σημαίνειν παρὰ τὸ γνωστόν, οὔτ'

ἄλλο τι καταλαμβάνεσθαι τοῦ βεβαιῶς γινώσκειν. Γαλην[ός], περὶ [τῆς] ἀρίστ[ης] διδασκαλ[ίας].

82 1 Cor.2.11.

83 1 Cor.2.7-8.

84 Ver.9-10.

85 As if Σῶμα had been a Corruption of Σῆμα.

86 [Cebes the Theban (*fl.* fifth century BC): Greek philosopher, disciple and friend of both Philolaus and Socrates, he features in Plato's *Phaedo* as one of the interlocutors seeking virtue and truth.]

87 Ὁρᾷς, εἶπε, παρὰ τὴν πύλην θρόνον τινὰ κείμενον ---- ἐφ' οὗ κάθηται γυνὴ πεπλασμένη τῷ ἤθει, καὶ πιθανὴ φαινομένη, &c. Κὲβητ[ος] πινακ[ίῳ].

88 1 Cor.2.16.

89 Rom.5.12.

90 Heb.10.1.

91 Luke 10.24.

92 2 Cor.3.12-13.

93 Ver.14.

94 Rom.16.25-26.

95 [Acroatic: '… those discussions in which more remote and subtile Philosophy was handed.' (T. Stanley, 1701, *Hist. Phil.* 232/1; as quoted in the *Oxford English Dictionary*, 1989, 2nd edition. Clarendon Press.)]

96 [Pythagoras of Samos (c.560-c.480 BC) was a Greek philosopher and religious leader who founded a philosophical and religious school. Pythagoreans believed – from observations of astronomy and music – that 'all things are numbers'. Pythagoras is famous for his proposal that the square of the hypotenuse of a right triangle is equal to the sum of the squares of the other two sides. The idea that the world can be understood through mathematics was vitally significant in the development of science and mathematics.]

97 Acts 20.20,27.

98 Rom.11.15.

99 [This paragraph is numbered [32] in the first edition. As there is also another paragraph [32] immediately before, we have changed this paragraph number.]

100 [This paragraph is numbered [34] in the first edition, but it should be [35].]

101 [By Mr H and Mr C, Toland might have been referring to:
George Hooper (1640-1727): DD 1677, Dean of Canterbury 1691, prolocutor of the lower house of Convocation 1701, Bishop of St Asaph 1702, Bishop of Bath and Wells 1703;
William Chillingworth (1602-44): godson of William Laud; although he disputed with Roman Catholics he embraced the Catholic Church in 1630, renouncing it in 1634; published *The religion of Protestants a safe Way of Salvation* 1638; taken prisoner while with the king's army 1643. According to Sullivan, Chillingworth was the first Anglican to oppose the Papist idea of infallibility by suggesting that reason is as effective a way to garner assent (Robert E. Sullivan, *John Toland and the Deist Controversy*, 1982, p.53).]

102 M. de Fontenelle.
[Bernard le Bovier de Fontenelle (1657-1757) popularized ideas and advances in science (the work of Copernicus) and philosophy (Descartes).]

103 Monsieur Perrault dans ses *Parallelles des Anciens & des Modernes.*

[Although Charles Perrault (1628-1703) is better remembered for his *Tales from Mother Goose* (1697), he was the leading champion of contemporary French writers in the 'quarrel between the ancients and the moderns', arguing for the superiority of moderns such as Molière over the classical writers of antiquity.]

104 [Clement of Alexandria (c.150-c.215) was a Greek theologian. He helped to found the Alexandrine tradition in Christian theology. His writings fuse Christian faith and Platonic Greek philosophy.]

105 Διὰ τοῦτο φωτισμὸς ἡ μαθητεία κέκληται, ἡ τὰ κεκρυμμένα φανερώσασα, ἀποκαλύψαντος μόνον τοῦ διδασκάλου τὸ πῶμα τῆς κιβωτοῦ.

106 [Saint Justin Martyr (c.100-c.165) is one of the most important early Christian writers. He studied in Peripatetic, Platonic, Pythagorean and Stoic philosophical schools before becoming a Christian. Justin tried to make a reasoned defence of Christianity to non-Christians. His works include his Dialogue with Tryphon the Jew. Justin was beheaded, probably in 165.]

107 [Tryphon, a.k.a. Tarfon: of priestly lineage, officiated in the Temple, he once took three hundred wives in a time of famine! Tryphon was bitterly opposed to Jews who converted to Christianity and swore he would burn every Christian book he came across: this included the Gospels. From *The Jewish Encyclopedia*, 1906, 12: 56-7).]

108 Exod.17.11.

109 Ἦν δὲ καὶ τοῦτο ἐπ' ἀμφοτέρων τῶν ἁγίων ἀνδρῶν ἐκείνων, καὶ προφητῶν τοῦ θεοῦ, νοῆσαι γεγενημένον· ὅτι ἀμφότερα τὰ μυστήρια εἰς αὐτῶν βαστάσαι οὐκ ἦν δυνατός· λέγω δὲ τὸν τύπον τοῦ σταυροῦ, καὶ τὸν τύπον τῆς τοῦ ὀνόματος ἐπικλήσεως.

110 Εἰ μή τι τοῦτο οὐκ ἐπίστασθε, ὦ φίλοι, ὅτι πολλοὺς λόγους ὁ θεὸς ἀποκεκαλυμμένους καὶ ἐν παραβολαῖς ἢ μυστηρίοις ἢ ἐν συμβόλοις ἔργων λελεγμένους, οἱ μετ' ἐκείνους τοὺς εἰπόντας ἢ πράξαντας γενόμενοι προφῆται ἐξηγήσαντο.

111 [Tertullian (c.155-220) was one of the greatest Western theologians and writers of Christian antiquity. His temperament was disposed to extremism, and his early – licentious – life was followed by advocacy of a harsh asceticism. Tertullian's writings have had a lasting influence on Christian thought in particular, and Western thought in general.]

112 Quotidiè obsidemur, quotidiè prodimur;
     __Si semper latemus, quando proditum est quod admittimus? Immo à quibus prodi potuit? Ab ipsis reis! Non utique; cum vel ex forma omnibus Mysteriis silentii fides debeatur. Samothracia & Eleusinia reticentur; quantò magis talia quæ prodita interim etiam Humanam animadversionem provocabunt, dum Divina servatur.

113 [Origen (c.185-c.254) is considered to be the greatest theologian of the early Eastern Church. When only eighteen, Origen succeeded Clement of Alexandria as head of the Alexandria catechetical school, where he had been a student. Eusebius states that he took Matt. 19:12 to mean that he should castrate himself. He preached widely even though he was not ordained. Demetrius, bishop of Alexandria, regarded this as a breach of discipline and ordered him to return to Alexandria. In 230 he was ordained priest by the bishops of Jerusalem and Caesarea. Demetrius then excommunicated Origen, deprived him of his priesthood, and exiled him. Origen attempted to synthesize Christianity with Greek

philosophy, in particular Neoplatonism and Stoicism.]

114 Εἰ δὲ δύναται διὰ συμβόλων καὶ τὴν ὁδὸν δεδηλωμένην τῶν ὁδευσόντων ἐπὶ τὰ θεῖα μαθεῖν· ἀναγνώτω τοὺς ἐπιγραμμένους Ἀριθμοῢς Μωυσέως, καὶ ζητησάτω τὸν δυνάμενον [αὐτὸν] μυσταγωγῆσαι ἐπὶ τὰ τῶν παρεμβολῶν τῶν υἱῶν Ἰσραὴλ ἀναγεγραμμένα.
Lib. 6. contra Cels[um]

115 Ὅρα δὲ εἰ μὴ τὰ τῆς πίστεως ἡμῶν ταῖς ΚΟΙΝΑΙΣ ΕΝΝΟΙΑΙΣ ἀρχῆθεν συναγορεύοντα, μετατίθησι τοὺς εὐγνωμόνως ἀκούοντας τῶν λεγομένων.
Lib. 3. contra Cels[um].

116 Col.2.8.

117 1 Cor.3.19.

118 1 Cor.1.22.

119 Rom.8.7.

120 2 Cor.10.4,5.

121 [*Blictri* is a nonsense word that was used by the ancient Greeks (David Berman, 'Eighteenth-Century Irish Philosophy', *The Field Day Anthology of Irish Writing,* ed. Seamus Deane, vol. 1, 1991, p.771).]

122 Heb.11.6.

123 Rom.10.14.

124 Ver.17.

125 Heb.11.1.

126 Rom.8.24,25.

127 Heb.11.13.

128 Joh.8.12&9.5.

129 Acts 13.47.

130 Eph.1.17.

131 Ver.18.

132 Eph.5.17.

133 Rom.14.5.

134 So Λογισάμενος *should be translated.*

135 Heb.11.17,18,19.

136 Ver.12.

137 Rom.4.19,20,21.

138 1 John 2.4,6.

139 Eph.4.14.

140 1 Cor.3.2.

141 Heb.5.12,13,14.

142 Mark 16.16.

143 1 Pet.3.15.

144 [A talapoin is a type of monkey.]

145 ['Sommonocodom' appears to be a nonsense word.]

146 Joh.4.42.

147 Rom.14.14.

148 1 Cor.15.58.

149 Mark 12.37.

150 1 Pet.1.9-12.

151 Acts 14.11,&c.

152 Rom.10.4.

153 Mat.5.17.

154 [Levites were members of the Israelite tribe of Levi. (Moses was a Levite.) They were a religious caste, whose members were Israel's priests. In early Israel the priesthood had a predominantly teaching function, because the laity were considered capable of carrying out sacrifices. 'Levite' eventually became the term for the lower-rank attendants who maintained the temple.]

155 Φρικτὰ, ἀπόρρητα μυστήρια.

156 [In Roman mythology, Ceres was the name of an Italic goddess. The name may be Etruscan in origin. It is possibly another name for Persephone, the daughter of Demeter. The cult of Demeter came from Sicily to Rome in the fifth century BC. In Greek mythology, Persephone was the beautiful daughter of Zeus and Demeter (goddess of agriculture). Hades (god of the underworld and brother of Zeus) was lonely in the underworld and Zeus told him to take Persephone as his wife. Persephone was a central cult figure in the Eleusinian Mysteries.]

157 Μυεῖσθαι.

158 Τελεῖσθαι.

159 Μυήσεις.

160 Τελειώσεις.

161 Τελειωτικὰ

162 Ἐποπτεῖαι.

163 Θέωσις.

164 Ἱεροτελεστής.

165 Sacerdos stipatum me religiosa cohorte deducit ad proximas balneas, & priùs sueto lavacro traditum, præfatus Deûm veniam, purissimè circumrorans abluit.
   Apul.
   Ter caput irrorat, ter tollit ad sydera palmas.
   Ovid.

166 Καθαρμοὶ.

167 ἐνήστευσα, ἔπιον τὸν κυκεῶνα.

168 _____Discedite ab aris,
   Queis tulit hesterna gaudia nocte Venus.
   Tibul.

169 Ah nimium faciles qui tristia crimina cædis,
   Fluminea tolli posse putatis aqua.
   Ovid.

170 Μυστήρια τὰς θύρας κλείσαντες ἐπιτελοῦμεν, καὶ τοὺς ἀμυήτους εἴργομεν.
   Homil. in Matth.
   [John Chrysostom (c.346-407) was one of the great eastern Fathers of the Church. John's eloquence in his writings and preaching gained him the name 'Chrysostom', which is Greek for Golden Mouth.]

171 Μυστήριον τὰ σεμνὰ σιωπῇ διασώσεσθαι..
   [Basil of Caesarea (c.329-79) is one of the Doctors of the Church. His writings include three books written against Eunomius, an Arianist.]

172 Ἀγνωσία σεμνότης ἐπὶ τελετῶν, καὶ νὺξ διὰ τοῦτο πιστεύεται τὰ μυστήρια.
   De providen.
   [Synesius (370-414): Neoplatonic philosopher, studied in Alexandria where he was both pupil and friend of Hypatia (female mathematician and Neoplatonist

who was stoned to death by a Christian mob on the orders of St Cyril [see Gibbon's *Decline and Fall of the Roman Empire*, ch.47]). He became a Christian in 409, and Bishop of Ptolemais in North Africa in 410. Incidentally, Toland was much taken with the murder of Hypatia and wrote about her in his *Tetradymus* (1720) as *Hypatia: or the history of a most beautiful, most virtuous, most learned and every way accomplish'd Lady; who was torn to pieces by the Clergy of Alexandria, to gratify the pride, emulation, and cruelty of their archbishop Cyril, commonly but undeservedly stil'd Saint Cyril.*]

173 Norunt initiati; "Ἴσασιν τοὶ μεμυημένοι τὸ λεγόμενον.

174 Θύρας ἐπίθεσθε βεβήλοις.

175 "Ὅσοι κατηχούμενοι προέλθετε, ἔξω περιπατεῖτε ὅσοι ἀμυήτοι.

176 [St Cyril of Jerusalem (c.315-c.386) was bishop of Jerusalem and a leading opponent of Arianism. One of the Doctors of the Church. Bertrand Russell calls him 'a man of fanatical zeal. He used his position as patriarch to incite pogroms against the very large Jewish colony in Alexandria. His chief claim to fame is the lynching of Hypatia' (from *The History of Western Philosophy, and its Connection with Political and Social Circumstances from the Earliest Times to the Present Day*, Routledge, London, 1946 (1961), p.365.]

177 Ἐν τοῖς ἱεροῖς ἡγοῦντο μὲν αἱ πανδήμιοι καθάρσεις, εἶτα ἐπὶ ταύταις αἱ ἀπορρητότεραι, μετὰ ταύτας συστάσεις, καὶ ἐπὶ ταύταις μυήσεις, ἐν τέλει δ᾽ ἐποπτεῖαι.
   Olympiodor[us].

178 Πρόκλαυσις.

179 Ἀκρόασις.

180 Ὑπόπτωσις.

181 Σύστασις.

182 Μέθεξις.

183 Act.24.14.

184 [Ulrich Zwingli (1481-1531) was a leader of the Reformation in Switzerland.]

A N

APOLOGY

F O R

Mr. *TOLAND,*

In a LETTER from Himfelf to a
Member of the Houfe of Commons
in *Ireland;* written the day before
his Book was refolv'd to be burnt
by the Committee of Religion.

To which is prefix'd a NARRATIVE
containing the Occafion of the faid
LETTER.

———————*Diis proximus Ille eft*
Quem RATIO *non* IRA *movet.* Claudian.

LONDON,
Printed in the Year MDCCII.

A NARRATIVE

Containing the Occasion of the following letter

I Promise not to give any account at this time of the Controversy occasion'd by Mr. *Toland's* Book, nor to enter into the Merits of the Cause on either side. His Adversaries seem not yet weary of writing against him; and when they have once done, it will be early enough then for him to reply, if he sees reason so to do: For it would be an endless labour to make *Answers* severally to so many as may concern themselves in this Dispute. My Design is only to shew what Treatment he receiv'd from some People in *Ireland*, as far as that may serve to set the *Letter* annex'd to this Narrative in its proper light. And I shall take care to insert nothing, but such notorious matters of Fact that no observing Person in *Dublin*, or I might say perhaps in the Kingdom, can pretend ignorance concerning them, or deny them to be true.

Mr. *Toland* was scarcely arriv'd in that Country, when he found himself warmly attack'd from the *Pulpit*, which at the beginning could not but startle the People, who till then were equal Strangers to him and his Book; yet they became in a little time so well accustom'd to this Subject, that it was as much expected of course as if it had been prescrib'd in the Rubrick. This occasion'd a Noble Lord to give it for a reason why he frequented not the Church as formerly, that instead of his Saviour JESUS CHRIST, one *John Toland* was all the discourse there. But how unworthy a Member soever of the *Christian Religion* Mr. *Toland* may be, he's still so sensible of the Obedience he justly ows to its most Divine Precepts, that he dares not allow himself to make any returns in the same Dialect to what was liberally utter'd against him in that place. We read, an *Archangel* was not permitted to rail against the very *Devil*[1]; and if Mr. *Toland* had not innumerable Passages of the *Gospel* to restrain him, yet the Reverence all Men ow to their own Persons join'd to the Rules of common Civility, would be powerful enough to keep him from bestowing any indecent Expressions or Reflections upon his Opposers. Nor is he such a Stranger to the former Ages or the present, as not to perceive that passionate or violent Proceedings never yet gain'd Credit to a *Cause*; nor produc'd any other Effects upon the Enemies of it, but to make 'em abhor it the more.

But when this rough handling of him in the *Pulpit* (where he could not have word about) prov'd insignificant, the *Grand Jury* was sollicited to present him for a Book that was written and publish'd in *England*. And to gain the readier Compliance, the Presentment of the *Grand Jury* of *Middlesex* was printed in *Dublin* with an emphatical Title, and cry'd about the Streets. So Mr. *Toland* was accordingly presented there the last day of the Term in the Court of *King's-Bench*, the *Jurors* not grounding their proceeding upon any particular Passages of his Book, which most of 'em never read, and those that did confess'd not to understand. Thus in the Reign of *Henry* VI one[2] *John Stephens* was presented by a Jury in *Southwark*, as a Man, say they, *we know not what to make of him, and that hath Books we know not what they are.* In the mean time those of either Sex who had any intimacy with Mr. *Toland*, or that favour'd him with their familiar Conversation, were branded as his Proselytes, and Lists of their Names industriously given about; altho those worthy Persons (for he always chose the best Company) had never discours'd him of Religion, nor had many of 'em then seen his Book. And so far was he himself from making his Opinions the Subject of his common Talk, that, notwithstanding repeated Provocations, he purposely declin'd speaking of 'em at all; which made his Adversaries (who slipt no handle of decrying him) insinuate that he was not the real Author of the Piece going under his Name. But if they were serious, and this was not another Artifice to make him own it, I would fain know what made them so angry with a Man whom they ought therefore to despise: For if there be any Poison (as I hope there is none) in that Book, the spreading of it in *Ireland* is wholly owing to the Management of those, who would be thought most to oppose it.

We must not forget that in a few days after the present *Lords Justices* of that Kingdom landed, the Recorder of *Dublin*, Mr. *Hancock*, presented Mr. *Toland* to their Excellencies after a very obliging manner; for in his Congratulatory Harangue in the name of his Corporation, whereof by the way he spoke not a word, he begg'd their *Lordships* would protect the CHURCH from all its Enemies, but particularly from the *Tolandists*, a Sect, I am sure, those Noble Persons ne'er heard of before. The late *Lords Justices*, the Earls of *Montrath* and *Drogheda*[3] were more neglected at least in the same Speech; tho all *Ireland* cannot without the blackest Ingratitude but acknowledg, that they never liv'd before under a more prudent, just, and peaceable Administration: For as they gave no occasions of Complaint in their Government, so were there no Murmurings against them but only of such, as, through a perpetual desire of Change, are always Enemies to their own and the Country's Happiness. Mr. *Toland* being thus made a *Heresiarch* in so publick a place, where all the Nobility and Gentry of the Kingdom then in Town were present, occasion'd every body to hunt for his Book which was very scarce; and his Enemies also took that Pretext of denominating all his Acquaintance *Tolandists*, how different soever they were from him or one another in their Sentiments.

From the *Pulpit*, from the *Jury*, and the *Court*, he must take his next turn at the *Press*, from whence there issu'd a Book said to be an Answer to him in particular, and to all others who set up *Reason* and *Evidence* in opposition to *Revelation* and *Mysteries*. This imports that Mr. *Toland* made *Reason* and *Revelation* contradictory. But how well the Author of the said Book, Mr. *Peter Brown*[4], senior *Fellow of Trinity College near* Dublin, has prov'd this or the rest of his Undertaking, is referr'd to the impartial Reader's Judgment. If hard Language would do instead of strong Arguments, we might easily determine who had the better end of the Controversy; and if you believe Mr. *Brown* himself, he assures you that *if it can be shewn where one Link of his reasoning fails, he'll make it up again so firm, that it shall never be undone.*[5]

113

Indeed, I don't believe Mr. *Toland* designs to give him any trouble of that kind, so that his *Reasons* are like to continue as good as ever they were. But Mr. *Brown's* Book comes now under Consideration as it was one of the Machines invented to render Mr. *Toland* dangerous or odious. And this he does not only by endeavouring all along to prove him *a most inveterate Enemy to all Reveal'd Religion;*[6] but he expresly solicits the Civil Magistrate to take a course with him, which looks not very generous in an *Answerer*, how much concern soever he may pretend for his Faith. In one place he says, *I have no more to do here but to deliver him up to the hands of our Governors. We may confute his Errors, but 'tis they only can suppress his Insolence; we only can endeavour to heal those already infected, 'tis they alone can hinder the Infection from spreading further.*[7] And afterwards he adds, *Here again I would deliver him into the hands of the Magistrate, not mov'd by any heat of Passion, but by such a* Zeal *as becomes every Christian to have for his Religion.*[8] I am fully satisfy'd this *murdering Zeal* is not inspir'd by Genuin *Christianity*; and as for his want of Passion, the *Inquisitors* themselves shew as much seeming Reluctance against killing or maiming of those whom they procure to be condemn'd for *Hereticks*. At the very instant they deliver 'em over to the Secular Power, they address themselves to the Magistrate in these terms; *We most earnestly beseech you, my Lord Judg, that for the love of God, and from a sense of Piety and Mercy, as well as out of regard to our Entreaties, you would neither inflict the loss of Life or Limb upon this miserable Creature.*[9] Tho at the same time, if the Judg should take the holy Fathers at their word, they would infallibly excommunicate him for his ready Obedience, whereof they are so fond in all cases but those of *Justice and Clemency*, which is the Motto of their Standard. Here we may observe how strangely Words of a good signification may be detorted to countenance very ill Actions. Thus to abuse a Man is in the Language of some term'd *Zeal*, and so it is to murder him in that of others; nor were the barbarous *Irish* wanting to sanctify their *Massacre* by that Name.

But lest the broaching of simple *Heresies* should not serve the turn, Mr. *Toland* must by all means be made the *Head of a Sect*, and of no ordinary one; for, if you credit Mr. *Brown*, he designs to be *as famous an Impostor as Mahomet.*[10] To confirm this Character, which was well enough invented to amuse the People with vain Terrors, there was a ridiculous Story handed about, whether true or false God knows; for Mr. *Toland* remembers nothing of the matter. 'Tis said in short, that about the fourteenth Year of his Age he gravely declar'd he would be the *Head of a Sect* e'er he was Thirty; and before he was forty he should make as great a stir in the Commonwealth as *Cromwel* ever did. *Risum teneatis.* Here's an old Prophecy found in a Bog with a witness, and which Mr. *Hancock* and Mr. *Brown* have labour'd to fulfil in part, that superstitious Folks might trepidly apprehend the event of the rest. Mr. *Brown* says, *The real design of this Man is plainly no other than what he* formerly declar'd, *and what he openly affects, to be the* Head *of a* Sect;[11] and doubts not but *he has a great deal more to say, whenever this new* Sect *of his becomes so numerous that they shall outbrave the Laws, and labour for a publick Reformation of the Mysterious Doctrines of the Gospel.*[12] Would any body believe this, did they not see it plainly own'd in Print? Nay he tells us that *he has trac'd this Heresiarch from the time he first gave out he would be* Head *of a* Sect *before he was thirty Years of Age, till he became an Author, and from thence to his coming into* Ireland *to spread his Heresies, and put his Design in execution.*[13] I assure him he wants two Years still of Thirty, and if his *Disciples* (as they're call'd) take not other measures than he did to erect that same Sect in *Ireland*, St. *Patrick* may securely possess his Apostleship in that Kingdom till Doomsday, which is an Honour Mr. *Toland* does not envy him. I ought not by any means to forget here the Sagacity of a certain Gentleman, who wonder'd at his Impudence for presuming to set up a *new Religion* in their Country, where he had not a foot of Land; which inclines me to believe he has met with better Records of the Apostles Possessions than Mr. *Toland* could in all his reading.

Well then, if all this won't do, what shall we make of him next? He must e'en be represented as dangerous to the Government; and truly so he's like to be if *Irish* Presages hold good, for their Prophecies were never worth a farthing. *How far Men in power,* says Mr. *Brown, according to their several Stations, are obliged to intermeddle in point of Conscience, I shall not now enquire. But sure I am in point of Policy it is*

*become no less than necessary: for the Writers of this strain have given broad
hints that they are as little friends to our Government, as our Religion. This
Man can say that* MAGISTRATES *are made for the* PEOPLE, *and
every one knows what Doctrines of* REBELLION *Men are wont to insinuate by this* SAYING.[14] O! is it thereabouts then? Why truly, the Doctrine of *Passive Obedience* was exploded by this same *Saying*, which Mr.
Toland acknowledges to be one fair Quotation. *James* the Second was
justly abdicated according to this Saying, because he was an Enemy to
the *People* for whom he was made a *King*; and our most Glorious Hero
William the Third, the Restorer of Universal Peace and Liberty, was
invested with the Supreme Power by the honest *People* of *Great Britain*,
for whose good he has indefatigably employ'd it ever since, in vindicat-
ing, settling, and enlarging their Civil and Religious Rights. Mr. *Brown*
has been pleas'd to say that Mr. *Toland* was proud of running down
three Kingdoms with one cross Question, which is, *How can a Man
believe what he does not know?*[15] and he that does so, knows not what he
believes. Now I would gladly be resolv'd by him, for whom the *Magistrates* are made unless for the *People*? Were they made for themselves?
or whether the *People* were made for the *Magistrates*? But he adds, *that
this sort of Men deserve to be look'd to, that their numbers grow formidable;*[16] and makes little doubt but *their design is at length to shew us, That
all Dominion as well as Religion is founded in Reason.*[17] Let him assure
himself they will never begin to shew that, for they have clearly prov'd
it long ago. What Dominion is not founded in Reason, must be doubtless unreasonable, and consequently Tyrannical. There was nothing
more reasonable than for Men first to unite themselves into Societies
for their mutual Peace and Security against the Violence or Fraud of
others. And as reasonable it was that they should agree upon certain
Rules, or frame Constitutions which were to be the known Standard of
every bodies Actions, and might serve for the Decision of all their Differences. That there should be Magistrates or indifferent Persons
appointed to preserve those Laws, and see 'em put in execution (not
leaving every Man to be his own Judg) is not less reasonable still. And
that all due Honour and Obedience should be paid to those Governors
by their Subjects, is likewise most highly reasonable; so that I fancy we
must necessarily conclude *all just Dominion to be founded in Reason.*

At length comes from the North a finish'd Master of such Politicks,[18] and he doubts not but Mr. *Toland* after all is a *Jesuit*. But his Book utterly destroys all the Principles of *Popery* and *Superstition*. That's nothing; for *Jesuits* to unsettle us will preach against their own Religion. Now if Mr. *Toland* be a *Jesuit*, he's certainly the most dangerous of the Order, and began extremely betimes. He was not sixteen Years old, when he became as zealous against *Popery* as he has ever since continu'd, and by God's Assistance always will do. From *Redcastle* near *Londonderry*[19] he went in 1687 to the College of *Glasco* in *Scotland*; and upon his departure from it the Magistrates of that City gave him Recommendatory Letters, wherein they took particular notice of his Affection to the *Protestant Religion*. The day before the memorable Battel of the *BOINE*, he was created *Master of Arts* at *Edinburgh*, and receiv'd the usual *Diploma* or Certificate from the *Professors*. Then he came into *England*, and liv'd in as good *Protestant* Families as any in the Kingdom, till he went to the famous University of *Leyden* in *HOLLAND* to perfect his Studies; and upon his return from thence lodg'd in a private House at *Oxford*, till about two Years ago he came to *London*, where 'tis well known his Company and Conversation were the farthest in the World from being *Jesuitical*. Notwithstanding the whole Series of his Education, as well as his own Genius, did thus run in the most opposite Channel to *Popery*; yet in *Ireland* that malicious Report gain'd upon some few, because his Relations were *Papists*, and that he happen'd to be so brought up himself in his Childhood, which was no more an Action of his own, than that he was born there. So his Countrymen treated him in this respect like his Majesty's good Subjects of *Guernsey*; who, when they are in *France* are call'd English Rogues, and in *England* French Dogs.

The last Effort, except the charge of *Socinianism*, to blast him, was to make him pass for a rigid *Nonconformist*. Mr. *Toland* will never deny but the real Simplicity of the *Dissenters* Worship, and the seeming Equity of their Discipline (into which being so young he could not distinctly penetrate) did gain extraordinarily upon his Affections, just as he was newly deliver'd from the insupportable Yoke of the most Pompous and Tyrannical *Policy* that ever enslav'd Mankind under the name or shew of *religion*. But when greater Experience and more Years had a little ripen'd his Judgment, he easily perceiv'd that the Differences were not so wide as to appear irreconcilable, or at least, that Men, who were sound *Protestants* on both sides, should barbarously cut one anothers Throats, or indeed give any disturbance to the Society about them. And as soon as he understood the late Heats and Animosities did not totally (if at all) proceed from a Concern for mere Religion, he allow'd himself a latitude in several things, that would have been matter of scruple to him before. His Travels increas'd, and the Study of Ecclesiastical History perfected this Disposition, wherein he continues to this Hour: for, whatever his own Opinion of those Differences be, yet he finds so essential an Agreement between the *French, Dutch, English, Scotish*, and other *Protestants*, that he's resolv'd never to lose the Benefit of an Instructive Discourse in any of their Churches upon that score; and it must be a Civil not a Religious Interest that can engage him against any of these Parties, not thinking all their private Notions wherein they disagree worth endangering, much less subverting, the Publick Peace of a Nation. If this makes a Man a *Nonconformist*, then Mr. *Toland* is one unquestionably. And so he is, if he thinks the *Dissenters* ought not to be molested in their Goods or Persons, nor excluded from any of their Native Rights, because they have a different Set of Thoughts from him or others, so long as none of their Principles are repugnant to good Government. He believes them likewise to be a true and considerable part of the *Protestant Religion* (for they have demonstrated themselves to be staunch *Patriots*) notwithstanding any Error or Weakness whereof they may be guilty in his Judgment. But this same reason will prove him as sound a Member of the establish'd Church of *England*; being perswaded the narrow Sentiments of a few about *Communion* is not any profest Doctrin of that Church: nor would there be any Separation from it in this Realm, were all others of his mind. 'Tis visible this Declaration is not made to curry Favour with one (as many do) while in their Hearts they are devoted to the other side. But Mr. *Toland's* Opinion being frequently demanded as to this Point, he now delivers it once for all; for he will never condescend to court any body of Men with preference to all others, further than he sees ground for it; and to this, as his settl'd Judgment, he's resolv'd to adhere, tho it should hazard the inevitable Ruin of his Fortune or Reputation with all Parties.

Atheism is now become so common an Accusation in every Person's mouth, who is displeas'd at the Rudeness of others for not complimenting him with their Assent to his Opinions, that, altho in it self be the most atrocious and unnatural Crime whereof a reasonable Creature can be guilty yet is it not otherwise minded than as a word of course which indicates a world of Inconsiderateness and Rancor. When Mr. *Toland* us'd to be traduc'd in *Ireland* for *Deism* with many other Opinions, and his Friends demanded of his Accusers where they made those Discoveries in his Writings, the ready Answer always was, that truly they had never read the Book, and by the Grace of God never would; but that they receiv'd their Information from such as were proper Judges of the thing. O how inseparable is *Popery* from *Ignorance*! And what is the source of all *Popery* but *Implicit Belief* wherever it is found? As to what the Author of the Letter to a Convocation-man says of a Congregation *de propaganda Infidelitate*, no body needs be asham'd of so good Company as the present Bishop of *Salisbury*,[20] the late Archbishop of *Canterbury*,[21] and the *Commons* of *England* themselves, whom he not only libels with most false and vile Insinuations, but even his Majesty's own Person as a Prince of no Religion, which none that had any Religion durst say of a King who is so great a Friend to it by his Patronage and Example. Mr. *Toland* was once writing an Answer to this Author; but he laid aside his Papers when he understood that such able Men had undertaken him, as the Reverend Dr. *Wake*, and the Ingenious Author of the Letter to a Parliament Man.

But some People not being satisfy'd, it seems, with all that past, and thinking Mr. *Toland* should never have enough on't, concluded at last to bring his Book before the *Parliament*. And therefore on Saturday the 14*th* day of *August*, it was mov'd in the *Committee of Religion*, that the Book entitul'd *Christianity not Mysterious*, should be brought before them, and accordingly it was order'd that the said Book should the Saturday following be brought into the *Committee*. That day the Committee sat not; but the next Saturday, which was the 28th day of *August*, there met a very full *Committee*, wherein this business was a great while debated. Several Persons eminent for their Birth, good Qualities or Fortunes, oppos'd the whole Proceeding, being of opinion it was neither proper nor convenient for them to meddle with a thing of that nature. But when this Point was without much Argument carri'd against them, they insisted that the Passages which gave Offence in the Book should be read; so those wonderful Objections were made which are clear'd in the *Letter* subjoin'd: and then the *Committee* was adjourn'd till the 4th of *September*. That day, after several Gentlemen had spoke to those Objections, they urg'd at last, according to Mr. *Toland's* own desire, that he should be call'd to answer in Person, to declare the Sense of his Book, and his Design in writing it. But this favour being peremptorily deny'd, an *Honourable Member* went to the Bar, and offer'd a *Letter* to be read which he had receiv'd that Morning from Mr. *Toland*, containing what Satisfaction he intended to give the *Committee*, had they thought fit to let him speak for himself. But this was likewise refus'd, and the *Committee* came immediately to those Resolutions, to which the House agreed, after some Debate, on Thursday following being the 9th of *September*, viz. *That the Book entituled* Christianity not Mysterious, *containing several Heretical Doctrines contrary to the Christian Religion and the establish'd Church of* Ireland, *be publickly burnt by the hands of the Common Hangman.* Likewise, *That the Author thereof* John Toland *be taken into the Custody of the Serjeant at Arms* (which he took care to prevent) *and be prosecuted by Mr. Attorney General, for writing and publishing the said Book.* They order'd too, *that an Address should be made to the Lords Justices to give Directions that no more Copies of that Book be brought into the Kingdom, and to prevent the selling of those already imported.*[22] Their Sentence was executed on the Book the Saturday following, which was the 11th of *September*, before the *Parliament-House* Gate, and also in the open Street before the *Town-House*; the Sheriffs and all the Constables attending.

One very singular Passage we must not omit, which is, that the same day the Book was to be condemn'd there came abroad a printed Sheet, wherein, to terrify any body from appearing publickly for Mr. *Toland*, were contain'd the following words: *Now let those consider this*, says the Writer of that Paper, *whether within doors or without; and whether the Vindication, or even the excusing this Book or the Author, or the ridiculing or otherwise baffling the just Prosecution or Censure of it and him, be not truly the denying of our Saviour before Men; and whether such may not assuredly expect to be deny'd of him in the presence of his Father and the holy Angels, and all the World at the last day.*[23] This strange Denunciation had no effect on those who all along appear'd in Mr. *Toland's* behalf, tho much out-number'd by those of the contrary Opinion. In the *Committee* it was mov'd by one that Mr. *Toland* himself should be burnt, as by another that he should be made to burn his Book with his own hands; and a third desir'd it should be done before the Door of the House, that he might have the pleasure of treading the Ashes under his feet.

I forbear making any remarks here either upon the design of burning Books in general, or this in particular; nor will I shew, as well I might, how fruitless this sort of proceeding has prov'd in all Ages, since the Custom was first introduc'd by the *Popish Inquisitors*, who perform'd that Execution on the Book when they could not seize the Author whom they had destin'd to the Flames. Neither will I insist upon the great Stop and Discouragement which this Practice brings to all Learning and Discoveries; but, without further Digression, I shall now leave the Reader to peruse Mr. *Toland's Letter*, and to judg for himself whether it would have given him satisfaction, had he been a Member of the *House of Commons*.

Mr Toland's Letter to a Member of the House of Commons in Ireland, &c.

Dublin, *Septemb.* 3. 1697.

SIR,

When the *Christian Religion* is attack'd by Atheists and others, they constantly charge it with *Contradiction* or *Obscurity*; and Mr. *Toland's* design in the Publication of his Book was to defend *Christianity* from such unjust Imputations, as he more than once declares in his Preface, and as he thinks it every Christian's Duty to do so, according to his Ability or Opportunity. If we might judg of his Performance by his profest Intentions, we should conclude it to be extraordinary good; but we must on the other hand reckon it as bad, if, without further Examination, we regard the strange Outcries that are made against it both from the *Pulpit* and the *Press*. That a Man should be run down because it is the fashion, or by *Interested* Persons, and such as are influenc'd by 'em, is nothing strange; for one way or other the like happens every day: but that a Book should be condemn'd by whole-sale, without assigning the particular Faults or Mistakes in it, and by many that never read it, is visibly unjust. What has contributed to make Mr. *Toland* (whom neither his Age, nor Fortune, nor Prefer-ment renders formidable) the Object of so much Heat and Noise, and after what manner his Enemies of all sorts have treated him under a zealous pretence, he's like very speedily to inform such of the World as will please to concern themselves. But not considering the Hon-ourable *House of Commons*, or your self in particular, among the num-ber of his *Adversaries* but as his *Judges*, he thinks convenient to clear those few Points which are reported to afford matter of Exception to some in the *Committee of Religion*. But, before this be done, he desires that two or three Particulars may be a little consider'd.

Mr. *Toland*, in the first place, is of opinion it portends much Happiness to the Nation, that the *Commons* (who have all the right imaginable to it) should take the cognizance of such things into their own Hands. And tho his Book should, as it's very probable, happen to fall under their Censure, yet his love to Mankind cannot but make him extremely pleas'd with the Consequences he foresees must necessarily follow from such an authentick Precedent in this Country, where it was most peculiarly wanting. Nor does he think it more reasonable for him to be angry at his private ill luck, than it would be for some to be out of love with *Parliaments* themselves (which is the best Constitution in the Universe) because they are *mistaken* sometimes, and that an Act is *repeal'd* in one Session which was establish'd in another; not considering that such an Inconvenience is infinitely overballanc'd by several excellent Laws, and by the Remedy that may likewise be had to this pretended Disorder from that very Court, upon better *Information* or *Temper.*

Secondly, Mr. *Toland* does not complain that he alone in the Kingdom is disturb'd for his Opinion, but is heartily glad that no more are troubl'd upon that account. For as he takes *Persecution* to be one of the chief Marks and Pillars of the *Antichristian Church*, so he looks upon an impartial *Liberty* of writing and speaking whatever is not destructive of *Civil Society*, to be the greatest advantage of any Country, whether the Learning, or the Commerce, or the very Peace and Tranquillity thereof be consider'd. Yet it cannot but look mighty odly to indifferent Persons, that all the *Dissenters* from the Establish'd Church, that the *Papists* who pervert Christianity it self, that several declar'd *Socinian*, ay and *Jacobite* Pamphlets should escape the burning Zeal of those, who so furiously prosecute one young Man only for the suspected Consequences of his Book, as if the very Being or Destruction of all *Religion* depended upon the fate of him, or his Writings.[24]

Thirdly, As for the *Errors* commonly laid to Mr. *Toland's* charge, they are so various and inconsistent with one another, that no Man of ordinary sense could possibly hold them all at a time; and being credited by his Enemies without book, he may with more Justice deny than they can affirm them. He's not therefore oblig'd to take notice of any thing but what is alleg'd in formal words, or plainly inferr'd from his Book. Indeed some Consequences an Author might not perceive, which should render him the more excusable; but Mr. *Toland* confesses he foresaw several Consequences of his Book, even to part of the Opposition with which it has met, tho not that (after the Pulpits, Presses, and Juries) the *Commons* of *Ireland* should likewise honour it with their Animadversion.

Now what is said to have been objected in the *Committee* is, First, That the very Title *CHRISTIANITY NOT MYSTERIOUS* is Heretical. Whether the Committee decrees a new or declares an old *Heresy*, Mr. *Toland* neither knows nor is much concern'd to understand, being conscious to himself of neither. If the *Title* be made good in the Book, 'tis orthodox or sound enough; and if not, yet he's still to seek for the *Heresy* of it. If it be an old Opinion, others would gladly be inform'd in which Century it was first taught, who the Author of it might be, or by what Council it was condemn'd: and if it be a new Notion, they desire likewise to know whether the *House of Commons* alone can decree it *Heresy*, being yet perfect strangers to any such Power claim'd by that Honourable Body.[25]

But 'tis affirm'd, that by his *Title* he rejects the *Mysteries* of the Gospel. If by *Mysteries* be meant the *Doctrines* themselves, he denies none of them; but that after Revelation they are not *mysterious* or obscure, he still maintains for the Honour of *Christianity*. A great many without doors very wisely conclude that he believes not the Doctrines, because he thinks they are *plain*, and therefore the more *credible*; for that's all he means by *not mysterious*. But some People, otherwise credulous enough, believe no body capable of rendring that clear and easy, which to themselves seems difficult or insuperable.

It was likewise objected, that he makes a doubt whether the *Scriptures* be of Divine Authority. That bare Expression, *If the Gospel be really the word of God*, imports no such matter, but very frequently the contrary; as for example, *If the Gospel be true, this frame of the World shall be dissolv'd*; which is not to question, but more emphatically to assert the truth of the Proposition. But this, I confess, is nothing to the case before us. The words in the Conclusion of the Book are these, *Nothing contradictory or inconceivable, however made an Article of Faith, can be contain'd in the Gospel, if it be really the Word of God: for I*

*have hitherto argued only upon this Supposition, for the Reason to be seen
towards the end of the Preface.*[26] The sense of the words then must be
determin'd by that Reason; and the Passage referr'd to in the Preface
is this, *viz. In the following Discourse, which is the first of three, &c. the
Divinity of the New Testament is taken for granted. In the next Discourse,
&c. I attempt a particular and rational Explanation of the reputed Mysteries of the Gospel. And in the third, I demonstrate the Verity of Divine Revelation against Atheists and all Enemies of Reveal'd Religion.*[27] Now is it
not something strange that a Man should question what he takes for
granted, and which the Method he follow'd would not permit him to
prove before his time, that is, not form the Conclusion before the
Premises? In one place he positively affirms the *Scriptures to contain
the brightest Characters of Divinity.*[28] But that the force of Calumny
may evidently appear, let this other Passage of the same Book be consider'd: *What we discours'd of Reason before,* says he, *and Revelation
now, being duly weigh'd, all the Doctrines and Precepts of the New Testament (if it be indeed Divine) must consequently agree with Natural Reason
and our own ordinary Ideas. THIS every considerate and well dispos'd
Person will find by the careful perusal of it; and whoever undertakes this
Task will confess the Gospel not to be HIDDEN from us, nor afar off, but
very nigh us, in our Mouths and in our HEARTS.*[29] But this whole
Chapter must have been transcrib'd, were all that's to our purpose in
it to be nicely quoted; for every word of it from No. 22 to the end, is a
Justification of the Method and Stile of the *New Testament.* Yet lest
any suspicion of Fallacy might remain where the Particle IF occurs, I
demand what Declaration can be conceived in stronger terms than
the following Passage; for you shall be troubl'd with no more, tho I
might easily cite forty others relating to this Head. The words are,
*Whether or no Christianity is mysterious, ought to be naturally decided by
the New Testament, wherein the Christian Faith is originally contain'd. I
heartily desire to put the Case upon this Issue, I appeal to this Tribunal; for
did I not infinitely prefer the Truth I learn from these sacred Records to all
other Considerations, I should never assert that there are no Mysteries in
Christianity. The Scriptures have engag'd me in this Error, if it be one; and
I will sooner be reputed Heterodox with these only on my side, than to pass
for Orthodox with the whole World, and to have them against me.*[30]

It was likewise objected that Mr. *Toland* shew'd not a due Respect to CHRIST, because he always stiles him in his Book barely CHRIST, or at most only JESUS CHRIST. If this be any Disrespect, the most Orthodox Divines are as guilty of it in their Writings; and the *Apostles* themselves speak of him without any additional Titles a great many times in the Gospel. 'Tis otherwise, I grant, when some special occasion requires them to be more express; and when Mr. *Toland* was declaring the Head of his Church, he says, *I am neither of* Paul, *nor of* Cephas, *nor of* Apollos, *but of the Lord JESUS CHRIST alone, who is the Author and Finisher of my Faith*.[31] And here I cannot forbear admiring how Mr. *Toland* should be deem'd an *Arian* or *Socinian*, seeing, for ought appears in his Book, he may lay a better claim to any other Sect, except the *Papists*, than to them; for these three are the only Parties he opposes by name. But if his Religion is to be really discover'd by his Book, 'tis utterly impossible he should be either an *Arian* or *Socinian*. They both of 'em (from different Notions) believe JESUS CHRIST to be a meer Creature-God, which Mr. *Toland* does not; and, to mend one Absurdity by a greater, they join in paying their Deify'd Creature Divine Worship, which Mr. *Toland* judges impious and ridiculous. His own words are these; *Tho the Socinians disown this Practice* (of admitting Contradictions in Religion) *I am mistaken if either they or the Arians can make their Notions of a Dignify'd and Creature-God capable of Divine Worship, appear more reasonable than the extravagancies of other Sects touching the Article of the Trinity;*[32] such as the Whimsies of EUTYCHES,[33] GENTILIS,[34] and the rest. In short, Mr. *Toland* had no natural occasion to declare his Sentiments relating to CHRIST's Person, that and the other particular Doctrines of the Gospel being the Subject of the second[35] and third Books he promises, and by which alone his Conformity or Dissent with the *Common Christianity* is to be discern'd. Nor had his Adversaries from the Press run into so many gross Mistakes, and been at the trouble of several no less unhappy than needless Conjectures, had they but Patience or Phlegm enough to attend the Publication of those Pieces.

It was objected also that he slighted the *Sacraments* (which is a term he never uses) by making them bare *Ceremonies*. That he cal'd 'em any where mere *Ceremonies* he absolutely denies, tho he now affirms with all Christians, that the Actions of *breaking Bread* and *washing with Water* are as much Ceremonial under the *New Testament*, as *Circumcision* or the *Passover* were under the *Old*. But when Mr. *Toland* had a just occasion to mention the *Sacraments*, tho not to declare his Opinion concerning their Nature or Efficacy, 'tis evident he speaks there of those numerous *Ceremonies* of Human Institution which were added to 'em by the mistaken Zeal or Prudence of the Primitive Christians, *who*, as he says, *not having the least Precedent for any Ceremonies from the Gospel, excepting Baptism and the Supper, strangely disguis'd and transform'd these by adding to them the Pagan Mystick Rites;*[36] and of these appending Ceremonies he gives a large Catalogue in that Chapter. But he's so far from making any comparison between *Christianity* and the *Orgies* of *Bacchus*, as was likewise alledg'd, that on the contrary he severely handles those who blended such Corruptions with pure Christianity. *Thus*, says he, *lest Simplicity, the noblest Ornament of the Truth, should expose it to the Contempt of Unbelievers, Christianity was put upon an equal level with the Mysteries of* Ceres, *or the Orgies of* Bacchus.[37] To this may be added another Passage where he affirms, *he could draw his Parallel between Heathenism and those early Superstitions much larger, to shew how Christianity became mysterious, and how so Divine an Institution did, through the Craft and Ambition of Priests and Philosophers degenerate into mere Paganism.*[38] Here you see, 'tis not the *Christian Religion*, but the unwarrantable *Additions* to it, wherein JESUS CHRIST never had any hand, which he compares with the *Mysteries* of *Ceres* and the *Orgies of Bacchus*. And what, pray, is the main body of the *Popish, Eastern*, or other Superstitions, but the continuance of those Rites of *Heathen* or *Jewish* Original which Mr. *Toland* justly explodes? Or is any body that draws a Parallel between *Heathenism* and *Popery* thought disaffected to Christianity? Indeed *profest* or *disguis'd Papists* will accuse him of such a Crime, but no *understanding Protestant* can ever be guilty of so much Weakness.

'Tis possible more Exceptions were made to Mr. *Toland's* Book in the *Committee*, or these not all in this Order; but these were all whereof he could inform himself, and of which he gives the most compendious and satisfactory account he can: being as ready to do the same in relation to all other Objections that shall fairly come to his knowledg. The greatest Hardship he complains of is, that, being an Inhabitant of *England*, he should be molested in *Ireland* (where he was only fortuitously born) for a Book he publish'd in another Country. His Errand hither, God knows, was neither to propagate nor receive any Doctrines, new or old; and as he was far from ever designing to fix his constant Residence here, so he thinks himself as liable to be disturb'd in any other place, whither his Curiosity or Business may lead him, as in this Kingdom; which is a way of proceeding hitherto unheard of in the World. I shall give you no further trouble when I have told you, that I resolve always to continue an unalterable Friend to *Liberty*, an Advocate for *Religion* without Superstition, a true Lover of my *Country*, and in particular, *Sir*, your most humble Servant,

JOHN TOLAND.

There was enough said in the preceding *Letter* concerning the *Socinianism* laid to Mr. *Toland's* Charge, and I doubt very much whether now there be any *Socinians* in England; I am sure, no considerable Body of them: for the Theology of the *Unitarians*, who vulgarly pass under that name, is very different from that of *Socinus*.[39] But these *Unitarians* in one of their latest Prints disown any Service intended their Cause by Mr. *Toland's* Book; and all Sects, we know, are ready upon the least apparent Conformity to augment their own Numbers, especially with such as they seem to value for their Learning or other Qualifications. In *The Agreement of the Unitarians with the Catholick Church* occurs the following Paragraph.

The (Bishop of *Worcester's*[40]) eighth and tenth Chapters, are imployed in opposing, and, as he thinks, in exposing and ridiculing some Interpretations of a few Texts of Scripture by the *Unitarians*; and attacking a few Paragraphs in Mr. *Toland's* Book, *Christianity not Mysterious*. I know not what it was to his Lordship's purpose to fall upon Mr. *Toland's* Book. But if he would needs attack the Book, he should have dealt fairly. He should have discuss'd the main Argument in it, and not carpt only at a few Passages; and those too so mangl'd and deform'd by his Representation of them, that I dare to affirm Mr. *Toland* does not know his own Book in the Bishop's Representation of it. I do not perceive, to speak truly, but that Book still stands in its full strength; if it has not also acquir'd a farther Reputation, by occasion of this so unsuccessful nibling at it. But suppose the *Bishop* had disarm'd the *Gentleman*, *what is that to us? Do we offer this Book against the Trinity of the Realists? Was it written with Intention to serve us? Does it contain any of our Allegations from Reason, against the Trinity of* Philoponus, Joachim, *and* Gentilis? We desire him to answer to the Reasons in our own Books against the Trinity of the *Tritheists*. But to these he says not a word, but only falls upon Mr. *Toland's* Book; *in which, or for which we are not in the least concern'd.* Nor do I think the Learned and Ingenious Author will hold himself to be interested to defend that *Christianity not mysterious* with which his Lordship presents us.[41]

So far that celebrated *Unitarian.*

A *good Temper* and *sound Judgment* usually go together, and if the absence of the former be no Demonstration that the latter is also wanting, yet questionless it creates a very reasonable suspicion of it; for a bad Cause is generally supported by Violence and ill Arts, while Truth establishes it self only by Lenity and Persuasion. This is so certain, that when an undiscerning Person happens to be engag'd on the right side, and employs Force or Calumny in its defence, we always find he does it infinitely more harm than good. That such as receive Gain or Honour by any thing should oppose those who go about to destroy it, tho with design to introduce a better in the room of it, is no great wonder tho it be manifestly unjust. Thus the Silversmiths of *Ephesus* headed by *Demetrius*[42] rais'd a mighty Tumult against the Apostle *Paul* for ruining their Trade, which was solely maintain'd by Lies and Impostures at the expence of the Peoples Credulity. The *Primitive Christians* were represented by the *Heathen Priests* as Atheistical, Rebellious, Incestuous, and in a word, polluted with all manner of Wickedness and Impiety; by which nefarious Artifices they procur'd those innocent Persons to be cruelly persecuted with Infamy, Confiscation, and Death it self in all its shapes. The *Waldenses*,[43] *Wicclifists*,[44] *Hussites*,[45] and the first *Reformers* were treated after the same manner by the Church of *Rome*; and when they could not seize their Persons, they never fail'd to load 'em with horrid, black, and monstrous Aspersions, that they might not be wanting to prejudice 'em all manner of ways, as if this had been the very

Method prescrib'd in the Gospel to reduce the Erroneous. Thus we read such accounts of *Luther* and *Calvin*'s Lives publish'd by the *Monks* of those Times, as paint 'em worse than Devils, and that make their Doctrine as different from what we know it to be, as the Historians were from telling Truth.

I am sorry to observe among us any Remains of that implacable and bitter Spirit, tho such as distinguish themselves by their eminent Vertues retain no tincture of so mean and base a Disposition. The Character which that most excellent Person the late *Archbishop* of *Canterbury* has left on record of the *Socinians* (when he was strenuously arguing against their Opinions) ought to be a Model which no body should be asham'd to imitate. He did not think to lessen his own Reputation, or to hurt his Cause, when he frankly acknowledg'd them *to be a Pattern of the fair way of disputing, and debating matters of Religion without Heat and unseemly Reflections upon their Adversaries. They generally argue matters with that Temper and Gravity,* says he, *and with that freedom from Passion and Transport which becomes a serious and weighty Argument: and for the most part they reason closely and clearly, with extraordinary guard and caution, with great dexterity and decency; and yet with smartness and subtlety enough, with a very gentle heat and few hard words: Vertues to be prais'd wherever they are found, yea even in an Enemy, and very worthy our Imitation.*[46] Yet this great Man, who so candidly represents his Adversaries, was himself most scurrilously and unworthily handl'd by his own and the Enemies of the Government. And here I must do Justice to Dr. *Payne*[47] lately deceas'd, who, as he tells the World in his Letter to the Bishop of *Rochester*, was desir'd by his Grace the present *Arch-bishop* of *Canterbury* to answer Mr. *Toland*; and why should not every body that thinks him in the wrong take the same liberty of writing against him, as he did to publish his Thoughts before? Now if Mr. *Toland*'s own Judgment ought to be receiv'd in this case, the Doctor has in his two Sermons said more against him than the Bishop of *Worcester*, Mr. *Norris*,[48] the Annonymous *Oxonian*, the Author of the Occasional Paper,[49] Mr. *Beverly*,[50] Mr. *Gailhard*,[51] Mr. *Browne*, or any other Answerer; and yet instead of treating him like a *Dominican Inquisitor*, he uses, with some little warmth, such Grave and Christian Language as shews his Metropolitan's Judgment and Moderation in pitching upon him, as well as his own Skill and Sincerity in the management of his Trust.

We must hold this *Mystery of Faith* (says Dr. *Payne*, speaking to his Auditory) with a *Christian good Temper*, and not lose that while we are contending for the other; nor let our Contentions grow so warm and intemperate, so fierce and cruel as to forget and violate the plain Morals of Christianity, while we are over earnestly disputing for the Faith of it; or perhaps *only for some false and mistaken, or at least some useless Opinions, and over-nice and subtle Controversies about it.* This has been the fault of those who have contended more for Victory than Truth, and more for their own Credit and Vain-glory than the Christian Faith; who tho they may be in the right, as 'tis ten to one that they are not (*for Truth seldom dwells with such a Spirit of Rage, and Pride, and Passion, but rather with a quite other Temper*) yet they greatly disserve the Cause they so unduly manage. And as they are never like to convince their Adversaries, so they give others just ground to suspect that *they supply want of better Reason and stronger Arguments with weak and impotent Calumny, with undecent and unbecoming Reflections.* This is as Criminal and as Unchristian as the *Error* or the *Heresy* they are so zealous against; and 'tis to be doubted '*tis rather a false Fire and a hypocritical Zeal, not for the Cause of God so much as their own;* and that *this is kindl'd not from the Altar, but some other place, and blown up by some private* PIQUE *and sinister Designs,* that thus blazes out to such an outrageous degree as to consume and destroy, not only *its Adversaries* if it were in its power, but even the most vital and substantial Parts of Christianity, even *Peace, Love,* and *Charity;* and contends for the *Christian Faith* with such a most *Diabolical* and *Unchristian Temper.* This is very far from the Spirit of Christ and Christianity; and however precious the Faith be, yet the Apostle tells us, *if we had all Faith, and understood all Mysteries, and all Knowledg, yet without Charity we are nothing,* however great we may be in our own Thoughts. And such a Zeal of Sowrness and Bitterness, as *it is generally without Knowledg, so it is always without Religion;* and tho it *hold the Mystery of Faith* (and do not rather pervert and corrupt it) yet, to be sure, this is not, according to the Apostle's Advice, *in a pure Conscience.*[52]

There needs no more to be added in this place but a sincere acknowledgment from Mr. *Toland,* that (notwithstanding any Prejudices he may be suppos'd to entertain against *Ireland*) he met there, and had the Honour to be acquainted with a great many worthy Gentlemen, who by their extraordinary Parts, Education, and Vertues, merit to be distinguish'd in any Country of the World. He knows several Men and Women (and doubtless there are or should be more) who don't confine all Salvation to the narrow Limits of a *Sect,* nor mistake the affected *Phrases* of any Party for the only true *Christianity:* who neither hate nor despise others for differing from them in *Opinion,* no more than in Features or Complexion; knowing that no body can believe as he pleases, and it were the highest Injustice to expect a Man should profess with his Mouth what in his Heart he detests: Persons who can live easily with all Men, as being of one Race, and fellow-Citizens of the same World; not denying any body the liberty[53] of improving the Happiness of the *Society* by his Invention, Learning, Industry, or Example: And who, in a word, are not willing to deprive themselves of real and certain *Advantages* for the sake of uncertain, contested, or useless *Speculations*; as if one that wants it should reject the profer'd Service of an honest and able Accountant, because he believes not a World in the Moon; or not allow an Ingenious Man's Conversation to be agreeable, for ridiculing the Fable of St. *Patrick*'s Purgatory. As for the *Publick Peace*, which is pretended to be endanger'd by a TOLERATION, it has been disturb'd or subverted in all Ages and Places of the World, not either by *Conscientious* or *Enquiring Men*, but by those who no less dogmatically than tyrannically *impose* upon their Understandings; and who, in spite of all their Disguises, appear to be much more concern'd for SOVERAIGNTY than REFORMATION. 'Tis likewise clear as the Sun they were Mr. *Toland*'s Enemies that made, or continue all the needless stir about his Book, and not his Friends, who only acted defensively for the *Common Liberty* of Mankind, but not upon his private account. Nor does he (who, one would think, should know it best) believe any Persons in *Ireland* or elsewhere favour'd him a jot the more for writing that *Treatise*; and if they did, he was never yet inform'd of this accessory Kindness either by themselves, or others by their Deputation: neither does he make returns of Love or Respect to any body living upon this mere Consideration.

Qui statuit aliquid, parte inaudita altera,
Æquum licet statuerit, haud Æquus est.
Seneca.

FINIS

Notes

1   Jude 9.
2   Bacon's *Historical Discourse of the Government of* England, *Part. 2. cap. 17. pag.* 161.
3   [Toland seems to use 'late' to mean 'former': both the 3rd Earl of Mountrath and the 3rd Earl of Drogheda were Lords Justices 1696-7. Charles Coote (1655-1709): 3rd Earl of Mountrath 1672; carried the Irish banner at the funeral of Queen Mary II – William's wife – 1694. Henry Hamilton-Moore (d.1714): 3rd Earl of Drogheda 1679; commanded a Williamite regiment at both the Battle of the Boyne and Limerick; also Lord Justice 1701-2 (from H.A. Doubleday & Lord Howard de Walden, *The Complete Peerage, or a History of the House of Lords and all its Members from the Earliest Times*, St Catherine Press, London, 1936, 9: 359-60 and 4: 463-5 respectively).]
4   [Peter Browne (1664?-1735): educated Trinity College Dublin, Fellow 1692, Provost 1699; wrote *A Letter in Answer to a book entitled Christianity not Mysterious* 1697, to which he may have owed his success: Toland boasted that he had made Browne a bishop (Bishop of Cork 1709) (from David Berman, 'Eighteenth-century Irish Philosophy', in Seamus Deane (ed.) *The Field Day Anthology of Irish Writing Vol. 1*, Field Day/Faber, Derry, 1991). According to Robert E. Sullivan, Browne believed that deism blended Socinianiam and Arianism (*John Toland and the Deist Controversy*, Harvard University Press, 1982, p. 207).]
5   Pag. 81.
6   Pag. 79.
7   Pag. 139.
8   Pag. 144.
9   Domine Judex, rogamus vos cum omni affectu quo possimus, ut amore Dei, pietatis & misericordiæ intuitu, & nostrorum interventu precaminum, miserrimo huic nullum mortis vel mutilationis periculum inferatis.
10 Pag. 162.
11 Pag. 164.
12 Pag. 166.
13 Pag. 121.

14 Pag. 172.

15 Pag. 122.

16 Pag. 172.

17 Pag. 173.

18 [Toland may be referring to William King (1650-1729), who was Bishop of Derry at the time, and was born in Antrim. Educated as a Presbyterian, DD Trinity College Dublin 1689, Dean of St. Patrick's 1689, supported the Whigs, Bishop of Derry 1691, Archbishop of Dublin 1703. He was a close friend of Jonathan Swift. His most famous work is *De Origine Mali* 1702; Alexander Pope used King's ideas in his famous poem *An Essay on Man*. His *State of the Protestants of Ireland under the late King James's Government*, 1691, was a powerful vindication of the Glorious Revolution (from David Berman, 'Eighteenth-century Irish Philosophy', in Seamus Deane (ed.) *The Field Day Anthology of Irish Writing Vol. 1*, Field Day/Faber, Derry, 1991).]

19 [Redcastle is in Co. Donegal.]

20 [Gilbert Burnet (1643-1715): Bishop of Salisbury 1689. Chaplain to Charles II (dismissed 1674), Visited William (Prince of Orange) 1686, advised Sophia of Hanover of the intended invasion of England, accompanied William when he landed at Torbay 1688, made bishop soon after, advocated toleration, censured by the Lower House of Convocation 1701, had charge of the Succession Bill 1701, attended King William on his deathbed.]

21 [John Tillotson (1630-94): Archbishop of Canterbury 1694, Published four letters on the Socinian controversy 1679-80 in answer to doubts on his orthodoxy. He was an innovative preacher, introducing clearness, brevity and addresses to reason (as can be seen by his quotation on the title-page of *Christianity not Mysterious*).]

22 Votes of the H. of C. of *Ireland*.

23 A Letter upon Mr. *Toland's* Book to J.C. Esq; *pag. 4.*

24 [This sentence was] *Left out in the Original Copy.*

25 [This sentence was] *Left out in the Original Copy.*

26 Pag. 170. [See p. 99 in this edition.]

27 *Pref.* p.24. [See p. 12 in this edition.]

28 Pag. 32. [See p. 36 in this edition.]

29 Pag. 46. [See p. 43 in this edition.]

30 Pag. 90,91. [See p. 63 in this edition.]

31 *Pref.* p.28. [See p. 12 in this edition.]

32 Pag. 25. [See p. 33 in this edition.]

33 [Eutyches (c.378-454): archimandrite (superior) of a monastery in Constantinople, supported Monophysitism (the idea that Jesus Christ had only one nature, rather than being both human and divine), also known as Eutychianism, and opposed Nestorianism (the two natures of Christ represented two distinct persons). He refused in 433 to accept the restored unity between the churches of Alexandria and Antioch, leading to his condemnation at a synod in 448 as a heretic. Under Emperor Theodosius II he was declared orthodox and was rehabilitated, but he was later condemned and exiled.]

34 [Gentilis or Alberico Gentili (1552-1601): Italian jurist and religious refugee in England, a founder of the study of international law, excommunicated for his heretical views and fled to England, settled at Oxford 1580.]

35   [Printed 'seeond' in original text.]
36   Pag. 160. [See p. 93 in this edition.]
37   *Ibid.*
38   P.168. [See p. 96 in this edition.]
39   [Unitarians believe that God is one person, the Father, rather than the Trinity's three persons in one. See p. 101, n.6 for a biography of Socinus and a discussion of Socinianism.]
40   [Edward Stillingfleet (1635-99): DD Oxford 1668, popular London preacher, Charles II's chaplain, Dean of St Paul's 1678, Prolocutor of Lr. House, Bishop of Worcester 1689-99, controversy with Locke about the Trinity 1696-7.]
41   P. 54, 55.
42   [See *Acts* 19:23-41.]
43   [The Waldenses are a tiny – mainly Italian – Protestant sect. They trace their origins to Peter Waldo (d. c.1218), who advocated voluntary poverty for the sake of following Christ. He sought papal recognition but was excommunicated for heresy in 1184. His followers developed as a religious society with their own ministers. They promoted religious discipline and moral rigour, and rejected the taking of human life under any circumstances. In 1208 a crusade was ordered against the Waldenses – and other groups such as the Albigenses – in southern France. Most Waldenses withdrew into the Alpine valleys of northern Italy. The Waldensian church is a member of the World Presbyterian Alliance.]
44   [John Wycliffe (c.1328-84) was a precursor of the Protestant Reformation. He called for a reformation of the wealth and corruption of the Church. Wycliffe's ideas were later disseminated in England by the Poor Preachers and the Lollards, and on the Continent by the Czech reformer Jan Hus.]
45   [Jan Hus (c.1372-1415) was a Czech religious reformer. He was critical of the wealth of the Church. His chief work was *De ecclesia* (1413). Condemned for heresy, he was burned at the stake. After his execution, Hus's teachings became the rallying point for Czech national self-expression.(NGME)]
46   *Four Serm. against the Socin.* p.57, 58.
47   [William Payne (1650-96): DD Magdalene College Cambridge 1689, wrote against Catholics and Unitarians.]
48   [John Norris (1657-1711): fellow of All Souls, Oxford. Argued with Quakers, propounder in England of the ideas of Nicholas Malebranche (1638-1715), a French Christian philosophe who believed that philosophy and religion are mutually dependent. According to Malebranche, ideas cannot come from the senses, nor from the soul itself; rather, God is the sole true cause of phenomena. Natural causes are merely apparent causes.]
49   [Richard Willis (1664-1734): DD Lambeth 1695, Bishop of Gloucester 1714, Bishop of Salisbury 1721, Bishop of Winchester 1723-4. *The Occasional Paper* was written in 1697 (Sullivan, p.342).]
50   [Thomas Beverley is probably the author of *Christianity the Great Mystery*, 1696. (Sullivan, p.339).]
51   [Jean Gailhard was the author of *The Blasphemous Socinian Heresie Disproved and Confuted, etc.*, 1697 (Sullivan, p.340).]
52   Dr. Payne's *Serm.* p.65, &c.
53   [Spelt 'liberby' in the original text.]

A
DEFENCE

OF

Mr *TOLAND,*

IN A

LETTER to Himſelf.

LONDON,
Printed in the Year M DC XCVII.

SIR,

I Have not the Honour to know you any other way than by your Writings and Character; but from thence I have entertain'd such an opinion of you, that I thought myself obliged to justify you to the World in such things as I judged capable of any defence, and to desire you to undertake your own vindication, where I found my self at a loss how to serve you.

Some time ago you obliged the World with a Book, Entitled *Christianity not Mysterious*; which I perceive has given abundance of offence here in *England*, and has drawn upon you the censure of the *Irish Parliament*. I have heard a great many violent things said against this Book by Men of all ranks and conditions, and a great many Pens have been ingaged in Writing it down; but, notwithstanding this mighty dislike, People have generally taken to it, I am very much disposed to believe that, if they had not been too much prejudiced to read it over with due care and attention, and wanted patience to stay for the other parts you promised, they would hardly have conceived such terrible apprehensions of your performance, and consequently would have been more moderate in their resentments.

The chief complaint I have met with is against the *Title* and *Design* of the Book. 'Tis an impudent thing, I am told, for a Man to publish to the World in huge Capital Letters, that *Christianity* is *not Mysterious*, when all Sects and Parties of *Christians*, have agreed to speak of the *Mysteries* of the *Christian Religion*; and a design to prove this seems to give the lye to all the *Fathers* and *Writers* of the whole *Catholick Church*, and to call them a Company of Ignorant Fellows, that did not understand any thing of the Religion they profess.

This is a severe charge indeed, but if you prove your point, I think, a very unjust one; for errours are to be opposed and confuted, be they never so ancient and venerable, and never so well established in the World; nay, the longer they have stood, and the wider they are spread, the more *Heroick* is the Adventurer, who lays his Pen to the root of them, and has the courage to give the first stroke towards their fall: And therefore the main Controversy betwixt you and the two Nations depends entirely upon the proof you have given of what you undertook to demonstrate to the World. If then it can be shewn that you have made good all you pretended to prove in your Book, you will be in a great measure justifyed, as to the *design* and *substance* of your Work, and we will see what can be said for the *management* of it afterwards.

Now I must needs own, notwithstanding there are so many eminent Names against me, that you have gone a great way towards proving the point you proposed to establish in your Book. *Christianity not Mysterious* is your *Title*, and your profest *Design* is to make it appear that there are *no Mysteries in the Christian Religion*; but then it is to be remembered that this Title belongs to the whole undertaking, which is to consist of three Parts, and 'tis as certain as any Maxim whatsoever that the design cannot be perfected before the conclusion of the Work.

All that you take upon you to do in the first part of your Work, which is out, is to acquaint us with the two different significations of the word *Mystery*; to shew that there are *no Mysteries in the Christian Religion* according to one sense of the Word, and to assure us there are none in the other sense of it, with a promise of proving it in the other Parts that are to come; and all this, with submission to better judgments, I humbly conceive you have performed to a tittle.

For, in the first place it must be allowed to be true that the word *Mystery*, does commonly signify *either something which we do not understand, because it is not discovered to us, or something that we cannot comprehend, or fully know after it is discovered.*

It is likewise as plain that there can be *no Mysteries in Christianity* in the first signification of the Word; because the whole *Christian Religion* being Revealed to us in the Scriptures of the *New Testament*, and there being no further Discoveries to be expected, it would be very Absurd to say, we do not understand any part of the *Christian Religion* upon the account of its not being Revealed to us; and therefore for Men who have this Notion of *Mystery*, to say *Christianity is*

Mysterious, is as much as to say, *Christianity is not Revealed*: which is so false and unwarrantable a Position, and so fully proved to be so by you, that I hope hereafter, whatever *Jews* or *Deists* may say, there will be no *Christians* to be found, that will dare to maintain the *Mysteriousness of Christianity* in this Sense.

But if we consider *Mystery* in the other sense of the Word, I must confess, all the *Christians* I have hitherto had occasion to Read of, or Converse with, have thought that there were *Mysteries in the Christian Religion*. Since therefore you appear to be somewhat Singular in your Notions upon this Point, if you please, we will take a more particular account of the *Popular* Opinion before we examine *yours*, that so we may be more capable Judges of the difference betwixt them, and of the present Controversie that has occasioned.

Now the *common* Opinion concerning the *Mysteries of the Christian Religion*, as far as I understand it, is in short this; That there are a great many things deliver'd to us in the *Scriptures* of the *New Testament*, which without *Revelation from God*, we should have known nothing at all of, and which, as they stand there Reveal'd to us, we know now but *in part*: Some of them we look upon to be of such a Nature, that we are not able in the present state of our Faculties, to conceive beyond such a Degree, and which we expect a further Comprehension of in another state of more Perfection, such as are the Doctrines of the *Trinity, Incarnation*, &c. others there are which are but in part Reveal'd to us, and which we are capable of knowing further in this state, if God had been pleased to give us a clearer and fuller Discovery of them, such as are the *Prophecies* contained in the *Revelations*, and other parts of Scripture.

This is the *Vulgar Faith*, to which *yours* being directly oppos'd, it must be this; That there is nothing in Scripture but what is fully discover'd to us, and what we fully comprehend; that we do not now *see through a Glass darkly*, but that we perfectly *know, even as we are known*.

This is *your* Opinion, and since you have kindly purposed and intended to make it ours too, I cannot imagine what reason any body should have to Condemn so generous a Design. For my part, I am not of that proud or invidious Temper to be uneasie under the Honour you are like to get by so Noble an Atchievement, as you are now upon; nor am I concerned who it is that informs me of any thing, when I am to be the better for his Information. If my Author be a good one, 'tis all one to me whether he be *Irish*, or whether he be *Greek*, or *Latin*, whether he have a long Beard, or none at all: and therefore, I cannot but think you have been a little hardly used, to be treated ill purely for such a design, as plainly tends to improve our Understandings, and enlarge our Knowledge. If indeed, you should fail in your Attempt, you could not possibly expect to save your self from a great deal of Scorn and Disgrace, and I cannot say the scurvy usage you would then probably meet with would be altogether unjust, for I think People have reason to take it ill to be put out of their way, and to be disturb'd in the peaceable Possession of Ancient Opinions, by new Doctrines that cannot make out their claim to be admitted.

But the World has no reason to cry out against you yet upon this account; for you are not yet come to the proof of your *New Divinity* in that part of your discourse which is already printed: you have only prepared the way and Skirmisht a little with some flying suggestions in order to lead on the main arguments with more force in the second part, which are to be backt and maintained by a strong reserve in the third. This is your design, and it is yet only a design; but you give us such mighty promises and assurances of bringing this design about, that there's no body can justly doubt but you are firmly perswaded of your own sufficiency to effect it; which is all you undertook to prove in your Book besides what is before mentioned. And therefore, having made good every thing you took upon you to do as farr as you are gone, I must needs say, 'tis a prejudging the cause to condemn you before the other parts you have promised are put out: whereupon I will suspend my judgment[1] of your work till I have it altogether, and will live in expectation of seeing all the supposed *Mysteries* of the *Christian Religion* unlockt, all the dark Prophecies of the New Testament unfolded, and all the hard and intricate passages of it made easy and plain, so that all *strife and contention shall cease from among us*, there shall be *no leading into captivity* by imposing false Notions upon us, *no complaining* any more of the difficulties of Religion. Oh what a glorious Scene will here be, and how happy should I think my self if I should live to see the day when the *Revelations* shall be as easy to be understood as any History of past matters of fact, when the *book with the seven seals*, shall be *opened*, and we shall certainly be inform'd of every thing that is in it; when we shall have such a clear and intelligible account of the *Trinity* that Dr. S. and Dr. Sh.[2] shall agree in, and all the *Unitarians* subscribe to; when a Man may be convicted of *Original Sin* as easily as he can of Murder; and the *Eternal Decrees of God* shall be plainer than *Acts of Parliament*!

I must confess I do not believe any thing of all this can be done, because no body has done any thing like it yet, and because I cannot conceive which way a Man could go to work if he would venture upon such an attempt: But this may be prejudice in me; for I am not to measure another Man's genius by my own, nor to despair of new discoveries which have escaped the greater capacities of our Ancestours: And therefore I don't think I have just ground to find fault with your work till I see it concluded ill; nor to be angry at the rashness of your design, till it is plainly discovered by your miscarriage in it; and, upon the same account I think others to blame who have too warmly and severely condemn'd the main *design* and *substance* of your Book.

In the next place then let us see what can be said in defence of the *Management* and *Conduct* you have observed in this affair. And here you must give me leave to deal freely with you, and let you know that, how much soever I am inclined to the favourable side, I cannot help thinking that there are some particulars, in which you have not taken such just and proper measures as the niceness of your Subject required; but where I want sufficient matter of Defence, or have not the sagacity to find it out; I hope you will take occasion to do your self justice.

There are several passages scattered through your Book, which are not so warily and cautiously expressed as they should have been; some of which have been taken notice of to you already in Print, and by the help of those, you might easily find out others, which to a curious and exact Reader would furnish the like matter of exception; and therefore I shall not trouble you with any remarks of this kind.

But that which, in my opinion, is the greatest oversight you have been guilty of, and which I judge you most to blame for, is the printing one part of your discourse by it self without the others. For a Paradox should never be asserted, but it should be at the same time thoroughly proved, and therefore it was not so prudently done of you peremptorily to assert that *Christianity* was *not Mysterious*, before you had perfectly confounded the *Mysteriousness* of it by dint of powerful Argument. You might easily have foreseen that the very Title of your Book, would shock a great many honest Christians, who came with an intention to read it, and very probably to such a degree, that they would not have the patience to go any further: But, if they did over-come their prejudices so far as to read it over, 'twas easy for you to have imagined what their resentments would be when they found a bold Title stand naked and unsupported by any proof. For to set the matter in a stronger light; suppose the Title of some Book had been *Christianity an Imposture*, can it be believed that a *Christian* Nation could have bore such an assertion as this, if it had not been irrefragably and unquestionably made out in the Book? And would not the Author, think you, have been justly censured for it? Had I therefore been one of your Friends, that you had been pleased to con-sult upon this occasion, it had been my advice to you to publish your whole Discourse together (if I had thought fit to advise the publish-ing any of it at all), and to recommend it to the World under a softer and more unexceptionable Title; and you should have reserved all your strong terms and hardy assertions till a full and convincing proof of your point had made way for their reception.

There is another mis-management I have heard objected to you, which I cannot wholly excuse you for, tho' I dont think it affects the main design of your Work so much as it is imagined by others to do; and that is the *obscurity* of your way of Writing. I have often heard it urged as an unpardonable thing for a Man to pretend to go about to prove that there's nothing in Christianity *Mysterious* in a Book where every thing is perplex'd and obscure, and where common easie Notions are deliver'd in such a manner as to be difficultly under-stood; but especially your Notions of *Reason*, and *Evidence*, and your account of the *Original* and *Progress* of our *Knowledge*, which seem to be taken out of a clear Writer, were thought to be so confused and so odly sorted together in your Book, that it was deem'd impossible for you to play your Game well with so ill a hand; upon which occasion it was said, that you must go to stock again, if you hoped to make any thing of it. And indeed I was not able to deny the charge; I could not help observing this fault my self, tho' I was willing to lay it upon my own Understanding, till I found my self oblig'd by the general consent of others to put it to your Account.

However, tho' I have been forced to allow your Book to be obscure, and in the Phrase of those that ridicule it, *Mysterious*; yet I do and will maintain to any Man that condemns it upon that account, that this can be no just prejudice to the Cause you have undertook. For if you can but certainly prove that *Christianity is not Mysterious*, 'tis no matter how obscure a Style you write in; if in clearing and brightning the dark parts of the Christian Religion, some obscurity should stick to the hand that does it, what Impeachment is that to the Work? Or if you should take all the *Mysteries* out of the Scripture, and put them into your Book, what's that to any body? 'Tis of Importance to have our Religion clear, but not your Book.

And since I have taken this freedom with you, give me leave to put you in mind of another thing, which I cannot tell how to account for; and that is the many Insinuations you have against the *Priests*, as if it was for their Advantage to have *Mysteries* in the *Christian Religion*. Several things of the same Nature I have met with in other Books that have come out of late, and I am puzl'd to know what all the Authors of them mean by their common cry against *Priests*, and laying all the Tricks and Mysteries of Religion at their Doors. I desire next time you write, you will be so kind as to inform me, what good end you propose to your self by a ridiculous Representation of the Order of *Priesthood*; and that, perhaps, may be a Key to let me into the design of those other Writers. I know very well that they are *Heathen*, and *Popish Priests*, that are commonly exposed and insulted in this manner; and I do not deny that a great many of them have deserved such usage; but why they should be made the common Subject of Railery now, in a Country where the *Priests* have freed themselves from the Bondage of *Superstition* and *Religious Craft*, where they have reduc'd Religion to its Primitive Standard, and con-

stantly propose it to the People in the plainest, and most simple
Dress; this I say looks very odd, and seems to have something either
of *Trick* or *Mystery* in it. For my part, I never read any one of our
English Divines who talks of any *Mysteries*, which upon consulting the
Scriptures, I did not find to be *Mysteries* there as well as in his Book;
and they are generally so far from making *Christianity* more *Mysterious* than it is, that they are rather guilty of the fault of venturing
upon too bold Explications of such things as they are not able to
comprehend. But pray what Honour, or Advantage is there to be got
by *Mysteries*? Suppose the *Arrian, Socinian*, or as you are pleas'd to
distinguish the *Unitarian Doctrines*, were received here, would not
they bring in as much Profit and Esteem to the *Arian, Socinian*, or
Unitarian Priests, as the *Orthodox Opinions* do to *ours*? I am afraid they
would hardly be contented with that scanty Provision, which
Nineparts in Ten of our Clergy subsist upon. What then can be the
meaning of so many Jests and Reflections upon the *Priests*, when
there is no present apparent likelihood, that *Heathenism*, or *Popery*
should prevail among us? Such abundance of care and caution as is
now used for our Safety, and such Zealous Admonitions as are now
given us to beware of being trickt and imposed upon, when there is
no manner of Danger to be perceived, looks very impertinent; but I
can hardly perswade my self that you, and so many other as considerable Writers that have appear'd of late in the Defence of our *Intellectual Liberty*, have perfectly thrown away your time and pains, and
been only very impertinent, though I must own, I think my self
sometimes obliged in Charity to believe so; because I cannot otherwise give my self any account of your behaviour, without ascribing it
to such reasons and motives as I am not willing to judge you acted
upon. Pardon me therefore, I intreat you, that I am rather inclined to
make a little bold with your understanding, and to think you impertinent, than to entertain any hard thoughts of your moral Character,
which every Man ought to be most tender of.

These are all Remarks I thought fit to trouble you with, upon your
Book Intituled, *Christianity not Mysterious*.

The next thing that appeared in Print, which was said to be yours,
was a *Preface* to the *Lady's Religion*; but your Name not being to it, I

am not certain it belong'd to you; and upon that account don't think my self obliged to undertake an express Defence of it, but shall content my self with making this one observation upon it, which, if you are the Author, will, I think, in some measure justify you from that untoward consequence, some of our zealous Clergy were apt to draw from your raillery upon the Priests, *viz.* That you was a sworn Enemy to their whole Profession; For by this *Preface*, if it be yours, it is certain that there are some *Priests* who have the honour of your acquaintance, and for whom you have a particular regard and esteem. 'Tis true indeed you are distinguishing in your respect to Men of that Order; and you are very much in the right of it: But if you meet with a Man of an *unprejudic'd emancipated understanding*, who is likewise a person of *strict integrity*, and *purity of behaviour*, and of *chast severe Morals*; you make him your Friend and Companion though a *Priest*, and you allow it to be his proper province to teach *Morality*; and who can blame you for giving a preference to Men of such *flagrant* and *extraordinary Merits*? This is such a proof not only of your judgment, but of the sincerity of your intention in every thing you do, as puts me in mind of an excuse for those severe things you drop now and then against the *Priests*, which I wanted just before, when I was discoursing with you upon this head; and that is, that you have dealt thus freely with them in general, in order to excite the emulation of those of a lower form in worth, and bring them up to the same pitch and Character with the *Author* of *the Lady's Religion*.

Your late *Apology* for your self, which is the only thing extant that is certainly yours, and remains to be considered, is written in such a manner as needs no further Defence. You have there sufficiently proved that the *Lay-men* are as improper judges of Religion as the *Priests*; and that a *Parliament* is altogether as fallible as a *General Council*: You have there likewise assured the World, that you are not to be over-ruled by censures, or convinced by Arguments; that you have as great an acquaintance among the Ladies, as among the Men; and that Dr. *Payne* writ the best of any Man that has yet entred the List against you.

But, as to the last of these assertions, give me leave to tell you, with the same freedom I have all along used, that I am not so intirely satisfied of the truth of this as of the former; and I the rather give way to my distrusts, because I am of Opinion it would be a more compleat Justification of your Book, to say that Dr. *Payne* had as ill success in his attempts upon it, as the other Answerers had. I must needs say, I took the *Bp.* of *Worcester*, Mr. *Norris*, and the *Author of the Occasional Paper*, to be Men of a superiour Character in Writing; but I allow you to have a peculiar tast and discernment in the choice of those *Priests* you are pleased to favour with your good Word; and therefore I inquire no further into the reasons and motives of your liking Dr. *Payne.*

All that I have further to observe to you upon your *Apology*, is that you are a little too much concerned for the treatment you have met with in *Ireland*, and too apprehensive of the consequences of it.

Papist, Impostour, and *head of a new Sect,* are only terms to flourish with; and you need not fear but the Gentlemen, who have bestowed this angry Rhetorick upon you, when they come to be better acquainted with you, and coolly examine their words by the severe rules of Truth, will change their language, and call in all their false and improper expressions.

When they consider well what laudable pains you have taken to rid your self of the first errours and prejudices of your Education, they may probably be under the temptation to fear, lest in throwing off *Popery*, you might strip a little too far, and not leave your self quite *Religion* enough. And in truth, I can't imagine what ground they could have to suspect you a *Papist* at all, unless it was because you had the peculiar fancy of Printing some part of the *Title* of your Book in *Red Letters*; and in your Opinion of the *Irish* understandings, that was perhaps occasion enough for such a Charge.

But those that call'd you *Impostour*, and compared you to *Mahomet*, had a further reach with them, which I am not able to fathom. However, I dare ingage to them, that they have no reason to fear you upon any such account; for if they will but take care to secure their *Old Religion*, they are in no danger of your imposing a *New* one upon them; for 'tis your business to take away and pull down, to mend and contract; and not to lay any new Foundations, where there has been too much Building already.

This no doubt they will quickly be sensible of, as soon as their first transports of Zeal have had their due time of assuaging; and therefore you need not trouble your self for such a strange undeserved imputation. Neither, as I think, have you any more occasion to be concerned for that other aspersion, of your being mark'd out and designed to be the *Ring-leader of a new Sect of Religionists*, that are to be called after your Name. I know you are not superstitious, and therefore I need not advise you to give little credit to any *Prophecy* of this kind; and for my part, except it had been foretold, and the Prediction confirm'd to me by unquestionable signs, I cannot believe such a thing will ever come to pass. What Mr. Recorder *Hancock* said in his ingenious Harangue, must not be understood rigidly according to the Letter; he had heard of a great many *Hereticks* that ended in ----*ists* and ----*ians*[3]; and he thought it a pretty short way of expressing *all the Gentlemen and Ladies, in and about* Dublin, *that favoured you with their Conversation*, to call them *Tolandists*. But this is a liberty that was always allowed to *Oratours*, and therefore you may be sure of keeping your Name within its just dimensions for the future, notwithstanding the *Recorder* of *Dublin* did once in a Figurative way, make bold to add a Syllable to it.

Thus, Sir, have I given you my thoughts of your *Writings* in short; I shall add one word or two more concerning your *Character*, and then beg your Pardon for the whole trouble together.

I have always been of Opinion, That the *General Character* of a Man is the best Interpreter of every thing he says and does; and I am very sorry to find I must now be forced to go by a new rule, if I take upon me to judge at all of your end, and intention in Writing what you have already Printed: For upon the best information I have been able to get, after a diligent inquiry, I find that the common Opinion of the World, and even that of your particular acquaintance, is such as renders what I am inclined to urge in your Defence perfectly ineffectual. And therefore, I will take this occasion to acquaint you how the matter stands betwixt me and my Friends, when you are the subject of discourse, and my charity puts me upon turning up the fairest side of things.

When they talk of *Veracity, Breeding, Discretion*, or any such qualifications as those, I wave the dispute as being foreign to the purpose:

But when they tell me you are look'd upon to be a *Deist*, or at best but a *narrow scanty Believer of Revelation*; when they assure me that not only the *Priests*, and some of the bigotted People that are rid by them, have this Opinion of you, but that the *Deists*[4] themselves take you to be in their interests; that the *Libertines* are fond of you, and caress you as one of their Party against all *establisht forms of Religion*; and that this cannot be only an artifice of theirs to make their strength appear more formidable, because you have said such things in their Company as gives them sufficient reasons to believe you of their Sentiments: When I am pressed hard with such accounts as these, my Answer is, That 'tis very difficult for me to conceive how any Man, that owns the least tittle of *Natural Religion*, can publickly and solemnly profess to the World that he is firmly perswaded of the Truth of the *Christian Religion*, and the *Scriptures*, when at the same time he does not really and sincerely believe any thing of them; and therefore since you have made such a profession as this, I think my self obliged to believe you so far, and upon that account, I should chuse rather to suppose that your intimate conversation with *Deists* and *Libertines*, and your seeming compliance with some of their opinions was by a mistaken policy carried on, and continued with a design of winning them over to the *Christian Faith*; this, I tell them, I had much rather imagine, than make your behaviour an Argument for calling your own *Christianity* in question: But with some seeming contempt of my Supine Charity, they answer me, that since I must be forced to call you *Fool* or *Deist*, they believe you would be best pleased with the latter Title; and they wonder I should be so unacquainted with the methods, used by the Enemies of our Religion, as not to know it is an usual Artifice with them to write booty, and to cover themselves with the profession of Religion, in order to undermine it more securely, and give their impiety an easier vent; for the truth of which observation they quote Mr. *Blount*[5], who in *the Oracles of Reason* plainly owns himself a *Deist*, and yet when he published his *Philostratus*, he would have pretended to take it very ill, if you had said he was not in earnest in all the encomiums he there bestows upon the *Christian Religion*, and *his Blessed Saviour*; though at the same time it was his design to have you believe him not in earnest.

Something I remember I said to this, but you being the best judge of your own intention, and the necessity of your own vindication in this matter, I shall leave the further reply to you.

Excuse me, Sir, for having detained you thus long with a *Defence*, which perhaps you may not very well like, though never so well meant: But I thought I could not doe you such impartial justice to the World, if I had shewed my self so blind and passionate a Friend, as to over-look all faults, and justify every thing with the same degree of Zeal. I am afraid my particular conduct in this matter, so different from the usual behaviour of those who ingage in the service of a Friend, or a cause, may give occasion to some to suspect that instead of defending you, I have been exposing you all this while to your Adversaries; and the same nice-jealousy you know some people have entertained of several that have seemingly writ in the *Defence of Religion*; but I can assure them that their suspicions are as ill-grounded here as there.

To be serious and plain with you, I have made as good a *Defence* for you as I could for my life; and though, I think at present, 'tis as good as the subject will bear, yet I heartily wish you may make a better for your self; in expectation of which I profess my self

Sir,

Your most humble Servant.

FINIS

Notes

1 [This is spelt 'jndgment' in the original text.]
2 [Possible candidates for 'Dr. S.' and 'Dr. Sh.' include:
John Sharp (1645-1714): DD Cambridge 1679, Chaplain to James II 1686 (suspended 1686-7), Archbishop of York 1691;
John Sheffield (1654?-1726): Nonconformist divine and a friend of John Locke, Presbyterian minister in Southwark 1697;
William Sheridan (1636-1711): DD Dublin 1682, Bishop of Kilmore 1682-93, Secretary to James II;
William Sherlock (1641?-1707): Opposed succession of William and Mary but later took the Oath in 1690, Dean of St Paul's 1691-1707, wrote a controversial treatise, *Present State of the Socinian Controversy*, 1698;
Thomas Smith (1638-1710): DD Oxford 1683, ejected from Magdalen as an anti-papist in 1688, refused to take oath to William and Mary;
Robert South (1634-1716): divine, strongly attacked William Sherlock in his *Animadversions* 1690;
William Stephens (1647?-1718): Whig divine, wrote *Account of the Growth of Deism in England* 1696;
Edward Stillingfleet (see p. 135, n.40.]
3 [Toland may be referring to Arianists and Socinians.]
4 [Deists believed that God was compatible with the scientific advances and rationalism of the Enlightenment. If God acted in a scientific manner, then there was no need for miracles. Moral law could be derived from natural law rather than from revelation through miracles or scripture. By contrast theists believed that God actively intervenes in the world by means of miracles. Deism flourished in the eighteenth century. Important figures in the history of deism include Anthony Collins (1676-1729), Benjamin Franklin (1706-90), Lord Herbert of Chorbury (1583-1648), Thomas Jefferson (1743-1826), Thomas Paine (1737-1809), Hermann Reimarus (1694-1768), Jean Jacques Rousseau (1712-78), Matthew Tindal (1657-1733), Toland, Voltaire (1694-1778) and George Washington (1732-99).]
5 [Charles Blount (1654-93): deist and author of books on free-thinking; regarded as a link between Lord Herbert of Chorbury (the founder of English deism) and Toland; committed suicide.]

VINDICIUS LIBERIUS:

O R,

M. *Toland*'s Defence of himfelf,

Againſt the late

Lower Houſe of Convocation,

and Others ;

W H E R E I N

(Beſides his Letters to the *Prolocutor*)

Certain Paſſages of the Book,

Intitul'd,

CHRISTIANITY NOT MYSTERIOUS,

are Explain'd, and others Correſted :

W I T H A

Full and clear Account of the Authors PRINCI-
PLES relating to CHURCH and STATE ;

And a JUSTIFICATION of the
WHIGS and *COMMONWEALTHSMEN*,
againſt the Miſrepreſentations of all their Oppoſers.

Dat Veniam Corvis, vexat C E NS U R A *Columbas.*

JUVENAL.

Being (I hope) releas'd from that irkſom and unpleaſant work
of *Controverſy and Wrangling about Religion*, I ſhall now turn
my Thoughts to ſomthing more agreable to my Temper.

Archbiſhop TILLOTSON.

L O N D O N :

Printed for *Bernard Lintott* at the Poſt-Houſe next
the *Middle-Temple-Gate* in *Fleetſtreet.* M.DCC.II.

After my Return from *Germany* I was very curious to know what had [*1*]
bin printed in my Absence; and guessing by the *English* Pamphlets I
saw in *Holland* that there were a great many publisht besides, I
order'd my Bookseller to send me 'em all Home, and was amaz'd to
perceive what a Task I had on my Hands. Som related to the *Commons*, som to the *Lords*, som to the new, and som to the old *Ministry*:
but none of any Sort were near so numerous, or written with greater
Heat and Spirit, than those relating to both Houses of CONVOCA-
TION.¹ I was deservedly Surpriz'd at several Things I met in the last;
but in those which justify'd the proceedings of the *lower House*, what
made the deepest Impressions on me was to find the most Reverend
the *Archbishop of Canterbury*, and the right Reverend the *Bishops*,
blam'd for doing nothing against heretical, impious, and immoral
Books, or protecting such from Censure; and that they had particularly Screen'd my self from I know not what perillous Circumstances,
tho His *Grace* and their *Lordships* are all Strangers to my Person, and,
I verily believe, as far from the Principles imputed to me by others, as
any the most orthodox Members of the *lower House*. I met with several Instances in my own Time, and read of a great many more, how
far the Force of Interest, Passion, or Design will carry People to
asperse their Adversaries, to vilify their Persons, and to render their
Principles or Intentions suspected, without more Regard to Sense or
Probability, than they commonly have to Justice or Truth: but I confess this to be one of the hardiest Attemts of the kind, and yet I
ought not to be startl'd at any Thing they have don against me, after
the Strange Usage which the *Bishops* on several Accounts have
receiv'd at their Hands.

But since the Publisher and the Compilers of the *Narrative of the* [*II*]
Procedings of the lower House have represented me as the Author of an
Atheistical and *Detestable* Book, which is to make me an Atheist and
detestable Person; and that the writer of *The Expedient Propos'd*

155

affirms, that my Lord *Bishop of* Salisbury *had too great an Influence on the upper House to Screen me, lest he shou'd be complain'd of next;*[2] I ow that Deference to the World, and that Justice to my self, as to give a particular Account of this Affair: for tho I am not so considerable (even in my own Opinion) as to think the Public shou'd be trobl'd about my Sentiments or privat Concerns, yet since certain Persons, for Reasons best known to themselves, have thought fit to make no small Stir about Me, and to represent me in very different Colors, somtimes as the Head and somtimes as the Tail of a Party; at one Time as a Man to be contemn'd, which yet they seem to fear shou'd happen, as well by the Number as the Virulence of their Answers; when they are in another Humor, I must straight be transform'd from a Pygmy to a Gyant, a destructive Monster whom Church and State must jointly consult by what Means to disarm or destroy; and lest the *Bishops* might think the Discussing of my Book below their Consideration, the *Narrative of the lower House* assures 'em that *the Cause was worthy their Endeavour.*[3] But be it which way they will, that I am as little or as great as they wou'd have me, yet conceiving my self to be publicly wrong'd and asperst, Equity and Law allow me the Benefit of a public Defence, tho my Enemies may add to their Crime by denying me a public Reparation. To reflect on Men's Persons when we oppose their Errors is not only expressly contrary to the sacred Precepts of the *Christian* Religion, but also to the common Dictats of Reason, and below the Dignity of human Nature. We are rather oblig'd to make the most candid Construction of their Designs, and if their words admit of a double Sense (which is hard to be always avoided in any Language), we ought to allow the fairest Interpretation of their Meaning. This is the practice of those who really love and esteem the Truth, who labor for the Reformation and not the Destruction of their Adversaries: for their Intentions can never be good who seem apprehensive lest those they attack shou'd be able to justify themselves, who aggravate their Errors or expose their Opinions under odious Names, who wiredraw their Expressions to Things that were never in their Thoughts, who charge 'em with Consequences they reject or did not foresee, who accuse 'em of impious or seditious Designs, who suspect the plainest Apologies they can make, and discover a hidden Poison in their words even when they are of their own prescribing.

Were I dispos'd to speak indecent and unmanly Language on this Occasion, I needed not to read our PLAUTUS[4] as MILTON[5] is said to have often don the better to rail at SALMASIUS,[6] I needed to go no farther than those very Pieces which have bin publisht on Behalf of *the lower House*; for if you consider the Dialect in which they treat those of the other Side, and what they positively or by Implication lay to their Charge, you wou'd not imagin you were reading Books that related to the Constitution of any *Church* in the world, much less that were written by Divines against Divines, by the *inferior Clergy* against the *Bishops* themselves, or such as espous'd their Cause and appear to have their Approbation. You meet in every Page with the Charge and Terms of *libelling, calumniating, bespattering, Detraction,* and *Slander*; of *Partiality, Disingenuity, Insincerity, Falsifying,* and *Prevarication*; of *Rudeness, Unmannerlyness, Ignorance, Disrespect,* of too much *Assurance,* and want of *Modesty*; of *false* or *partial Quotations, Misrepresentations* of Matters of Fact, *Insinuations* against Som as Betrayers of the Church, against others as mere *Tools* ready to say or do or write any Thing for *Preferment,* and the *Discontents* of those are not forgot who are angry at their *Disappointments*; there are little pitiful *Stories* plainly told or obscurely[7] hinted; somtimes they rake into the Pedegree, mean Beginning, Youthful Slips, or common Indiscretions of their Adversaries; and, in a word, you meet with a Treatment and stile that abundantly favor of this World, and have not the least Rellish of Heaven. But nothing Scandalises me like certain base and low Expressions, as when Doctor KENNET[8] is made to personat a Quack-Doctor or Mountebank in the *Remarks upon the Temper of the late Writers about Convocations*[9]: and in the same Book is very intelligibly (I will not say how truly or gentilely) call'd a mercenary Dog; for what else can be the Meaning of these Words? *He was resolv'd to write for Himself, and against Som Body. Whether Mr. ATTERBURY[10] or Som else had fallen in his Way, his Teeth were alike ready Set to fasten upon any one, at whom his Masters shou'd think fit to play him.*[11] Tho these Gentlemen profess to be *Christians,* and that we know 'em to be *Divines,* yet they somtimes forget of what Spirit they are; and I hope

[*III*]

157

their Doctrin may gain more Friends to the *Church*, than I am sure such Language or Examples ever can: For my own Part, how much soever I am provok'd, I shall not indulge my Passion, nor Sanctify Malice by their Authority, having learnt to forgive my Enemies, and being persuaded that the Cause of Religion the least of all others needs the Aid of Force or Calumny to Support it.

[*IV*] I shall therefore to the best of my Knowlege fairly relate what concerns my self in their Writings, pleading my Justification where I think I am injur'd, and ingenuously owning my Mistakes where I am convinc'd there's Reason for so doing. In the beginning of *March* 1701, I was inform'd by common Fame that the *lower House of Convocation* had appointed a Committee to examin Books lately publisht against the *Christian* Religion or the establisht Church of *England*. Som people seem'd mightily pleas'd with this News on my Account, exulting beforehand at the *Censure* I was sure to incurr, and positively telling what it shou'd be with the Consequences of the same, long e'er it became the Subject of Debate. In nothing on Earth did there more appear the Spirit of a Party, especially if it be consider'd that the Persons who show'd their Zeal and Joy on this Occasion were not more remarkable than their Neighbours for Knowlege or Practice, and that they were most if not all of 'em absolute Strangers to me. Som little Time after, I heard indeed that two Books of my Composition were under the Consideration of that Committee, wherupon I did immediatly write a Letter to the reverend Dr. HOOPER, Dean of *Canterbury* and *Prolocutor*[12] of the *lower House of Convocation*, either to give such Satisfaction as shou'd induce 'em to stop their proceedings, or desiring to be heard in my own Defence before they past any *Censure* on my Writings. This Letter (which I understand to have bin only privatly shown to som of the Members) was variously represented. Som said it was a rude and menacing Piece, maintaining the *Socinian* Heresy, and fit to be burnt with the Book, if not with the Author: others reported that it was a direct Submission, a mean Complyance, and a very humble Recantation. Now supposing it had bin a Submission (tho I knew no Obedience to be due to them, and was ignorant with what Errors they charg'd me), yet none of my Adversaries ought to have bin displeas'd at it, unless they were sorry lest by so doing I shou'd escape those Inconveniences into which my Obstinacy might bring me; and none of the Clergy ought to reflect on any Man's Retracting as a mean Compliance, since *Recantation* is all the *Inquisition* it self requires, and that the preaching of *Repentance* is at least half a *Clergyman's* Business. But that every Reader may judg which of the two Reports were better grounded, or whether Neither of 'em had any Ground at all, here follows the Letter it self for their satisfaction.

For the reverend Dr. Hooper, D. *of* Canterbury, *and* Prolocutor *of the* [V] *lower House of Convocation.*

Reverend Sir,

In the Post, which you so deservedly Supply, tis no Wonder if you are often addrest by persons (as I am) wholly unknown to You; tho Fame has made me no Stranger to your great Learning and Moderation. I have bin inform'd by several People, that *the lower House of Convocation* has order'd a Committee to examin what Books have bin lately written or publisht against the *Christian* Religion and the three *Creeds*, or to this Effect; and that, among many others, two Pieces, wherof I am the Author, are now under their Consideration. That in those Books there may be som singular Opinions, and such as are not authoriz'd by the common Approbation, I will not deny: for I had not only the same Liberty with all others of writing in a free Contry, but might also make what new Discoveries I was able towards the better understanding of Religion, of Law, of History, or any other Faculty. And indeed He trifles extremely with the World, who is not convinc'd, that, at least, he makes Things clearer than they were; if He explodes no vulgar Errors, detects no dangerous Fallacies, nor adds any stronger Light or Proof to what was generally receiv'd before. Those and such like are the real or pretended Motives of all Authors, of *Divines* as well as others; and they actually advance new *Notions, Expositions,* and *Hypotheses* in their Books every Day, without being decry'd for their Innovations, or suspected to undermine Religion. Tis not to be suppos'd therfore that the *Convocation* is displeas'd with me for differing sometimes with others (which I can show the most eminent of their Members to have don) but for writing, as it's given out, against the *Christian* Religion or the Three *Creeds.* The Truth of this Charge I positively deny, or that there is any Reason or Color for it in any of my Books. CHRISTIANITY NOT MYSTERIOUS cannot relate to the three *Creeds,* since it do's not treat particularly of any *Article;* notwithstanding that such as never saw it are made to believe it directly attacks the *Trinity,* and openly defends the *Socinian* Principles, which the Author has always believ'd not only to be false, but also wholly groundless and ridiculous. As for the *Christian* Religion in general, that Book is so far from calling it in Question, that it was purposely written for its Service, to defend it against the Imputations of Contradiction and Obscurity, which are frequently objected by its Opposers. There is nothing blameworthy in this Design, nor ought any Persons to be angry with me for professing that I understand the *Christian* Religion, how *mysterious* soever it may seem to them: and, I am sure, the better any Man comprehends a Thing, the more He has to say for it, and the greater Reasons to believe it.

Som Passages in my Book, which were disputed, I have explain'd in an *Apology* apart: and were my Principle erroneous or my Performance insufficient, yet my Intentions were Sound and Orthodox. As for AMYNTOR, every Body knows how Mr. BLACK-HALL[13] drew me in to write it, when no such Purpose had ever enter'd into my Head before. This Book consists of Matters of Fact, and som *Observations* on them. The *Facts* are all or most of them collected out of the *Fathers* of the *Church*, Men for whom the *Clergy* profess a great Veneration, and the best Editions of their Works have bin made or procur'd by *Divines*. What lies dispers'd and scatter'd in those Volums, is neither better nor worse being extracted and laid together in their natural Order. But if the bare Quoting of *Facts* be any Fault, I may pretend, I hope, to as good Quarter as Mr. DODWELL;[14] not that I wou'd promote any *Censure* against that worthy Person, but that what is not reckon'd amiss in him may not be thought criminal in Me. But the *Facts*, I may reasonably suppose, are not likely to be made an Objection to any Body; and I have even convinc'd my Adversaries that by the *Spurious Pieces*, mention'd in MILTON's *Life*, I did not mean any books of the *New Testament*. Tis confest I have shown som Consequences which have bin drawn from the pretended *Sacred Books*, of which I have given a Catalog in AMYNTOR; but that I approve of 'em there or any where else dos by no Means appear. On the contrary, in the Sixty-fifth Page, I affirm that *it had much more becom Mr. BLACKHALL's Profession to appear better acquainted with these Things, and commendably to spend his Time in preventing the mischievous Infer-ences which Heretics may draw from hence, or to remove the Scruples of doubting but sin-cere Christians, than so publicly to vent his Malice against a Man that never injur'd him,* &c. And as to som Remains of the *Apostles* which the *Fathers* thought unquestionably theirs, and wherof I had so favorable an Opinion as to offer som Arguments to prove 'em genuin; yet, in the fifty eighth Page, I declare that I *shall not be too hasty to make a final Decision of this Matter with my self, lest I incur the dreadful Curse which the Author of the* Revelation *pronounces against such as shall add or take away from that Book. Let Mr. BLACKHALL be assur'd, that, if He must needs have me to be a Heretic, I am not unteach-able; tho I wou'd not have it reputed Obstinacy, if I shou'd not Surrender without satisfacto-ry Reasons. Instead therfore of censuring and calumniating (which ought not to be reckon'd Virtues in any Order of Men, and least of all in the Ministers of the Gospel) let such as are better inlighten'd endeavour to extricat the erroneous out of these or the like Difficulties,* &c. This is what I thought necessary to suggest in general concerning those two Pieces of mine, which have bin made the Occasion of so much noise. I was but five and twenty Years old when I wrote the first, which ought to be Excuse enough for any unadvis'd Expressions; and the last I was plainly forc'd to publish in my own Vindication, having bin openly traduc'd to the honorable *House of Commons*. For many important Reasons I have firmly resolv'd never hereafter to intermeddle in any *religious Controversies*, but to keep my self (as now I am) very easy and contented; *provided always I be not con-strain'd (as before) to write in my just Defence, which I shall think my self more oblig'd to do in Relation to the Animadversions of a public Body, than against any privat Person how con-siderable soever.* There is nothing less equitable or more ineffectual than condemning of Books by wholesale, without assigning the particular Places which contradict Reli-gion, the Laws, or good Manners. I cou'd easily show the ill Effects of such Procedings in *Convocations* and other *ecclesiastic Assemblys* in all Ages, were I not sure that you understand the History of these Things much better than I can pretend to do. I have collected occasionally in my Reading such Passages as relate to the expunging, castrat-ing, suppressing, burning, or other Ways of censuring Books among the *Heathens, Jews,*

Christians, and *Mahometans*: And were such Materials digested into a Volum on this Subject, to represent the Matter at one View to the Reader, the World wou'd be astonisht at most of the Circumstances; which convinces me that the less of this is practis'd the better it is, and more for the Honor of Religion. This I say not with Regard to my self, being prepar'd for whatever happens; but were it becoming me to advise a Person so much my Superior in all Respects, I wou'd desire you to countenance as little as may be against others a Thing which has all the Appearance of Severity to make the Party odious that use it, and none of the intended Effects to reconcile or intimidat, but rather to provoke their Enemies. There are other Methods more just and reasonable to secure the *establisht Religion*, of which I own my self a Member, as finding it after due Consideration to be the best in the World, tho in many Respects coming short of Perfection. It will not be long before I have Opportunity to acquaint the Public with my Reasons for this Profession, both to undeceive those who are pleas'd to question my Religion in general, and because I adher'd to no peculiar Society before, but only occasionally join'd with all *Protestants* indifferently, against the Superstition, Idolatry, and Tyranny of *Popery*. But not to digress, when this Letter is but too prolix already, tho the *Convocation* pretends to no Authority over Men's Persons, yet, if you think fit to intimat your Desire of any further Satisfaction in these Matters, I shall readily wait on you wherever you please to appoint me. In the mean Time, I hope you'll attribute nothing I have said to any greater Assurance, than what I ought to have of my own Innocence and your Justice. If I have bin misinform'd about the Procedings of your House, I beg Pardon for giving you this Troble; but if the Matter of Fact be true, I have don no more than is necessary. Wishing therfore a happy Conclusion to the Determinations of that *Assembly* where you make the greatest Figure, I am,

    Reverend Sir,
    Your most humble Servant,
    Jo. Toland.

To this Letter the Prolocutor was pleas'd to send me a short Answer, containing, that my Information was true about the Committee, and that they had com to som Resolutions about my Book which they were expected to report suddenly: that his Business was to manage the Debates of the House, and to moderat any Disputes that might arise about wording their Questions; in which Cases, if he might be capable, he concludes with his Offers to serve me. As well therfore to justify my self from the different Reports about my first Letter, as to leave them no Color or Pretence of not fully understanding my Design, I thought fit after due Consideration to send him this second Letter. [VI]

Reverend Sir,
I thankfully acknowlege the civil Offers in your Answer; nor did I doubt before of your Justice, tho I cou'd pretend no Title to your Favor either by Friendship or Merit. But

you seem to mistake my Design, for I wrote to you as a public Person, in Order to communicat my Letter to the *Assembly* over which you preside, or at least to the Committee: that in so doing I might give 'em full Information and Satisfaction; or, that if they proceded to any *Censure*, it shou'd be a Part of my *Defence*. My Resolutions of Silence about these or the like Matters for the future are honestly meant, and were fixt a long Time before the Meeting of the *Convocation*, as som Persons of great Worth and Honor can testify. This is all that cou'd be expected from one who cannot be brought to *recant* those Errors which he never held, how ever uncharitably imputed to him by others. As the Deference I paid to the *Convocation* is no more than their Due, and the farthest imaginable from Soothing; so I hope no Body takes for Rudeness, what I was oblig'd to say in my own Vindication. Flattery is as much below me, as it is above me to menace: but in Dealing plainly within the Bounds of good Manners, I can never dispense with my self. The space of a Month shall convince the World of my Sincerity in performing what I promis'd you with Respect to the *establish't*[15] *Church*, which I really think to be the best national[16] Constitution on Earth, and admirably suted to our civil Government: and if my Judgment in this or any other Case may be thought of any Weight, it is more becoming me to declare it now, than at any Time of my Life before. But referring to what I shall[17] publish on this Subject, I desire the Favor of You to impart this and my former Letter to your *House*, if they continue resolv'd to *censure* my Books. And for the rest, I question not but you in particular will act answerably to your great Character, in Pursuance of your Trust, for the Interest of Religion, the Honor of the *Church of England*, and with no ill Intentions towards,

Reverend Sir,
Your most humble Servant,
Jo. Toland.

[VII] Having receiv'd no Answer to this *Letter* (which I now understand was no more communicated to the *House* than the Other) I took it for granted that I had given 'em intire Satisfaction both as to my Writings and Principles. And who wou'd not have thought so? for I cou'd not imagin I had to do with TIBERIUS,[18] or such other *Tyrants*, who procede with no Regard to the Justice of the Cause, but only aim at oppressing and condemning the Person accus'd. Nor was I to look on *the lower House of Convocation* as on the *Popish Inquisition*, tho even in that inhuman, execrable, and *Antichristian* Court, a Man is always allow'd to be heard at his own Desire. Neither did I dream in the least but that my *Letters* had bin under the Consideration of the *House*, so far was I from suspecting they were accidentally or advisedly supprest. I took all the Steps on my Side that cou'd be expected or demanded. The Design of my Book was controverted, I plainly declar'd it; My Faith in general was question'd, I profest it to be the *Christian* Religion; and there being a Doubt what Communion I prefer'd, I own'd it to be that of the *Church of England*. But in Case these Answers might not give full Satisfaction, I offer'd personally to appear in their Assembly, which indeed was more than they cou'd require by Law, yet being voluntarily offer'd by me, they cou'd not pretend to run any Risk in accepting it. Having therfore never heard from them afterwards, I made no Doubt but all this Controversy was happily at an End, and that I shou'd not hear again of these Matters except by the Congratulations of my Friends, that the Members of *the lower House*, being undeceiv'd from the false Reports and perverse Glosses of my Enemies, had set me right with their Brethren in the Contry, as in Justice and Charity they were bound to do.

But, to my extreme Surprize, in perusing the *Narrative* drawn up [*VIII*] by Order of *the lower House*, I found, that, without any regard to my *Letters*, they had proceded so far as to draw a *Representation* against me to *the upper House*, and to send to their *Lordships* certain *Positions* they had condemn'd in the Book intitul'd, CHRISTIANITY NOT MYS-TERIOUS. In the *Narrative* it is call'd a *detestable* Book,[19] and the Publisher more than once terms it *Atheistical*.[20] Now, 'tis well known the Book has bin examin'd by the late learned Lord *Bishop* of *Worcester*, by Mr. NORRIS, Dr. PAINE, Dr. BROWNE the present Provost of *Dublin* College, by the Author of *the Occasional Paper*, by the Author of *the Gentleman's Religion*,[21] by Dr. BEVERLY, by Mr. BECKENSALL[22] of *Oxford*, and others; of these som taxt it with Forms of Speaking out of the common Road, others thought it favor'd *Socinianism*, and a very few charg'd it with Principles tending to *Deism*: but not one of 'em ever spoke of discovering *Atheism* in it, when neither the whole Discourse nor any Part of it can have any Sense or Meaning, but as they are founded on the Being of a Deity. People ought to be very tender and reserv'd in accusing a Man of any Thing that manifestly turns to his Disadvantage; but making one pass for a Traitor, a Parracid, or Murderer, are nothing, even in the Eys of the World, to charging him with *Atheism*: for such a Person is not only justly lookt upon as one that has no Reason or Reflection, but likewise as under no Tyes of Conscience, of Obligations or Oaths, when he has an Opportunity of doing Mischief; and so not to be trusted in any privat or public Capacity. Besides that a great many People, when they are confidently told by those on whose Judgment and Sincerity they depend (such as their *Spiritual* Guides) that any Man is an *Atheist*, they presently conclude him guilty of all those Immoralitys which they take to be the natural Consequences of his Opinion, and without further Examination they actually charge him with all the ill Things that com into their Heads. This is taken on Trust by others, and so let the Person be innocent as a Child, yet his Vindication will never probably reach so many as are prejudic'd against him, wherby the more ignorant Sort are made to abhor him, and his crafty Enemies thus securely gratify their Malice or Revenge. *Tis no matter for Truth, calumniat stoutly, somthing will stick.*

[*IX*]   I cou'd produce many Instances to this purpose from the antient *Philosophers*; the *Heathen Priests* represented the *primitive Christians* as *Atheists* both in Doctrin and Practice, and the People at their Instigation treated 'em as such; the first *Reformers*, with their followers, met with the same unjust Measure from the *Papists*; and, at this present Time, when the *Inquisitors* can make no other Accusation good against their Prisoner, they take Care to Charge him with *Atheistical* Notions and the most enormous Crimes, wherby he's straight condemn'd by the public Voice, and all Men's Ears are stopt against any Thing that can be said for one they conceive to be such a wicked Wretch. GOD forbid I shou'd think the Intentions of those who stil'd my Book *atheistical* and *detestable* to be quite so bad; however, those Epithets carrying with them so terrible an Impression, they shou'd have consider'd better before they made use of 'em. But in their Excuse, and to my Comfort, the Danger is not so great in *England*, where the generality of the People are so well instructed, and so clearsighted in all Affairs, as to judg for themselves, yielding neither an implicit Belief nor Obedience to any single Man or public Society. Besides that the Sowerness of som and the Rashness of others in *religious Controversies* have made this Word so common an Opprobry, and to be so thrown out at Random on the least Difference about one another's Opinions, that it ordinarily signifys no more than Man's being passionatly displeas'd against those who dissent from him, and on such occasions it imports as much as an angry Bully's calling every one he meets *Son of a Whore*, tho it were his Brother or a Woman. But for the Sake of those who may lay a greater Stress on this Word, I solemnly profess to the World, and make my Appeal to Heaven, that in writing CHRISTIANITY NOT MYSTERIOUS, I neither doubted my self of the Wisdom, Goodness, or Power of GOD; nor in the least intended to bring others into any Scruples about his Attributes or Existence: and, whatever Errors or Mistakes there may be in that Treatise, yet I challenge all my Accusers to discover any Thing in the same directly or indirectly, exprest or imply'd, as tending to *Atheism*, which I execrate and abhor from the Bottom of my Soul; or if any of *the lower House* thought me to be truly guilty of this most heinous of all Crimes, why wou'd they not hear me at my own Request, when I might either vindicat my self from this foul Aspersion, or be throly convinc'd of so dangerous an Error in such a numerous and learned Assembly of *Divines*?

But this is a Favor (tho others may call it a Piece of Justice) [X] wherof it seems I was not worthy; and I am afraid, from my Observation on som Men's Temper and Designs, that even for finding Fault with their procedings, and for questioning the Equity or Legality of any Thing they have don, I may still be counted little better than an *Atheist*, at least very temerarious and presumptious, as it formerly happen'd to the famous *Monsieur* ARNAUD.[23] He affirm'd that having carefully perus'd JANSENIUS's Books,[24] he cou'd not find therein those *Propositions* condemn'd by the *Pope*, tho he himself did likewise condemn the same *Propositions* wherever he met 'em, and wou'd have don it in JANSENIUS cou'd he have found 'em there. Threescore and eleven *Doctors* undertook his Vindication, and som of 'em declar'd, that (notwithstanding the strict Search they had made) they cou'd never find any such *Propositions* in JANSENIUS, but many that were quite contrary: wherfore they earnestly[25] intreated that if there was any *Doctor* present, who had discover'd 'em there, he wou'd be pleas'd to show them; but this they cou'd never obtain. On the other Side were fourscore *Secular Doctors* and about half as many *Mendicant Fryers*,[26] who, without ever examining whether what *Monsieur* ARNAUD affirm'd were true or false, condemn'd him as *temerarious for saying he was not satisfy'd those Propositions were in* JANSENIUS, *when the Bishops had before declar'd they were there.* And why may not I, or any that appears in my Defence or Excuse, be as well counted *temerarious* for affirming that there is no *Atheism* in my Book, after it is declar'd to be there by the publisher of the *Narrative*, who was likewise a Member of *the lower House*? In one Thing the *lower House* has outdon the *Sorbonne*; for there *Monsieur* ARNAUD or any other might freely Discourse, tho they were artfully stinted to half an Hour by those who had no Mind they shou'd have Time enough to justify themselves; but here I was not allow'd to speak at all. There is a Thing, I must observe, wherin they are both agreed, it being easier to find Votes than Arguments, and that is to CENSURE: *For*, as my Author observes,[27] *the Censure how censurable soever it may be in it self, will for som Time have its Effect. And tho tis certain there will be so much Pains taken to show its Invalidity, that it will be at last discover'd; yet it is true withall, that at the Beginning it will have as great an Influence over most People, as if it were the justest Censure in the World.* It suffices that it be publisht in the News Paper, or cry'd about the Streets. *How few are there that will read it? how few of those that do read it, will understand it? how very few will perceive that it answers not the Objections? And who do you think will concern himself so much in the Business, as to undertake the Examination of it to the Bottom?*

[*XI*]   But not to digress too far, *the lower House* without any previous Consultation with the *Bishops*, without expecting the KING's *License*, and without any Regard to the two *Letters* I sent 'em, came to formal Resolutions about CHRISTIANITY NOT MYSTERIOUS; and on the Report of a Committee appointed for examining of Books lately written against the Truth of the *Christian* Religion, they did, about the twentieth of *March*, send a *Representation* to the *Bishops*, praying their Lordships *Concurrence to their Resolutions*, with *their Advice and Directions what effectual Course might be taken to suppress this Book and all other pernitious Books already written against the Truth of the* Christian *Religion, and to prevent the Publication of the like for the future.* Their Resolutions contain, that, *in their Judgment, the said Book is of pernitious Principles, of dangerous Consequence to the* Christian *Religion, written on a Design (as they conceive) and tending to subvert the Fundamental Articles of the* Christian *Faith:* that *the Positions extracted out of it are, together with diverse others of the same Nature, pernitious, dangerous, scandalous, and destructive of the* Christian *Faith.* In Answer to that Part of the *Representation* which concern'd a *Censure*, their *Lord-ships*[28] declar'd (*April* the Eighth)

That on their consulting with Council learned in the Law concerning heretical, impi-ous, or immoral Books, and particularly concerning this Book sent up to them from *the lower House*, they do not find how, without a *License* from the KING (which they had not yet receiv'd) they cou'd have sufficient Authority to *censure judicially* any such Books: but on the contrary they were advis'd that by so doing both Houses of *Convoca-tion* might incur the Penalties of the Statute of 25. of H.8.

And this Opinion their *Lordships* receiv'd from able Lawyers after desiring their Resolution of these two[29] Questions; First, *Whether the* Convocation's *giving an Opinion concerning a Book that is heretical, impious, and immoral, is contrary to any Law?* to which they receiv'd an Answer in the Affirmative: Secondly, *Whether the Position* (they had extracted out of CHRISTIANITY NOT MYSTERIOUS) *were such an Opinion as is contrary to any Law?* to which it was answer'd in the Negative. Nor did they content themselves with this Advice, but they inquir'd besides what had bin[30] formerly don in such Cases, and found that on a Complaint being exhibited against som Books by the *lower* to the *upper House*, in the year 1689, the learned in both the Laws were of Opinion they cou'd not procede judicially in such Mat-ters.

But the *Narrative* affirms that *they were as far from proposing to their* [*XII*] Lordships *to censure the book judicially, as they were from presuming so to censure it themselves;*[31] and that they desir'd not the punishment of the Author. Yet[32] *certainly in the Sense of Mankind* (as the Author of *the History of the Convocation* justly observes) *to declare a Judgment of certain* Positions, *to be pernitious, dangerous, scandalous, and destructive of the* Christian *Faith: and to com to formal* Resolutions *hereupon, and to pray their Lordship's* Concurrence *to these Resolutions, is as much a judicial* Censure *as one House cou'd possibly pass without the other; and it is as much aiming at* a concurrent judicial Censure *of the whole Synod, as any Words cou'd well prescribe.* The same Author says, that[33] *the Report first agreed on in the Committee was much more judicial, and that, before it was brought to the House, a Mitigation of Judgment was obtain'd with great Difficulty.* But to evince that it was not out of Ten-derness to my Person, or from a Spirit of Moderation, that they deny

167

JOHN TOLAND

their having aim'd at a *judicial Censure*, the Publisher of the *Narrative*
says *they were sufficiently discourag'd now from desiring the Punishment
of the Author, from the Reception that the Address of the lower House met
on such an Occasion in the Year* 1689.[34] Tis from Want of Incouragement then, and not of Inclination, that the Author was spar'd; nor
did certain Gentlemen make a Secret of what, upon the passing of a
concurrent Censure, they expected shou'd be don by the *Parlament*,
which they said was wholly in their Interest, and wou'd not stick at
making a Precedent to oblige 'em. *Sed pudet Hæc——*

Nec semper feriet quodcunque minabitur Arcus.

The Narrative affirms that *had a judicial Censure bin desir'd, tho
som eminent Lawyers were against it, there are others, perhaps as eminent, who are of a contrary Opinion.*[35] I doubt not at all but there be
Lawyers as well as *Divines* that are ready to give any Opinion to gratify their Ambition or Revenge, which ought to be no Argument
against the Usefulness or Necessity of those excellent Professions,
since there was found a treacherous, false, and ambitious Brother
even among the 12 Apostles. In CHARLES I's Reign, we had *Lawyers*
who were forc'd to fly their Contry for advancing the King's Preroga-
tive above the Liberty of the Subject, and the known Laws of the
Land. It was a *Lawyer*, who, in the Year 1675, wou'd persuade the
House of Lords that the *Oath* then endeavor'd to be impos'd for
utterly inslaving the Nation to *Popery* and *Tyranny* was only a *Moderat Security to the Church and Crown*, tho it imported that it was not
lawful for *Englishmen* upon any Pretence whatsoever to take up Arms
against the King or those commission'd by him (which was to swear
Subjection to his Army) and that they wou'd not at any Time
endeavor the Alteration of the Government, either in Church or
State. In the late Reigns there were *Lawyers* who went the utmost
Lengths to subvert our Constitution, who under the Appearance of
legal Forms favor'd all the villanous Machinations against our Religion and Government, who wrested and perverted the Laws against
all those whom the Court had a Mind to destroy, who by their nau-
seous and venal Rhetoric, Scurrility, Threats, and false Suggestions,
procur'd som of the best Blood in *England* to be barbarously spilt.

Questionless such of these Men as are yet alive wou'd be gladly imploy'd to condemn the Authors of any Pieces that expose the arbitrary and extravagant Procedings of those Times, or that justify the Principles of the late most happy *Revolution*, wherby GOD has mercifully deliver'd us from the Hands and Tongues of such sanguinary Monsters. Tis no wonder if som of 'em incourage a Censure now against my Book, when they harangu'd others out of their Lives for only writing such Things in the late Reigns as never went farther than their Closets, and which are sufficiently prov'd to have bin no Crimes by the Reversal of their Attainders under his present Majesty. It is not *Scribere est Agere* with me, for I have not only publisht but own'd my Books. But I have no small Satisfaction to find those Men no Friends to my Person, who were such notorious Enemies to their Contry: tho I admire that any of 'em should offer to discover my Sentiments by the old infamous Practices of forc'd Consequences and Innuendos, when I am able to give so good and positive an Account of their wicked Notions in their own Words, as they were printed by Authority in certain *Tryals* that are not forgot, how much soever they may be forgiven. But I shall despise their Malice, as the Lenity of the present Reign has overlookt their Punishment: for tis a true Observation, that

—————————————— Nunquam
Sanguine Causidici maduerunt Rostra pusilli.

But tis suggested that the *Bishops* wou'd do nothing against Books [*XIII*] of ill Principles, on which the Authors of the *Regale* and the *Expedient Propos'd* largely insist, nor is it forgot by the Publisher and Compilers of the *Narrative*. The *Archbishop*'s saying that several Obstructions and Stumblingblocks were laid in their way to censure my Book, those words *Obstructions* and *Stumblingblocks* are printed in a distinct Character in the *Narrative*,[36] tho his Grace hereby meant nothing else but the *Statute* beforemention'd, or the irregular Procedings of *the lower House*, notwithstanding the *Prolocutor*'s hoping the Stumblingblocks were not of their laying, wheras indeed they plainly were. And as if they fear'd that this Charge of neglecting such Books in general, or favoring me in particular, shou'd not appear popular enough by their Report, Doctor JANE[37] propos'd that there shou'd be som Marks or Signification in the Acts of their House, that the *Archbishop* and *Bishop*'s Answer given to them in Relation to my Book was insufficient; and accordingly (as it appears from their *Minuts*) *they decreed that the Committee shou'd in their Answer represent the* Archbishop *and* Bishop's *Answer to that Book as insufficient, and* insinuat *that this House is not satisfy'd concerning the Opinion of their Counsil learned in the Law:* And the Publisher of the *Narrative* says that *the Bishops made use of a far fetcht Reason for doing nothing in it.*[38] But this Representation of Things will obtain its due Character with all fair and impartial Readers, when it is consider'd that their *Lordship*'s actually receiv'd the Charge of *the lower House,* they inquir'd for Precedents in the like Case to regulat their Procedings, they advis'd with able Lawyers about it, and, finding they cou'd not *judicially censure* the Book themselves, they recommended the Business to the *Bishop* of the Diocese wherin the Author had or shou'd have his Residence. Yet further, they appointed a Committee of *Bishops* to examin it, who reported[39] that *they had found therein several dangerous Positions, and one in particular which they lookt on as the Foundation of all the rest, of which the* lower House *had not taken notice,* wherof in due place. I thought myself oblig'd to give this Account by Reason of the Justice I ow to any that is wrong'd or asperst on my Account, as well as to show the candid and serious Proceding of the *Bishops,* who, tis manifest, had no personal Regard to me or my Writings, no Interest, Fear, or Affection to byass them, and are blam'd in Effect for nothing else, but for not proceding in a passionat and arbitrary Manner, against common Equity and the Laws of the Kingdom, to the Scandal of the *Reform'd Religion* which abhors Persecution, and for not exposing *themselves* and *the lower House* to a *Præmunire.*

[XIV] But to load the *Bishops* still with more odium on my Account the Publisher of the *Narrative* says, that, *why their* Lordships *were not as free to give their Opinion concerning that* Atheistical *Book of* TOLAND, *as they were of a few Words let fall in a Book writ upon State-matters only, reflecting upon the Disposal of som Preferment, he shall not presume to inquire.*[40] The Matter of Fact is this. Two Days after *the lower House* had made their Representation of my Book, the *Archbishop* did pro-

duce another Book in *the upper House*, and after reading a Paragraph
in the fortieth Page of the same, his *Grace* and the rest of the *Bishops*
agreed that the following Paper shou'd be fixt over several Doors in
Westminster Abbey.

March 22. 1701. Wheras this Day a Book, intitul'd, *Essays upon*, I. *The Balance of
Power*. II. *The Right of making War, Peace, and Alliances*. III. *Universal Monarchy, &c*.
was brought into the *Jerusalem* Chamber, where his Grace the *Archbishop* of *Canterbury*, and the rest of the Suffragan *Bishops* of his Province, were assembl'd in *Convocation*, in the fortieth Page of which Book are these Words, *Are not a great many of us able
to point out to several Persons whom nothing has recommended to Places of highest Truth,
and often to rich* Benefices *and* Dignities, *but the open Enmity which they have, almost
from their Cradles, profest to the Divinity of* CHRIST? It is desir'd by the said *Archbishop*
and *Bishops*, that the Author himself, whoever he be, or any one of the great many to
whom he refers, wou'd point out to the particular Persons whom he or they know to be
lyable to that Charge, that they may be proceded against in a judicial Way, which will
be esteem'd a great Service to the *Church*: otherwise the abovemention'd Passage must
be lookt upon as a public SCANDAL.

I shall not presume, on my Part, to inquire why the Publisher of the
Narrative brought in this matter on Occasion of my Book, or what
was his Design in joyning together Things so widely different in their
Nature. But as for any Respect to Persons, or Parity in the Subject,
the *Bishops* are already vindicated by him that wrote *the History of the
Convocation*, who says that *their* Lordship's *Paper was not the judging or
resolving upon any Matter of Doctrin, but the taking Notice of a vile*
Slander *cast upon the* King, *and the* Church, *and the* Bishops: *nor was it
directly a censuring even of that* Slander, *but only challenging the Author
of it to make it good, or to let it be reputed a public* SCANDAL. *And it had
really this Effect; for the reputed Author never offer'd a word to justify
that Passage.*

But worse than all the Artifices of the Publisher of the *Narrative* is [XV]
the Motive, which many apprehend did ingage som of *the lower
House* to single me out from all those obnoxious Authors wherof they
so loudly complain'd before, and whom they made a principal Reason
for calling a *Convocation*. My Book by their own Confession has only
a certain mischievous Tendency, which they had the great Sagacity
to discover: but there was a numerous Company of other Books that
openly avow'd their Design, opposing the Doctrin of the *Trinity*, with
several other Articles of the *Church*, expresly and by Name, som of

'em rejecting the *Scriptures* themselves; yet not a Word against any of these, tho in all Men's Judgments they ought to have preceded mine, whether we consider their Subject or the Time of their Publication. I cou'd likewise produce, were it necessary, their mutual Threatnings of one another before the Meeting of the *Convocation*. Dr. SHER-LOCK was to be call'd to an Account for *Tritheism*, Dr. SOUTH for differing in Terms and agreeing in Notions with the *Socinians*, Dr. WAKE[41] for betraying the Rights of *Convocations*, and other eminent *Clergymen* for unsound Principles, neglect of Disciplin, or som desperat Conspiracy against the *Church*. But when they had their Will, and a *Convocation* was call'd, all this mighty Noise ended only in a design against a poor *Layman*, Dr. SOUTH and Dr. SHERLOCK being join'd in the same Committee to examin his Writings, and on that Occasion were very good Friends: tho most People are agreed it wou'd have don the *Church* more Service either to reconcile the Opinions of these two Doctors about the *Trinity*, or (if this cannot be) to declare which of them (if either) is Orthodox, lest the Followers of the other persist in a damnable Doctrin.

[XVI]   Now they must give others Leave to guess at Designs as well as themselves, and therfore many Persons believe that really and truly the Reason of falling on me first, was to draw in the right reverend the Lord *Bishop of Salisbury* afterwards, it being apparently invidious to fall on his Lordship alone, and thinking they might easily obtain a *Censure* against me, without much insisting on matter of Legality or Form; as those who strive to break in upon the *Toleration* level all their Artillery against the *Quakers*, as being the weakest Sect, and well knowing that if they can abridg these of their Liberty, their Reasons will as forcibly extend against all the more considerable Dissenters,

Concidit infelix alieno vulnere TOLAND.

Those of *the lower House* hasten'd the *Bishops* to a Resolution in my Case, *because* (as they say) *they*[42] *were at a stand what was fit to be don with Relation to the other Books under their Consideration*; and yet we do not find that afterwards they meddl'd with any besides *the Exposition of the thirty nine Articles*. The Author of the *Expedient propos'd* speaks out, and says, that, *not discourag'd by the Answer they receiv'd about* my Book, *they further complain'd of an Exposition of the thirty nine Articles*—— and *that they had Cause to suspect that the Author had too great an Influence on* the upper House *in screening* me, *lest he shou'd be complain'd of next.*[43] Yet whoever considers that he was one of the Committee of *Bishops* who found dangerous Positions in my Book, will think I have little Reason to thank his *Lordship* for any Favor he show'd me on that Account. But this both Nature and Religion oblige me to forgive, nor will I out of any personal Disgust conceal what I think in Justice due to that venerable and learned *Prelat*. I wonder'd many a Time to find any *Divines* of the *Church of England* industrious to vilify and discredit his excellent *History of the Reformation* to a greater Degree of Spite and Chicanery than the *Papists* themselves; tho the Sincerity, Disinterestedness, and Accuracy of that noble Work continue Proof against the joint Attemts of all its Enemies, nor perhaps on so severe a Scrutiny from so many Hands, and such different Quarters, were fewer Defects ever found in any History, and those consisting in one or two mistaken Names and Dates, from the Want of Manuscripts or other necessary Informations, but not one Omission appearing to be out of Fraud or Design. I am likewise surpriz'd to find so many People at this Time lessening his Services in the late Reigns, when it is notorious that for his steddy adhering to the *Protestant* Cause, and opposing to his Power the Conspiracy against our Government, he was often in Danger of his Life, defam'd, outlaw'd, and prosecuted to such a Degree as oblig'd him to seek for shelter in another State. We all know how much he contributed in *Holland* to the late *Revolution*, both by his Interest and Conversation there, and by the several *Tracts* he sent from thence to incourage the People here, and to warn 'em of their Danger; so that if Mr. JOHNSON[44] had Reason to say that he himself had laid the Bridg on which the *Prince of Orange* came over, it cannot be deny'd but Doctor BURNET was one of the strongest Arches to Support it. But *hinc illæ Lachrymæ*. This is the great Crime of both these Gentlemen; and the Enemies of the present Government will never forget or forgive them, no more than they'll do the *Dutch*, which ought to induce its Friends to have 'em in the greater Reverence and Esteem: and for my own Part, I declare that had the *Bishop* don me a particular Injury, or bin guilty of those little Stories which his Enemies publish and aggravate with so much visible Rancor, I cou'd heartily draw a Vail over his human Frailties, and not only forgive but honor him for his public and extraordinary Services to this *Church* and *Nation*.

[*XVII*]   The *Bishop* of *Sarum*[45] is not the only Person whose Zeal and Courage against *Popery* in the late Reigns, are now ungratefully lessen'd or forgot. Of this the false and virulent Libels against the present and the late *Archbishops* of *Canterbury* are palpable Instances, not to mention som base Insinuations against both of 'em in the Books of certain Authors who were under more than one Obligation to defend them. But opposing of *Popery* at that Time seems now in som Men's Opinion to be no such extraordinary Merit. The Publisher of the *Narrative* acknowledges *there was a Time when the Word* Popery *carry'd Terror in its very Sound; and any Opposition made to it had the Power of Charity to cover a Multitude of Faults:*[46] *but*, says he, *that is long since, the Charm is now worn out*—— *What peculiar Hazards our* Bishops *ran of their Lives and Fortunes he confesses himself not able to judg; but this he is sure of, that thro God's Mercy they have escapt with both.*[47] This Gentleman's own ludicrous and unconcern'd Way of writing, and the Pleas of those he undertakes to defend, convince me of our Danger from *Popery* more than ever. I thought the Pains and Expence of keeping out the late King JAMES for so many Years, the renouncing of the pretended *Prince of Wales*[48] in all our Addresses, and the Preparations for the insuing War, were intended to save us from *Popery* as well as from *Tyranny*; but all these Endeavors must be very needless if there's no Danger of restoring *Popery*, or if *Popery* be no dangerous Thing. The Historian of the *Convocation* takes Notice[49] of a *Popish* Writer who dedicated a Book to the *Prolocutor* wherin he not only labors to expose our *Reformation*, which he charges with Schism, calling it the *Cranmerian* Heresy,[50] and by other opprobrious Names; but he also proposes an Expedient for us to be restor'd to the *Catholic* Communion, affirms that King JAMES was cast out with a Trick, and complains that no Proofs are produc'd about the Birth of the *Prince of Wales*. *This Book*, says the Writer of it in a Postscript, *was printed, tho not to be publisht but only for Members of the Convoca-*

tion. But however such a Dedication might be put upon the *Prolocutor* without his Knowlege, yet since they were so hot on the Scent of pernitious Books, I have Reason to ask with my Author, *Why such a Dedication was not Solemnly renounct and disown'd in the lower House? Why the Writer was not reprov'd for inscribing such a Libel to them? Why som Care or other was not taken to remove all Suspition of any Part of the House being concern'd in such a public Scandal?*[51] Why did they not likewise show som Marks of their Displeasure against another Author, a Nonjurant Divine, who, in his *Case of the Regale*, proposes our entring upon a Treaty with the Church of *France*, and *so far to reconcile our Differences as not to hinder our Communion:*[52] he complains, that *the* English *Convocation not being suffer'd to sit while that of* France *lasted, render'd any Treaty betwixt them impracticable*, and som other Things to the same or a worse Purpose. I shall not inquire how those Writers escapt, when such a Noise was made about me, unless it be that *Jacobites* are to be us'd more tenderly than *Williamites*, that *Popery* has lost its Terror with som People in good Earnest, or that my Errors were not real but personal, their Prejudices being more against the Writer than his Book; which was likewise my Lord of *Sarum*'s Case, as one of their own Members observ'd, putting the Question,[53] *If his Lordship had drawn up the* thirty nine Articles, *whether they wou'd not have bin as much blam'd as his* Exposition?

In the Representation of *the lower House* to the *Bishops* tis desir'd [*XVIII*] that som effectual Course may be taken to suppress my Book, and to stop any further spreading of the same; when there was not one of 'em to be found in any Bookseller's Shop in *England*, I having refus'd my Consent to make any Edition of it since the second in the same Year with the first, 1696. When I perceiv'd what a Stir was made about it, and what real or pretended Offence it had given, all I cou'd do was not to publish any more of 'em; and so willing I was both to live quietly my self, and to let others injoy their Opinions undisturb'd, that, in Spite of all Provocations and unfair Usage, I never defended the same against any Answer made to it directly or indirectly, excepting my *Apology* against the *Irish Parlament*, whose Proceedings were exactly of a Piece with those of the *English Convocation*. The Book therfore being thus in a Manner supprest and forgot, the Publication of it having bin six Years ago, and I not since maintaining the same Opinions in any other Writings, it seem'd an uncharitable and unnecessary Proceding to most People, that after so long a Time I shou'd be question'd for mere Speculations, which expresly justify none of the Sentiments laid to my Charge, and the Consequences of others being by me deny'd, or frankly renounc'd where I did not foresee them. But those of *the lower House* have extracted several *Positions* out of it, that (as they affirm) are of dangerous Consequence, and tending to the Subversion of the *Christian Faith.* I will by no means go about to justify every Thing in this Book, and the Wonder is not so great if either as to many of the Contents, or the Publication of the Whole, one of my Years and little Knowlege then of the World had bin too hasty, unadvis'd, and not throly settl'd in all his Notions. If we were all to be call'd to a strict Account for the Follies, Indiscretions, Oversights, and Omissions of our Youth, I believe I cou'd charge many of my Adversaries with much less pardonable Faults than any in my Writings; I cou'd not only collect a huge Store of erroneous Doctrins for the *Convocation* to censure, but likewise alledg Facts as well as Notions which now they neither can nor will offer to defend. But this being neither just nor *Christian,* I leave it to such as have no Charity nor Humanity; and am prepar'd to acknowlege whatever I have don amiss in that Book, or on any other Occasion whatsoever. I peruse it with as little partiality, as if it were written by any in *America; refrigerato Inventionis amore, diligentius repetitum tanquam Lector perpendo.*

[*XIX*]   Nevertheless I must not, neither ought or can I, accuse my self of Opinions I never believ'd nor maintain'd, such as *Arianism, Socinianism,* or the like; and whatever may be untenable in the Book (which we shall see anon) I plainly assert that of those *Positions* censur'd by *the lower House* som are falsly represented, som are undoubtedly true, and none so bad as they make 'em. The Design imputed to me in the whole I utterly deny and renounce, as I have already largely don towards the Beginning of this Discourse. The first *Proposition* is unfairly represented, and bears a quite different Sense in the Book. It is This. *I conclude that neither* GOD *himself, nor any of his Attributes, are Mysteries to us for Want of an adequate Idea.*[54] Who wou'd not think now but that I pretended to have an Adequat Idea of GOD, and that my finit Capacity comprehended all his infinit Perfections? But I was in that Chapter positively proving the contrary, and showing that we knew not the real Essence of any Thing in the World, let alone of GOD: that Things were only known to us by their Properties, yet that we had not a distinct View even of all the Properties of any Thing at once: that every Pebble and Spire of Grass being in many of their Properties, and altogether in their Essence, above our Understanding, nothing ought to be peculiarly call'd a *Mystery* on this Account, since every Thing was so: and that therfore when we knew as many of the Properties of any Thing as made us understand the Name of it, and as were useful and necessary for us, this was enough for our present Condition, and we might be reasonably said to comprehend it. Accordingly I acknowledg'd there in express Words, that *we know not the Nature of that eternal Subject or Essence wherin infinit Goodness, Love, Knowlege, Power, and Wisdom coexist:* and that *as we knew nothing of Things but such of their Properties as were necessary and useful, we might say the same of* GOD; *for every Act of our Religion is directed by som of his Attributes without ever thinking of his Essence: our Love to him is kindl'd by his Goodness, and our Thankfulness by his Mercy, our Obedience is regulated by his Justice, and our Hopes are confirm'd by his Wisdom and Power.* At last from several Reasonings to this Purpose, I conclude that nothing is a *Mystery* because we know not its Essence, since it appears that it is neither knowable in it self, nor ever thought of by us. In a word that it was too general a Notion, making all Things Mysteries alike; wheras somthing more particular was intended by the Word, since one Thing was a *Mystery* and not another. So I declar'd my self fixt in the Opinion that *what infinit Goodness has not bin pleas'd to reveal to us, we are sufficiently capable to discover our selves, or need not understand it all.* But this in the Opinion of *the lower House,* is atheistical and detestable, dangerous, pernitious, scandalous, and destructive of the *Christian* Faith. Nevertheless, I declare my self under my Hand to be still of the same Mind, that Things are improperly call'd *Mysteries* because we are ignorant of their Essence, if we understand so many of their Properties as are necessary or useful: and whoever infers from hence, that I pretend to have an adequat Idea of GOD, may as well charge the holy *Scriptures* with, saying that there is no GOD, or that JESUS CHRIST was a Winebibber and a Glutton: for ten thousand Blasphemies and Absurdities will follow, either upon taking a few Words of any Author without showing their Connection with the rest of his Discourse; or by culling Expressions that lie in different Places, and tacking 'em together to make up a Proposition wherof the Writer never thought, or which he may execrat and abhor.

[XX]   As for the Second *Proposition*, I shall here set down the intire Passage, and then explain it. *Revelation*, c.17.v.5-7.[55] *Upon her forehead was a Name written*, MYSTERY, BABYLON THE GREAT, *&c. And the Angel said ---I will tell thee the* MYSTERY *of the woman.*

This He performs too in the following Verses, which you may consult. Nor is it undeserving our particular Notice, that MYSTERY is here made the distinguishing Character of the false or *antichristian* Church. MYSTERY *is a Name written on her forehead*; that is, all her religion consists in MYSTERY; She openly owns, She injoins the Belief of MYSTERIES. And, no Doubt on't, as far as any Church allows of MYSTERIES so far it is *antichristian*; and may with a great Deal of Justice, tho little Honor, claim Kindred with the scarlet Whore.

This is crudely spoken, and not strictly true, as som of my Answerers have explain'd the Word *Mystery*. The Sense that I oppos'd all along, was, when MYSTERY *is made to signifie a Thing of its own Nature inconceivable, and not to be judg'd of by our ordinary Faculties or Ideas, tho never so clearly reveal'd.*[56] This is the Refuge of the *Papists* to defend all their absurd or inconceivable Articles, and it is obvious to every Reader that I had their Notions very much in my View, which might lead me somtimes into Expressions that were too general, as now I take this *Position* to be; for som of my Answerers having disclaim'd that Sense of the word *Mystery*, and professing that the *Church of England* means no more by it than a Doctrin wherin tho there appears no Contradiction, and that it is clearly understood in Part, yet that a great Deal of it is still above our Comprehension, which we are bound to believe on the Credit and Authority of the Revealer. In this Sense my Words are not true of the *Reform'd Churches*, and are only applicable to *Papists, Mahometans, Heathens*, and such others. The Author of the *Occasional Paper*, Num. 3. ingenuously owns that *my chief Arguments are directed against those who denote by the word* MYSTERY *a Thing so far above us, that we do not at all conceive what is meant by it, nor have any Notion of the Matter*; and *he believes I shall hardly find any in the* Church of England *that talk in such a Manner.*[57] He says, what I approve, that *a Doctrin may be said to be* above Reason *when we can from the* Revelation *apprehend it only in Part, know so much of it as may answer the wise Ends of the* Revelation; *but for other Parts of it they may be quite out of our Reach and above our Apprehension, so that we cannot form any clear and distinct Ideas of the whole Doctrin; and such Points as these are chiefly what we call* Mysteries *in Religion.*[58] Afterwards he hopes we may still agree, *For if I but grant him such Points as these, where we apprehend but in Part, but however so much as may be of good Use and Service to us; He will on his side gratify me by rejecting all Doctrins of which we can apprehend Nothing, and of which we can make no Use.*[59] I do in all Sincerity shake Hands with this Author, acknowledging his Moderation and fair Dealing in the whole Controversy, which shows him to love the Truth and not to hate a Man he took for his Adversary, but who is to be consider'd by him as such no longer. Before I have don I shall yet further own what I have profited by his Information, and convince him, that the charitable Opinion he has more than once exprest of my Intention, was not wholly without Ground; nor cou'd this Difference have so long subsisted, had others treated me in their Writings with the like Humanity and *Christian* Temper.

It was upon the same Foot with the former *Proposition* that I [XXI] asserted *Contradiction* and *Mystery* to be only two emphatical Ways of saying *Nothing*, as is evident from the Scope of the whole Passage, which runs in these Words:

The Subject of *Faith* must be intelligible to all, since the Belief thereof is commanded under no less a Penalty than Damnation. *He that believeth not shall be damn'd.* But shall any be damn'd for the Non-performance of Impossibilities? Obligations to believe do therefore suppose a Possibility to understand. I show'd before that *Contradiction* and *Nothing* were convertible Terms; and I may say now as much of *Mystery* in the Theological Sense: for to speak freely, *Contradiction* and *Mystery* are but two emphatical Ways of saying Nothing. *Contradiction* expresses Nothing by a Couple of Ideas that destroy one another, and *Mystery* expresses *Nothing* by Words that have no Idea at all.[60]

179

In like Manner is to be understood the Fourth Position concerning *Faith*; and I shou'd accordingly have corrected those Passages were I to make any further Editions of that Book.

[*XXII*]   The last *Position* is misrepresented like the First. *Here's enough to show how* Christianity *became* Mysterious, *and how so divine an Institution did, thro the Craft and Ambition of* Priests *and* Philosophers, *degenerat into mere* Paganism.[61] These Words indeed are mine; but without attending to the Discourse immediately foregoing (from which they are a Conclusion) they must needs sound harshly to many good and pious Men, who may be Strangers to the things wherof I treat in that Place. I was giving a brief Account of the manifold Superstitions, mysterious and useless Rites, that the new-converted *Heathens* introduc'd into the *Christian* Religion, which did a World of Injury to the plain Dress and beautiful Facility of the *Gospel*. They increast by Degrees to such a Number that the Sacraments of *Baptism* and the *Lord's Supper* were transform'd by their Means to Rites very different from their first Institution. I mention particularly the Milk and Hony, the Unction, white Garment, frequent Questions and Responses, Salt and Wine, Lights, Exorcisms, Exsufflations, and Crossings, added to *Baptism*. By the same Means did the *Lord's Supper* in succeeding Ages grow up into the absurd and monstrous Doctrin of *Transubstantiation*. I produce those superstitious Observations in public *Pennance*, which brought it at length to privat *Confession*; and pointed to the first Footsteps of that spiritual Empire to which the *Clergy* have erected themselves in the Church of *Rome*. Of these Ceremonies som are very useless, som very ridiculous, others very profane, a few of 'em very innocent, and all together very burden-som, if not intolerable. I think still I had Reason to say that *such Things never fail to take off the Mind from the Substance of Religion, and to lead Men into dangerous Mistakes*; of which there is the clearest Demonstration from *Popery*, wherin those and a great many other Ceremonies are daily us'd after the Manner of the *Heathens*, and the practical Part of their Religion dos scarce consist in any Thing else. I did say therfore that the divine Institution of *Christianity* did thus degenerat into mere *Paganism*; but this cannot affect any Church where *Christianity* is taught and practis'd without those Disguizes,

where the holy *Scriptures* are made the only Foundation and Model
of Religion, and where neither the Worship nor Disciplin are over-
whelm'd by those Ceremonies of *Heathen* or *Jewish* Original. For my
Part, I think the Church of *Rome*, and som Eastern Sects, to be in
these Things, as well as in their Idolatry, Frauds, and Tyrannical
Impositions worse than *Pagans*; and that their assuming the Name of
CHRIST, without imbracing the Purity of his Doctrin, cannot be of
any Effect to Sanctify their superstitions, no more than a Man who
forcibly takes away the Goods of another is ever the less a Robber,
because he pretends to borrow them, or NERO was the more a Friend
to Liberty tho he was created *Consul* and *Tribun* of the People.

It was of the *Clergymen* who introduc'd and countenanc't such   [*XXIII*]
Practices, and who set up the most abominable of all Tyranys in the
Church, that I have so frequently complain'd; but never against the
whole Order, as it sufficiently appears by the last paragraph of the
Preface, which being a full Vindication against the Calumny of being
their Enemy, I shall transcribe in this Place.

To all corrupt *Clergymen* who make a mere Trade of Religion, and build an unjust
Authority upon the abus'd Consciences of the *Laity*, I'm a profest Adversary; as I hope
every good and wise Man already is, or will be. But as I shall always remain a hearty
Friend to pure and genuin Religion, so I shall preserve the highest Veneration for the
sincere Teachers thereof, than whom there is not a more useful Order of Men, and
without whom there cou'd not be any happy Society or well constituted Government
in this World; to speak nothing of their Relation to the World to com, nor of the double Esteem they deserve for keeping proof against the general Infection of their Profession. But I have no Apprehensions from the Sincere; and if the designing Party discover their Concern by their Displeasure, it may well serve for a Mark to distinguish
them, but will not be thought an Injury by Me.[62]

As for that *Position* which My Lords the *Bishops* extracted out of   [*XXIV*]
my Book, and which they look upon as the Foundation of all Errors
they conceive to be contain'd therin, I freely acknowlege that on
mature Consideration it appears to my self unwarily exprest, beyond
my Intention, and (as the author of the *Occasional Paper* justly
observes) contrary to other Passages which are very clear and express.
It bears a Sense I can by no Means approve, no more than any Thing
that is a direct Consequence from it. Instead therfore of saying that
REVELATION *was not a necessitating Motive of Assent, but a Means of
Information*,[63] I ought to have said, REVELATION *was not* only *a neces-*

sitating Motive of Assent, but likewise *a Means of Information.* The most distinct Ideas in the World are not a sufficient *Ground of Persuasion,* for they prove no more then that such a Thing may be; but to be convinc'd that it dos actually exist, we must have our own Experience, or the Authority either of divine or human Testimony. This the Writer just now cited evinces beyond all Dispute. Therfore after having thus corrected this *Position,* and whatever depends upon it, I declare notwithstanding that I shall never consent or contribute to any more Editions of that Book (leaving the *Lower House of Convocation* to answer for any further spreading of it by reason of the Noise they have made about it) neither will I defend what may be objected against it by any Persons whatsoever, desiring it may no longer be consider'd as a Work I wholly approve, unless I wou'd still continue to be five and twenty, and obstinatly justify all the undigested Notions, all the Rashness and Indiscretions of such an Age. On the contrary, if I have really given any public or privat Scandal by that Book, if I have disquieted the Minds of particular Men, or disturb'd the general Peace of the Church, I am truly sorry for it, and humbly Pardon for the same of GOD Almighty and all good Men. I defended my self before from the horrible Charge of *Atheism,* which is not only the Denyal of GOD, but also of the future Existence and Immortality of the Soul, of the Rewards attending the Good, and the Punishments due to the Wicked; all which I stedfastly believe. I have no Doubts concerning the Excellence, Perfection, and Divinity of the *Christian Religion* in general as it is delivered in the holy *Scriptures,* and I willingly and heartily conform to the Doctrin and Worship of the *Church of England* in particular. As to my thoughts about our Communion with other *Protestants,* and the *Toleration* of such as dissent from us, I have largely deliver'd 'em before in *Anglia Libera,* and shall now insert the Passage here,[64] to avoid the Repetition of the same Things in other Words.

[XXV][65]   Tho Such as call their *Religion* under Examination do often differ in their Notions about it, yet in all Contries of the World the greatest Part of the People give themselves up to the public Leading in divine Things as well as in other Matters; and this they do whether the generally receiv'd Opinions happen to be true or erroneous. It were to be earnestly wisht, no doubt, that every Region were free from Error, and had sincerely receiv'd the Truth; but tho Men deny themselves this Happiness by indulging their Vices, minding nothing but their Business, or for Want of Consideration: yet *Religion* it self is not more natural to Man, than it is for every Government to have a *national Religion*; or som public and orderly way of worshipping GOD, under the Allowance, Indowment, and Inspection of the Civil Magistrat. It was the highest Favour this Iland cou'd receive from Heaven to be delivered from the intolerable Yoke of *Popish* Superstition, and to have the purer Worship of God imbrac'd by the Majority of the People. And tho *Protestants* in general are unhappily divided among themselves about som Articles of more or less Importance, yet they are all agreed about the main Points of Religion, and jointly abhor the Idolatry and Tyranny of the *Romish* Clergy. Wherfore (after the numberless Artifices of the common Enemy to encrease their Divisions) I hope they are all now com to so good an Understanding and so charitable a Disposition, as to allow, that altho each of 'em may think his own Disciplin and Doctrin to be better than any of the rest; yet that, when he happens to be in another Contry, he may safely join with the *Protestants* of that place, without any Danger to his Soul or Scandal to his Profession. But as to our own Kingdom in particular (where the different Sects are more numerous Bodies, with Relation to one another, than in[66] any other Place) the *National Church* is much the best Constitution in it self, naturally allows of a more generous Latitude than the others, and is infinitly the most accomodated to our Civil Government, which is a material Point in the Disciplin of every *National Church*. But supposing that any of the rest might equal it in these Respects, yet being already and so long establisht, it were the highest Folly as well as Injustice in the Government to change it on this Account, especially since it has at least as few Errors as any other Church in the World. But I also declare that by approving the *National Church*, and owning my self a Member of the same, I do not think it a Doctrin of this Church to persecute or disturb those of another Religion which dos not teach or practise any Thing that's cruel, immoral, or profane. The Liberty of the Understanding is yet a nobler Principle than that of the Body, if this be not a Distinction (as they say) without a Difference; and where there is no *Liberty of Conscience* there can be no *Civil Liberty*, no Incouragement for Industry, no proper Means of rendring the Contry populous, no Possibility of Men's freely informing themselves concerning the true Religion, nor any Refuge or Protection for the Distrest, which is the greatest Glory of free Governments. But as the *National Religion* ought not to oppress the *Dissenters* from it in their Persons or Possessions, nor to exclude 'em from any Privileges in the State to which they have a Right by Birth, Naturalization, or otherwise; so the *tolerated Religions* must maintain their own Teachers (their Dissent from the Public being voluntary) and not pretend to the Places of Worship, or to the allow'd Maintenance, nor to any other Rights or Emoluments of the *National Church*, under Pain of being accounted Hypocrits grasping at Dominion instead of designing Reformation, to have their Liberty taken away, and their Persons to be put out of the Protection of the Government. But whatever Indulgence may be due to other Persuasions, *Papists* ought not to be tolerated in any free State, because they not only deny Liberty to all others, and pronounce 'em eternally damn'd; but also because they are Subjects to a foren Head whose Authority they prefer to that of their native Magistrats, and that their Doctrin of Dispensation leaves 'em under no Tyes of Oaths or other Ingagements, as their allowing no Faith to be kept with *Heretics*, makes 'em incapable of holding any Fellowship on the Square with such as are not reckon'd *Orthodox* by their infallible Head, another Doctrin inconsistent with all privat Faith or public Society.

Sad Experience has put these Things beyond Question in every Part of the World; and therfore they can never be too much consider'd by the States of the *Reform'd Religion*. We can never be too much put in mind of the Genius of their Persuasion, and what we are always to apprehend from them. Wherfore I hope I need not spend many Words to persuade *Englishmen* that *Popery* in general is an Extract of whatever is ridiculous, knavish, or impious in all Religions; that it is Priestcraft arriv'd at the highest Perfection; that it contains peculiar Absurdities, never known in any other Persuasion; and that it is the most insolent Imposition that ever was made on the Credulity of Mankind, &c.

[XXVI]   Thus have I given ample Satisfaction, I hope, to all good *Christians* who are Lovers of Docility, Moderation, and Truth. I have likewise kept my Word with the late *Lower House of Convocation*, having told 'em in my first Letter (which in my Second I said shou'd be Part of my *Defence*) that *I thought my self more oblig'd to write in Relation to the Animadversions of a* Public Body, *than against any* Privat Person *how considerable soever*. The Opinion of many People generally obtains more Weight than that of any one Man, besides that I knew with whom I had to do; wheras a nameless Writer may throw out at Random whatever comes in his Way without any Regard to Truth or the Merits of the Cause: yet he is conceal'd from the Hands of Justice and the Resentments of his Adversary, which in Matters of Fact takes away his Credit with all Men of Justice or Honor; since no Body is secure from the Accusation of any Guilt, when the Reputation of his Accuser is no more to be known, than his Person is accountable. Tis som Comfort if you have not a generous Adversary, to meet with a considerable one:

Optat Aprum aut fulvum descendere monte Leonem.

But I see no Ground to think the late *Lower House of Convocation* was freer from Error, Passion, or Interest, than the antient *Councils*, and other *Ecclesiastic Assemblies*, of whose Procedings we are inform'd by History, where we find that they were often summon'd to serve the Ends of a Faction or som great Man; and somtimes when they were not, that there reign'd among 'em a great Deal of scandalous Partiality, indecent Warmth, and cruel Animosities, of perverse Contentions and Wranglings, of mere worldly Design and Interest, which made the Issue of such Assemblies seldom to prove for the

Good of Religion or the Peace of the State, and to be extremely dreaded by som of the brightest Luminaries of the Church. Being compos'd of Men obnoxious to all Sorts of Passions, they cou'd no more be infallible all together, than any one of 'em was in his single Capacity. Tis but a small Number, a very small Number of those *Synods* that had any Right (as may be seen by their Determinations) to arrogat to themselves those Words of the *Apostles* in their Consult at *Jerusalem, It seems Good to the* Holy Ghost *and to us*. In the Hymns of our Church the *Holy Ghost* is truly stil'd the GOD *of* PEACE *and* LOVE; and were I not convinc'd before from the Nature of the Thing, and by the Writings of the most eminent Reformers, that the *Holy Ghost* dos not necessarily and extraordinarily preside over every *Synod*, I shou'd have abundant Satisfaction about it from the Procedings of the late *Lower House of Convocation*.

That I am not overconfident of my own Judgment is clear at least [*XXVII*] from this present Discourse, and I shall pay all reasonable Deference and Submission to the deliberat, serious, prudent, impartial, and peaceable Deliberations of any great Number of Men; but yet without they inlighten my Understanding and convince my Judgment, it is impossible for me to give them my Assent in perplext or dubious Matters, much less to be sway'd in any Thing by their bare Authority against the clear Persuasion of my own Mind. As that excellent Person Dr. TILLOTSON, the late *Archbishop of Canterbury*, says, *It is neither Immodesty nor a culpable Singularity for a Man to stand alone in the Defence of the Truth*, in his admirable Sermon concerning *Stedfastness in Religion*.[67] In the same Discourse he has these Expressions: *If all the great Mathematicians of all Ages*, ARCHIMEDES, *and* EUCLID, *and* APOLLONIUS,[68] *and* DIOPHANTHUS,[69] *&c. cou'd be suppos'd to meet together in a* General Council, *and should there declare in the most solemn Manner, and give it under their Hands and Seals, that twice* two *did not make four, but five; this wou'd not move me in the least to be of their Mind. Nay I, who am no* Mathematician, *wou'd maintain the contrary, and wou'd persist in it without being in the least startl'd by the positive Opinion of these great and learned Men: and shou'd most certainly conclude, that they were either all of 'em out of their Wits, or that they were byass'd by som Interest or other, and sway'd against the clear Evi-*

dence of Truth, and the full Conviction of their own Reason, to make such a Determination as this. They might indeed over-rule *the Point by their* Authority, *but in my* inward Judgment *I shou'd still be where I was before.*[70] And to show that a Man ought not to be put out of Countenance by the Name of a *Church,* or be born down by the Number of a *Council,* he cites the concurrent Judgment of Mr. HOOKER[71] in his deservedly admir'd Book of *Ecclesiastical Policy. Altho ten thousand* General Councils (says that most learned Divine) *shou'd set down one and the same definitive Sentence concerning any Point of Religion whatsoever, yet one demonstrative Reason alledg'd, or one Testimony cited from the Word of* GOD *himself to the contrary, cou'd not chuse but oversway them all: in as much as for them to be deceiv'd is not so impossible, as it is that demonstrative Reason or divine Testimony shou'd deceive.* And again, *That the Authority of Men shou'd prevail with Men, either against or above Reason, is no part of our Belief. Companies of Learned Men, tho they be never so Great and Reverend, are to yield unto Reason, the weight wherof is no Whit prejudic'd by the Simplicity of the Person which doth alledg it; but, being found to be sound and good, the bare Opinion of Men to the contrary must of necessity stoop and give place.*[72] This he conceives to be the Judgment of the *Church of England* as well as his own; so did CRANMER, JEWEL,[73] CHILLINGWORTH, with the most applauded and respected Writers since the *Reformation.* I need say no more to justify this *Defence* of my self against the late *lower House of Convocation,* against the *Narrative* drawn up by their Order, and the *Publisher* of the same who was likewise one of their Members, and may be presum'd to speak their Sense. Their Procedings against my Book I conceive to have bin neither fair in themselves, nor warranted by their own Privileges, but expresly against a *Statute*; not to insist again on the satisfaction offer'd 'em in my *Letters,* and that none of the *Positions* (however otherwise erroneous) were contrary to any Law of this Realm.

[XXVIII]   Thus I have don with the *Convocation*; and shou'd have don Writing, did I not think this a fit Place to set People to rights about another Objection which has bin commonly join'd to the Charge of *Heresy* against me, which is, that *I am a great Common-wealths-man,* the Truth wherof I freely own, and value my self upon being so. Ever since I knew what it was to be a Member of civil Society, or to concern my self about the Nature of Government, I have bin wholly devoted to the self-evident Principle of *Liberty*, and a profest Enemy to *Slavery* and *arbitrary Power*. I have always bin, now am, and ever shall be persuaded that all Sorts of Magistrats are made for and by the People, and not the People for or by the Magistrats: that the Power of all Governors is originally conferr'd by the Society, and limitted to their Safety, Wealth, and Glory, which makes those Governors accountable for their Trust: and consequently that it is lawful to resist and punish Tyrants of all Kinds, be it a single Person or greater Number of Men; for the Case was just alike to the People of *Denmark* (for Example) whether their *House of Commons* had assum'd an unlimitted Authority to themselves, or conferr'd such a Power (as they did) on their King. I am therefore evidently and avowedly a *Common-wealths-man*. Tis true, that in the late Reigns all those who espous'd the Liberty and defended the Constitution of their Contry against the manifest Incroachments and despotic Councils of our Kings, were by the Court flatterers and Pensioners nicknam'd *Common-wealths men*, by which they insinuated 'em to be irreconcileable Enemies to regal Government, and men, who, if they did not design a downright *Anarchy*, yet were intirely for a *Democracy*. That I am of any such Principle I positively deny, and assert it to be a Calumny rais'd by som of those who were formerly more than ordinarily remarkable in abbetting and incouraging the destructive Measures of the Court. The contrary appears in every Thing I ever wrote, having never bin for a *Democracy* which I think to be the worst Form of a *Common-wealth*, tho a thousand Times better than any Sort of *Tyranny*. In *Anglia Libera*, I declare that *I mean by the word* Common-wealth *not a pure* Democracy, *nor any particular Form of Government; but an independent Community, where the* common-weal *or Good of all indifferently is design'd and pursu'd, let the Form be what it will.*[74] Before this, in the *Art of governing by Parties*, I fully deliver'd my Sense of our own and all other Governments in these Words.

All the world knows that *England* is under a free Government, whose supreme legislative Power is lodg'd in the King, Lords, and Commons, each of which have their peculiar Privileges and Prerogatives; no Law can pass without their common Authority or

187

Consent; and they are a mutual Check and Balance on one another's Oversights or Incroachments. This Government is calculated for the Interest of all the Parties concern'd, which are all the Inhabitants of *England*; wherfore it depends on their good Will, and is supported by their Wealth and Power. But in *absolute Monarchy* all Things are only subservient to the Pleasure or Grandeur of the *Prince*, who therfore by Force of Arms maintains his Dominion over the People, on whom he looks but as his Herd and Inheritance, to be us'd and dispos'd as he thinks convenient. In Opposition to such *arbitrary Governments*, those have bin call'd *Common wealths* where the common Good of all was indifferently design'd and pursu'd. But tho' they agree in their main End, yet they often differ about the Means, in the Names of their Magistrats, and som other Circumstances. Thus the two Kings of *Sparta* had no more Authority than a Duke of *Venice*; and the Stadtholder of *Holland*[75] has more real Power, tho less State and Dignity, than either of 'em. A *Common-wealth*, when the Administration lies in the People, is call'd a *Democracy*; when tis solely or for the most Part in the Nobility, tis then an *Aristocracy*; but when tis shar'd between the Commons, the Lords, and the supreme Magistrat (term him King, Duke, Emperor, or what you please) tis then a *mixt Form*, and is by POLYBIUS,[76] and many judicious Politicians among the Antients, esteem'd the most equal, lasting, and perfect of all others. In this sense *England* is undeniably a *Common-wealth*, tho it be ordinarily stil'd a *Monarchy*, because the chief Magistrat is call'd a KING. Such as are afraid therfore that *England* shou'd become a *Common-wealth*, may be suspected not to understand their own Language; and those who talk of making it one, may dream of turning it into an *Aristocracy* or *Democracy*, but can never make it more a *Common-wealth* than it is already. This is our admirable Constitution.[77]

And, to bring no more Instances, in the Preface to HARRINGTON's *Life and Works*,[78] I say, that if

a *Common-wealth* be a Government of *Laws* enacted for the common Good of all the People, not without their own Consent or Approbation; and that they are not wholly excluded, as in *absolute Monarchy*, which is a Government of *Men* who forcibly rule over others for their own privat Interest: then it is undeniably manifest that the *English* Government is already a *Common-wealth*, the most free and best constituted in all the world. This was frankly acknowledg'd by King JAMES the First, who stil'd himself *the great Servant of the* COMMON-WEALTH, and it is the Language of our best Lawyers.

[XXIX] This is the Sense in which I own my self a *Common-wealths-man*, and in which I take *England* to be now a *Common-wealth*. This is what I mean by being a *Whig*, and what I have ever understood from all those People call'd *Whigs*, either by themselves, or by their Enemies; and if any that ever was reputed a *Whig* has thought or acted otherwise let the Fault remain his own, and not be imputed to such as disclaim all Practises inconsistent with their Professions. If there be any who approve at present what they condemn'd in the late Reigns, who envy those Privileges to others which they justly demanded then as the Rights of all Mankind, these were never truly concern'd for *Liberty*, but only wanted more indulgent Masters, and such as wou'd be partial in their Favor, whatever Hardships they might lay on other People. For such Sort of Persons (whoever they may be) I have nothing to say;

Tu quoque pro Dominis, & Pompeiana *fuisti, Non* Romana *Manus.*

But then let not the whole Party suffer for the Faults of a few, nor the Miscarriages of any be made the Consequence of a Principle they disown or disgrace; I mean the Principle of a *Common-wealths-man*, to which I am firmly resolv'd to adhere, and will openly defend so Noble a Cause tho all the world shou'd desert or be asham'd to own it. From this Principle it is, that the *Whigs* were no less zealous and seasonable in setting the Crown on King WILLIAM's Head, than they have bin hearty and constant ever since to defend his Person, to support his Right and Dignity against all foren or domestic Enemies, and that they are always ready to put him in a Capacity of maintaining the Honor of the Nation, of assisting our Allies, and Protecting the *Reform'd Churches.* Acted by the same Principle, they have so unanimously promoted and confirm'd the Title of her *Royal Highness* the *Princess* ANNE *of Denmark,* to whom they have never bin wanting in their Respects on any Occasion, contrary to the malitious Insinuations of a certain Tribe, whose detested Cause must be upheld by Falshood where it fails of violence: but the Interest of that illustrious *Princess* has ingag'd her (no Doubt) to study the Constitution of this Kingdom too well to be deceiv'd by such chimerical Infamations; and questionless she's better inform'd by her faithful Servants than to believe the *Whigs* had ever any Thoughts to her Disadvantage, much less that they made indecent Reflections on Her in public Places, this being the most notorious Calumny that cou'd be utter'd, and which they defy any one credible Witness to prove. Nor needs she require a better Demonstration that the Genius of the People is intirely fixt in the Principle of *Liberty,* than the Endeavors of the *Jacobites* to persuade the World that the *Republicans* have thrown away their old Opinions, and that they have taken 'em up, which is plainly valuing themselves (how undeservedly soever) on those good Qualities which they have discover'd to be acceptable to the Nation. And she cannot be ignorant that none of those are sincerely her Friends who oppose the Oath of *Abjuration*,[79] it being impossible that any shou'd favor her Title who scruple renouncing that of the pretended *Prince of Wales* (these being utterly irreconcilable and incompatible) wheras the *Whigs*, were they so madly dispos'd, cou'd not violat the Establishment of her Right, without unsettling all the Securities they have for their present or future Happiness, without unravelling all they have hitherto desir'd or obtain'd, without exposing themselves to the Fury of their most implacable Enemies, and without incurring the Hatred of all the World for their palpable Hypocrisy, in having so much Respect to Persons, and none at all to Things. And perhaps it is not unworthy her *Highnesses* Consideration, whether such as endeavor to possess her with these pernicious Jealousies, have not a Design to put her in good Earnest on such Measures, as may lose her the Confidence of her best Friends, in a Way sufficient to justify their Conduct, and yet not gain one of her Enemies to fortify or maintain her Interest. Tis from this same Principle of *Liberty* that the *Whigs* have bin so forward and active in providing for the Succession of the Crown, and settling it in the *Protestant Line* on the most excellent Princess SOPHIA and her Issue in the House of *Hanover*; which is no Sign they are for a *Democracy* or Enemies to Kingly Government, this being the most numerous princely Family in *Europe*: and being Strangers, tis fit they shou'd know, that all the Enemies to his present *Majesty*, or their *Succession*, are such as formerly past for the greatest *Royalists*, and carry'd the Preference and Pretences of *Monarchy* so high as to make its Original of *Divine Right* exclusive to all other Governments; wheras, such as were in those Days branded with the Name of *Commonwealths-men*, are unalterably loyal to King WILLIAM, and prepar'd to sacrifice their Lives and Fortunes in Maintenance of the Succession in the *Protestant Line* against the pretended *Prince of Wales*, and all other Pretenders, their open or secret Abettors. This is the naked Truth, and GOD grant the Persons concern'd to make a right Use of it.

[XXX]   Such Sort of Men are *English Republicans*, nor are they improperly distinguish'd by this Denomination. A COMMONWEALTH, says

CICERO,[80] *is the* Common-weal *of the People, when it is well and justly manag'd, whether by one* King, *a few* Nobles, *or the whole* People. *But when the* King *is unjust (whom I call a* Tyrant) *or the* Nobles *are unjust (whose Combination is a* Faction*) or the* People *themselves are unjust (for whom I find no usual Appellation unless I call 'em* Tyrants*) then it is not a faulty* Common-wealth, *but really none at all: for it is not the* Weal of the People, *when a* Tyrant *or a* Faction *disposes of 'em; and the* People *themselves are no longer a* People *when they becom unjust, because they are not* (according as *People* are defin'd by Legislators) *a Multitude associated by Consent of Laws, and a Communication of Advantage.* A COMMONWEALTH therfore is the general Denomination of all *free Governments*, and I think the particular Form of the *English Commonwealth* to be the best in the World. Now I expect som of my Readers will be startled at the very Sound of a COMMONWEALTH, a Word they have bin taught to hear with Abhorrence, and to which from their Infancy they have bin accustom'd to annex the most dreadful Ideas of *Anarchy, Confusion, Levelling, Sedition*, and a Thousand other terrible Things: wheras it really signifies Liberty and Order, equal Laws, strict and impartial Justice, a wise and liberal Education; a sober and frugal Management in privat Oeconomy, an upright and disinterested Administration of the public Revenues; the natural Soil of Industry, Wealth, and Power, of ingenious Arts and useful Inventions; a Nursery of capacious, daring, and gallant Spirits, an Example of noble and generous Actions, a Promoter of great and glorious Undertakings; a Place where the *Natural Religion* is duly maintain'd and piously observ'd, with an allow'd Toleration to *innocent Dissenters*, where Vice is severely punisht (tho it can never be totally extirpated) where Virtue is amply incourag'd (tho it be still the greatest Recompence to it self) and where the Merit of *deserving Citizens* obtains those honorable Characters and lasting Monuments after Death, which their own Modesty or the Envy of others might happen to deny 'em alive. Yet such are the Ignorance and Prejudices of som Persons, that when they talk of *the Commonwealth of England* they mean the Time of our last *civil Wars* and even the Tyrannical Usurpation of OLIVER CROMWELL: wheras they might as well understand by *the Commonwealth of Rome*, the Tumults of CINNA,[81] MAR-

IUS,[82] or SYLLA,[83] the Contests of CAESAR and POMPEY,[84] of
OCTAVIUS[85] and ANTONY for the Monarchy, their bloody Proscriptions, and most impious Treason against their Contry. But (as I clearly demonstrated before) we mean by this Word *the antient and present Constitution* of England *under King, Lords, and Commons*, which is to all Ends and Purposes a *Commonwealth*, a Name we are not asham'd to own, nor will ever be compell'd to quit no more than the Thing. And if after all this, any shou'd think the Expression novel or improper, let him be determin'd by the better Authority of Sir THOMAS SMITH, one of the most learned Men of his Time (principal Secretary of State to King EDWARD the VI and likewise to Queen ELIZABETH of immortal Renown), who on the Entreaty of som eminent Foreners, having written an Account of the *English* Government, which is highly valu'd abroad as well as at Home, he has in the very Title justly stil'd it, THE COMMONWEALTH OF ENGLAND.

[*XXXI*]   I shall not give any more Troble to my self or others by making this *Apology* much longer: for I am so far from being concern'd at the frivolous Remarks or scurrilous Treatment of nameless, envious, and mercenary Libellers, that as I have never hitherto contributed to give them any Reputation by taking notice of their notorious Falsities, or those poor Stories, which, supposing 'em to be true, are very impertinent: so I cannot but think the better of my self to be abus'd in the good Company to which I am join'd of late in all the Libels against the Government, and which might temt me to imagin I was as considerable as a certain *Lawyer* wou'd needs make me, from whose Family Sir WILLIAM JONES[86] has prophesy'd *the Leprosy of Eloquence* shall never depart. But all I have hitherto written or may write hereafter is sufficiently confuted, not by the old fashion'd Way of *soft Words and hard Arguments*, but by the new fashion'd Method of *much Railing and no Reasoning*. My Religion and Politics are eternally baffl'd, and there's no Remedy for it, since those, who are resolv'd to be in the Wrong if I am in the Right, have strenuously and learnedly asserted that I am a Son of a Whore, that I am *Antichrist*, that I had not a good Title to set up a new Religion in *Ireland* where I have no Land, that at fourteen Years of Age I foretold I shou'd be Head of a *Sect* before thirty and a greater Statesman than CROMWELL before forty, that altho my Enemies think me a Fool my Friends do nothing of Moment without my Advice, that scarce six Men in the Nation being of all my Opinions yet I have a great many Followers among the modern *Whigs*, and that I am the Head of all the *Arians, Socinians, Deists*, and *Infidels* in the three Kingdoms. I ought to beg Pardon for repeating such nonsensical and contemtible Stuff, but I produce this Specimen of the Generosity of som Men's Temper, and the Formidableness of their Opposition. I believe the Author of *Whiglove and Double*[87] wou'd vouchsafe to smile himself, if I shou'd seriously go about to prove against him, that the Cloaths in which I went to *Hanover* were made in *England* and not in *Holland*: but his affirming (tho never so falsly) that they were bought with *Dutch Mony*, is no disservice to any Man's Reputation in these suspitious Times, from one who is thought to know so well how *the French Mony* has bin dispos'd of; tho (as far as his Word may be taken in this Matter) yet, without a constant Principle and Practice against *France*, I shou'd not think my Credit secure even by *an Act of a Parlament*: for do we not all know that it was made penal by *an Act of Parlament*, to say King CHARLES II was a *Papist*, when much the greatest Part of the Nation were convinc'd of the Contrary, and that if he was not guilty he needed no such Law to stop his Subjects Mouths? And was not Sir THOMAS PILKINGTON[88] in an Action of *Scandalum Magnatum* fin'd a 100000 Pounds, for saying the late King JAMES (when Duke of *York*) was a *Papist*, which serv'd but to make all those believe the Thing who might doubt of it before? But perhaps it will be objected here that I fail in Point of Gratitude, since certain Persons were lately grown so tender to me of a sudden, as to do all they cou'd to conceal my receiving of som foren Gold; and when it cou'd no longer be kept a Secret thro my own Folly (as the Receivers of *French Gold* will call it) and the Officiousness of my Friends, then they endeavor'd to extenuat the Crime, affirming boldly (at which they are the best in the World) that it was all Silver gilt; and when this Excuse was render'd vain by the Weight of the Pieces and the extraordinary Fineness of the Impressions, they kindly suppos'd they might be bought by my self, tho on any other Occasion they wou'd not allow me to have any Mony or Lands. These, every Body may remember were the Turns their Malice and Envy gave to those *gold Medals* which *their Highnesses the Electress Dowager* and the *Elector of Hanover* were pleas'd to present to me as a Princely Acknowlegement for the Book I wrote about *the Succession*, in Defence of their Title and Family. Nay, so shameless were the same Persons that they reported I was banisht the Court of *Hanover*, before I arriv'd indeed in the Contry, for preferring (no Doubt) *the Protestant Line* to the pretended *Prince of Wales*, and for espousing the *Electoral* House, against their Treachery, Bigottry, and Corruption. But after This was contradicted by all the Letters from thence, they ventur'd to give out, that my LORD MACCLESFIELD[89] wou'd not see me there, which a certain Gentleman in *Surry* swore to one who did not believe him to be true of his own Knowlege, for that he had heard it in *Garraway's* Coffee-House; yet the contrary is so manifest, that no Friend I have in the world cou'd more effectually recommend me than my Lord had the Goodness to do particularly to *her Highness*, who besides those *Medals* (which my Enemies wou'd be glad to have on a less creditable Account) condescended to give me likewise the *Pictures* of her self, the *Elector*, the young *Prince*, and of her *Majesty* the Queen of *Prussia*, knowing the extraordinary Veneration and Affection I have for the whole Family, and which their conspicuous Virtues will put beyond all Suspition of Flattery. Nor is it out of any Disrespect to them, nor from any Fear of their Enemies, that I have not yet publisht my *Observations* on that Court and Contry, the Characters of the chief Persons, the Nature of the Government, the particular Account of My Lord MACCLESFIELD's Reception and Entertainment, and the great Honors paid to the whole *English Nation*; but such Reasons have oblig'd me to keep those Papers yet in my Closet, as will justify my Conduct when ever there shall be Occasion for Printing them. My *Lord* treated me all the while in that Court, and afterwards in *Holland*, with greater Kindness and Confidence than I cou'd by any Means pretend to Merit; he was so much my Friend as to recommend and present me at *Loo* to the KING, who is as much belov'd and rever'd by the Princes I had the Honor to see there,[90] as the best of them can be by their own Subjects. But my particular Loss in his *Lordship*'s Death must be join'd with that of his Contry in one that was inviolably true to its Interest, and sincerely zealous to promote its Welfare abroad as well as at Home. As for his good Opinion or Intentions, I refer my self to Ey-witnesses that wou'd scorn to ly for mine or any Body's Service, My Lord SEA AND SEALE, my Lord MOHUN,[91] Captain TYRRELL,[92] and the Reverend Mr. SANDYS; appealing more especially to the last for my Behavior and Conduct with Respect to Religion or Morality, and giving him my hearty Thanks in this place for all his good Advice, which, I hope, he will not think wholly thrown away.

I have mention'd these Things to show that it is no Wonder I shou'd be misrepresented in *nice Speculations* or *intricat Deductions* by such as will venture to contradict *Matters of Fact* publicly known in so many Places and to so many People, and which it is so evident I do not affect to relate here out of Vanity, that I shall make no other Apology for it, but that of DAVID to his angry Brother, *Is there not a Cause?*[93] How often have the same Set of Men positively attributed Books to me, of which they well knew I was not the Writer, tho at the same Time they valu'd themselves for the Zeal in their Answers against me on this Account! GOD be prais'd I am fully convinc'd the true Religion approves not of these wicked Practices; for if it had, I wou'd really chuse to be of no Religion (as my Enemies falsly report) than be guilty of such dishonorable and inhuman Actions, and I declare that I wou'd rather at any Time be the Object than the Author of the like Calumnies. Once for all therfore I tell my Adversaries and Answerers (as I did on another Occasion[94]) that I was sensible before I wrote, I cou'd not escape the Displeasure of three Sorts of Persons: such as are resolv'd to be angry at whatever I do; such as neither rightly understand me nor any Body else; and those, who, without any particular Spite against an Author, yet to get a Penny will pretend to answer any Book that makes a considerable Noise or Figure. Therefore I find my self oblig'd beforehand to disclaim all Explanations made of my Meaning, beyond what is warranted by the express Words of my Book; having constantly indeavor'd not only to write intelligibly, but so as that none can possibly misunderstand me. I renounce all the Designs that may be imputed to me by such as are

[*XXXII*]

so far from being admitted into my Secret, that they were never in my Company; but I specially disown whatever is said by those who first presume to divine my Thoughts, and then to vent their own rash Conjectures as my undoubted Opinions. I slight their Artifice, who, when unable to object against the Point in Question, labor to ingage their Adversary in Matters wholly besides the Purpose; and, when their Evasions have no better Fortune than their Attacks, fall to railing against his Person because they cannot confute his Arguments. I am as much above the Malice of som, as they are below my Resentments; and I wou'd at any Time chuse to be rather the Object of their Envy, than of their Favor. I know that to enterprize any Thing out of the common Road is to undergo undoubted Envy or Peril; and that he, who is not beforehand resolv'd to bear Opposition, will never do any great or beneficial Exploit: yet tis no small Incouragement to me, that, from the Beginning of the World to this Time, not a single Instance can be produc'd of one who either was or wou'd be eminent, but he met with Enemies to his Person or Fame.

TO CONCLUDE therfore (being now arriv'd to Years that will not wholly excuse Inconsideratness in resolving, or Precipitance in Acting) I firmly hope that my Persuasion and Practice will show me to be *a true Christian*, that my due Conformity to the public Worship may prove me to be *a good Churchman*, and that my untainted Loyalty to King WILLIAM will argue me to be a *stanch Commonwealthsman*; that I shall continue all my Life a Friend to *Religion*, an enemy to *Superstition*, a Supporter of *good Kings*, and (when there's Occasion) a Deposer of *Tyrants*.

Tu ne cede Malis, sed contra audientor ito.

FINIS

The Judgment of the Socinians *concerning the Book, entitul'd* Christianity not Mysterious, *deliver'd in* the Agreement of the Unitarians with the Catholic Church. *Pag. 55.*

I Know not what it was to his *Lordship's* Purpose (meaning Dr. STILLINGFLEET *the late Bishop of Worcester*) to fall upon Mr. TOLAND's Book. But if he wou'd needs attack the Book, he shou'd have dealt fairly, he shou'd have discust the main Argument in it, and not carpt only at a few Passages; and those too so mangled and deform'd by his Representation of them, that I dare to affirm Mr. TOLAND does not know his own Book in the *Bishop's* Representation of it. I do not perceive (to speak truly) but that the Book still stands in its full Strength, if it hath not also acquir'd a farther Reputation by Occasion of this so unsuccessful Nibbling at it. But suppose the Bishop had disarm'd the Gentleman, *What is that to us? Do we offer this Book against the* Trinity *of the* Realists? *Was it written with Intention to serve us? Doth it contain any of our Allegations from Reason against the* Trinity *of* PHILOPONUS,[95] JOACHIM,[96] *and* GENTILIS? We desire him to answer to the Reasons in our Books against the *Trinity* of the *Tritheists:* but to these he saith not a Word, but only falls upon Mr. TOLAND's Book, *in which or for which we are not in the least concern'd;* nor do I think the learned and ingenious Author will hold himself to be interested to defend that *Christianity not Mysterious* which his Lordship presents us with.

Notes

1 [Convocation: the Synod of Anglican clergy from the province of either Canterbury or York. Sullivan states that there was a High-Church majority in the lower
house, while the upper house inclined more towards Latitudinarianism and
Whiggery. He suggests that Toland was used by the lower house to strike at the
more liberal upper house (p.10). In both 1698 and 1701, the bishops were reluc-
tant to move against the author of *Christianity not Mysterious*, feeling it would
cause grave civil disturbance to attack not just deists, but also – eventually – Dissenters and other non-Anglican Protestants. They suggested that they needed a
royal writ before they could move against Toland (Sullivan, pp.264-7).]

2 Pag. 21.

3 Pag. 53.

4 [Titus Maccius Plautus (c.254-184 BC): ancient Rome's greatest comic dramatist;
he has been a strong influence on the development of both comedy and romantic
drama in the West since the Renaissance.]

5 [John Milton (1608-1674): poet. Toland published his *Life of John Milton* in
1698. *Eikon Basilike* was thought to be written by Charles I, and had many High-
Church devotees. Milton – who had published pamphlets against episcopacy –
wrote (in his capacity as Latin secretary to the Council of State) a reply in
Eikonoklastes, 1649. Toland showed in his *Amyntor; Or a Defence of Milton's Life*,
1699, that *Eikon Basilike* was a forgery, being actually written by the Bishop of
Worcester, John Gauden (1605-62) (Sullivan, p.135).]

6 [Claudius Salmasius (1588-1653): French classical scholar, he was not allowed to
succeed his father as magistrate as he was a Protestant; professor at Leiden 1631,
Wrote more than eighty works; expert in Latin, Greek, Hebrew, Arabic, Persian
and Coptic. Salmasius is most well known on account of his controversy with
Milton. He believed in the divine right to rule of kings; Milton didn't. He wrote
Defensio pro regio Carolo I, 1650; Milton responded with *Pro populo Anglicano
defensio contra Claudii anonymi, alias Salmasii defensionem regiam*, 1651.]

7 ['obscurely hinted' were joined together in the original edition.]

8 [White Kennett (1660-1728): one-time patron of Toland (Sullivan, p. 5).
Although Sullivan says that Kennett was Bishop of Lincoln the *Concise Dictio-
nary of National Biography* disagrees, calling him Bishop of Peterborough 1708.
Supporter of the Revolution, DD 1700, chaplain-in-ordinary to Queen Anne.]

9 Pag. 34.

10 [Francis Atterbury (1662-1732): chaplain to William and Mary. Opposed Eras-
tianism (the state having primacy over the church. Thomas Erastus (1524-83)
was a Swiss Protestant theologian, chaplain-in-ordinary to Queen Anne, Bishop
of Rochester and Dean of Westminster 1713, sympathetic to Jacobites and
imprisoned in the Tower 1720, went to France and served the Old Pretender
(James II's son, and father of Bonnie Prince Charlie). He believed that to be English was to be Anglican (Sullivan, p. 60).]

11 Pag. 47.

12 [Prolocutor: Chairman.]

13 [Offspring Blackhall (or Blackall) (1654-1716): chaplain to William, Bishop of
Exeter 1708. Blackhall gave the Boyle Lectures in 1700, in which he was
obsessed with the papist threat and saw links between papists and deists. He
attacked Toland in a speech to the House of Commons in 1699, stating that
Toland denied the authenticity of the Gospels. Toland rebuffed him, and Blackhall retracted his accusation (Sullivan, pp. 135, 236-40).]

14 [Henry Dodwell 'the elder' (1641-1711): scholar and theologian, fellow of Trinity College Dublin, deprived of his professorship of history at Oxford for refusing
to take the oath of allegiance 1691, returned to the established church in 1710.]

15 [Spelt establish'h in the original text.]

16 [The space between these two words is missing in the original text.]

17 *In* Anglia Libera, *sect.* 14.

18 [Tiberius Julius Caesar Augustus (42 BC-AD 37): the second emperor (r. AD 14-
37) of Rome.]

19 Pag. 51.

20 P.17.19.

21 [Edward Synge (1659-1741): author of *A Gentleman's Religion* (1693-8). Bishop
of Raphoe 1714, archbishop of Tuam 1716, opposed the Toleration Bill 1719.
David Berman states that *A Gentleman's Religion* was a direct response to *Christianity not Mysterious*, even though Synge to some extent shared Toland's views
on rationalism and deism. He was the son of a bishop, and two of his sons were
bishops ('Eighteenth-century Irish Philosophy', in Seamus Deane (ed.), *The Field
Day Anthology of Irish Writing, Vol. 1*, Field Day/Faber, Derry, 1991, pp. 770,
804.). The playwright John Millington Synge (1871-1909) and the scientist John
L. Synge are descended from the same family.]

22 [Thomas Beconsall: a harsh critic of Toland's, author of *The Christian Belief*, 1696
(Sullivan, pp. 244, 339).]

23 *The Provincial Letters, or Mystery of Jesuitism*, Lett. 1.
[Henri Arnaud (1641-1721): Waldensian pastor at La Tour, the chief Waldensian village in Piedmont. He organized those who had been expelled to Switzerland by the Duke of Savoy 1686; attempted to return but was forced back by
French and Savoyard troops 1687-8; duke let them back 1689 but expelled them
again 1696 when Arnaud became pastor of Dürrmenz-Schönenberg in Württem-
berg.]

24 [Cornelis Jansenius (1585-1638): Dutch-Flemish theologian. Denounced the
Jesuits as Pelagians; Bishop of Ypres 1631; fame rests on his main work (published
two years after his death), *Augustinus, seu doctrina Sancti Augustini de humanae
naturae sanitate, aegritudine, medicina, adversus, Pelagianos et Massilienses*. In the

199

Augustinus, Jansenius strictly interpreted one part of Augustine's philosophy to argue for predestined salvation for the chosen few. In this sense Jansenism resembles Calvinism. It was strongly opposed by the Jesuits.]

25 [Spelt 'earuestly' in the original text.]
26 [Friars living solely on alms.]
27 *Letter* 3.
28 *History of the Convocation*, pag. 112.
29 *Ibid*. Pag. 113.
30 *Ibid*. Pag. 112,113.
31 Pag. 52.
32 *Pref.* pag.24.
33 Pag. 129.
34 Pag. 19.
35 Pag. 53.
36 Pag. 60.
37 [William Jane (1645-1707): DD 1674, regius professor of divinity at Oxford 1680-1707, prolocutor of the lower house of Convocation 1689. Son of Joseph Jane (1600-1660) who defended *Eikon Basilike* against Milton 1651.]
38 Pag. 16.
39 *History of the Convocation*, Pag. 114.
40 Pag. 19.
41 [William Wake (1657-1737): DD Oxford 1689, Bishop of Lincoln 1705, Archbishop of Canterbury 1716, negotiated with the French Jansenists with a view to union 1717-20.]
42 *History of the Convocation*, Pag. 119.
43 Pag. 21.
44 [Samuel Johnson (1649-1702): Whig divine, fined and whipped for circulating his *Humble and Hearty address to all English Protestants in the present Army* 1686, awarded pension and bounty by King William.]
45 [The origins of Salisbury date back to Old Sarum, an early Iron Age fortification just north of modern-day Salisbury. Before the building of Salisbury cathedral, the episcopal see was housed at Old Sarum. The cathedral is sited in a valley south of Old Sarum. Salisbury town is also called New Sarum.]
46 Pag. 16.
47 Pag. 17.
48 [The son of James VII and II, James Edward was Prince of Wales and known as 'the Old Pretender'. After the death of his father, he was recognized as king of England and Scotland by France and Spain. He tried to invade Britain twice, in 1708 and 1715. He was the father of Charles Edward Stuart ('Bonnie Prince Charlie' or 'The Young Pretender').]
49 *Preface*, Pag. 30.
50 [Thomas Cranmer (1489-1556): Archbishop of Canterbury 1533, allowed divorce of Henry VIII from Catherine of Aragon (wife 1) 1533, pronounced his marriage to Anne Boleyn (wife 2) null and void 1536, supported divorce from Anne of Cleves (wife 4) 1540, told Henry VIII of the infidelity of Catherine Howard (wife 5) 1541. Although he admitted the supremacy of the pope and the truth of all Roman Catholic doctrine (except transubstantiation), he was still burned at the stake.]

51   *Ibid.* Pag. 31.
52   P.263, 2 *Edit.*
53   *History of the Convocation*, Pag. 114.
54   Pag. 80. 2 *Edit.* [See p. 60 in this edition.]
55   Pa. 106. [See p. 73 in this edition.]
56   Pag. 67. [See p. 53 in this edition.]
57   Pag. 15.
58   Pag. 16.
59   Pag. 26.
60   Pa. 139,140. [See p. 84 in this edition.]
61   Pag. 168. [See p. 96 in this edition.]
62   2 edn Preff., Pag. 30. [See [pp. 13-14n in this edition.]
63   Pag. 38. [See p. 37 in this edition.]
64   *Pag. 94. &c.*
65   [This chapter was incorrectly labelled XXIII in original text.]
66   [The space between these words was omitted in the original text.]
67   Pag. 28.
68   [Apollonius of Perga (*fl.* 250-220 BC): Greek mathematician. In his most famous work – the Conics – he introduced the terms ellipse, hyperbola and parabola. He also made great contributions to Greek astronomy.]
69   [Diophantus of Alexandria (*fl.* middle of third century): a Greek mathematician, he introduced an algebraic symbolism which used an abbreviation for the unknown quantity. (*NGME*)]
70   Pag. 18.
71   [Richard Hooker (1554?-1600): theologian, admitted to Corpus Christi College in Oxford by influence of John Jewel, Bishop of Salisbury. Major work: *The Laws of Ecclesiastical Politie* (1574-7), praised by Swift for its style. (*CDNB*)]
72   Pag. 25.26.
73   [John Jewel (1522-71): Bishop of Salisbury 1560, notary to Cranmer 1554, aligned himself with Anglicanism and not Puritanism; Richard Hooker was a *protégé*.]
74   Pag. 92.
75   [The Dutch Republic was known as the United Provinces of the Netherlands in the seventeenth century. The ruler was called the Stadtholder of Holland. Prince William became Stadtholder in 1672: it seems William was also a republican!]
76   [Polybius (c.200-c.118 BC): Greek historian of Rome. A friend of the Roman general Scipio, he accompanied him to Spain and Africa, where they saw the destruction of Carthage in 146 BC. (*NGME*)]
77   Pag. 31.
78   [James Harrington (1611-77): political theorist, best-known work is *The Commonwealth of Oceana*, 1656. He argued that a strong middle class is essential to a stable political life. He was imprisoned twice: during the English Civil War (1649) and in the 1660s. Harrington's works were edited by Toland and published in 1700.]
79   [Signing the Oath of Abjuration meant that the signee disclaimed any right to the Crown of England on the part of descendants of the (Old) Pretender.]
80   Respublica Res est Populi, cum bene ac juste geritur, sive ab uno Rege, sive à paucis Optimatibus, sive ab universo Populo. Cum vero injustus est Rex (quem Tyrannum voco), aut injusti Optimates (quorum Consensus Factio est) aut injus-

tus ipse Populus (cui Nomen usitatum nullum reperio nisi ut ipsum Tyrannum appellem) non jam vitiosa, sed omnino nulla Respublica est: quoniam non Res est Populi, cum Tyrannus eam Factiove capessat; nec ipse Populus jam Populus est si sit injustus, quoniam non est Multitudo Juris Consensu & Utilitatis Communione sociata.

[*from:* Fragment. Cicer. ex lib. 3. de Repub. apud Augustin. de Civ. Dei. l. 2. c. 21.]

[Marcus Tullius Cicero (106-43 BC): Orator, politician and political theorist. Champion of the Roman Republic. A powerful influence on nineteenth-century liberalism and still widely read today. A great hero of Toland's. Toland translated some of Cicero's work.]

81 [Lucius Cornelius Cinna (c.130-84 BC): Roman politician and rival of Lucius Cornelius Sulla.]

82 [Gaius Marius (157-86 BC): Roman military man and politician, he combined with Cinna to capture Rome from Sulla.]

83 [(Toland misspells Sulla here.) Lucius Cornelius Sulla (c.138-78 BC): dictator of Rome in 82-1 BC. His bloody career inspired Pompey and Julius Caesar to seek the kind of power that was incompatible with republicanism.]

84 [Gnaeus Pompeius, a.k.a. Pompey the Great (106-48 BC): great military leader. Pompey became jealous over Caesar's success in Gaul and helped Cicero return from exile. Fought against Julius Caesar in Rome's civil war of 49-48 BC. Early attempts to avert civil war failed. Caesar crossed the Rubicon and forced Pompey's retreat to Greece. Pompey fled to Egypt, where he was assassinated.]

85 [Gaius Octavius, a.k.a. Augustus (63 BC-14 AD) was the first Roman emperor.]

86 [Sir William Jones (1631-82): lawyer and MP, directed 'Popish Plot' persecutions.]

87 [There is no record of a book with such a title in either the Library of Congress or the British Library. The *British Library Catalogue* (1975) has *The Lord Whiglove's Elegy: to which is added A pious epitaph upon the late bishop of Addlesbury* (1715), by Edward Ward (1667-1731). Ward was a humourist who kept a tavern in London. He published many coarse poems satirizing both Whigs and the low-church party. The above-mentioned book is a satire in verse on Lord Wharton and Bishop Gilbert Burnet. Like Burnet, Thomas, 1st Marquis of Wharton (1648-1716), was quick to declare for Prince William: he joined him at Exeter. His place in the history of Irish music is assured by his publication in 1687 of 'Lilli Burlero, Bullen-a-la', an anti-Catholic song (still used by the BBC World Service to announce the news). Wharton is said to have boasted that he sang King James off his throne. Indeed, Burnet says that 'The whole army, and almost all people were singing it' (*History of his own Times*, 1723-34). Wharton was Commissioner for Union with Scotland 1706, and Lord Lieutenant of Ireland 1708-10. Baron of Trim. Acquired Rathfarnham Castle.]

88 [Sir Thomas Pilkington (d.1691): Lord Mayor of London and a strong Whig, imprisoned 1682-6 for *scandalum magnatum*, Lord Mayor 1689-91, knighted by William 1689.]

89 [Charles Gerard, 2nd earl of Macclesfield (1659?-1701): sent to the Tower on suspicion of treason 1683, acquitted, sentenced to death 1685, pardoned 1687, Lord Lieutenant of Lancashire 1690, went bail for Lord Mohun 1692, envoy-extraordinary to Hanover in 1701: Toland's boss on that occasion.]

90 ['where' was originally printed, but the 'w' was crossed out and overwritten – by hand – with 't'.]

91 [Charles Mohun, 4th Baron Mohun (1675?-1712): duellist, twice tried for murder before he was twenty; his wife's uncle was Earl of Macclesfield. He accompanied Macclesfield to Hanover in 1701 to present the Garter to the Elector of Hanover; presumably this is when he met Toland.]

92 [James Tyrrell (1642-1718): historical writer, JP and deputy-lieutenant for Buckinghamshire; deprived by James II for not supporting the Declaration of Indulgence 1687; very close friend of John Locke.]

93 1 *Sam.* 17.29.

94 *In* Harrington's *Life*, Pag. 40.

95 [John Philoponus a.k.a. John the Grammarian (*fl.* sixth century AD): Alexandrian philosopher and theologian, his name means 'lover of work': the *philoponoi* looked after places of worship. His theological works are clearly Monophysitic (expressing the idea that Christ had one nature rather than being both human and divine). Monophysitism was widespread in the Eastern Church. In 560 Askusnages proposed that the three persons of the Trinity were actually three Gods. Even the Monophysites rejected this, and many rejoined the Catholic Church. Both the Jacobite and Armenian Churches derive from Monophysitism.]

96 [Joachim de Floris (1145-1202): Italian mystic theologian; after a pilgrimage to the East as a youth he became a Cistercian monk. He propounded a mystical interpretation of the Scriptures, and divided the history of mankind into three parts: Age of Law (or the Father), Age of the Gospel (or the Son), and Age of the Spirit. His ideas were seen as millenarian, and spread widely. His teachings on the Trinity were condemned by Lateran IV as tritheistic.]

Critical Essays
_____

JOHN TOLAND: AN IRISH PHILOSOPHER?

Richard Kearney

John Toland was condemned by the Irish parliament and denounced from church pulpits all over Ireland after the publication in 1696 of *Christianity not Mysterious*. Threatened with arrest, Toland fled abroad (not for the first time). Then only twenty-six, he was to spend the remainder of his years in exile philosophizing, publishing and polemicizing on the burning issues of his time. On his death-bed in 1722, Toland signed one his last books, *Pantheisticon*, with what he claimed was his original baptismal name, Janus Junius Eoganesius – a signature indicating his place of birth on the Inishowen peninsula in Co. Donegal in accordance with native Gaelic practice. Beside his baptismal name he added the pseudonym *Cosmopoli*, meaning 'one who belongs to the world'.

But who was John Toland? Those who have tried to answer this question have generally given up in despair. Pierre Des Maizeaux, who embarked on a biography shortly after Toland's death, found the materials insufficient. The intervening two-and-a-half centuries have not improved matters, as Robert Sullivan admits in his mammoth study of the man: 'Toland habitually covered his tracks, and the bulk of his papers have been destroyed. Coming across the order 'burn this' on the charred fragment of a letter concerning Toland, a researcher must wonder how much [else] has been lost besides.'[1] Toland himself proposed some solution to this anticipated dilemma – 'If you would know more of him [he wrote of himself] Search his Writings' (*caetera scriptis pete*).[2] But this, as we shall see, is no solution. Toland's final self-description, inscribed in a Latin epitaph on his grave in Putney churchyard, declared that he would rise again, 'yet never to [be] the same Toland more' ('*At Idem futurus Tolandus nunquam*'). But who, one is compelled to ask, is the *same* Toland? *Which* Toland are we talking about? Even in death, John Toland continued to tease and mystify.[3] He chose, it would seem, to remain an enigma.

I

While no definitive portrait of Toland is possible, a rough identikit can be pieced together from the odd records (and rumours) that have survived. Here is a list of some of the most salient features. Born a Gaelic-speaking Catholic in Donegal, Toland went on to acquire nine other languages, and as many other religions, as he journeyed through Britain and the continent. A shepherd-boy until the age of fourteen, he was known as 'Eoghan na leabhar' (Eoghan of the Books). He became a scholarship student at Redcastle school in Derry and converted to Protestantism in 1686 before proceeding to study divinity in Glasgow University at the age of seventeen. After three years there, Toland travelled on to the universities of Edinburgh (1690), Leyden and Utrecht (1692-4). But his philosophical and theological inquiries did not stop there. Toland's intellectual itinerary was also to take in such disparate centres of cosmopolitan learning as Hanover, Berlin, Dusseldorf, Vienna and Oxford. Toland spent much of his life seeking to restore, or reinvent, a noble genealogy for himself, going so far as to suggest that he was the descendant of old Gaelic aristocracy (the Uí Thuathalláin) and persuading Irish Franciscans in Prague to certify his story.

Privately insecure, improvident and racked by self-doubt, Toland's public persona was one of bold self-assertion. His prolific publications soon made him a subject of international debate: Locke supported him, as did Leibniz, who championed him as '*Un homme d'esprit et de savoir*'. Other luminaries of the period, including Swift, Berkeley and Defoe, became scornful adversaries. Denounced as a drunken braggart, apostate waif, spoiled Jesuit and subversive infidel,

Toland went on to become one of the leading 'free thinkers' of his time, publishing over one hundred books, inventing the term 'pantheist' and establishing himself as 'the founding father of modern Irish philosophy'.[4]

But the enigmas do not end there. A strident spokesman for republican virtue – publishing editions of Cicero, Milton, Harrington and the regicide millenarian Edmund Ludlow – Toland was, simultaneously, a darling of the royal court of Hanover. He was alleged to be a secret agent of Prussian monarchy and amorous confidant of the Electress Sophia, who received him alone in her room for several hours a day and rewarded him with 'gold medals and other curiosities of considerable value'.[5] A defender of English liberties against Jacobite plots, Toland was himself accused of Jesuit conspiracy and disloyal adventurism. Branded an atheist, he was obsessed with religious questions, displaying a particular proclivity for pantheistic, Rosicrucian and Latitudinarian movements (and spending considerable time studying the mystical doctrines of Giordano Bruno). A cosmopolitan idealist, Toland never abandoned his Irish roots and returned again and again to the claim that the ancient Irish Church of the Culdees was the most genuine form of Christianity. In fact, Toland was to devote several scholarly studies to the Gaelic tradition. These included (i) extensive research for an Irish dictionary conducted in Oxford in 1694; (ii) a compendious *History of the Druids*, published posthumously in 1726 and containing a Breton-Irish-Latin dictionary as well as *A Critical History of the Celtic Religion and Learning*; and (iii) *An Account of the Druids, Vaids and Bards of the Ancient Gauls, Britons, Irish and Scots*. Toland's researches on the Gaelic tradition also comprised work on an old Irish manuscript, written in Armagh in 1138, that was stolen from the Bibliothèque Royale in Paris by a renegade priest called Jean Aymon who befriended Toland in Amsterdam in 1709.

This last text merits some comment, as it contains revealing passages about Toland's attitude – however disguised in scholarly detachment – about his native culture. An account of the manuscript was published as part of *Nazarenus* in 1718. The full title of the text is *The relation of an Irish Manuscript of the Four Gospels, as like-*

209

wise a Summary of antient Irish Christianity and the Reality of the Keldees (an order of Lay-religious) against the two last Bishops of Worcester. Though the manuscript was originally catalogued in the Bibliothèque Royale as a Latin text with Anglo-Saxon glosses, Toland was able to correct the error and decipher the meaning of the Old Irish script. He concluded that it epitomized the tolerant free-thinking spirit of the *Céle Dé* (or Culdee) movement, which Toland identified as the original form of Irish Christianity. Indeed, Toland appears to take mischievous pleasure in his commentary, quoting claims from certain ancient scribes which he himself could never advocate directly. For example, we find him citing the sentiment of the monk Cummian that 'Rome errs, Jerusalem errs, Alexandria errs, Antiochia errs, the whole world errs; but the Irish alone ... are right!'[6] Later in the same text Toland rehearses another ancient opinion to the effect that the Irish 'were to all others a harmless race, and to the English (whom they entertained, furnished with books and instructed gratis) a most friendly nation ... the Saxons were indebted to them for their letters, no less than their learning'.[7] An Irish cultural patriot *avant la lettre?*

It is certainly tempting to read a certain *apologia pro sua viva* in Toland's choice of opinion. And this suspicion is strengthened when, several pages later, Toland identifies his own persecution with that of his compatriot and predecessor Johannes Scottus Ériugena. Ériugena's book, writes Toland, 'was, by the authority of the Pope and the Council of Verceil, flatly condemned, [this being] the only way they had to confute it'. And he adds, significantly, that 'this method of answering is successively practiced *to this day* by the promoters of error everywhere, and by those who prefer interest to truth'.[8]

Lest there be doubts about Toland's own sentiments on the matter, we need only turn the page to find him citing Eric of Auxerre's celebration of Irish scholars in exile: 'Why should I mention Ireland, not fearing the danger of the sea, and removing almost all of it with a flock of philosophers, to our shores; whereof of how much any one excels the rest, he undergoes a voluntary exile; and by so much the readier is he to stand before our most wise Solomon and to devote himself to his service.'[9] Toland praises the ancient monks who 'were of no order, nor indeed men in Orders at all', who founded schools 'among the Picts, Anglosaxons, Germans, Burgundians, Switzers and French: as who has not heard of Sedulius, Columba, Columbanus, Colmannus, Aidanus, Furseus, Kilianus, Gallus, Brendanus, Claudius, Clemens, Scotus Erigena, and numberless others?'[10] These secular monks were, according to Toland, 'Western latitudinarians' before their time – anti-hierarchical and non-sacerdotal, courageous of mind and adventurous of spirit.

It is little wonder that the exiled Toland should choose to identify with these migrant Irish minds, just as the exiled James Joyce would do two centuries after him in his famous Trieste lecture.

II

In addition to the explicitly Irish dimension of Toland's biography and bibliography, the question of whether he was an 'Irish' thinker might be extended to some of his philosophical writing where no ostensible Irish content is in evidence. We might ask, moreover, if it actually matters whether Toland is called an 'Irish' thinker or not? And if it is true that Irish bishops were calling for his books to be burnt in 1697, surely things have changed in three hundred years? Yes and no.

Let me take an example. On 12 May 1985 the Bishop of Limerick, Jeremiah Newman, delivered an address on the occasion of the International Year of Youth. It was a nine-page typescript distributed to the press and reported widely in the Irish media. In his address Bishop Newman singled out John Toland as a thinker who did not 'represent the Irish mind as such'. His rationalist scepticism regarding church doctrine rendered him, in the Bishop's view, a more appropriate listing for the histories of 'English' philosophy. Bishop Newman went on to express indignation at 'what is going on at present in our country by way of changing … our Catholic inheritance' – citing as example the inclusion of Toland as an Irish philosopher in a book I had edited called *The Irish Mind*. The particular essay on Toland was, Bishop Newman insinuatingly observed, written by a 'non-Irish contributor' – namely Dr David Berman, a self-confessed atheist of American-Jewish origin and an expert of eighteenth-century Irish thought. The following is an extract from the Bishop's diatribe:

[This book] purports to explore the intellectual tradition of the Irish people, that is us – yes us. Who else could claim to be Irish? But apart from one chapter on the medieval Catholic scholar, John Scotus Eriugena, this book is devoted almost entirely to a type of thinking that is *anything but typically and traditionally Irish*. In the sphere of philosophy, it manages to concentrate on figures with names such as Molesworth, Hutcheson, Clayton, Dodwell, Skelton and Toland. One has only to consult any thorough history of English philosophy to find most of these names included in it, which means or should mean that they do not exactly represent the Irish mind as such. Indeed, I could not but find annoying, as well as quite unscholarly, the statement by a non-Irish contributor to the book to the effect that the 18th-century rationalist John Toland is, quote, 'the father of modern Irish Philosophy'.[11]

This statement begs as many questions as it raises. In particular it recalls the controversial (and in my view untenable) distinction made by certain cultural nationalists between the 'Irish Irish' and the 'non-Irish Irish' – that is, between the real Catholic Irish and the rest. This is surely what Bishop Newman has in mind when he states that most of the thinkers mentioned in Berman's article belong to 'English' (not Irish) intellectual histories, and represent a threat to Ireland's genuine 'Catholic inheritance'.

This dual complaint by the Bishop sadly illustrates how 'exclusivist Catholic nationalism can go hand in hand with English cultural expropriation'.[12] The philosophers mentioned by Berman were each of them born, bred and published in Ireland. Their only allegedly non-Irish characteristic was their non-Catholicism. The one true 'Irish' philosopher the Bishop cites as typical of our 'Catholic inheritance' is Johannes Scottus Ériugena – a thinker who had his books banned in Rome and was placed on the Index by successive Popes: the charge against him being, ironically, the same as that brought against Toland a thousand years later, namely pantheism. Moreover, if we were able to take the Bishop's equation of Catholic and Irish to its logical conclusion, we would have to say that Toland was in fact 'Irish' for as long as he was Catholic (up to the age of fifteen, approximately), but became 'English' when he converted to Protestantism and left Ireland for Glasgow University in 1687.

According to the rigid criteria of exclusivist Catholic nationalism, then, Toland is both Irish and non-Irish. In other words, he upsets the distinction itself and therefore cannot be tolerated. If he is not pure Irish he must be English. Toland's complex Irishness, like that of most Irish thinkers of the period, defies a narrow logic of identity; it epitomizes the defiance of an excluded middle. Indeed, Toland himself seems to have been aware of the anomaly created by his hybrid character, and playfully exploited his own self-presentation to his public. In addition to his puzzling epitaph, mentioned above, the question of his baptismal name – *Janus Junius* – also carries connotations of ludic doubleness. Alan Harrison notes that Toland claimed to have been christened a Roman Catholic with the name Janus Junius. Harrison suggests it is more likely he was christened Seán Eoghain, and that 'Janus Junius' was a pseudonym, an 'elaborate verbal joke', invoking, among other things, the two-faced god Janus.[13]

The ploy of double-coding was no doubt a strategy of survival adopted by Toland to escape condemnation as a 'free-thinker'. Several commentators besides Harrison have recognized this, and Toland's acknowledgment of the esoteric/exoteric distinction in such works as the *Pantheisticon* (1720) and the *Tetradymus* (1720) confirms it. Fear of persecution, Toland states in the latter, leads authors to become 'supple in their conduct', 'reserved in opening their minds' and even 'ambiguous in their expressions'; a view already anticipated in *Letters to Serena* (1704) and in his claim in *Christianity not Mysterious* to 'propose his sentiments to the World by way of Paradox'.[14] This was, of course, a practice adopted by many freethinking minds of the age, from Locke to Voltaire, eager to avoid censure. But there is more to Toland's doubleness, I would argue, than a strategy of survival or *succès de scandale*. We also witness here a telling symptom of Irish intellectual culture since the seventeenth century. Perhaps one of the reasons why Toland presented himself as a *contradiction* (as Leibniz and others noted) was because the Irish mind was a cleft-mind? Not uniform but pluriform. Not homogeneous but diverse. Anglo *and* Gaelic. Catholic *and* Protestant. Native *and* planted. Regional *and* cosmopolitan.

I am not claiming that no other European cultures of the period experienced similar divisions, only that Ireland was arguably a more accentuated version of such conflict to the extent that it was at once a brutally colonized country (particularly since the introduction of the Penal Laws) and one of the most advanced centres of elite intellectual culture (especially in the Pale). Toland's doubleness was undoubtedly a general feature of persecuted Enlightenment rationalists, but it also bore the birthmarks of his cultural-historical origins. This is true of all thinkers, no matter how universalist or cosmopolitan their thought, and certainly true of Toland, who was consciously aware of his 'Irish' identity and devoted several works to the study of it, most notably the *History of the Druids* mentioned above. In short, while I am not saying that Toland's doubleness was uniquely or exclusively Irish, I am saying it was Irish to *some* extent, and that this extent is not insignificant.

III

Does this offer a supplementary perspective from which to review the ambiguities and duplicities that proliferate in Toland's writings? Does it help explain why Toland deploys so many pseudonymous ruses that, in Sullivan's words, he is 'never able to assert his long-obscured person over his obscuring personas'?[15] Why he conceals esoteric meanings behind exoteric modes of argument, saying indirectly what cannot be said directly? Why he defends Enlightenment rationalism against religious sectarianism and superstition but devotes several of his major writings to a defence of ancient Celtic Christianity? Why he was such a zealous supplicant of patronage from English, Dutch and German royalty, while remaining a dyed-in-the-wool 'commonwealthman' whose heroes were invariably radical republicans – Brutus, Milton, Sidney, Ludlow and Harrington? Why, finally, Toland was able to support the Protestant Succession after the 1688 Revolution against popish conspiracies yet proudly invoke his own Catholic descent and, when it came to the crunch, appeal to the Irish Franciscans in Prague to authenticate his Gaelic origins? (The

Latin certificate, dated 1708 and signed by the clerical superiors of the College, O'Neill and O'Devlin, would have offered Toland a carte blanche to visit other Irish Catholic colleges in Vienna, Rome and Louvain – places where Irish learning was still fostered and where priests and professionals were trained before they returned to Ireland to work for the Catholic cause during the Penal times.)[16]

Several commentators have suggested connections between Toland's strategic duplicity and his Irish background. Alan Harrison, for example, describes him as a 'threshold figure' in line with the Irish paradigm of the 'trickster'.[17] Stephen Daniel observes that Toland's ruses are a kind of anti-colonial deconstruction: 'On the periphery of the English experience, Toland is the Irish anomaly, the spokesman for alterity within national or linguistic unity.'[18] David Berman, as we shall see below, relates Toland's critique of Christian mysteries to an attack upon the Penal Laws imposed on Ireland by English rule. Toland's compulsion to conceal his native subversiveness behind a veneer of respectability would certainly go some way to explaining his device of camouflaging his real message behind an ostensibly innocuous public pronouncement. Indeed, Toland's deployment of the esoteric/exoteric strategy ranks him, in Daniel's phrase, 'among the foremost eighteenth-century theorists of discretion'.[19]

This discretion, I am suggesting, derives at least in part from Toland's deep-rooted need to develop hidden layers of meaning in order to challenge the official discourses of power that prevailed during his time. The hermeneutic tricks deployed by Toland at the level of biblical, political and linguistic exegesis were marginal strategies to outwit and out-manoeuvre the orthodox centres of authority.

One wonders, moreover, if this persona of wandering trickster, peripheral rebel, unpredictable Irishman-in-exile, was not in fact typical of many another Irish intellectual in the eighteenth century and after? Does one not find similar devices of irony, subterfuge and satire in the writings of Swift, Burke and Congreve, or later again, of Wilde and Shaw, Beckett and Joyce? Indeed is Joyce's description of *Finnegans Wake* as a narrative perpetually 'between twotwinsome minds', a double-sided story inviting us to have 'two thinks at a time', not itself a twentieth-century reinscription of that subversive Irish mind epitomized by Toland? Is it an accident that Toland's own experience of peripheral difference and exile issued not only in appeal for tolerance of different perspectives, but also in his spirited defence of foreigners and Jews in England?[20] A position that anticipates Joyce's own empathy with outsiders and abhorrence of imperial conformity as manifested in his choice of a Jew, Leopold Bloom, as a central character of his celebrated novel?

Toland was by no means the only Irish thinker of his time to exemplify the double role of Janus responding to crises of identity and authority. The multiple divisions of Irish cultural life – Protestant and Catholic, Planter and Gael, Irish-speaker and English-speaker, conformist and dissenter – were also evidenced in the controversies surrounding Irish philosophy for most of the eighteenth century. The 'golden age' of Irish philosophy stretching from 1690 to 1760 was, as David Berman observes, deeply informed by questions of power and revolt in Ireland. To follow Berman's own genealogy, most of the proponents of theological representationalism (the theory around which the dominant school of Irish philosophy developed) were responding directly or indirectly to the radical implications of Toland's rationalist critique of Christian mysteries in *Christianity not Mysterious*. Such prominent thinkers as Edward Synge, William King, John Ellis, Philip Skelton, Thomas McDonnell, and finally Edmund Burke, all felt obliged to respond to Toland's insinuation that the existing authorities – both clerical and political – had no fundamental basis for claiming that the Establishment 'represented' God's rule on earth. One immediate consequence of this insinuation was that the Penal Laws upholding Ascendancy power in Ireland were devoid of philosophical foundation. As Berman succinctly points out: 'Toland's non-mysterious, tolerant deism threatened the sectarian basis of the Ascendancy.'[21]

Irish philosophers responded in different ways to this challenge. Some, including theological representationalists like Berkeley and Swift, reacted negatively to Toland's argument – the latter even vilifying Toland as 'the son of an Irish priest' and 'the great Oracle of the anti-Christians'.[22] Burke too expressed considerable hostility to Toland, preferring Berkeley's argument for an emotive rather than cognitive model of belief in his *Philosophical Enquiry into the Origin of our Ideas of the Sublime and Beautiful* (1757). Many other Irish minds, most notably Francis Hutcheson, Robert Clayton and Thomas Emlym, followed in Toland's footsteps. The point, however, is not to adjudicate between the sides, but to show how the key philosophical debates that raged in Ireland in the eighteenth century betrayed a deep sense of cultural and political division within the island – and in its relationship to the neighbouring island. No matter what side of the divide one came down on, one could not but be aware that division existed. Thus while Swift, for example, may have railed against Toland when wearing his hat as establishment Protestant, he railed against the injustices of English interference in Ireland when wearing his hat as Irish colonial nationalist. This double stance was shared by Berkeley and other Anglo-Irish thinkers of his time.

Many Irish intellectuals *since* the eighteenth century have also shown ambivalence towards their identity. The recurring allusions to masks, mercurial allegiances, pseudonyms, esoteric codes and double-layered ironies from Swift and Congreve to Wilde and Yeats is not adventitious. Perhaps, as Andrew Carpenter argues in his thesis of the 'double vision',[23] this cleft mentality is a specific characteristic spawned by eighteenth-century Irish culture? Or perhaps it has more ancient origins in Irish cultural history, as suggested by Vivian Mercier in *The Irish Comic Tradition* (1962) and Thomas Kinsella in 'The Divided Mind'?[24] Either way, such a mentality is omnipresent in Toland's work, and is arguably a general feature of the 'golden age' of Irish philosophy running from the publication of *Christianity not Mysterious* in 1696 to Burke's essay on the *Sublime and Beautiful* in 1757.[25]

IV

The choice of Burke as the major culminating figure of this period offers an opportunity, in conclusion, to comment upon the recurrence in his writings of the cleft mentality so prominent in Toland. In his biography of Burke, *The Great Melody*, Conor Cruise O'Brien argues that Burke's intellectual career was deeply informed by his native experience of 'doubleness', growing up in Ireland with his mother's Catholic family (the Nagles) near the Blackwater in County Cork, yet obliged to hide this distinguishing birth-mark as he doffed the official mask of the Protestant establishment in order to function, like his convert father before him, as a legitimate legal authority. This masking strategy was, of course, to become even more pronounced as Burke became a leading public figure in Irish and British affairs.

Taking a metaphor from Seamus Heaney's 'Cure of Troy', O'Brien describes Burke's experience of doubleness as a 'Philoctetes wound'. He traces its scars through Burke's split allegiances in Trinity College (where he felt obliged to adopt debating strategies of indirection to avoid exposure) to his tormented efforts to revoke a death penalty imposed on one of his Nagle relatives and, more generally, to support the Catholic Relief Act of 1778. But the most dramatic expression of Burke's Philoctetes complex was his famous speech against the Penal Laws in Ireland to the Bristol Guildhall in September 1780. This was an extraordinarily deft and passionate speech which carried with it a major threat to his seat in Parliament. Referring to the event, O'Brien writes:

This is the closest glimpse we get of the festering wound of Philoctetes ... When Burke speaks of 'infection' and 'corruption' in this context, he necessarily has his own family and personal situation most uncomfortably in mind. He loathes the Penal Laws, not merely for being unjust, but because of the false position in which the combined effects of the laws, and fear and worldly ambition, have placed the Burkes. This is what 'frets him with feverish being'; and is clearly fretting him right there in the Guildhall, in the probably perplexed presence of the discontented burgesses of Bristol.

O'Brien goes on to suggest that a

lesser person, circumstanced as he was, would have turned his back on Ireland altogether, and this would have been wholly to the advantage of his political career in Britain. It would have freed him from the 'Jesuit' albatross, which he carried around his neck throughout his political career. It would almost certainly have saved his seat at Bristol, whose retention would have enhanced his consequences in the House of Commons.[26]

Above all, O'Brien argues, Burke would have been perceived as a more normal person by his English contemporaries if he had 'lived down' his Irish connection. Such a suppression of his Irishness would have left him a free run to pursue high office undisturbed. 'Edmund Burke chose otherwise. He often spoke in the persona of an Englishman, but he never dropped Ireland altogether, which was the only way he could have induced Englishmen to take him seriously as one of themselves. Specifically, he failed to drop the cause of Irish Catholics, the most compromising, and the most disabling, by far, of all his Irish associations.'[27]

While such conflicts of allegiance may not have been as dramatic for most other Irish thinkers of the period, they were, I would suggest, never very far from the surface. And nowhere more so, in my view, than in Toland. Here Burke's Philoctetes complex finds parallels in the litany of split identities that, as noted above, ghosted the Donegal heretic's life. I rehearse them here by way of résumé. Toland was at once Irish and non-Irish, Gaelic-speaking and English-speaking, Catholic by birth and deist by choice, native and cosmopolitan, devotee of ancient Celtic sects and champion of Enlightenment reason, inventor of countless pseudonyms yet never forgetful of his original Irish name.[28] Born and bred on the Inishowen peninsula yet a traveller through eleven capitals of Europe. Speaker of ten languages yet forever fascinated by his native tongue, whose ancient wisdoms he explored in numerous tracts. Sworn enemy of religious orthodoxy yet obsessed with the intellectual origins of religion. Author of *Christianity not Mysterious*, yet there was rarely a Christian more mysterious. In short, the Philoctetes wound of divided loyalties was as tormented for Toland, the founder of the 'golden age' of Irish philosophy, as for Burke, its ultimate exponent.[29] What is certain is that neither of them enjoyed the luxury of being able to say with Rousseau in *The Confessions*: 'I played no part: I became indeed what I appeared.'[30] Resembling and dissembling, masking and unmasking, the play between reality and appearance, were to remain hallmarks of their Irish psyche.

So where does all this leave Bishop Newman's criterion of what is *typically and traditionally Irish*? From such a viewpoint, Toland – like every other major Irish thinker – is neither typical nor traditional. Certainly Newman's sectarian claim flies in the face of any generous

definition of Irishness that embraces the numerous intellectual traditions of Catholic, Protestant and Dissenter. I would go further than
this, however. I would argue that in a telling if oblique way, John
Toland *is* a typical Irish thinker in that his genius for dual forms of
identity epitomizes a crucial feature of Irish culture, nowhere more
dramatically manifest than in the eighteenth century.

Perhaps, as John Toland reminds us, the truest Irish mind is one
open to a multiplicity of minds? If this be so, then the Irish mind is at
its best when differentiated into diverse minds. Its greatest resource is
the preference for complexity over uniformity. That such a hypothesis challenges the orthodoxy of narrow Irish nationalism, which seeks
to exclude Irish scientists and philosophers from its essentialist cate-
gory of belonging, is undeniable. But that is what the hermeneutic
retrieval of historical and cultural memory is all about – a conflict of
interpretations as to who and what we are. That such self-interpreta-
tion muddies the waters and blurs certain essentialist boundaries
between Irishness and Britishness is a risk worth taking. All reminders
that we are a hybrid, mongrel, mixed-up group of peoples are to be
welcomed, especially at the historical juncture at which we find our-
selves some three centuries after Toland.

These are some of the lessons to be learned from that ambidex-
trous adventurer, John Toland, christened Janus Junius Eoganesius in
the parish of Clonmany, Co. Donegal, in the year 1670, and, to this
day, one of Ireland's finest philosophers.

NOTES

1   Robert Sullivan, *John Toland and the Deist Controversy* (Harvard University Press
     1982), p. 1.
2   *Ibid.*
3   *Ibid.*, p. 40. See also J.G. Simms, 'John Toland (1670-1722), A Donegal Heretic',
     Irish Historical Studies, XVI, 63 (1969), pp. 304-20; P. Des Maizeaux, *A Collection
     of Several Pieces of Mr John Toland* (London 1972); S.H. Daniel, *John Toland: His
     Methods, Manners and Mind* (Kingston and Montreal 1984); Günter Gawlick,
     Introduction to critical bilingual (German-English) edition of *Christianity not
     Mysterious* (F. Frommann Verlag, Stuttgart-Bad Cannstatt 1964), pp. 5-21; L.
     Stephen, *English Thought in the Eighteenth Century*, vols 1 and 2 (Smith and Elder,

London 1881), pp. 4-28; Richard Kearney, 'John Toland: Ancestor of Liberty but Follower of no Man' in *Fortnight* 297 (1993), pp. 2-4; Sean Kearney, 'John Toland, 1670-1722: An Ulster Freethinker' in *The Humanist* 3(6) (1996), pp. 10-14, where the author lays particular emphasis on Toland's cosmopolitan and European-republican thinking; Alan Harrison's biography, *Béal Eiriciúil as Inis Eoghain: John Toland (1670-1722)* (Coiscéim, Dublin 1994), which contributes new information on Toland's life but ultimately concedes that it remains an enigma; and the special Toland issue of *Revue de Synthèse*, vols 2-3, 1995, Paris.

4   David Berman, 'The Irish Counter-Enlightenment' in R. Kearney (ed.), *The Irish Mind* (Wolfhound Press, Dublin 1984), pp. 119-40. See also Berman's other articles, 'John Toland' in G. Stein (ed.), *The Encyclopedia of Unbelief* (New York 1985), pp. 669-70; and 'Disclaimers as Offence Mechanisms in Charles Blount and John Toland' in M. Hunter and D. Wootton (eds), *Atheism from the Reformation to the Enlightenment* (Clarendon Press, Oxford 1992), pp. 255-72.

5   See Sullivan, *op.cit.*, pp. 16, 29.

6   Toland, *An Account of an Irish Manuscript of the Four Gospels in Nazarenus* (second edition, London 1718), p. 2. See A. Harrison's analysis of this document in his article 'John Toland and the Discovery of an Irish Manuscript in Holland', *Irish University Review*, vol. 22, no. 1 (1992), pp. 33-9.

7   *Ibid.*, p. 18.

8   *Ibid.*, p. 23.

9   *Ibid.*, p. 24.

10   *Ibid.*, pp. 32-3.

11   See *Irish Independent* report on Bishop Newman's address, 13 May 1985.

12   D. Berman, 'Irish Philosophy and Ideology', *The Crane Bag* (9)2 (Dublin 1985), p. 159.

13   A. Harrison, 'John Toland and Celtic Studies', in C.G. Byrne, M. Harry and P. O'Siadhall (eds.), *Celtic Languages and Celtic Peoples: Proceedings of the Second North American Congress of Celtic Studies* (Halifax, Nova Scotia 1991). See also A. Harrison, 'John Toland's Celtic Background', in the present volume, for a fuller discussion of the associations of the pseudonym.

14   Quoted in Sullivan, *op.cit.*, pp. 44-5 (p. 5 of Preface to *Christianity not Mysterious*, present edition).

15   *Ibid.*, p. 39.

16   Harrison, 'John Toland and Celtic Studies', p. 562.

17   *Ibid.*, p. 555.

18   Stephen Daniel, 'The Subversive Philosophy of John Toland', in *Irish Writing, Exile and Subversion*, ed. P. Hyland and N. Sammells (Macmillan, London 1992), p. 5. Sean Kearney has much to say about Toland's dissident and iconoclastic free-thinking, particularly as it translates itself into a 'republican' suspicion of inherited authority and hierarchy, political or ecclesiastical. This is epitomized in Toland's support for republican figures like Ludlow, Milton and Harrington and his bold statement in favour of popular sovereignty as embodied in a common-wealth: 'I have always been, now am, and ever shall be persuaded that all sorts of magistrates are made for and by the people and not the people for or by the magistrates ... I am therefore and avowedly a Commonwealthman' (cited in S. Kearney, p. 11).

19   *Ibid.*

20   *Ibid.*

21   Berman, 'The Irish Counter-Enlightenment', p. 137: 'Consider now the birth of Irish philosophy in Toland. He was christened Janus Junius and, appropriately

enough for his background, posed a two-faced threat to the ascendancy: born a Roman Catholic, he became a Dissenter at fifteen. But Toland's most threatening face was shown in *Christianity not Mysterious*. His attack on Christian mysteries and his defence of natural or deistic religion represented a fundamental challenge to the ascendancy establishment. For if there were no Christian mysteries then there could be nothing to separate the rival Christian religions or sects. And then there could be no basis for the Penal Code. The success of deism or natural religion would be fatal to the ascendancy. Deism's belief in a few fundamental religious doctrines and little or no ritual, and its emphasis on morality and toleration, could hardly fail to soften or erode the Penal Code. At any rate, historians have agreed that this is what did happen, but that it happened late in the eighteenth century in Ireland. An attitude of scepticism was fatal to the Penal Code. If we allow that Toland's deistic thinking represented a threat to the material well-being of the ascendancy, then we can explain not only the fury unleashed against him (and Emlym and Clayton) but also the distinctively counter-enlightenment character of most of Irish philosophy.' For further discussion of this rationalist-irrationalist debate in Irish philosophy see also Berman, *George Berkeley* (Oxford University Press 1994); and J.G. Simms's lament that 'the prophet of rationalism [Toland] was without honour in his own country' (*op.cit.*).

22 Berman, 'Irish Philosophy and Ideology', p. 150.
23 Andrew Carpenter (ed.), 'Jonathan Swift (1667-1745)', in *The Field Day Anthology of Irish Writing*, vol. I (Field Day Publications, Derry 1991), pp. 327-94.
24 Thomas Kinsella, *Davis, Mangan, Ferguson? Tradition and the Irish Writer* (Dublin 1969).
25 Berman, 'Irish Philosophy and Ideology', p. 150.
26 Conor Cruise O'Brien, *The Great Melody* (Sinclair-Stevenson, London 1992), p. 83.
27 *Ibid.*
28 Toland was, as mentioned at the outset, probably descended from the Uí Thuathalláin sept of Inishowen in Donegal, a satellite family of the once powerful O'Neills and closely associated with the schools of traditional Irish learning (see Alan Harrison's essay in this volume).
29 And, we might add, for Irish thinkers such as Berkeley and Swift who, as noted, also bear witness to countless divisions of fidelity – between resident country and foreign crown, between sympathy for their dispossessed Catholic compatriots and loyalty to their own class, between colonized nation and colonizing empire, powerlessness and power, poverty and privilege.
30 J.J. Rousseau, *The Confessions* (Penguin 1953), p. 300.

THE IRISH FREETHINKER

David Berman

John Toland was born in County Donegal in 1670. 'Educated from my cradle in the grossest superstition and idolatry', as he says in the Preface to *Christianity not Mysterious* (1696), he threw off Roman Catholicism at the age of fifteen by his 'own reason, and such as made use of theirs'. From his conversion in 1685 – an imprudent time, given the known religious predilections of James II – Toland's life is marked by considerable activity, both external and intellectual.

From 1687 to 1690 he attended the University of Glasgow, where he aligned himself with the Presbyterians. His original conversion was probably to Presbyterianism, and not to Anglicanism as some claim, since in his 1697 *Apology* for himself he speaks of 'the Dissenter's worship [gaining] extraordinarily upon his affections, just as he was newly delivered from [Popery]'. From Glasgow he went to Edinburgh, and received an MA in 1690. He then moved to London, where he so impressed the Dissenters that they sent him to the University of Leyden to 'perfect his education', as his biographer Pierre Des Maizeaux puts it.[1] In Holland he studied under Spanheim and Leclerc and became a latitudinarian.

Benjamin Furley, John Locke's Dutch correspondent, described Toland in 1693 as 'a free-spirited, ingenious man'. This characteristic free-spiritedness brought with it the abiding practical problem of Toland's life; for, continues Furley, 'having once cast off the yoke of spiritual authority ... has rendered it somewhat difficult for him to find a way of subsistence in the world'.[2] Having neither family fortune, as had Anthony Collins, nor an Oxford fellowship, as Matthew Tindal had, Toland was thrown upon the generosity of aristocratic patrons, such as the Duke of Newcastle, Prince Eugene of Savoy, Lords Shaftesbury and Molesworth, and the Earl of Oxford, who employed him variously as an editor, political pamphleteer, biographer, and probably a 'general' spy.

As Toland's background was obscure, so his prospects were generally uncertain, and he was forced to live by his wits and his pen. That he was an incessant writer and controversialist is amply shown in Giancarlo Carabelli's two-volume bibliography of his writings and replies to them; it runs to over five hundred pages, and lists more than a hundred works by or attributed to him.[3] Toland was perhaps the first professional freethinker. Eliminating prejudice and religious intolerance was, by his own account, one of the main aims of his life. Most of his writings, and probably the best of them, are directed against established religion – not, of course, that he ever avowed this. Officially he claimed, as in *Vindicius Liberius* (1702), to be a loyal member of the Church of England, anxious only to eliminate abuses of religion. However, critics such as Samuel Clarke saw him, rightly, as one of Christianity's most powerful enemies.

After leaving Holland, Toland spent some time in Oxford, using its library facilities. From there he moved to London, where early in 1696 he published his most influential work, *Christianity not Mysterious*. This short and forceful book made him notorious; it also began, or helped to initiate, the so-called deist debate. *Christianity not Mysterious* was also the great seminal act in Irish philosophy; indeed, it brought Irish philosophy into being, and continued to haunt it until its demise in the late 1750s. If anyone can be described as the father of Irish philosophy it is Toland, although he was its hated father.[4]

In *Christianity not Mysterious* Toland applied the Lockean theory of meaning to religious mystery, arguing that since mysteries such as the Holy Trinity do not stand for distinct ideas, Christianity must either employ meaningless doctrines, or else be non-mysterious. Thus the Christian mysteries were for Toland as meaningless as 'Blictri'– a traditional nonsense word – because like 'Blictri' they did not stand for any distinct ideas. For, writes Toland, 'if we have no ideas of a thing, it is ... lost labour for us to trouble our selves about it: For what I don't conceive, can no more give me right notions of God, or influence my actions, than a prayer delivered in an unknown Tongue can excite my devotion' (§ 11, ch. 1).

Reason is supreme for Toland. There are no dark spots or mysteries. Toland is a militant rationalist. But he is not a rationalist in the manner of Spinoza or Leibniz. His rationalism is not metaphysical but rather – perhaps following Locke – epistemological. It is not that the world, or existence, has no cognitive dark spots, but that our understanding need have none. We can be absolutely certain about our ideas or how things appear to us. Our assent, and its degrees, are a function of the evidence. And while our understanding does not know all that can be known of what is, we can be certain of what we perceive and conceive. Thus we do not know the real inner nature of bodies, but we do know what we perceive of them – their nominal essence, as Locke called it. Hence there is no reason for scepticism or for regarding our understanding of the world as in any way mysterious. We must give our assent to that which we know; that which we do not know is meaningless and should be of no concern to us. Hence, Toland's epistemological rationalism, as it may be called, vanquishes all mysteries or things above our understanding. His position is based on Locke's theories of meaning and nominal essence and his epistemological standpoint. But the synthesis and the shocking conclusion that Christianity is not mysterious are distinctively Toland's. As Alexander Pope nicely put it in a suppressed couplet from the *Essay on Man*:

> What partly pleases, totally will shock:
> I question much if Toland would be Locke.[5]

The reaction to Toland's book was fierce, and nowhere more so than in Ireland. In 1697 Toland paid a visit to the country of his birth, and within a short time, as we are informed by Locke's Dublin friend, William Molyneux, he had 'raised against him the clamour of all parties'; the clergy, especially, were 'alarmed to a mighty degree against him'.[6] His book was burned by the common hangman, and it was even moved by one member of the Irish House of Commons 'that Mr Toland himself should be burnt'.[7] Yet for all that, his book drew creative replies from Peter Browne (whom Toland drolly claimed to have made a bishop), Edward Synge, and William King.[8]

It is not clear why Toland returned to Ireland. There is some evidence that he expected a political appointment. Possibly he also wished (notwithstanding his protests in his *Apology*) to encourage or even lead a return to the tolerant deistical Christianity of the ancient Irish, the 'Western Latitudinarians', as he described them in his *Nazarenus: or, Jewish, Gentile, and Mahometan Christianity* (1718). Like many Irishmen, Toland looked to the past for inspiration; and he found it in the Gaelic religious life prior to the tenth century. That century brought a 'stupendous change' to the Irish people; they became 'barbarous', Toland argues, from a corrupt brand of Christianity. Before this the 'Irish deny'd all communion with the [Roman] Church'; their 'faith consisted in a right notion of God, and the constant practice of virtue'. These 'Western Latitudinarians', Toland says, had the 'tolerating principle'. Whether or not Toland wished to revive Western Latitudinarianism, he did boast, according to Browne, that he would become 'the *head* of a sect'.[9] But his plans came to nought, and he was forced to flee to England, where he published his *Apology*, which deals with his reception in Dublin and contains much of the meagre information we have on his early life.

Toland's concern for civil liberty, another professed aim, begins to appear in his editions of John Milton's *Works* (1698) and James Harrington's *Oceana* (1700), and in his own *Anglia Libera* (1701), a book that encouraged the British government to send him with a delegation to Hanover, where he is said to have gained the esteem of the future ruling family of England. In 1702 he revisited Hanover and also travelled to Berlin, where he engaged in philosophical discussions with the Queen of Prussia, to whom he addressed his *Letters to Serena* (1704).

The rationalism of *Christianity not Mysterious* is continued in the *Letters to Serena*; but whereas the first book may be described as deistic, the *Letters* are pantheistic. Once again, however, this is not Toland's avowed view. In fact, in the penultimate section of Letter

226

Five, 'Motion Essential to Matter', he expressly repudiates Spinoza's pantheism and affirms that there is an immaterial, presiding intelligence, which is responsible for the formation of plants and animals. But, as F.A. Lange has suggested in his *History of Materialism*, this caveat should be seen as an application of the esoteric/exoteric distinction, a subject Toland discusses at length in *Tetradymus* (1720), where he claims that the distinction is 'as much now in use as ever; tho' the distinction is not so openly and professedly approved as among the ancients'.

That Toland was a pantheist in 1704 – and hence that the penultimate section of 'Motion Essential to Matter' was designed for exoteric use – is borne out by the following: In *Socinianism Truly Stated*, a pamphlet printed in 1705, Toland signs himself 'a Pantheist' (the first recorded use of the term – at least in English); and the logical tendency of the fifth Letter to Serena is toward pantheistic materialism, since allowing motion to be essential to matter undermines the most compelling reason for positing a transcendent cause of the world, as active matter does not need a cause or First Cause. In the exuberant poem *Clito*, first printed in 1700, Toland explicitly develops and takes seriously a pantheistic theory. Moreover, his statements on key doctrines in the *Letters to Serena* are basically the same as those in the poem and in his later *Pantheisticon* (1720; English trans. 1751), where he openly professes pantheism.

The third Letter to Serena is a 'History of the Soul's Immortality', in which Toland argues that the doctrine was invented by Egyptian priests for their own selfish interests. The drift of the Letter is clearly irreligious, but once again in the penultimate section Toland issues a religious caveat. His strategy here bears comparing with that of David Hume, who, in the final paragraphs of his essays 'Of the Immortality of the Soul' and 'Of Miracles', issues a similarly crude religious caveat. A concluding 'Bounceing [sic] compliment', as Toland observes in *Tetradymus*, 'saves all'.

In 1707-9 Toland visited Prague and the Hague, where he published his *Adeisidaemon*, directed against superstition, and *Origines Judaicae*, in which he suggests that Strabo was a sounder historian of the Jews than Moses. Leibniz commented critically on these works in letters to Toland, which were printed in the second volume of *A Collection of Several Pieces of Mr. John Toland* (1726). In addition to writing numerous political pamphlets, such as *Reasons for Naturalizing the Jews* (1714) and *The State Anatomy of Great Britain* (1717), which continue his plea for religious toleration, Toland planned a number of 'grand works', among them a history of the Druids, which appeared in a modest form in his posthumous *Collection*.

Nazarenus is Toland's most significant contribution to biblical scholarship. It looks back to a controversy started by his *Life of John Milton* (1698), where he defended Milton's view that *Eikon Basilike* was not written by Charles I, as claimed, but was a pious fraud composed by Charles's chaplain, Gauden. Toland then suggested that this recent forgery helped to explain the acceptance in earlier times of 'supposititious pieces under the name of Christ and his apostles', a thesis he then defended in *Amyntor* (1699), in which he lists more than seventy spurious Gospels, Epistles, Acts, etc. Toland said that he was not calling into question the canon of the New Testament; but few, if any, took this seriously.[10] In *Nazarenus* he anticipates the so-called 'higher criticism' in placing early Christianity firmly in a Jewish context. He argues that the first Christians – the Nazarenes, Ebionites, or, as he calls them, 'Jewish Christians' – were obliged to keep the Levitical law, and that although true Christianity was perverted by the heathenism of the Gentile Christians (who were not meant to keep the Levitical law), it can be extensively reconstructed from the Gospel of Barnabas.

In 1720 Toland had printed *Pantheisticon*, his most exotic work, which contains material that was taken to be a burlesque of the Christian liturgy, as it was printed in red and black. Whether there were pantheistic societies that used this liturgy, as he suggests, is not known. Some scholars think that his pantheism is closer to that of Giordano Bruno (whose works he translated) than to that of Baruch Spinoza, who is criticized in the fourth of the *Letters to Serena* (although the criticism cannot be taken at face value). In 1720 Toland also published *Tetradymus*, which, apart from the study of the esoteric/exoteric distinction, contains an essay on the murder of Hypatia, a naturalistic account of the pillar of cloud and fire mentioned in the Exodus, and a defence of *Nazarenus*.

Toland's impact on his generation was widespread and varied: few prominent writers of the time were not goaded by him. Toland's cosmopolitan reputation is nicely shown in one of Lady Wortley Montague's letters, where she says that she met a Turkish Effendi in Belgrade, who surprised her by asking whether she had any news of Mr Toland.[11] Yet many of Toland's contemporaries affected a condescending attitude towards him, which has been continued, unjustly, by Leslie Stephen's influential *History of English Thought in the Eighteenth Century* (1876), and more recently by Robert Sullivan in his otherwise useful study *John Toland and the Deist Controversy* (1982). Other commentators rightly feel that, given Toland's undoubted powers, his intellectual contribution might have been more solid and powerful than it was. There is something swashbuckling about Toland's work: he was, as it were, an Irish adventurer in scholarship, the bravest Irish freethinker. And like many adventurers, his last years were bedevilled by financial worries, as a result of losing money in the South Sea scheme, whose secret history he helped to write.[12]

Yet when Toland died on 11 March 1722 he was, according to Des Maizeaux, 'without the least perturbation of mind', having a few days earlier written an epitaph that concludes: 'if you would know more of him Search his Writings'.

NOTES

This is a revised and expanded version of an article on Toland that originally appeared in G. Stein (ed.), *The Encyclopedia of Unbelief* (Buffalo, Prometheus Press, 1985), copyright 1985 by Gordon Stein.

1   John Toland, *A Collection of Several Pieces of Mr John Toland* [...] *with Some Memoirs* [by Pierre Des Maizeaux] *of his Life and Writings* (London 1726), vol. 1.

2   In *The Correspondence of John Locke*, vol. 4 (Oxford 1979), ed. E.S. De Beer, pp. 710-11.

3   Giancarlo Carabelli, *Tolandiana: Materiali Bibliografici per lo Studio dell'Opera e della Fortuna di John Toland (1670-1722)* (1975) and *Errata, Addenda e Indici* (1978).

4   See my 'The Irish Counter-Enlightenment', in R. Kearney (ed.), *The Irish Mind* (Dublin 1985).

5 *The Works of Alexander Pope*, ed. W. Warburton (1757), vol. 3, p. 32.

6 *The Correspondence of John Locke*, vol. 6 (1981), letter of 27 May 1697, p. 132.

7 *An Apology for Mr Toland* (London 1702); p. 121 in the present edition.

8 While George Berkeley, the central figure in Irish philosophy, does not explicitly refer to *Christianity not Mysterious* in any of his extant works, it seems reasonably certain that he is reacting to it in *Alciphron* (1732), Dialogue vii, and in entry 720 of the *Philosophical Commentaries*, where he seems to refer specifically to Toland: 'When I say I will reject all Propositions wherein I know not fully ... This is not to be extended to propositions in the Scripture. ... In this I think an Humble Implicit faith becomes us just ... such as a popish peasant gives to propositions he hears at Mass in Latin. This proud men may call blind, popish, implicit, irrational, for my part I think it more irrational to pretend to dispute at cavil & ridicule holy mysteries i.e. propositions about things out of our reach ...' (see Berkeley, *Philosophical Works*, ed. M.R. Ayers, Everyman, 1989, p. 321).

9 Browne, *Letter in Answer to a Book entitled Christianity not Mysterious* (Dublin 1697), p. 199.

10 See my 'Disclaimers as Offence Mechanisms in Charles Blount and John Toland', in *Atheism and the Enlightenment* (Oxford 1992), ed. M. Hunter and D. Wootton, and 'Hume and Collins: Two Ways of Lying Theologically', in *Aufklärung und Skepsis* (Stuttgart-Bad Cannstatt 1995), ed. L. Kreimendahi.

11 See J. B. Bury, *A History of Freedom of Thought* (1913), p. 134.

12 Toland, *Collection of Several Pieces*, vol. I, p. 404.

CHRISTIANITY NOT MYSTERIOUS
AND THE ENLIGHTENMENT

Philip McGuinness

John Toland is the one who is closest to the type of the Enlightenment philosopher.

Franco Venturi[1]

I

'John Toland, quel homme étrange!' exclaims Paul Hazard in *La Crise de la Conscience Européene*, a magnificent survey of the origins of the Enlightenment.[2] Hazard places Toland in the pantheon of those who founded the Enlightenment, along with Baruch Spinoza (1632-77) and John Locke (1632-1704).[3] He regards Toland as both anticlerical and antireligious. No one could seriously doubt the former charge. Toland reserved much venom for those who practised what he called 'priestcraft': elevating the use of mystery and ritual to preserve their position of privilege.

As for Toland being antireligious, the jury is still out. David Berman believes Toland to have been an atheist.[4] Others offer a markedly different analysis. For example, Silvia Berti suggests that Toland attacked institutional Christianity from a Judaeo-early-Christian standpoint rather than an atheistic one.[5] Justin Champion argues that although Toland and his freethinking contemporaries were certainly challenging Church of England hegemony in the 1690s, they had a vision of a new and reasonable civic religion for a country only recently freed from monarchical and religious absolutism. That is to say, Champion sees Toland as a builder rather than a destroyer.[6]

These problems of interpreting Toland mirror the problems of defining and delimiting the Enlightenment. Until the 1960s, the Enlightenment was viewed in the English-speaking world as principally a French and German and eighteenth-century phenomenon. In the past thirty years, a torrent of scholarship has shown that the roots of the Enlightenment lie in England and Holland. Between 1687 and 1690, three extremely important events delimiting the origins of this movement occurred. Isaac Newton published his *Principia* in 1687. In 1690 John Locke published his *Essay Concerning Human Understanding* (herein *Essay*),[7] and at the Boyne the republican William of Orange defeated the loyal Irish who fought for James II. The defeat of King James was the most decisive political event in Europe between the Polish-Lithuanian defeat of the Turks at the gates of Vienna in 1683 and the French Revolution in 1789. At last a large and powerful European country was in the hands of the Enlightened! The pent-up creative energy that had been stored in the Dutch Republic by such English exiles as Locke, such French Huguenot refugees as Pierre Bayle, and such Dutchmen as Spinoza, was exported to England. It is surely no exaggeration to say that the Enlightenment was brewed in Holland, bottled in England, and uncorked in France and Germany.

What does 'the Enlightenment' mean? Perhaps Immanuel Kant (1724-1804) came closest by describing it in 1784 as 'man's intellectual coming-of-age, emancipating himself from the guardianship of Classical learning and Church theology, learning instead to understand himself and his environment through the use of his own reason'.[8] Thinkers such as Kant and Moses Mendelssohn also saw that the unlimited use of reason by individuals would wreak havoc upon the existing social, religious and political order. This conflict between individuals thinking without limits while belonging to a society embedded (as all societies are) with traditions and authority is well seen in the outrage that greeted the publication of *Christianity not Mysterious*, despite Toland's protestations of loyalty to Protestantism and King William.

A glance at recent books on the Enlightenment suggests that there were as many Enlightenments as there are students of the

Enlightenment.[9] The older 'High Enlightenment' saw the Enlightenment as emanating from a few major figures such as Montesquieu (1689-1755), Voltaire (1694-1778) and Kant. Isaiah Berlin also saw a Counter-Enlightenment, which included Giambattista Vico (1668-1744) and others.[10] Peter Gay regarded the Enlightenment as the Age of Atheism.[11] Margaret Jacob has proposed *two* Enlightenments: a conservative 'Newtonian' Enlightenment and a 'Radical' Enlightenment comprising Pantheists, Freemasons and Republicans.[12] She sees the European Enlightenment as 'a coherent intellectual milieu' originating in 1690s England.[13] Many of the more recent English-language studies on the Enlightenment have re-evaluated Toland's contributions to the Republic of Letters, elevating his importance in the process.[14] Jacob, for instance, regards Toland as a vital link between the late Renaissance and the Enlightenment, citing Toland's crucial part in disseminating and reinvigorating the vitalist and Hermetic ideas of Giordano Bruno (1548-1600).[15] We can visualize the period from the publication of Newton's *Principia* in 1687 to Toland's putting his name to the second edition of *Christianity not Mysterious* in 1696 as a crucial time when the solid foundations for the Age of Reason were laid.

II

And so to *Christianity not Mysterious*. Toland's book owes a great deal to Locke's *Essay*, especially Book IV.[16] As John Biddle has put it, 'the substantive and verbal similarities between the views set forth at the beginning of Toland's book and those of the *Essay* leave no room to doubt his dependence on Locke'.[17] According to Toland, four 'Means of Information' are available: experience of the senses and of the intellect, and human and divine authority. These correspond, respectively, to Locke's categories of sensation, reflection, human testimony and divine revelation. For both philosophers, more credibility is to be placed on discoveries made by either the senses or the intellect than on knowledge from authority.[18] Locke suggests that if a proposition is not contradicted, one can accept it in faith. Toland disagrees.[19] He states that

God ... has endu'd us with the Power *of suspending our Judgments about whatever is uncertain; and of never assenting but to clear Perceptions.*[20]

Locke suggests that knowledge of an object's properties does not imply knowledge of that object's essence. Toland also accepts this:

As we know not all the Properties of things, so we can never conceive the *Essence* of any Substance in the World.[21]

This has dramatic implications for Christianity: we can know God exists through some of His properties, but we can know nothing of His essence. Thus we cannot verify the Trinity.

The intertwining of these Lockean ideas with Toland's refusal to assent 'but to clear perceptions' galvanized the Bishop of Worcester, Edward Stillingfleet, into action. Stillingfleet had not found anything subversive of Church of England doctrines in Locke's *Essay*. By 1696 Stillingfleet was deeply embroiled in the Socinian[22] controversy. He had just completed his *Discourse in Vindication of the Doctrine of the Trinity* when *Christianity not Mysterious* was published.[23] A pamphlet war ensued between Stillingfleet and Locke, with Stillingfleet accusing Locke of paving the way for Toland's attack on Christianity.[24] Locke responded by defending his *Essay* and distancing himself from Toland. Danger lurked around the corner for anyone who loudly proclaimed their heterodoxy: in 1697 Thomas Aikenhead was hanged in Edinburgh for insulting the Trinity and scriptural authority.[25]

It is worth digressing to examine the personal relationship between Locke and Toland. Locke supported the attempted exclusion in 1683 of James (then Duke of York, and later James II) from the succession to the throne. When this attempt failed, Locke left England for Holland. He returned to England with the Princess of Orange (later Queen Mary II) in 1689. While in Holland, Locke stayed in the house of the free-thinking Quaker Benjamin Furly.[26] Furly's house in The Hague was a meeting place for advocates of freethought and reason. If Holland was a small oasis of freedom surrounded by tyranny, perhaps we can see The Hague as a late seventeenth-century version of *Casablanca*, with Furly's house doing a more than passable impersonation of Rick's.

Toland went to Holland in 1692, with the intention of studying in Leyden and Utrecht. On his return to England in 1693, he carried a letter of introduction to Locke from Furly, who obviously thought highly of Toland:

> I find him a freespirited ingenious man; that quitted the Papacy in James's time when all men of no principles were looking towards it; and having now cast off the yoak of Spiritual Authority, that great bugbear, and bane of ingenuity, he could never be persuaded to bow his neck to that yoak again, by whomsoever claymed; this has rendered it somewhat difficult to him, to find a way of subsistence in the world and made him ask my counsel ... I entreat you, sir, to be assistant to him whenever you can; not for my sake but for his own worth.[27]

By May 1694 it was rumoured that Toland was writing a book purporting to show that Christianity had no mysteries. Locke might well have received Toland's manuscript of *Christianity not Mysterious* before April 1695, because he returned 'Mr T.'s Papers' to John Freke, a mutual scholarly acquaintance.[28] Thus Locke was probably aware that Toland was writing a controversial book based on his own epistemology in the *Essay*. It is still uncertain whether Locke's *The Reasonableness of Christianity* (which appeared in August 1695, while Toland's book, though dated 1696, appeared around Christmas 1695) was written in reply to *Christianity not Mysterious*, or whether Toland was responding to Locke's book.[29] Peter Gay sees the publication of the two books as a defining moment in the history of ideas:

> There are moments in intellectual history when a small change in quantity produces a change in quality, when the addition of a new shade to a seemingly continuous spectrum produces a new color. ... nothing could demonstrate more forcibly than these two books the strange illogic that governs the history of ideas. Toland claimed to be a disciple of Locke, and he was right; Locke repudiated Toland, and he too was right ... Locke had tried to prove that Christianity was acceptable to reasonable men; Toland, that what was mysterious and miraculous about Christianity must be discarded – and in that single amendment the essence of revealed, dogmatic religion evaporated.[30]

In *Christianity Not Mysterious* Toland argues that 'nothing should be called a Mystery, because we have not an adequate Idea of all its Properties, nor any at all of its essence'.[31] He then trawls through the New Testament discussing every usage of 'mystery'. He concludes that '*Mystery* in the whole *New Testament* is never put in for *any thing inconceivable in it self*'.[32]

The concluding chapters of *Christianity not Mysterious* trace the history of the use of mystery in Christianity. Toland sees the early Christian Church as propounding the ideal Christianity. As attempts were made to win over converts, the Church compromised with pagan practices in order to attract those who loved ritual and mystery:

Thus lest *Simplicity*, the noblest Ornament of the Truth, should expose it to the Contempt of Unbelievers, *Christianity* was put upon an equal Level with the *Mysteries* of *Ceres*, or the *Orgies of Bacchus*.[33]

As the philosophers and the powerful became Christians, Christianity became debased by 'vain Subtilties', and by those who 'continu'd *Pagans* in their Hearts'. The acceptance of Christianity by Emperor Constantine as the official religion of the Roman Empire marked the destruction of true Christianity. By contrast, the coup d'état that brought William of Orange to the throne of England signalled – for Toland – the beginning of a glorious age of reason, and *Christianity not Mysterious* was meant as a foundation stone for the erection of a concomitant reasonable religion.

Pagan and Christian mysteries have much in common, according to Toland: the same vocabulary; the same preparations to initiations, similarly hidden from the public; and the Fathers of the Church rarely 'speak intelligibly of their *Mysteries* before Unbelievers'. In effect, Toland is saying that where mystery exists in Christianity, it has been placed there by corrupt clerics to preserve their own power.

Christianity not Mysterious sparked off a violent flurry of pamphlets from such eminent churchmen and intellectuals as Thomas Beconsall, Thomas Beverly, Peter Browne, Edmund Elys, Jean Gailhard, Gottfried Wilhelm Leibniz, John Norris, William Payne, Edward Stillingfleet and Edward Synge.[34] *Christianity not Mysterious* was ordered to be burned by the Irish Parliament on 11 September 1697. Toland, ever the serial controversialist, wrote *An Apology for Mr Toland* and *A Defence of Mr Toland* by way of reply. In 1702 he defended himself against the Lower House of Convocation with his *Vindicius Liberius*. Toland's deconstruction of priestcraft and mystery threatened the Church of Ireland ruling class in Ireland, which was foisting a religious *apartheid* state upon Catholics and Presbyterians by means of the Penal Laws. Browne, Synge, William King and George Berkeley all reacted against Toland's promiscuous use of reason. Significantly, all four were clergymen. David Berman has seen their writings as a Counter-Enlightenment movement.[35]

III

Like a pebble splashing into water, *Christianity not Mysterious* created ripples that spread outwards and onwards into the headwaters and backwaters of eighteenth-century Europe. Toland's book has been described as 'the signal gun of the deistic controversy' in England.[36] In brief and simplistic terms, deists maintained that God ordered the world through rational means, and divine interventions such as miracles did not occur. Morality should thus be based on natural law rather than revelation. Deism spread through Europe via coffee-houses and salons. It was influential in freemasonry, and many eighteenth-century republicans such as Maximilien Robespierre, Benjamin Franklin, Thomas Jefferson and Thomas Paine found in deism a vital counterweight to the idea of divine right.[37]

The most representative figure of French Enlightenment deism is Voltaire (1694-1778). Voltaire described Toland as 'a fiery and independent spirit; born into poverty, he could have made his fortune had he been more moderate'.[38] French deism, which had linked up with the writings of Toland and others, was much more aggressive than its English counterpart, giving rise to 'the birth of a race of men whose sole spiritual nourishment was anti-clericalism'.[39] As late as the 1760s, Toland was still being translated and paraphrased in French by Baron d'Holbach, and Montesquieu had read Toland's *Letters to Serena*.[40] Denis Diderot's materialism was influenced by Toland.[41]

Deism and the ideas of the French *philosophes* were very influential in Germany, being deeply embedded in the court of Frederick II.[42] Johann Gottfried Herder was interested in Toland, and saw in him 'the well-read man, the clear head, the impassioned questioner and examiner'.[43] Gotthold Ephraïm Lessing, a leader of the German

Enlightenment (*Aufklärung*), was also a deist but of a very different type from Voltaire. While Voltaire and his ilk arrogantly believed in the uniqueness of their age, Lessing saw the light of enlightenment as

having been shining ... from remotest times. What the present age had done had been to strengthen it .... For the rest it was a fact ... by them established. For Lessing it was a becoming .... For the others it meant the inevitable defeat of metaphysics and religion; for Lessing it was a metaphysic in itself, and almost a religion.[44]

This passage is extremely helpful to us in understanding the concerns of Toland. Toland was obsessed by the history of Christianity because he believed that 'primitive' Christianity was more true to God than the contemporary variants.[45] He saw Moses as a republican and claimed that if Moses had been able to establish a government in Judaea, it would have lasted to eternity.[46]

In Ireland the subversive nature of Toland's ideas called forth theological and philosophical responses well into the eighteenth century. George Berkeley used the emotive theory in his *Alciphron* to argue that such doctrines as the Trinity were both meaningful and mysterious.[47] Edmund Burke was repulsed by deism. He preferred revelation to reason. Both the deists and Rousseau rejected God's will, in his eyes. In short, deists were atheists. Burke rather witheringly dismissed freethinkers in the following terms:

At present they repose in lasting oblivion. Who, born in the last forty years, has read one word of Collins, and Toland ... and that whole race who called themselves Freethinkers?[48]

This is surely unjust to Toland, who was as devoted a supporter of the Glorious Revolution of 1688 as was Burke.

John Toland was influential to some degree in the Scottish Enlightenment. Clandestine debates on religion, politics and philosophy took place in the graduate clubs of Glasgow. Many of the protagonists became members of the professional classes in mid-century Scotland. The rhythm of dissent in Enlightenment Scotland was beaten out by Ulster students who were persecuted at home by the Penal Laws. Radical freethinkers such as Toland were discussed in these debates. Francis Makemie (1658-1708) – a Donegalman and founder of Presbyterianism in the United States – might have known Toland when the latter was a student at Glasgow.[49] George Turnbull taught at Aberdeen University in the 1720s. He tried to engage Toland in correspondence.[50] Francis Hutcheson was influenced by Toland.[51]

Even in Sweden, John Toland's name sent shivers down the Establishment's spine. As late as 1755 some of his writings were still banned, as were the works of other deists. (Hutcheson's books suffered the same fate.) Frängsmyr recounts how one theology student – although describing Toland as 'that most impious philosopher' – was still accused of overemphasizing reason in his dissertation.[52]

IV

Two of this century's most important philosophers have suggested that the Enlightenment is still incomplete.[53] Michel Foucault regarded modernity as an attitude of mind rather than as a period of history, perhaps echoing Lessing in this respect. This attitude involves acceptance of one's own reason rather than someone else's authority. We are linked to the Enlightenment by 'the permanent reactivation' of this attitude, which Kant shared[54] (see earlier quotation). Jürgen Habermas regards the driving force behind the Enlightenment as 'the will to knowledge', and judges this as 'an impulse worthy of preservation'.[55] Both philosophers see enlightenment as being a personal process: the individual decides whether to follow the dictates of his own reason or to cling to hand-me-down solutions and systems. To be liberated or to be incarcerated, this is the choice facing us.

Kant's seminal essay *Was ist Aufklärung?* ends with the exhortation '*Sapere aude*': have the courage to know. John Toland's life can be read with profit as a series of impatient transgressions of cultural and religious barriers. He was truly possessed by the desire to know. The world was quickened into reason, pure reason by pioneers of free enquiry such as Toland. He ranks, with Swift, Berkeley, Burke, Joyce and Beckett as a seminal Irish figure in European culture.

NOTES

1 Franco Venturi, *Utopia and Reform in the Enlightenment* (Cambridge University Press 1971), p. 57.

2 From Paul Hazard, *La Crise de la Conscience Européene 1680-1715* (Librarie Arthème Fayard, Paris 1961 (1935)), p. 135.

3 Hazard says (trans. P.McG.): 'The great war of ideas took place before 1715, even before 1700. The achievements of the Enlightenment pale into insignificance beside the aggressive audacities of the *Tractatus theologico-politicus*, or the awe-inspiring daring of the *Ethics* [both by Spinoza]. Neither Voltaire nor Frederick II of Prussia ever reached the anticlerical and anti-religious frenzy of the likes of Toland; without Locke, d'Alembert would not have written the *Discours prélimi-naire* in the *Encyclopédie*; the fierce philosophical tussles were not more rough than those that engulfed Holland and England' (p. 419).

4 David Berman, 'Disclaimers as Offence Mechanisms in Charles Blount and John Toland', in M. Hunter & D. Wootton (eds), *Atheism from the Reformation to the Enlightenment* (Oxford University Press 1992).

5 Silvia Berti, 'At the Roots of Unbelief', *Journal of the History of Ideas*, 56 (1995), p. 573.

6 Justin Champion, *The Pillars of Priestcraft Shaken: The Church of England and its Enemies, 1660-1730* (Cambridge University Press 1992).

7 Incidentally, Locke was on friendly terms with the Irish politician-philosopher William Molyneux. Molyneux referred to Locke in his *Dioptrica Nova* (1692), and Locke repaid Molyneux in kind by enlarging the second edition of his *Essay* to include a discussion of 'Molyneux's problem': whether a man born blind would be able to distinguish between a sphere and a cube if his sight were restored. (This is discussed in J. R. Milton, 'Locke's Philosophy of Body', in Vere Chappell (ed.), *The Cambridge Companion to Locke* (1994), pp. 19-20. Correspondence between Locke and Molyneux offers interesting insights into the character of Toland, whom both knew. Joep Leerssen writes that 'Molyneux's book [*The Case of Ireland's being Bound*] may count as one of the first instances of the effect of Enlightenment thought on the British political scene'. (See Leerssen's, *Mere Irish and Fíor-Ghael: Studies in the Idea of Irish Nationality, its Development and Literary Expression prior to the Nineteenth Century* (Cork University Press/Field Day, Cork 1996 (1986)), p. 298.

8 As paraphrased by Hugh Dunthorne, *The Enlightenment* (The Historical Association, London, 1991), p. 7.

9 Fuller considerations of the origins and nature of the Enlightenment as well as extensive bibliographies can be found in three relatively short books: Dunthorne, *op. cit.*; Dorinda Outram, *The Enlightenment* (Cambridge University Press 1995); and Roy Porter, *The Enlightenment* (Macmillan, London 1990).

10 See Isaiah Berlin, 'The Counter-Enlightenment', in Henry Hardy (ed.), *Against the Current: Essays in the History of Ideas* (Hogarth Press, London 1979), pp. 1-24.

11 Peter Gay, *The Enlightenment: An Interpretation. Volume I: The Rise of Modern Paganism* (Knopf, New York 1966); and *Volume II: The Science of Freedom* (Knopf, New York 1969).

12 Margaret C. Jacob, *The Radical Enlightenment: Pantheists, Freemasons and Republicans* (George Allen and Unwin, London 1981).
13 *Ibid*, p. 6.
14 See Champion, *op.cit*.; Robert Rees Evans, *Pantheisticon: The Career of John Toland* (Peter Lang, New York 1991); F.H. Heinemann, 'John Toland and the Age of Enlightenment', in *Review of English Studies*, 20(78) (1944), 125-46; Jacob, *op.cit*.; and Porter, *op.cit*.
15 Jacob, *op. cit*., pp. 32-7.
16 Chappell, *op. cit*., p. 20.
17 John C. Biddle, 'Locke's Critique of Innate Principles and Toland's Deism', in *Journal of the History of Ideas*, 37 (1976), p. 419.
18 Robert E. Sullivan, *John Toland and the Deist Controversy: A Study in Adaptations* (Harvard University Press 1982), p.123.
19 Biddle, *op.cit*., n. 41.
20 John Toland, *Christianity not Mysterious* (1696), section 1, chapter 4; p. 29 in the present edition.
21 *Ibid*., section 3, chapter 2; p. 61 in the present edition.
22 Socinianism is the name given to anti-trinitarianism (or unitarianism), which asserts that God is one person, the Father, rather than three persons in one, as the doctrine of the Trinity states. Socinus raised doubts about the divinity of Christ and came into conflict with the teachings of both Catholic and Protestant churches. His Racovian Catechism (1605) stated that Christ was a man who received divine power as a result of his blameless life and miraculous resurrection.
23 Chappell, *op.cit*., p. 22.
24 Biddle, *op.cit*., p. 421.
25 Sullivan, *op.cit*., pp. 10-11. For a comprehensive account of Aikenhead's life and death, see Michael Hunter, '"Aikenhead the Atheist": The Context and Consequences of Articulate Irreligion in the Late Seventeenth Century', in M. Hunter & D. Wootton (eds), *Atheism from the Reformation to the Enlightenment* (Oxford University Press 1992).
26 John Marshall, *John Locke: Resistance, Religion and Responsibility* (Cambridge University Press 1994), p. 331.
27 Furly to Locke, 19 August 1693. MS Locke c.9 f.108 (Lovelace Collection of Locke MSS in the Bodleian Library, Oxford).
28 Summarized from Biddle, *op.cit*., p. 418.
29 See Biddle, *op.cit*., pp. 418-22.
30 Gay, 1966, *op.cit*., p. 327.
31 See *Christianity not Mysterious*, section 3, chapter 4; p. 86 in the present volume.
32 *Ibid*., section 3, chapter 3; p. 73 in the present volume.
33 *Ibid*., section 3, chapter 5; p. 93 in the present volume.
34 A detailed list of pamphlets written against *Christianity not Mysterious* is found in Günther Gawlick (ed.), *John Toland*: Christianity not Mysterious; *Faksimile-Neudruck der Erstausgabe London 1696 mit einer Einleitung von Günther Gawlick und einem textkritischen Anhang*, (Friedrich Frommann Verlag [Günther Holzboog], Stuttgart-Bad Cannstatt 1964), pp. 22-4.
35 See David Berman, 'The Irish Counter-Enlightenment', in Richard Kearney (ed.), *The Irish Mind: Exploring Intellectual Traditions* (Wolfhound Press, Dublin 1985), pp. 119-40.

36   As quoted by Evans, *op.cit.*, p. 5.

37   Roger L. Emerson, 'Deism', in Philip P. Wiener (ed.), *Dictionary of the History of Ideas*, vol. 1 (Scribner's, New York 1973 (1968)), pp. 646-52.

38   'C'était une âme fière et indépendente, né dans la pauvreté il pouvait s'élever à la fortune, s'il avait été plus modéré.' As quoted in Heinemann, *op.cit.*, p. 125.

39   Paul Hazard, *European Thought in the Eighteenth Century: From Montesquieu to Lessing (La Pensée Européene au XVIIIème Siècle: De Montesquieu à Lessing)* (Meridian Books, Cleveland 1963 (1946)), p. 415.

40   Gay, 1966, *op.cit.*, p. 383.

41   See Lester Crocker, 'John Toland et le Materialisme de Diderot', *Revue d'histoire litteraire de la France*, 52 (1953), 289-95.

42   Frank E. Manuel, *The Eighteenth Century Confronts the Gods* (Harvard University Press 1959), p. 284.

43   Gawlick, *op.cit.*, p. 24. See J.G. Herder, *Adrastea IV* 2 (1802), in B. Suphan (ed.), *Sämtliche Werke (Collected Works)*, vol. 24, (1886), pp. 93-4.] Quotation translated by Eugene Dyche, 'The Life and Works and Philosophical relations of John (Janus Junius) Toland 1670-1722' (unpublished Ph.D. thesis, University of Southern California 1944), p. 82; from Herder's *Sammtliche Werke, vol. 25*, 1802 (1803), p. 93.

44   Hazard (1963), p. 433. Incidentally, Peter Gay (1966, p. 380) states that Lessing was impressed with Christob Mylius, a journalist who publicly praised 'the learned Toland'.

45   See the essays by Alan Harrison and Richard Kearney in this volume for discussion of Toland and early Christianity.

46   Discussed in Berti, *op.cit.*, p. 568. See John Toland, *Nazarenus: Jewish, Gentile or Mahometan Christianity, Appendix I* (London 1718), p. 2.

47   David Berman, 'George Berkeley', in Stuart Brown (ed.), *Routledge History of Philosophy, Volume V: British Philosophy and the Age of Enlightenment* (Routledge, London 1996), pp. 139-40

48   Quoted in Ian Harris, 'Rousseau and Burke', in Brown, *op.cit.*, p. 372.

49   Discussed by Dyche, *op.cit.*, p. 81.

50   M.A. Stewart, 'The Scottish Enlightenment', in Brown, *op. cit.*, pp. 276-7.

51   See my 'Looking for a Mainland: John Toland and Irish Politics' in this volume.

52   Tore Frängsmyr, 'The Enlightenment in Sweden', in Roy Porter & Mikulá Teich, *The Enlightenment in National Context* (Cambridge University Press 1981), pp. 167-8.

53   See the discussion in Outram, *op.cit.*, pp 10-13.

54   Michel Foucault, 'What is Enlightenment?', in Paul Rabinow (ed.), *The Foucault Reader* (New York 1984), pp. 45-56.

55   Jürgen Habermas, 'Taking Aim at the Heart of the Present: On Foucault's Lecture on Kant's *What is Enlightenment?*', in D.C. Hoy (ed.), *Foucault: A Critical Reader* (Oxford 1986), pp. 103-19.

JOHN TOLAND'S CELTIC BACKGROUND

Alan Harrison

In a recent book Kenneth Craven has suggested that John Toland's *Christianity not Mysterious* was the real target of Jonathan Swift's *Tale of a Tub*. He goes further and ascribes the volatile nature of the two to their Celtic background.[1] Whatever about Craven's first suggestion (which is argued with fascinating detail and a great deal of passion), the second assertion has no validity at all in the case of Swift but is central to an understanding of John Toland. In this essay I will give a short account of Toland's Gaelic background and attempt to assess his competence and interest in the field of Celtic Studies.

There is not enough space to attempt a full biography of John Toland here,[2] and there are still many gaps in the information we have of the worlds he inhabited at different periods of his life, but I believe it will be worthwhile to follow the lifelong interest he had in his mother tongue and in the cognate Celtic cultures. I will look at his whereabouts during the various periods of his life and give an account of the opportunities he would have had to follow these interests.

Toland was born in a remote part of Ireland, the Inishowen Peninsula, at a time when the country would have been 90 per cent or more Irish-speaking. In the *History of the Druids*, which was published posthumously in 1726, he asserted that he had a special advantage in understanding the origins and ritual of the druids because he was raised in a part of the country where he had not only spoken the language from childhood, but also had managed to learn to read the older forms of it. He claimed that such a competence was necessary to understand the ancient documents written in Irish, and also led to a knowledge of the other Celtic languages. There are two important aspects to this claim. Firstly, it meant that he was by origin one of the 'native Irish' or 'Popish natives' – who at the time of his birth comprised about three quarters of the total population of between one and a half and two million – for whom Irish was their first and, in the case of many, their only language. Secondly, it identifies him as being among to the very few Irish-speakers who acquired a reading and writing competence in their own language. It is practically impossible now to estimate the number of those who were literate in Irish in the second half of the seventeenth century, but it was never a large number, being confined to those born and trained in the schools of traditional learning, which had been the mainstay of Gaelic scholarship for centuries.

The Irish version of his family name is 'Uí Thuathalláin' (the grandsons or descendants of Tuathallán). The name Tuathallán occurs in the Irish annals but it is not possible now to identify the particular individual who gave his name to the family.[3] They were probably subjects of one of the local noble families, the O'Dohertys or the O'Donnells or the O'Neills. There is some evidence that they were traditional historians or bards, and that is the most likely explanation of John Toland's competence in the written language.[4] It is important at this stage to point out that the orthography of Irish was more a reflection of the historical development of the language than a guide to contemporary pronunciation. And if this was true about the contemporary written forms it was even more so in connection with the older forms of Irish, which, as we will see, Toland was able to read. By the time of Toland's birth the traditional schools had nearly disappeared, so the only ones who could read and write were the remnants of the scholarly families or those who had learned from them for interest's sake. We will see later on that the Franciscans in Prague gave Toland a certificate validating his claim to be a member of an ancient and respected Inishowen family. They were prepared to do this despite the fact that he was by this time notorious for his heretical views and well known for his anti-Catholicism. I will anticipate my suggestion here that his knowledge of Irish and the probable connection with a bardic family were enough to overcome the suspicion that his fellow-countrymen would have felt about such a renegade. The surname 'Toland' occurs both in Inishowen to this day and in parts of Co. Mayo where some of the family migrated in the seventeenth century. What all this shows clearly is that in the eighteenth century a man named Toland, from Inishowen, claiming to be an Irish-speaker, was very likely telling the truth. He never sought to hide this aspect of his origins, and as we will see he often tried to capitalize on it. It is also interesting that even in his own day Toland was under some pressure to establish his claim to be a native Irishman, and that he sought and received assistance from Irish Franciscans on the continent to do this.

We are told in some accounts of his life that he was christened a Roman Catholic with the name 'Janus Junius'. Toland himself is the origin of this claim. In *Pantheisticon* the title-page tells us that it was written by 'Janus Junius Eoganensis' ('Janus Junius from Inishowen'), and in an unpublished letter he recounts how the other pupils in school used to laugh at his name so that he adopted the Christian name 'John' to avoid their teasing. There are several reasons why this is probably fiction. As Robert Sullivan has pointed out, it was unlikely that such Christian names would have been allowed in the late-seventeenth-century Catholic church anywhere, let alone in Irish-speaking Ireland. He may, however, have been christened 'Seán Eoghain'. Both of these Christian names occur in Irish and derive from different forms of John. Indeed 'Eoghan' is the name of the eponymous saint for whom Inishowen is named, and naturally many children in that region were (and are) called after him. It should also be noted that Irish uses a patronymic system of naming, even to this day, whereby a child is recognized by his/her father's name rather than (or sometimes as well as) by his/her surname. Thus 'Seán Eoghain' (or 'Eoghan Sheáin') would mean 'John's John'. It might not be too fanciful to suggest that 'Janus Junius' was an elaborate verbal joke on Toland's part, echoing the anglicized version of his name. At the same time it would indicate two important facets of his nature and personality: 'Janus', the two-faced god of the Roman household, indicating his propensity for looking at things in more than one way; and 'Junius', recalling the name of Junius Brutus, reputed founder of the Roman republic, which in terms of Toland's political philosophy was an ideal period. It is surprising how often the name 'Janus Junius' is accepted without any regard to its improbability in the Irish tradition, or to the clear evidence we have of Toland's efforts to hide or otherwise influence the record we have of his life and origins.

After receiving help towards his schooling, probably from a Protestant benefactor, Toland renounced his Catholicism and in 1687 went to Scotland where he continued to study, first at Glasgow University and then at Edinburgh University, where he was awarded the degree of MA. This was a seminal period in the formation of his religious and political views and it also whetted his appetite for controversy and debate. It may also have been during this period that his interest in mysticism and Masonic-type societies was awakened. Despite the lack of real evidence, both of these areas deserve more study, as his actions and ideas from this period seem to have laid a blueprint that he followed for the rest of his life. In this paper I want to draw attention to another aspect of his sojourn in Scotland, namely the cultural connections between Gaelic Ireland and the Highlands and islands of Scotland. In both Glasgow and Edinburgh Toland would have encountered speakers of Scottish Gaelic and others who had an interest in the language for antiquarian purposes. There was, and is, a certain mutual intelligibility between the two languages, both of them being dialects deriving from a common medieval version of Irish. Until the demise of the traditional Gaelic learning in the seventeenth century, the whole area of Ireland and the aforementioned regions of Scotland had constituted a unified cultural entity, with practitioners of the various branches of scholarship moving freely within the whole area. Given his Gaelic background, it is more than likely that Toland met some of those who were to the fore in Gaelic scholarship in Scotland, people like Martin Martin, who wrote an account of the Hebrides, or the Reverend John Beaton, who was one of those who assisted the great Celtic scholar Edward Lhuyd when he visited Scotland.[5] It can certainly be argued that Toland had other fish to fry while he was in

Scotland, and this is true. But given his later tendency to capitalize on anything in his intellectual armoury to advance his name or his causes, he must have used this period to become more acquainted with the Scottish version of his native tongue and to look for manuscript remains there written in the common ancestor to both Irish and Scottish Gaelic.

The first concrete evidence we have of Toland's interest in Celtic studies appears in a letter written by Edward Lhuyd in 1694.[6] Lhuyd was a Welshman born in Oswestry on the English border in 1660. He had come to Oxford in 1682 and remained there until his death in 1709. He worked as an assistant in the Ashmolean museum until 1691, when he was appointed curator. He began a research project on the Celtic countries that was originally planned to embrace many aspects of scholarship from the natural sciences to antiquities. He soon understood the importance of the languages in this research and began by focusing on them. Just before Toland arrived in Oxford, Lhuyd had written:

I am now at some spare hours learning Irish, that I may be the better critic in the British [Welsh and Cornish], in case I should ever be concern'd in the History of Wales. But I can not learn that there is any Dictionary, Vocabulary or Grammar of that language extant, nor one man in this town that can read it; w[hi]ch makes the task somewhat difficult.[7]

Lhuyd must have welcomed the coming of Toland, which he announced in another letter:

One Mr Tholonne [sic] is lately come hither (but as yet I am not acquainted with him) with a design to write an Irish dictionary & a dissertation to prove the Irish a colony of the Gauls.[8]

Toland came to Oxford having spent nearly two years at Leyden, where he worked under the famous classical and biblical scholar Bernhard Spanheim. We have a letter from Toland written at the time in which he declares his intention to use his competence in Hebrew and Irish to gain entrance to the Oxford libraries:

The place is very pleasant, the Colleges are exceeding fine, and I must confess I never saw so much of the air of a University before. I ly under great obligations to the Gentlemen who recommended me, both for the advantageous Character they were pleas'd to bestow upon me, and the suitable reception I met with: Mr CREECH in par-

ticular has been extraordinary civil to me, and did me the honor to recommend three
or four of the most ingenious men in the University to my acquaintance, who accordingly visited me. The like did Dr MILL amd Mr KENNET. This I look upon as very
obliging, and so I take it, but it is very troublesome, and somewhat a la mode de
France: for I am put into as great agonies as Sir LIONEL JENKINS to answer the
expectations of those grand Virtuosos; especially some of their Antiquaries, and
Linguists who saluted me with peals of barbarous sounds and obsolete words, and I in
return spent upon them all my Anglo-Saxon and old British Etymologies; which I
hope gave them abundant satisfaction: Hebrew and Irish, I hope will bear me out for
some weeks, and then I'll be pretty well furnish'd from the Library, into which I was
sworn and admitted yesterday only: for it was not to be done, without being first propos'd in Congregation.[9]

Though it would seem that Toland would have been just the sort of
person who could have helped Lhuyd in his Irish researches, there is
no evidence that he did so. We don't know how well they became
acquainted, but later in *The History of the Druids* Toland claimed that
he had met and discussed his opinions with Lhuyd. In some later letters the Welshman speaks both admiringly and disapprovingly of
Toland – admiring his natural ability but shying away from his arro-
gance and his tendency to involve himself in the hustle and bustle of
religious and political argument, especially in establishments like the
Oxford coffee-houses. In one letter he wrote: '[he is] one of excellent
parts, but as little share as may be of modesty or conscience; and one
of the best scolds I ever met'.[10] One very interesting connection
between the two men is that they both received encouragement from
the Rev. John Mill, an eminent biblical scholar and from 1685 until
his death in 1707 Principal of St Edmund Hall at Oxford University.
At the end of *The History of the Druids* Toland published a
Breton/Latin/Irish dictionary which, he says in a note in Latin, he
had received as a gift from Mill. And in his preface to his Celtic
researches published in his *Archaeologia Britannica* in 1707, Lhuyd
expresses his thanks to Mill in the following words:

And here I ought not to forget that the first helps I even had in the Study of the Irish,
were from the Reverend Dr *John Mill*, Principal of *Edmund-Hall* and Prebendry of
Canterbury, whose Character for promoting any useful studies (tho' they should be of a
Different Nature from those Generally in request) is so well known, that nothing need
be added, unless by a Hand more adequate to the subject.[11]

Lhuyd is, of course, the father of Celtic linguistics, so it is fascinating to see his name connected to Toland regarding comparative methods of studying languages through their mutual connection with John Mill.

It is likely that Toland was already writing *Christianity not Mysterious* while at Oxford. From there he was drawn to London, probably to pursue his connection with John Locke and his circle. Whatever brought him to London at this time, it was to be a place where he spent the greater part of the rest of his life. Not only was he drawn there by his interest in the life of other intellectuals but he also revelled in the political and religious controversies that centred there. For an Irishman interested in Irish and the other Celtic languages there was much to attract him in London in the 1690s and after. There were large numbers of native Irish living there, and there was much Irish and other Celtic material in the libraries of the great collectors. For example, there were manuscripts of Irish origin in Irish and Latin in the Royal Library, the Cottonian Library, the collection of John Bridges, Duke of Chandos, and later on in the Harleian Library. London was also the place where one could lobby for recognition and a government post. Toland came to Ireland after the publication of *Christianity not Mysterious* (published anonymously late in 1695 with a 1696 imprint, and then published under his name in the summer of 1696), hoping to be appointed to a secretaryship under John Methuen, the new Lord Deputy. We know that he came with letters of introduction from Locke and was therefore welcomed by the latter's friend William Molyneux. His admission of the authorship of *Christianity not Mysterious*, combined with his immoderate behaviour, caused both Locke and Molyneux to disown him. Molyneux, of course, was one of the important members of the Dublin Philosophical Society and in this capacity had helped the Irish antiquarian Roderic O'Flaherty. Later, in *The History of the Druids*, Toland showed that he was familiar with O'Flaherty's most famous work, *Ogygia*, and it is possible that he met him as Edward Lhuyd did later when he came to Ireland in 1699. Toland also mentions Irish manuscripts that were in the Library of Trinity College, Dublin, and it is very possible that he would have consulted them himself. However, his notoriety guaranteed that his stay in Ireland would be short-lived and that he would be unable to meet with success in either his ambitions for employment or his desire to pursue his studies there.

From 1701 to 1710 Toland spent long periods on the continent. He was one of those chosen to present and explain the Act of Settlement to Sophia, Electress of Hanover. Not only did he play a major part in this diplomatic work but he made the most of his opportunities to widen his circle of intellectual and political friends, for example Gottfried Leibniz, who was not only a great mathematician but also a keen student of religion and philosophy, and Prince Eugene of Savoy, better known as a soldier, who shared with Toland an interest in esoteric societies, republicanism and books. Again, a fuller study than is possible here of his movements and his relationships during this period is a desideratum in Toland studies. I will confine myself to two events from this phase of his life that throw a light on his lifelong interest in his mother tongue and in all the cognate cultures of the Celtic peoples.

I have already mentioned his encounter with the Irish Franciscans in Prague. The Franciscans are important in seventeenth- and eighteenth-century Irish history for a number of reasons. They were to the fore in bringing Counter-Reformation teaching to Ireland, and by this missionary work they ensured that the Reformation had relatively little impact on the native population. They founded houses all over the continent – Louvain, Salamanca, Padua and Prague – in which young Irish friars were trained in post-Tridentine theology before being sent back to Ireland. And they engaged in the scientific study of the Irish language and its antiquities, and also used the language as a means of instruction. Through the Franciscans and some of the other regular orders for Catholics who remained in Ireland there was a network of international intellectual contacts.[12] So when Toland arrived in Prague in 1708 he sought out the Franciscans and received the following certificate from them (translated from the Latin):

We whose names are below testify in writing that Mr John Toland originates from a good, noble and ancient family, who have lived for many hundreds of years as history and the continuing memory of the kingdom shows, in the peninsula of Inishowen, near Londonderry in Ulster. To affirm this stronger, we, who come from the same country, have written this in our own hands at Prague in Bohemia, on this day 2 January 1708.

> John O'Neill, superior of the Irish College
> Francis O'Devlin, Professor of Theology
> Rudolph O'Neill, Lecturer in Theology. [13]

This certificate is interesting on several counts. If we study the names of the friars, two O'Neills and one O'Devlin, we recognize immediately that they were not merely compatriots in the sense of being Irishmen, but that they probably came from Toland's home territory. They would have been able to speak to each other in Irish, using their local dialect. If Toland's family had been, as I have suggested earlier, one of the exclusive clans of traditional learning, he would have been even more acceptable to the Irish friars, given their scholarly interest in Irish. There is some evidence that Toland repaid the friars' generosity in kind. In a letter of introduction written by him for O'Devlin the same month he wrote:

I have nothing to add to what I did myself the honor to write to your Excellency per post, but that the Countess of STERNBERG is not the only person at Prague to whom I am particularly oblig'd: for the very reverend Father Guardian, and the rest of the worthy members of the Irish Convent, were not more disposed to do me all the good offices of humanity, than they were forward to shew me the most zealous affection of Country-men. Yet I did not receive half that satisfaction from their many civilities to my own person, as I was charm'd with their putting round the Queen's health in full Refectory, where a great many strangers were present, and of several nations as well as different Religions. Nor did I find 'em less easy and well-bred upon this last article than in other things; tho' I frankly told 'em my sentiments, and, perhaps that I might sometimes, to improve by the discourse of ingenious persons, carry matters further than Reason or the Reformation will allow. But I must do that justice to the bearer of this Letter, Father Francis o Devlin, Lector of Divinity, as to own my own self not a little pleased with his courteous behaviour and good literature. The least I cou'd therefore do in return of so much kindness and friendship, was to recommend him, according to his own desire, to a person of your Excellency's extraordinary candor and capacity, not doubting by my own experience, but that during his stay in Vienna, you'll not only favor him with your protection (he being a good Imperialist, without which I wou'd not espouse him) and be ready to forward or countenance him in all lawful occasions. But I am confident his own merit will prevail farther than anything I can say in his behalf. [14]

It is not clear to whom this is addressed but I believe it may have been Prince Eugene or Baron de Hohendorf, the Prince's aide de camp. What I find particularly interesting in these exchanges between Toland and the friars is the fact that the brotherhood of language and common culture overcame the natural antipathy one would expect between the orthodox Catholic clergy and a renegade Catholic.[15] Did Toland request the certificate and how did he use it? He might have simply been proud to have his ancestry authenticated, but it is probable that he asked these friendly compatriots to provide him with it in order to use it as a 'passport' when he visited other centres of Irish clerics.

The second important encounter from this period in Toland's life revolves around an early manuscript of the gospels written in Latin in Ireland about the year 1138 by an Irish monk named Mael Brigte.[16] In the second letter that forms part of his *Nazarenus* Toland announced the discovery in Holland of this manuscript, which is now known as 'The Gospels of Mael Brigte' or 'Harl. 1802'. *Nazarenus* consists of two letters written to an important patron whom Toland calls 'Megaletor'. This name can help us to identify his patron when we add it to circumstantial evidence in the text itself. 'Megaletor' is Greek, probably Homeric in origin, and means 'great-hearted one'. It first occurs in a Toland context in the version of Harrington's *Oceana* edited by Toland in 1700. It seems in this context to refer to the ideal leader in the ideal egalitarian state. So Toland's 'Megaletor' must have been worthy of recognition as a leader and have had an interest in republicanism. The person who best fits this description of Toland's acquaintances in Holland at this time was Prince Eugene of Savoy. He was a patron of learning and an avid book-collector, and he was involved in 'Masonic-type' societies of the kind that would have appealed to Toland.[17] There are many direct and indirect references to Prince Eugene in Toland's correspondence and in the papers he left when he died.[18] The circumstantial evidence in *Nazarenus* is as follows: The first letter addressed to 'Megaletor' informs him of a manuscript written in Italian which purports to be the Gospel of Barnabas, a lost apocryphal book. In the letter Toland, who always had an interest in apocrypha, both authentic and forgeries, raises the possibility of this actually being a book of pseudo-scripture and enters into a discussion of the acceptability of this version of the Christian message for Mohammedans. The actual letter was written in 1709 but in the book, published ten years later, Toland introduces the fact in the preface and in an appendix that this esoteric manuscript is now in the possession of Prince Eugene. It is not hard to see Toland acting in the letter as an agent who has discovered material his rich and powerful patron might buy. It is reasonable to suppose that he was doing the same in the other letter but this time a sale was not made. The relationship between Toland and figures like Prince Eugene and his aide de camp Baron de Hohendorf would be worth following. I have suggested above that the Prince was one of his correspondents when he was in Prague and would have probably recommended Toland to friends of his there and in Vienna.

The second letter, also written in 1708 to 'Megaletor', introduces the Irish manuscript of the Gospels. The text of this manuscript is essentially that of the Vulgate. There are also many notes of commentary, variant readings in Latin, and glosses, colophons and commentaries in Irish. Much of it is hard to decipher. Toland uses this material to launch into a discussion of the original Irish Christianity, which he depicts as a religion free from 'priestcraft' and the supremacy of the Pope. He mentions in this respect the Culdee movement in the early Church in Ireland and Scotland between the eighth and twelfth centuries. If my suggestion that the letters were written to Prince Eugene is right, Toland was using his special knowledge of Irish language and history to present another manuscript dealing with 'original' but unorthodox versions of Christianity in the hope that his patron would buy it.

It appears that this manuscript had been stolen from the Bibliothèque Royale in Paris previously by one Jean Aymon, 'an adventurer and renegade priest'.[19] We are not told how it came to be in Paris, but it could have been brought there by the many Irish, priests and soldiers, who had followed the Stuart king there after the Battle of the Boyne in 1690. Much 'Irish' material in French libraries dates from this migration. The following extract from *Nazarenus* gives a good flavour of the combination of erudition and polemic that was typical of John Toland:

[...] be pleas'd to understand, that in the beginning of the same year, 1709, I discover'd at the Hague *a manuscript of the four Gospels* (then lately brought from France) all written in the Irish characters, which were mistaken for Anglosaxon, but the whole text in the Latin tongue. Some little thing in Irish itself is here and there mixt among the NOTES, which are very numerous, and other passages in the Irish language occur also else-where [...] I have set it in its true light, beyond what most others had an opportunity of doing, the Christianity originally profest in that nation [...] which appears to be extremely different from the religion of the present Irish.[20]

The linguistic notes by Toland are accurate and display a sure familiarity with the subject. But most modern scholars of early Christian Ireland would not be satisfied with his special pleading and his selective use of facts. For example, his thesis about the religion of the Culdee movement is essentially the same as that of James Ussher, the celebrated Archbishop of Armagh, in the seventeenth century. It is a thesis that appealed to Protestant apologists (and still does to their equivalents today) by asserting that there was an original Celtic Christianity which always differed from Roman Catholicism, making it possible to see the Reformation as a return to old values rather than a schism. Toland had advanced the idea that the Christianity represented in this manuscript, especially in the variant readings and in the Irish glosses, allowed freedom of conscience and was itself a form of egalitarian republicanism. There is very little probability that these traits were a reality in monastic Ireland at any time. The important point for us to remember is that Toland's linguistic competence and his scholarship were always part of the intellectual arsenal that he used in his polemic. The polemic was always more important than the scholarship.

What did Toland gain by presenting these manuscripts to his patron? He would have earned the goodwill of both the sellers and buyers and have promoted his reputation as a man well-informed in esoteric material. Prince Eugene might actually have paid him for these services. To say this is not to accuse him of venality; he marshalled his resources cleverly to survive in the lifestyle he had chosen. As I said above, it seems that 'Megaletor' was not interested enough in the 'Gospels of Mael Brigte' to buy them (perhaps, even if he had been willing, Aymon was not an easy person to deal with). When Toland returned to London in 1710 Aymon still had the manuscript. It was finally bought for the Harleian Library by Humfrey Wanley, the librarian, along with other 'stolen' manuscripts, most likely at the instigation of John Toland.[21] Toland is not mentioned in Wanley's correspondence or in his diary in connection with the purchase, but we would not expect him to be because of his notoriety and because he had by this time fallen out with the Harley family. Like many of his other works *Nazarenus* was attacked on many sides, and with typical force he rejected all accusations and was especially contemptuous of any that questioned his mastery of the Gaelic Irish sources.[22]

Nazerenus belongs to both the period when Toland was on the continent and the period when he had returned to London: he wrote the original letters in 1709 and published the book in 1718. After he returned to London in 1710 there is little evidence that he travelled again, though there is a suggestion in *The History of the Druids* that he visited Ireland about the year 1715. We can be sure from his surviving correspondence from that period that his interest in Celtic languages continued to be part of the intellectual ammunition he was prepared to use in the promotion of his ideas and his causes. The publication of two books points to this interest: Dermot O'Connor's translation of Geoffrey Keating's *History of Ireland* (*Foras Feasa ar Éirinn*) and Toland's own *History of the Druids*.

Dermot O'Connor was an Irish scribe and heraldic artist who had been employed in 1720-1 by an Irish cleric, Anthony Raymond, to transcribe, translate and explain material from Irish manuscripts.[23] Raymond, a friend of Jonathan Swift, was Anglican Vicar of Trim, Co. Meath, from 1705 until his untimely death in 1726. He tells us in his papers that he learned Irish in order to carry out his pastoral duties in his parish, which, according to him, although only thirty miles from Dublin, consisted of a population of 750 families of which two thirds knew no English at all. He became interested not only in the vernacular but also in the manuscript remains of the history and literature. He planned to publish a translation of Keating; when he found that deficient he decided to publish a general history that would be basically a corrected version of the Irish original. In order to do this he became acquainted with the native scholars in Dublin and Meath and paid them for their help. O'Connor, it seems, was recommended to him as a scribe and was employed in that capacity for about a year. When they fell out in 1720 O'Connor went to London, where we find him early in 1721 touting for a sponsor for a translation of Keating's history. The book duly appeared in January 1723 and there ensued a fierce controversy about it in the public prints, in pamphlets and in private correspondence. The main attackers of O'Connor and the translation were Raymond and a Thomas O'Sullevane. O'Sullevane had been an associate of Humfrey Wanley, the librarian of the Harleian Library, and it was O'Sullevane who first attacked the translation (before it was published) in the anonymous preface to *The Memoirs of the Marquis of Clanricarde* (1722). Both of these suggested that Toland had assisted in the translation or in its publication and accused him of making suggestions that changed the original in ways that supported his views regarding paganism. If this is the case, which seems likely, we can say that the nature of his tampering with the original text to suit his own interpretations of religion and belief is in keeping with other examples we have of his use of his specialist knowledge of Celtic cultures.

The History of the Druids was first published in the collection of Toland's writings prepared by Pierre Des Maizeaux in 1726, four years after Toland's death. Like *Nazarenus* it consists of letters he had written earlier to one who he hoped would support his efforts to publish this material. Robert Molesworth is the addressee this time; the letters were sent to him in 1718. The correspondence between Toland and Molesworth shows that they had become good friends by this time. When he wrote to Molesworth, Toland himself recalled his discussions long before with Lhuyd:

I presume to acquaint your Lordship with a design, which I form'd several years ago at Oxford, and which I have ever since kept in view [....] 'Tis to write the History of the Druids, containing an account of the ancient Celtic religion and Literature [....] Tho' this be a subject, that will be naturally entertaining to the curious in every place; yet it does more particularly concern the inhabitants of antient Gaul (now France, Flanders, the Alpine regions, and Lombardy), and all of the British Islands, whose antiquities are here partly explain'd and illustrated, partly vindicated and restor'd.[24]

This is evidence of a lifelong interest in the subject and we can safely say that he would have used all opportunities to add to his knowledge and to refine the work he had planned.

Having signalled his intentions in the passage above, Toland proceeds in the letter to establish his own suitability to treat the subject as an Irish-speaker and as one who has constantly pursued study of it. He gives a description of the Celtic languages that could be used today with very little change.[25] He quickly comes to the point of his interest in the Celtic languages, namely to use material in them to elucidate the religious beliefs of the Celts. Once again his scholarship is marshalled in the cause of his attacks on orthodox religion. His interest in the Celts and their religion was not inspired by scholarship alone, but was also affected by his desire to establish the 'truth' of positions he had taken. He saw the druids as the forerunners or exemplars of the priesthood:

In the mean time I do assure you, My Lord, from all authors, that no Heathen Priesthood ever came up to the perfection of the Druidical, which was far more exquisite than any other system; as having been much better calculated to beget ignorance, and an implicit disposition in the people, no less than to procure power and profit to the priests, which is one grand difference between the true worship and the false. This Western Priesthood did infinitely exceed that of ZOROASTER and all the Eastern sacred polity; so that the *History of the Druids*, in short is the *complete History of Priestcraft*, with all its reasons and ressorts.[26]

In another fine passage he anticipates his detractors and cleverly turns their criticism against them:

For true religion does not consist in cunningly devis'd fables, in authority, dominion, or pomp; but in spirit and in truth, in simplicity and social virtue, in a filial love and reverence, not in a servile dread and terror of the Divinity. [...] But if in clearing up antient rites and customs, with the origin and institution of certain religious or civil societies (long since extinct) any communities or orders of men, now in being, should think themselves touched; they ought not to impute it to design in the author, but to the conformity of things, if indeed there be any real resemblance: and in case there be none at all, they should not make people apt to suspect there is, by crying out tho' they are not hurt. I remember, when complaint was made against an honourable person that, in treating of the heathen Priests, he had whipt some Christian Priests on their backs; all the answer he made, was only asking, *What made them get up there?* The benefit of which answer I claim beforehand to myself, without making or needing any other apology.[27]

What an elegant way to say 'If the cap fits wear it'!

In another passage he deals with the assertion that St Patrick had ordered the burning of manuscript books 'stuft with the fables and superstitions of heathen idolatry'.[28] This leads Toland to a discussion of the Christian tendency to persecute authors and burn books that they do not approve of, saying that it is an example that is followed by Christians 'better ... than any precept of the Gospel'. Though he does not spell it out for us in this passage, Toland is likely using this evidence of prejudice by the Irish 'Apostle' to resonate with the unfairness of clerics in his own times who ordered the burning of *Christianity not Mysterious*. Once again the scholarship is subordinate to the polemical message. Any of his contemporaries who read that passage would have made the connection between this argument and the treatment that had been meted out to his most famous book, and they would have understood the subtext of tainting Irish clerics who attacked *Christianity not Mysterious* with the same criticism that St Patrick deserved for his wanton destruction of scholarship and learning.

Apart from what Toland says about the ancient history of Ireland and his use of the Celtic languages, there is another feature in *The History of the Druids* that is interesting and innovative, namely his references to what we can call folk beliefs and customs. These came from his own experiences and memories. Let us look first of all at his account of ritual fires on St John's Eve in June:

Thus I have seen the people running and leaping thro' the St John's fires in Ireland, and not only proud of passing unsing'd: but, as if it were some kind of lustration, thinking themselves in a special manner blest by this ceremony, of whose original nevertheless they were wholly ignorant in their imperfect imitation of it.[29]

Another passage deals with foretelling the future by means of happening to see a raven with a white wing feather. Toland himself points out the illogicality of such a belief, 'But I am persuaded all I did or could say ... would have made little impression on them.' This observation of his countrymen and their nature shows Toland to have been a keen observer and adds considerable charm to his writing.

In conclusion, Toland spent much of his life away from his native land and he was focused on the intellectual and political life of England and Europe. The Irish language was his mother tongue and he showed himself to have been a considerable scholar in it. This itself distinguished him from most Irishmen and gave him access to a brotherhood of learning that had a network in Europe through the Catholic houses belonging to the regular clergy, especially the Franciscans. There is evidence that he capitalized on this connection and he also freely made use of his specialist knowledge of Irish and the Celtic cultures to support his views. His contribution to Celtic studies is not great – not as important as that of Edward Lhuyd, for example. But he was original and innovative for his day and his scholarship does not deserve to be completely forgotten. Nor should his Celtic origins and his polemic use of Celtic material be forgotten by Tolandians.

NOTES

Some of the material in this article has appeared in A. Harrison, 'John Toland (1670-1722) and Celtic Studies' in *Celtic Languages and Celtic Peoples: Proceedings of the Second North American Congress of Celtic Studies* (ed. Byrne, Harry & Ó Siadhail, Halifax, Nova Scotia, 1989), pp. 545-76; and A. Harrison, 'Sur les Origines Celtes de John Toland' *Revue de Synthèse*; 4e S. (Nos. 2-3, avr.-sept., Paris 1995) pp. 345-55.

1   Kenneth Craven, *Jonathan Swift and the Millennium of Madness* (Leyden, New York, Cologne 1992).
2   All the usual sources for Toland's life were consulted for this article. See the general bibliography in this volume.
3   Edward MacLysaght, *The Surnames of Ireland* (Dublin 1978), p. 287.
4   A. Harrison, *Béal Eiriciuil as Inis Eoghain: John Toland (1670-1722)* (Dublin 1994).
5   See the entries for these and other contemporaries in D. Thomson (ed.), *The Companion to Gaelic Scotland* (Oxford, 1983), *passim*.
6   For Lhuyd's life see R. Gunther, *Life and Letters of Edward Lhuyd: Early Science in Oxford*, vol. 14 (Oxford 1945); J.L. Campbell & D. Thomson, *Edward Lhuyd in the Scottish Highlands 1699-1700* (Oxford 1963).
7   Gunther, p. 217.
8   *Ibid.*, p. 249.
9   P. Des Maizeaux (ed.), *A Collection of Several Pieces of Mr. John Toland* (London 1726), vol 1, pp. 292-3.
10 Gunther, p. 278.
11 E. Lhuyd, *Archaeologica Britannica* (Oxford 1707).
12 See the discussion of the Franciscans and Irish scholarship in A. Harrison, *Ag Cruinniú Meaala* (Dublin 1988).
13 The Latin text is quoted by Des Maizeaux (ed.), vol. 1, pp. v-vi.

14 Des Maizeaux (ed.), vol. 2, pp. 381-2.
15 Francis O'Devlin, incidentally, returned to Ireland in 1714 and we find him among the coterie of Irish scribes, writers and scholars working in Dublin in the early eighteenth century. See Harrison (1988) for a discussion of this group.
16 A more detailed account of this episode is given in A. Harrison, 'John Toland and the Discovery of an Irish Manuscript in Holland', *Irish University Review* 22 (1992), pp. 33-9.
17 See a discussion of these movements in M. Jacob, *The Radical Enlightenment: Pantheists, Freemasons and Republicans* (London 1981).
18 For example in 1712 Toland seems to have proposed to Prince Eugene that he sponsor an edition of the works of Cicero. See Des Maizeaux (ed.), vol 1, pp. 231-96.
19 C.E. and R.E. Wright (eds), *The Diary of Humfrey Wanley* (London 1996), p. 439.
20 *Nazarenus*, p. x.
21 P.L. Heyworth, *Letters of Humfrey Wanley* (Oxford, 1989), pp. 265-7, 275-8, 294, 429-30. See also my review of this book in *Eighteenth-Century Ireland* 5 (1990), pp. 196-8.
22 For example in *Magoneutes* which occurs as the fourth part of *Tetradymus* (London, 1720) p. 173.
23 See Harrison (1988), chapter 4, and my forthcoming *The Dean's Friend*, for a discussion of this episode.
24 Des Maizeaux (ed.), vol. 1, p. 4.
25 Des Maizeaux (ed.), vol. 1, pp. 6-7.
26 Des Maizeaux (ed.), vol. 1, p. 8.
27 Des Maizeaux (ed.), vol. 1, pp. 15-16.
28 Des Maizeaux (ed.), vol. 1, pp. 57-8.
29 Des Maizeaux (ed.), vol. 1, p. 79.

LOOKING FOR A MAINLAND:
JOHN TOLAND AND IRISH POLITICS

Philip McGuinness

I

Picture a hillside in Ardagh townland, near Clonmany on the
Inishowen peninsula, about three hundred and fifteen years ago.[1] The
view is magnificent: to the west stand the two great sentinels of
Errigal and Muckish, austerely guarding Gaelic Ireland; to the south
lies Slieve Snaght and beyond are the Laggan lowlands of east
Donegal, prosperous and Presbyterian. The spire of St Columb's
Church of Ireland cathedral in Derry calls the privileged to prayer to
the south-east, while the white cliffs of Islay and the Paps of Jura
beckon us northwards over the sea to Scotland.[2]

On our hill, a boy is reading. Perhaps his cattle are wandering away
and getting lost; it concerns him not, his mind is fixed on the book.
He is absorbing all of its learning like a sponge, preparing for the next
battle with Father Sheils, a local priest who regards him as devilish in
his erudition. For this is *Eóghan na leabhar* (Owen of the books),
known to the world as John Toland.[3] As he trod his path through life
he would call himself many other names, and be called many things
too: atheist, Jesuit and Mahometan Christian to name a few.[4]

This essay is an exploration of the complex relationship between
John Toland and Ireland. Toland was a political animal, born and
bred in the Ulster Plantation and nourished by both the
Cromwellian Commonwealth and the Europe-wide conflict between

Catholic and Protestant states.[5] Ireland was transformed in the last
quarter of the seventeenth century by the struggle between James II
and William of Orange (the politico-religious context of Ireland and
Britain in Toland's early life is discussed below). Toland, in turn,
played a significant role in the world of politics and in the transmission of ideas in the eighteenth century. An inveterate polymath,
Toland moved with ease from the study of the Scriptures to politics
to physics. Few scientists today would regard Toland as a serious scientist, yet his natural philosophical musings remind one of the early
Greek philosopher-scientists. His response to Newton's physics offers
us an interesting example of how science itself is often in thrall to
conservative social forces.[6] And what of Toland the writer? He
writes elegantly, impressing with his erudition and wit and avoiding
vulgar invective. As Catholic, Anglican, Dissenter and freethinker,
Toland fits uncomfortably into any narrow pigeonholing of Irish
writers. This literate servant of the rich and powerful in England is
in every splinter of Stephen Dedalus's cracked looking-glass.

II

The above fragment from Toland's youth may be apocryphal, but the
available evidence strongly points to his birthplace being the townland of Ardagh, near Clonmany.[7] One commentator has suggested
that Toland was of French origins, but it is unlikely he could have
spoken and read Irish and have been aware of the history and pre-
history of Ireland unless he grew up there.[8] It is possible that Toland
was the bastard son of an Irish priest, born to a prostitute.[9]

To anyone interested in antiquity, history and religion, Inishowen
is a fascinating place. The last land bridge between Ireland and
Britain is thought to have run from Inishowen to what is now the
island of Islay.[10] Comprising both the north-eastern arm of County
Donegal and the diocese of Derry, Inishowen was formerly part of
Cenél Eoghain, whereas the remainder of Donegal was Cenél
Conall.[11] Inishowen also marked the westernmost extent of the
always precarious Norman foothold in Ulster.[12] Although part of the

Ulster Plantation, it has always been mainly Catholic. Even today, Inishowen is still replete with paradox: it is the northernmost part of Ireland yet politically in the South, and its largest town – Derry – is cut off from its western hinterland by the border. The Bogside is as much Inishowen as is Malin Head.

As a child, Toland would certainly have been aware of the Grianán of Aileach, the jewel in Inishowen's archaeological crown. The nerve-centre of the northern Uí Néill kingdom before it split into Cenél Eoghain and Cenél Conaill, this magnificent stone fort is an umbilicus into a tribal, druidic Ireland. It is ironic that St Patrick is supposed to have converted and baptized Eoghain in a nearby well: the king of the Uí Néill was a descendant of Niall of the Nine Hostages, reputed abductor of Patrick from the English Lake District. Another of that monarch's lineage was St Colmcille (Columba), founder of the monastic centres of Derry and Iona.

In Toland's parish in the 1670s, the brothers McLaughlin were performing one of the most remarkable religious double acts in Ireland: Daniel was rector in the local Church of Ireland parish whereas Peter was Catholic parish priest![13] The Anglican church was built on the site of a former Columban monastery.[14] It seems that many of the Clonmany Protestants were local conformists: David Dickson reports that 36 per cent of parish clerks and church wardens in Church of Ireland parishes in north Inishowen had local surnames such as McLaughlin and O'Doherty.[15] More recently, John Barkley, a Malin man and Presbyterian minister, humorously describes harmonious integration between Catholic and Presbterian during his childhood in the early years of this century only a few miles away from Toland's birthplace.[16]

Such idyllic ecumenism was not to be found everywhere in Ireland at the time. The seventeenth century in Ireland was one of extreme upheaval. Before the battle of Kinsale in 1601, England's grip on Ulster was minimal. Ulster was *Ultima Thule*: contemporary maps of Ireland are hopelessly inaccurate west of the Bann and north of the drumlin belt from Armagh to Sligo. The departure of the O'Donnell, O'Neill and Maguire chieftains from Ireland in 1607 left much of Ulster rudderless, and England was free to impose its will on the *tabula rasa* that was west and central Ulster. The influx of English and lowland Scots settlers decisively changed and shaped Ulster so that today Ulster sits uneasily with its sister provinces. It is often said in Ulster that 'Protestants got the land and Catholics got the view', creating a wound of fear and loathing that still suppurates. While many of the Irish limped sullenly to the hills (some returning to the fertile valley in 1641 to wreak havoc), others conformed to the new dispensation: Maginnis is as much a northern name today as is McGuinness, for example.

The ethno-political reality of Ulster can be viewed as patchwork-like, with each townland having its own unique narrative of fear and amity. The complex interdigitation of religion, land ownership and outside political pressures has had a varied signature on different areas of Ulster, and would later on give us republicanism from east Ulster Presbyterians, Orangeism from mid-Ulster Episcopalians and Defenderism from south and west Ulster Catholics. Ulster is still both the most Gaelic *and* the most British part of Ireland. The effect of such tensions on an Ulster Catholic of humble – and possibly ille-gitimate – origins searching for advancement may only be guessed at, but the ability of John Toland to be a Dissenter in Scotland, a free-thinker in Holland, a Catholic in Prague and a defender of both the Protestant faith and the Irish Protestant parliament in England must derive at least in part from his early years in Ulster, swimming in the cross-currents of an uneasy plurality of allegiances.

A restless maverick, Toland was both 'a mick on the make' – to extend Roy Foster's memorable phrase back two hundred years – and his own worst enemy. He was a relentless propounder of heterodox religious and political ideas, but this radicalism, coupled with an unwillingness to defer to a person's social status, effectively precluded upward mobility. On the one hand he seems to have used his conver-sion to the Church of Ireland aged fifteen as a means to escape the Romish backwaters of Clonmany.[17] By contrast, a sympathetic con-temporary, Benjamin Furly, saw Toland as conforming to the Anglican Church when it was neither profitable nor popular, the Catholic James II having become King of England in 1685.[18]

John Toland's early studies in Glasgow and Edinburgh were in

theology. Having arrived in Glasgow from Redcastle, he soon dis-
carded any Episcopalian tendencies – having been refused patronage
by the Archbishop of Glasgow – and plunged into the religious ferment brewing on the streets of Glasgow.[19] James II's accession to the
throne had threatened to overturn the Established Church in favour
of the Catholic cause. The spectre of wholesale transfer of land ownership as well as an end to freedom of worship was also anathema to
northern Dissenters who remembered 1641, and this accounts for
their support for Parliament and King William. The university was a
stronghold of the Dissenters, and Toland was granted a certificate
that described him as 'ane true Protestant and loyal subject' as a
reward for joining the Glaswegians on the barricades against the
Jacobite soldiers during the Glorious Revolution of 1688-9.[20]

Meanwhile, the Episcopalians were divided. On the one hand
they felt they had to support the monarchy come what may, but this
was equivalent to sawing away the branch upon which they loftily
presided over Catholic and Dissenter.[21] The situation was resolved by
the arrival of William of Orange and the flight of James to France.[22]
William came from Holland, the most enlightened and tolerant
country in Europe at the time, and Toland supported William as a
harbinger of toleration. (It should be noted in William's favour that
his surrender terms – via Ginkel, another Dutchman – at the Treaty
of Limerick for the Catholics were reasonably magnanimous. It was
the infuriated Protestant Ascendancy[23] that passed the Penal Laws
against both Catholic and Dissenter in Parliament from 1694
onwards.)[24]

John Toland received his MA from Edinburgh University the day
before the Battle of the Boyne.[25] Thus ended his education in the
Celtic kingdoms. He was later to travel south to London and onward
to Oxford and Holland to continue his education, his memory 'fired
with images of bigotry, persecution and student rioting'.[26] He seems
to have returned to Ireland only once afterwards, in 1697, when it is
thought he was hoping for preferment in Dublin governmental circles. After the burning of *Christianity not Mysterious*, he left Ireland
for good, deriving later intellectual sustenance from the libraries and
royal courts of England and mainland Europe.[27]

John Toland's writings were as influential in his day as they are neglected now. He left us what John Hewitt has called 'a now-unfrequented legacy of excellently disputatious prose'.[28] This was not the case in his lifetime: as both a political pamphleteer and a religious polemicist he was read all over Europe, although he made very little money out of his endeavours. John Toland is important in English history as a transmitter of the political ideas of the Commonwealth-Protectorate (1649-60) into the eighteenth century. He is the epitome of the Augustan Age: we find him re-editing the works of Milton, Ludlow and Harrington at the turn of the century.

When we view Toland's life and writings from an Irish perspective, his credentials as a progressive – obvious in England – become ambiguous. Radicalism and Anglicanism were compatible in eighteenth-century England but much less so in Ireland: Dissenters and Catholics alike felt the rigour of the Penal Laws passed by the Episcopalian parliament in Dublin. Toland was both a Protestant and an opponent of privilege based on mystery rather than reason. To evaluate Toland's legacy to Ireland in English political terms will not suffice if we are to fairly assess his contribution. We can see this contribution more clearly if we view him as both Radical and Reactionary; an either-or view of his political outlook will not suffice.

III

Toland was well known among progressives in Dublin. One of the few prominent Episcopalian Irish radicals was Robert Molesworth, who – along with the Quaker William Penn – was probably one of Toland's few lifelong friends. He wrote one of the most important political tracts in his time: *An Account of the State of Denmark* (1694). Through an analysis of absolutism in Denmark, Molesworth attempted to point out the risks to English freedom. Although a supporter of the penal laws, he later became more supportive of the Catholics of Ireland.[29] Molesworth was also on very good terms in later years with Francis Hutcheson (see below), who frequented his home at Swords. He was a patron of Toland, who dedicated his

Account of the Druids (in the 1726 *Collection*) to him. Toland repaid this friendship in typical fashion by publishing correspondence between Molesworth and the third Earl of Shaftesbury in 1720 – against the wishes of Molesworth. (Shaftesbury, a deist, was friendly for a time with Toland, who also surreptitiously published a manuscript by him in 1699.[30] We find Shaftesbury's name on the title page of Hutcheson's *Inquiry*.) Robert Molesworth is a vital link in the transmission of republicanism into Ireland from James Harrington (via Toland) to Francis Hutcheson. Ian McBride calls Molesworth 'the original commonwealthman'.[31]

Toland was also acquainted with William Molyneux when he was in Dublin grubbing around for preferment in 1697. Like Toland, Molyneux knew John Locke and corresponded with him for many years. One such letter contained Molyneux's – and Ireland's – most famous philosophical puzzle, known as Molyneux's problem: would a blind man be able to differentiate between a cube and a sphere by sight alone if his sight was restored, having known them previously by touch? (Molyneux believed he would.) Molyneux also made important contributions to the study of optics in his *Dioptrica Nova* (1692). His *The Case of Ireland's being bound by Acts of Parliament in England stated* (1698) analyzed the effect of English legislation on industry in Ireland. This book, along with Molesworth's *Account* and Toland's *Christianity*, acutely perturbed the edifice of Ascendancy Ireland. It is from one of Molyneux's letters to Locke that we find an all-too-familiar portrait of an indiscreet Toland:

> I do not think His management since he came into this Citty [Dublin] has been so prudent; He has raised against him the Clamours of all Partys; and this not so much by his Difference in Opinion as by his Unseasonable Way of Discoursing, propagating and Maintaining it. Coffee-houses and Publick Tables are not proper Places for serious Discourses relating to the Most Important Truths.[32]

We can dimly perceive the occasional interaction between the ideas of Toland and some of the most influential citizens of the Ulster Enlightenment. John Toland became a Dissenter while studying in Glasgow. He then continued his studies in Edinburgh and Leyden in Holland. These three centres of learning were a sort of theological Ulster Way for many northerners, denied education in

Trinity at the time because of their religious convictions. (Of the twenty-five Presbyterian ministers and probationers involved in the 1798 rebellion whose origins are known, twenty-three were known as *Scotohiberni*, i.e. educated in Scotland.[33]) One such wandering northerner was Rev. Samuel Haliday. He became minister at Belfast First Presbyterian Church at Rosemary Street ('Belfast First') in 1720 but refused to sign the Westminster Confession of Faith. (This had been enacted by the Synod of Ulster in the wake of the Thomas Emlyn affair (see below) as an attempt to signal to Dublin Castle that Presbyterians would not threaten matters of Church and State in Penal Law Ireland.) Haliday's grounds for refusal were that such a document was human-made. His refusal to sign led to a split in Presbyterianism between Subscribing and Non-Subscribing adherents, a split which lasts to this day. Holland was then probably the most liberal country in Europe and the heterodox religious climate of Leyden must have left its mark on both Toland and Haliday.[34]

Haliday was succeeded in Belfast First by Rev. Thomas Drennan (1696-1768), father of William Drennan (1754-1820). We will return to William Drennan later, but at this stage Francis Hutcheson (1694-1746) deserves a mention. Friend of Samuel Haliday, Hutcheson was born in Drumalig, between Carryduff and Temple crossroads in Co. Down, and educated in Glasgow. He achieved fame as professor of Moral Philosophy at Glasgow University and educated many Irish Presbyterians, some of whom played an obstetrical role in both the American War of Independence and in the United Irishmen. (The constitution of the USA was based to a large extent on that of the American Presbyterian Church, founded by the Donegalman Francis Makemmie (1658-1708).) Many Ulstermen signed the Declaration of Independence and Benjamin Franklin had read some of Hutcheson's writings.[35]

Before his time in Glasgow, Francis Hutcheson – with the help of Thomas Drennan – set up an academy in Dublin in the 1720s, whose pupils included William Robertson, the first Unitarian.[36] Most of Hutcheson's important political and philosophical works were written in Dublin.[37] It was Hutcheson who first wrote about the function of government as providing the greatest happiness for the greater number, anticipating Jeremy Bentham and John Stuart Mill. Hutcheson was strongly influenced by James Harrington (1611-77), endorsing Harrington's ideas in his lectures at Glasgow. He sub-scribed to the Dublin reprint in 1737 by James Arbuckle and William Bruce of Toland's edition of Harrington's *Oceana*. One assumes that Hutcheson supported the publication of Toland's ver-sion of Harrington's works because he felt that Toland was also important enough to be published. When Hutcheson writes in his *Inquiry Concerning the Original of our Ideas of Virtue or Moral Good* that 'All strict attachment to party, sects, factions, have but an imperfect species of beauty', we surely see the influence of Toland.[38]

If Belfast First was a vital (Scottish) component of the roots of Irish republicanism, then Dublin's Wood Street Presbyterian congre-gation was also important in introducing English republican and the-ological ideas to Ireland. This church had actually been set up by Cromwell in the 1640s. 'The Presbyterian Pope', Dr Daniel Williams, who had been minister at Wood Street, helped raise money for Toland to study in Holland in the early 1690s.[39] One of Wood Street's earlier ministers, Thomas Emlyn, was jailed for non-belief in the Trinity in 1702. He might well have been at the receiv-ing end of the backlash that followed the publication of *Christianity not Mysterious* six years earlier.[40]

In 1720 Toland privately published *Pantheisticon*. Written in Latin, *Pantheisticon* can be viewed as an attempt to create a liturgy for a pantheist sect. Some contemporaries regarded it as lampooning the Anglican liturgy; others felt that Toland had finally realized that rit-ual – and, therefore, liturgy and a priest caste – was necessary for a sect. (He had earlier repudiated his youthful outpourings on religion as seen in *Christianity not Mysterious* at the turn of the century, regarding them as his 'juvenile thots'.[41]) It is not the sort of book that one would expect respectable citizens and churchgoers to have in their possession, unless that church itself was a radical one. It is sur-prising, then, to find not only that the names of two of Belfast's most respectable inhabitants – Alexander Haliday (1728-1802) and William Bruce (1757-1841) (nephew of the publisher William Bruce) – are inscribed as owners on a copy of it, but that this same

copy of *Pantheisticon* had actually been the property of a church –
Belfast First. The ownership of such a book speaks volumes for the
spirit of tolerance that was found in some Presbyterian churches in
late eighteenth-century Ireland.[42] (It would be of value to know
whether Toland's writings were disseminated in the Reading
Societies that were found over much of Presbyterian Ulster.[43])

Alexander Haliday was, of course, the son of the above-mentioned
Samuel Haliday. He trained as a doctor in Glasgow and corresponded
with both Edmund Burke (1729-97) and Richard Brinsley Sheridan
(1751-1816) about a play – in the Ciceronian style – that he had
written; both found it to be an excellent piece of writing. (Toland was
also a great fan of Cicero, translating some of his political writings –
see Bibliography.) Alex Haliday was a close friend of the 1st Earl of
Charlemont (1728-99), organizer of the 1782 Dungannon
Convention and a General in the Irish Volunteers. In 1770 Haliday
reputedly saved Belfast from being burned by mediating between the
Hearts of Steel (the Co. Antrim tenantry) and the militia.[44]

Dr William Bruce, the other name in the Belfast First copy of
Pantheisticon, was minister at Belfast First from 1790 to 1831. He also
set up the Belfast Royal Academy. Born in Dublin and – unusually for
a Dissenter – educated in Trinity, his father Dr Samuel Bruce was
minister at Wood Street. A member of the Lisburn True Blues
Volunteers, in later years he was a moderate on the Belfast political
scene and he wrote *Belfast Politics* with Henry Joy (which was dedicated to Alex Haliday). Bruce was related to both Hutcheson and Henry
Joy, whose father Francis (1697-1790) founded the *Belfast Newsletter*,
the oldest newspaper in the British Isles.[45] Commander of the Belfast
Volunteers, Henry Joy was also related to Henry Joy McCracken
(1767-98) who led the Antrim United Irishmen in 1798.

Another eighteenth-century radical who was familiar with
Toland's writings was Alexander Stewart (1700-81). Born near
Moville, he represented Derry in the Irish House of Commons, and
was an elder in the Belfast First congregation. He built up a fine col-
lection of radical books in his lifetime, including such authors as
Bayle, Cicero, Emlyn, Harrington (*Oceana*), Hobbes, Hutcheson,
Locke, Milton, Molesworth, Shaftesbury, Voltaire and Toland.[46]

Stewart was the executor of the will of the elder William Bruce, and he erected a monument over the grave of Hutcheson.[47] He was the grandfather of Lord Castlereagh (1769-1822). Castlereagh was a relentless pursuer of the 1798 rebels in Co. Down, but he also supported both the enfranchisement of Catholics and state payment of priests. From his estate at Mount Stewart on the shores of Strangford Lough, Castlereagh planned both the Act of Union between Britain and Ireland and the Congress of Vienna. The fortunes of the Stewart family are illustrative of the changing political allegiance of many Presbyterians in Ulster in the eighteenth century. The Stewarts became members of the Established Church. Alexander's son, Robert (father of Castlereagh), was a champion of the radicals in his youth but later supported the government.[48]

Any discussion of the Ulster Enlightenment is incomplete without mentioning William Drennan. Doctor and poet and a friend to both Alex Haliday and William Bruce, Drennan is remembered for his description of Ireland as 'The Emerald Isle'. Although Theobald Wolfe Tone gave the Society of United Irishmen its title, it was Drennan who first proposed such a society.[49] The late eighteenth century also saw the flowering of Freemasonry in Ireland.[50] Drennan adopted the language of Freemasonry in his writings in 1784, implying that he might well have joined the Craft.[51] Indeed, his preferred name for the United Irishmen – The Irish Brotherhood – is redolent of Masonic language. A Masonic lodge in Penal Law Ireland was practically the only institution where Catholic and Protestant could meet as equals. Many of the heroes of the Enlightenment – Voltaire, Goethe, Mozart and Benjamin Franklin – were Masons, as were many Irish radicals. A.T.Q. Stewart has said:

Once the fact of Masonic involvement in the Volunteer movement is realised, its extent becomes staggering .... It explains what has always been seen as something of a mystery about Irish politics in the 1780s, why the old asperities between Protestants and Catholics seemed suddenly to melt, and both persuasions, especially in the North of Ireland, seemed eager to create a new Irish nationality, one more liberal than the 'Protestant nation' or a hypothetical theocracy dominated by the Catholic Church.[52]

Margaret Jacob has argued that John Toland is a key figure in the spread of radical Masonry in the early eighteenth century. She suggests that a document in Toland's manuscripts outlining a meeting of pantheists (The Knights of Jubilation) in the Hague in 1710 was actually describing a meeting of a Masonic lodge.[53] There are many similarities between the development of Freemasonry and societies of pantheists in England and Holland.[54] It is possible that Toland's *Pantheisticon* was the tract for some sort of Masonic ritual: the liturgy in this book is of a civic religion. Viewed as a Masonic tract, it is not surprising to find *Pantheisticon* in the possession of some of Belfast's leading citizens.

The Age of Reason found many northern Dissenters ready to unite under 'the common name of Irishman' with their Catholic and Protestant fellow-islanders. Along with the peregrinations of the early Christian monk-missionaries across Europe, the Ulster Enlightenment is the greatest achievement of the Irish intellect, a monument to individualism and inclusiveness. Terry Eagleton has described its legacy thus:

> ... the richest radical culture which Ireland has ever known. Other oppositional currents in the country – O'Connell, Sinn Féin – may have proved more politically effective; but none can remotely rival the philosophical ambitiousness and intellectual fertility of this extraordinary period, with its complex blending of Lockeian rationalism, classical republicanism, radical Presbyterianism and political libertarianism. Its preoccupations range from the soul to the state, from sentiment to the nature of civil society, from the springs of consciousness to the sources of political authority. Contemporary Ireland, both north and south of the border, stands under the judgement of this precious heritage, and has yet to catch up with its past.[55]

The above quotation reads like a résumé of Toland's literary output. John Toland is a vital link in the transmission and development of ideas that contributed to the Enlightenment all over Europe. He was admired by Voltaire, and debated with Leibniz, Locke and Bayle. He has been described as 'a true Enlightenment thinker', 'the initial Freethinker in England', 'a major intellectual and political bridge ... from the seventeenth to the eighteenth century' and 'a great European ... astonishingly modern'.[56] It is fitting that Toland is known as the 'father of Irish philosophy'.[57]

IV

A hallmark of Toland's writing is his sympathy for minorities. While living in London and Holland, he mixed freely with French Huguenot refugees.[58] (Many of these Huguenots had left France after the revocation in 1685 by Louis XIV of the Edict of Nantes, which had guaranteed religious toleration for French Protestants.) Toland was voluble in his philo-semitism: in his *Reasons for Naturalizing the Jews* (1714) he argued that encouraging Jewish immigration into Great Britain and Ireland would harness their creative and entrepreneurial skills for the good of the entire country. This attitude was astoundingly tolerant for its day. Toland may well have been influenced by *Oceana*: Harrington's 1656 book urged a Jewish plantation in Ireland in an attempt to improve the country's economic wellbeing.[59] Judaism was regarded by Toland as being closer to early Christianity – which Toland regarded as more pure – than its contemporary counterpart.[60] Silvia Berti suggests that Toland's criticism of Christianity owes more to 'a rationalistic and scathing utilization of the polemic spirit of Judaism' than to 'a total, atheistic condemnation of the Judeo-Christian tradition'.[61] What the Huguenots and the Jews shared, in Toland's eyes, was a freedom from priestcraft and a consequent intimacy with rational progress. Toland renounced Catholicism and became a Protestant in order to position himself at the vanguard of this counter-movement. This conversion was seen in another light by one of the few Irish commentators on Toland – William Doherty – who regarded Toland as 'joining the English Party'.[62] This also appears correct: Toland wanted to become more English than the English themselves. His political preoccupations centre around one big issue: how to preserve Protestant hegemony in England and keep the unholy threat from both France and Rome at bay. Many of his publications reflect this concern in their titles, for example: *The Jacobitism, Perjury, And Popery Of High-Church Priests* (1710), *An Appeal To Honest People Against Wicked Priests* (1713) and *The Probability of the Speedy and Final Destruction of the Pope* (1718).

The position of Huguenots and Jews in Ireland was fundamentally different than in England. The (Protestant) minority in Ireland held the reins of power over the impoverished Catholic majority. Toland saw this minority as being the only hope for progress in Ireland. In a 1720 pamphlet entitled *Reasons ... Why the Bill ... Entitul'd, 'An Act for the better Securing the Dependency of the Kingdom of Ireland upon the Crown of Great-Britain' Shou'd not Pass into a Law*, Toland opposed any attempt by London to dilute the power of the Irish Parliament:

... attempts have been lately made to shake off the subjection of Ireland into, and dependance upon, the Imperial Crown of this Realm, which will be of dangerous consequence to Great-Britain and Ireland .... The Protestant inhabitants of Ireland abhorr from their hearts the thoughts of such Attempts. They count it their chief happiness, to be inseparably united and annex'd to the Crown of England, now of Great-Britain.[63]

... whereas the People of Ireland were wont to have justice near at hand and even at their own doors, they must hereafter ... be forc'd, to their unspeakable loss of time and expense, besides the danger of the Seas, to come over hither, whenever they conceive themselves aggrieved by the Chancery there. This wou'd soon impoverish the richer part of that Nation, while the poorer sort must be totally depriv'd of Justice, as not being able to come and sue for it in England. ... Ireland wou'd thus become ... the most deplorable scene of wrongs in the Universe.[64]

In opposing the shackling of a Protestant parliament for a Protestant people, Toland is anticipating the stances taken by both the Orange Order towards the Act of Union in 1801 and the Unionist Party towards the abolition of Stormont in 1972. His usage of 'the People of Ireland' excludes Catholics; they are merely referred to as the 'native Irish' elsewhere (see below). Few – if any – commentators have discussed the significance of *Reasons* in Toland's political thought. Caroline Robbins, for example, suggests that Toland 'supported the claims of the Irish to have laws of their own devising',[65] but she does not discuss *Reasons* in her book *The Eighteenth-Century Commonwealthman* (1959), an influential survey of the origins of republican thought in England, Ireland, Scotland and America. This overlooking of what is perceived to be one of Toland's minor works has led to erroneous interpretations of Toland's views on Ireland.

The following quotation from *Reasons* firmly places Toland's sentiments with the post-1690 elite in Ireland:

Nothing shou'd be attempted that might bring about the possibility of a Union of civil interests between the Protestants and Papists of Ireland, whose antipathies and animosities all sound Politicians will ever labor to keep alive.[66]

Its tone suggests that Toland was only too happy to see the fomenting of sectarian hatred in Ireland as a strategy for maintaining Protestant hegemony. *Reasons* was issued during the passing of the Penal Laws, which – despite Toland's beliefs in toleration – he avoids discussing. He may be making an oblique reference to religious persecution in Ireland when he takes on the pseudonym 'Patricola' in *The State-Anatomy of Great Britain* (1717): Patricola can be translated as 'hedge-priest' (an oblique reference to the workings of the Penal Laws against priests in Ireland?) or, perhaps, 'lay-priest' (Toland as head of a pantheist sect?).[67]

It is instructive to compare a sample of the political writing on Ireland that emanated from radical England in the seventeenth century in order to place Toland's supposed radicalism towards Ireland in perspective. Consider William Walwyn's 1649 address to the Cromwellian troops about to depart for their Irish tour of duty:

It has come to a pretty pass with most of your great officers. They would have you to obey their commands, thought to the killing and slaying of men, without asking a reason; and as the church of Rome holds the poor ignorant Papists in blind obedience … so would they have it with you, to be led this way and that way … into Ireland …. [But] he that runs to kill men merely upon authority or others' judgements or for money is condemned of himself in his conscience as a murderer, be the cause what it will, and first or last shall not escape the judgements of God.[68]

Nowhere does Toland emulate the fiery rhetoric of this English Leveller on English policy in Ireland. Toland may have actually been a belated supporter of Cromwell's policy in Ireland: Pierre Des Maizeaux – compiler of Toland's *Collection* – mentions stories about Toland that suggest that Cromwell was one of the teenage Toland's heroes.[69] Des Maizeaux calls this 'a ridiculous Story', but given Toland's admiration for Commonwealthmen such as Milton, Harrington and Ludlow it may not be a completely outlandish one. It is difficult to imagine an Irish Catholic – born only twenty-one years after the slaughter of Drogheda – supporting the man responsible for that massacre unless that person had an overwhelming sense of loathing for his own background and culture.

John Toland may have been the first person to use the terms 'West Britain' and 'North Britain' to describe Ireland and Scotland, respectively. In 1701, six years before the Act of Union joining Scotland to England and Wales, he suggests in his *Limitations for the Next Foreign Successor, Or A New Saxon Race* that:

... the Names of *English*, *Scots*, and *Irish* should be diffused, and that the distinction should be South, North, and West Britains.[70]

Later on he says:

As for Ireland in particular ... it's unreasonable that our own Offspring who conquered that Country, or our Children or Brethren who from time to time transplant themselves thither, should be looked upon to be in the same condition with the native Irish whom they conquered, and lose the Birthright of *Englishmen* ...

Again we see a refusal to even contemplate the idea of the 'native Irish' (Catholics) as equal to members of the ruling class. This quotation is extremely revealing of Toland. He has hidden his 'mere Irish' origins and considers himself to be English ('our own Offspring'). His 'People of Ireland' have the 'Birthright of *Englishmen*'. There is a question-mark over Toland's familial origins, and his complete identification with England may be an attempt to cover up his chequered origins. If so, this dissimulation was not entirely successful: he was accused by Swift, among others, of being both a priest and the son of a priest.[71]

In his haste to cover his familial tracks with a veneer of acceptability as judged by English society, Toland gives us an insight into the meaning of Britishness that is still relevant today. In the first quotation above from *Limitations* he is quick to suggest the subordination of Englishness, Irishness and Scottishness into Britishness, but then his suggestion that the colonizers should keep their 'Birthright of *Englishmen*' gives the game away. I suggest that Toland saw Britishness *in Ireland* as an identity that someone from the periphery could aspire to, but those at the centre – the Episcopalians of Ireland – had no incentive to dilute their English background with the possessors of wild shamrock manners.[72] Thus the question of Britishness did not arise for the Ascendancy: this ruling class are often called the *Anglo*-Irish, and rarely – if ever – known as the *Brito*-Irish.[73] Unfortunately for them, the Irish Episcopalians were perceived *from England* as also being at the periphery. As the eighteenth century progressed, the imbalance in relations between Ireland and England seems to have increased anti-English sentiment among the Ascendancy. Some re-evaluated their identity, accepting this marginality and admitting a ray of greenish light into the big house.[74] Indeed, we find today that the two communities in Northern Ireland seem at times to be united only in their distrust of perfidious Albion.

Many of Toland's writings were published before the Act of Union in 1707 when British nationality was invented. In his concerns over the military and religious threat from France and Rome, and his interest in English commerce and trading – as seen in his 1696 translation of Davanzati's *A Discourse upon Coins*, and his own *Propositions for uniting the two East-India Companies* (1701) – Toland anticipates the concerns of this new nation. In her marvellous book *Britons: Forging the Nation 1707-1837*, Linda Colley suggests that the roots of Britishness lie in Protestantism, empire and war:

> It was their common investment in Protestantism that first allowed the English, the Welsh and the Scots to become fused together, and to remain so, despite their many cultural divergences. And it was Protestantism that helped to make Britain's successive wars against France after 1689 so significant in terms of national formation. A powerful and persistently threatening France became the haunting embodiment of that Catholic Other which Britons had been taught to fear since the Reformation in the sixteenth century. Confronting it encouraged them to bury their internal differences in the struggle for survival, victory and booty.[75]

Protestantism, by doing away with papish superstition, guaranteed more civic freedoms to Britons (apart from Catholics in Britain and Ireland) than to peoples elsewhere. Moreover, the supremacy of a Protestant state translated – in Toland's eyes – into deserved world hegemony:

> … the whole Variety of things wherewith the Earth is stock't had bin principally design'd for our profit or delight, and no more of 'em allowed to the rest of Men, than what they must necessarily use as our Purveyors or Labourers. [London is] a new Rome in the West [deserving] like the old one, to become the Sovereign Mistress of the Universe.[76]

One would be hard pressed to disentangle the strands of Britishness and imperialism in Toland's world-view.

The other element of Colley's Holy Trinity of British identity is war. Britain and France were at war for sixty-four of the one hundred and twenty-seven years between 1689 and 1815. France was adept at using the Jacobite threat against Britain, for example in 1690 and 1745. John Toland was not behind the door when it came to virulent anti-French pamphleteering: see *Dunkirk or Dover* (1713), or his 1707 translation of Schiner's *A Phillipick Oration to Incite the English against the French*. Toland, by his enthusiastic embrace of Protestantism, Francophobia and proto-imperialism, is one of the earliest persons to see himself as completely British.

Despite the hostile reception accorded to *Christianity not Mysterious* in 1696-7, Toland managed to write his way back into royal favour, even meeting King William. In 1701 he was entrusted to carry the Act of Succession to Hanover. In that Act, the throne was to pass to Sophia, wife of the ruler (or Elector) of Hanover and a Protestant. Her son became George I, since Sophia died before Queen Anne. The Act of Succession is expressly anti-Catholic:

all ... persons that were or afterwards should be reconciled to or shall communion with the see or church of Rome or should professe the popish religion or marry a papist should be made ... forever uncapable to inherit possess or enjoy the crown and government of this realm.

This law is still in force today. In attempting to understand why such a law was necessary we must consider the strategic position of England in the early eighteenth century. England at this time was much weaker than in the nineteenth century, and was surrounded by Catholic Ireland, Spain and France. This fact, combined with the fear of the Catholic Stuarts someday reclaiming the Scottish monarchy, caused the Act of Union between England and Scotland to be forced through in 1707.

John Toland's interest in early Christian Ireland parallels his interest in Judaism: both helped him argue that corrupt priestcraft had polluted the contemporary Christian Church. The following quotations from his *Nazarenus* (1718) give a flavour of this polemic use of the past to serve his present purpose:

... the genuin Christianity of the ancient Irish: for the Irish and the albanian Scots, with the Western Britons, were the last of the European nations that submitted to the hierarchy, ceremonies, and doctrine of the Roman Church; tho they became the most eager sticklers for it, with all its superstitions, in after times of ignorance. ... And so farr, in effect, were they from acknowledging any subjection to the Church of Rome, or implicitly conforming to its Decrees; that, on the contrary, they did in very many things strenuously oppose it ... the Religion which the aboriginal Irish profest, especially before the ninth century, was not that, wherof the bulk of their posterity are so fond at this day ... [Their] faith consisted in a right notion of God, and the constant practice of virtue: for the enormities which render'd 'em afterwards infamous, if not literally barbarous (begging my country's pardon for the expression) ensu'd upon their changeing the purity and simplicity of their faith, into gross Idolatry and endless Superstitions .... They did not in the least acknowledge the headship of the Roman Church .... Neither did they own the supremacy of any other Church on earth, managing all their affairs, both civil and religious, within themselves .... Yet so many things remain'd among the Irish ... opposite to the Religion and Government of Rome (in spite of all the ignorance, bigottry, and barbarity, to which by that time this same Rome had reduced them) that Pope ADRIAN the fourth, in his *brief* to King HENRY the second in the year 1154, for encouraging him to undertake that conquest, alleges for his motives in so doing; *the enlarging the bounds of the Church* (which is a very singular expression, if Ireland had been of his Church before) *the declaring the truth of the Christian faith to those unlearned and rude people*[77] ... which were the real Heretics (according to the bad sense of the word) the Romanists or the Irish? or whether any thing can be more preposterous in these last, than to be so mighty fond of the Pope, who together with their Clergy, betray'd the country to the English?[78]

Clearly, Toland sees Ireland's first Christians as Protestants. One senses a profound admiration for the early Irish Christians. The above passage is typical of Toland's writing. He is a revisionist *par excellence*, harnessing the past in a polemical way to prove his thesis. In this sense he is a very Irish writer.

V

John Toland has set us what seems an unresolvable paradox: the profound truths of toleration and reason embedded in his writing have informed some of the most radical thinkers of eighteenth-century Ireland and Europe, yet he also appears as a leading strategist of Protestant sectarian politics in Ireland. It is as if Toland were having his cake in Garvaghy and eating it in Drumcree. Can we reconcile our picture of Toland as both Radical and Reactionary in Ireland?

That Toland can belong in both categories illustrates the complexity both of Toland's thought and of the political situation then and now. The resolution of this apparent conundrum lies also in Toland's complex background. He was never perceived to be firmly in one camp during his lifetime. This is evident from the reaction to *Christianity not Mysterious* in Ireland. Toland wanted to belong to the Irish ruling class: he hoped to gain preferment in Dublin. After *Christianity not Mysterious* the Dublin establishment wanted nothing to do with him. This proponent of tolerance completely misread the way his book would be received. Rejected and a refugee, the rest of Toland's life was spent dealing – unsuccessfully – with this setback to his ambitions. His marginal and impoverished status forced him to depend upon patrons, probably affecting the objectivity and quality of analysis he could offer on any particular issue.

It is difficult to untangle what Toland really thought of Irish Catholics. A reading of his works suggests that he assumed radicalism was possible only if Catholicism was kept underfoot, hence his opposition to France, Rome and the 'native Irish'. He destroyed Robert Harley (1661-1724) – his former patron – in *The Art of Restoring* (1714) because of the latter's suspected Jacobite tendencies. On the other hand, his description above of the Pope as 'having betray'd the country to the English' perhaps suggests someone who has not quite severed the bonds of emotional attachment to his tribe. Perhaps he believed that Irish Catholics were really Protestants, but his writings show no evidence of his attempting to rouse Irish Catholics from their papist slumbers. Indeed, this obvious gap in his religious and political concerns may well exist because Toland tried so hard to escape from this – ultimately his own – milieu.

John Toland shares his anti-Catholicism with many eighteenth-century Irish Republicans. Wolfe Tone, for example, regarded the Catholic clergy as 'tyrants of the people and slaves of Government'.[79] However, one could not seriously argue that Tone was hostile to Catholics. His republicanism was political in its origins and thus universally applicable to persons of all religious denominations: Tone wanted to unite Protestant, Catholic and Dissenter. By contrast, Toland's republicanism was religious in its roots and emanated from seventeenth-century Protestant England. In Toland's political philosophy, one could not be both Catholic and republican: a Catholic would always have allegiance to Papal Rome before Ciceronian Rome and was therefore an untrustworhy citizen. This is why Toland advocates the extension of English rule in Ireland by keeping the sectarian pot boiling: it was necessary for the advancement of his species of republicanism. Compare this to Tone's wanting 'to break the connection with England'! The significance of American independence was huge for the development of republicanism in Ireland. *Separatism* became deeply embedded for the first time in the Irish body politic. The French Revolutionary success brought *universalism* into republicanism; this is not a feature of Toland's republican outlook. Both Tone and Toland were not hostile to the idea of a monarchy. William of Orange was actually the head of a republic – the Dutch Republic. He is also the most republican monarch to have ruled Britain. For both men, republicanism did not imply social revolution. Tone came from the colonizing class; Toland aspired to it. Neither devoted much of his writings to 'the men of no property'.[80]

J.G.A. Pocock elegantly distinguishes English republicanism from the French variant as follows:

> If Louis XVI in 1793 was executed for being a king ... Charles I in 1649 was executed for failing to be a king.[81]

He is implying that English republicanism was the result of regicide whereas French republicanism was the cause. Pocock regards James Harrington's *Oceana* (1656) as 'the English republican classic'.[82] He also states that 'Harrington's republicanism is more Machiavellian than Platonic because of its concern with the *de facto*'.[83] Toland's republicanism was also very sensitive to immediate political preoccupations. This concern with the tactical rather than the strategic helps to explain why the republican Toland can also be a fervent Williamite monarchist.

Even when apparently non-sectarian political movements have broken through the hate-ridden surface of Irish politics, the roots of such movements may well be thoroughly infused with religious bigotry. In the late eighteenth century we find anti-Catholic sentiment among some of the Ulster United Irishmen, even though that organization espoused the ideal of uniting Protestant, Catholic and Dissenter under the common name of Irishman. For example, the Rev. Thomas Ledlie Birch – and many Dissenters – saw the French

Revolution as a victory more for anti-Popery than for liberty, equality and fraternity.[84] Marianne Elliott reports that Tone was disturbed at the anti-Popery evident among Presbyterians celebrating Bastille Day at Belfast in 1792.[85]

If we are confused about Toland and his natal identity, his thoughts on Protestantism are no less complicated. To see Toland simply as a leading ideologue of Protestantism and Britishness is to ignore what I would call his 'pure radicalism'. Toland believed that Protestant sects could also produce popes:

> Since Religion is calculated for reasonable Creatures, 'tis Conviction and not Authority that should bear Weight with them. A wise and good Man … knows no Difference between Popish Infallibility, and being oblig'd blindly to acquiesce in the Decisions of fallible Protestants.[86]

And:

> … there may very well be such a thing as Protestant Popery.[87]

Toland implied that popery was found not just in religion but in all fields where the professional use of mystery occurred, for example medicine, politics, philosophy and law.[88] He considered popery to be the attempt by the powerful – whether in politics or religion – to constrain the thoughts of the individual and to try to destroy the power of other sects or parties:

> Popery in reality is nothing else, but the Clergy's assuming a Right to think for the Laity.[89]

We now approach the true significance of the reaction in Ireland to *Christianity not Mysterious*. To suggest that the post-1690s Irish ruling class were as much adherents of popery as were the Catholics was the ultimate heresy because it decisively undermined the justification for Protestant rule. If all Christian churches were equally fallible then there was no moral basis for the Penal Laws. Toland put it thus in his *Apology for Mr Toland* (1697), which he wrote to defend himself in the immediate aftermath of the burning of *Christianity not Mysterious* in 1697:

> … all Dominion as well as Religion is founded in Reason. … What Dominion is not founded in Reason, must be doubtless unreasonable, and consequently Tyrannical.[90]

No wonder the Dublin elite burned it and hounded Toland out of the island. One commentator describes the impact of Toland on such privileged circles:

An Irish peer gave it as a reason why he had ceased to attend church that once he heard something there about his Saviour Jesus Christ, but now all the discourse was about one John Toland.[91]

Toland may also have burned his bridges with the Anglo-Irish over the Standing Army controversy.[92] Briefly, Cromwell's New Model Army had proved so unpopular in England that a genuine fear of standing armies remained after the Restoration. This fear grew by leaps and bounds when James II gained the throne. Here was a Catholic monarch with an army that could threaten Protestant life and property. The victories of William in 1690 and 1697 did not wholly allay these fears: the comprehensiveness of the Treaty of Rijswik increased foreboding. In 1697 a pamphlet war ensued, initiated by the Irishman John Trenchard in his *Argument, Shewing, that a Standing Army Is inconsistent with A Free Government, and absolutely destructive to the Constitution of the English Monarchy*. John Somers and Daniel Defoe advocated maintenance of William's army. Toland weighed in with *The Militia Reform'd; Or An Easy Scheme Of Furnishing England with a Constant Land-Force, capable to prevent or to subdue any Forein Power; and to maintain perpetual Quiet at Home, without endangering the Publick Liberty* (1698), which suggested a compromise between the two Whig factions; the eventual solution – the army reduced to seven thousand Englishmen – approximated Toland's suggestions.[93] The idea of reducing the size of the army was anathema to the Irish Episcopalians, who depended on a large and permanent English army to secure their position.[94] (It is surely no coincidence that rebellions occurred soon after the rise of Volunteer, nationalist and loyalist militias in Ireland in 1782 and 1914.) Once again, Toland had bitten the Ascendancy hand which he had hoped would feed him.

A.T.Q. Stewart once said that in Ireland 'all history is applied history'.[95] It would also appear that all philosophy is applied philosophy on this troubled island: *Christianity not Mysterious* sparked off the

most productive era in Irish philosophy, which included such luminaries as George Berkeley, Francis Hutcheson and Edmund Burke.
What was really being debated, however, was the ownership of political power. With the re-alignments of both Catholic, Protestant and
Dissenter in Ireland, and Catholic and Revolutionary in France,
towards the end of the eighteenth century, Toland has become an
Irish radical in spite of himself.

VI

In John Toland's world-view, everything flows. To worry about
beginnings and endpoints is to completely miss the point of what life
and nature is about:

> All things are in a perpetual Flux, nothing permanent or in every Regard the same for
> one Moment. But none of them is so visibly subject to such Variations, as Kingdoms,
> States, and (in a word) all sorts of *Governments*.[96]

Erection of classificatory systems and the cordoning off of knowledge
into specialities form no part of Toland's philosophical speculations:
they merely delay the underlying change. Reason was the tool to free
up the logjam that inevitably resulted when people unhesitatingly
accepted the arguments of clergy and politicians. Many commentators
have stated that John Toland was the first to use the word pantheism.
This is untrue. He was certainly the first person to use the word *pantheist*, at least in English. There is a difference. Toland constructed no
rigid system of thought: he was a philosopher of *process*, not of *product*.
This distinction is crucial in understanding the great contribution of
Toland to the world of ideas. Toland's migrations of the mind allow
him a pivotal role in the investigation of mental boundaries.

Does this make Toland a revolutionary or an evolutionary? It
depends on one's perspective. I have already discussed his hostility
to what he called Popery among both Catholic and Protestant clergy. To those who put their faith in ideologies, whether religious or
political, or to those whose purpose was to keep power by manipu-
lating the faithful, Toland was a revolutionary. However, he saw
himself as a healer of political differences (as is seen by his interven-

tion in the Standing Army controversy). Toland believed that truth was plural, and that it was not possible for any two people to use their reason in a debate and agree: the purpose of debating was to clarify the quality of one's own opinions. Everyone is born different and each travels his own path through life: why expect agreement about the important issues of God and government? To accept completely the opinions of another was to give up the use of reason.

When considering historical characters such as Toland, it is vitally important that what Thomas Bartlett has called 'the burden of the present' is lifted from our deliberations.[97] Great events and ideas intervene between us and them and the fog of the past becomes nearly impenetrable. The past is indeed a different country. Irish republicanism has been transformed by eighteenth-century American separatism and French universalism, nineteenth-century Catholic confessionalism, and twentieth-century universal suffrage. It is now a very different brew from Toland's elitist, freethinking and headily sectarian potion. Yet Toland speaks to us across the centuries. He is a pivotal figure in the construction of both British identity and – by implication – Irish identities.

It is interesting to compare Toland's career with those of Jonathan Swift (1667-1745) and Daniel Defoe (1660-1731). All three vied for patronage from the powerful in London, indeed all were employed as writers at various times by Robert Harley (to all intents and purposes the 'Prime Minister' of Britain from 1710 to 1714).[98] In their pamphletic venting of spleen we see the origins of modern journalistic polemicism. Whereas Defoe and Swift are now best remembered by the public for their novels, Toland languishes in obscurity. John Toland also deserves to be remembered both for his contribution of a new word – *pantheist* – to the English language and for being one of the first – if not the first – to describe Ireland as West Britain. His relentlessly heterodox mind needed a new word to characterize it: John Locke coined the term *free-thinker* in order to describe Toland.[99]

Seamus Heaney has recently proposed a way of placing Irish writers in literary and political context in Ireland with the idea of the *quincunx*: a diamond with fortifications at each point and a central node.[100] Heaney places Edmund Spenser – the horse Protestant – in Kilcolman Castle, Co. Cork; W.B. Yeats – representing Gaelic

Ireland – at Thoor Ballylee, Co. Galway; Louis MacNeice – the Ulsterman – at Carrickfergus Castle, Co. Antrim; and James Joyce – the European modernist – at Sandycove Martello Tower, Co. Dublin. Each of these artists, Heaney suggests, has looked into 'the tower of prior Irelandness' – the centre of the quincunx – and seen a differently imagined Ireland. If it is necessary to sympathize with all sides in order to truly understand Ireland then I suggest that Toland has a foothold in all four camps: he was a loyal Protestant; an Irish-speaker and Catholic at birth; an Inishowen man and Dissenter; and a European cosmopolitan. It may not be so fanciful to see the Grianán of Aileach at the centre-point of Heaney's quincunx, with Toland's free spirit restlessly wandering there.[101]

An examination of the tensions in Toland's life allows us, per-haps, to view the conflict in Northern Ireland in slightly less parochial terms. I have already alluded to the religious imprint on the monarchy. Meanwhile, the Irish Constitution is suffused throughout with Catholic irredentism. Consider the following quota-tion from the Preamble:

In the Name of the Most Holy Trinity ...We, the people of Éire, Humbly acknowledg-ing all our obligations to our Divine Lord, Jesus Christ, Who sustained our fathers through centuries of trial ...

Expecting Northern Ireland to solve its political problems alone is unrealistic if the sectarian nature of both states is not tackled by London and Dublin: Churchill's dreary steeples lie in Anglican England as much as in Fermanagh. It is a hopeful sign when Prince Charles can see the role of the monarch as being a 'Defender of Faiths' and not just merely Protestant.[102] Perhaps a comprehensive separation of Church and State in both countries could free up orga-nized religion, caught vice-like in the suffocating middle-ground between God and Caesar. Toland's thoughts on 'true religion' seem appropriate here:

For true religion does not consist in cunningly devis'd fables, in authority, dominion, or pomp; but in spirit and in truth, in simplicity and in social virtue, in a filial love and reverence, not in a servile dread and terror of the Divinity.[103]

All around us we see the crumbling of the old reassuring power blocs. The Soviet empire has imploded. De Valera's 1937 constitution is more anachronistic with each passing day. The Christian Churches are being challenged and revitalized from without and within. The growth of integrated schools and *gaelscoileanna* are offering exciting new ways of educating our children. Sensuality has re-entered music and dance. The pustulating atavisms of green and orange may just be able to live with each other. Nonetheless, a time of change is also a time of great stress in one's belief system. We should not jettison unthinkingly all our old shibboleths and embrace new versions of what Vaclav Havel has called 'cheap ideological utopias'. The problem remains: how to get from A to B?

John Toland, philosopher of process, would laugh at such a question. He would point out that A and B do not exist but that he knows how to get there anyway! He would suggest we take reason to heart in our religion and tolerance as a benchmark in our political dealings. Three hundred years after it first appeared, perhaps this new edition of *Christianity not Mysterious* may help us on the way to our destination. In any case, if it is better to travel hopefully than to arrive, such a challenging work is necessary to animate that journey.

NOTES

Parts of this essay appeared in the *Times Literary Supplement* (18 Sept. 1996) and *Irish Studies Review* (summer 1997). The title derives from a phrase used by Colm Tóibín in his essay 'On (Not) Saying What You Mean', *London Review of Books* (10 Nov. 1995).

1 The grid reference for Ardagh is C3849, and C3746 for Clonmany (both in the Irish Republic).

2 Inishowen is only thrity-three miles from Islay.

3 William J. Doherty, *Inishowen and Tirconnell: Being some Account of Antiquities and Writers of the County of Donegal* (Dublin 1895), p. 150.

4 See bibliography for details of the pseudonyms that Toland used.

5 I use 'Protestant' as a blanket term for those who followed the tenets of the Reformation. 'Anglican' is used to describe members of the Church of Ireland, the Church of England and the Episcopal Church in Scotland.; 'Episcopalian' is interchangeable with 'Anglican'. 'Dissenter' is another (older) term for Presbyterian.

6 See my '"Perpetual Flux": Newton, Toland, Science and the Status Quo' in this volume.

7 Doherty 1895, pp. 149-50.

8 See Letter from Dr Edmund Gibson, Fellow of Queen's College, Oxford, to Rev.

Dr Charlett, Master of University College, Oxford, 21 June 1694. The relevant section is reprinted in F.H. Heinemann, 'John Toland, France, Holland, and Dr. Williams', in *Review of English Studies* 25(100) (1949), pp. 346-7. Heinemann states that Gibson knew Toland. Toland states that he learned Irish in his childhood and he discusses some Inishowen antiquities: the cairns at Fahan and Inch, and the standing stones at Clonmany (*Collection of Pieces*, vol. 1, pp. 21, 68 and 105).

9 Stephen H. Daniel, *John Toland: His Methods, Manners and Mind* (McGill-Queen's University Press, Montreal 1984), p. 5; Leslie Stephen, 'John Toland', in Sydney Lee (ed.), *Dictionary of National Biography*, Vol. 56 (Smith, Elder & Co., London 1898), p. 438; and Isaac Disraeli, *The Calamities and Quarrels of Authors* (Routledge, Ware and Routledge, London 1859), p. 156.

10 Jonathan Bardon, *A History of Ulster* (Blackstaff Press, Belfast 1992), p. 4.

11 These Ulster chieftancies would later give us Tyrone and Tyrconnell.

12 At Northburgh, now Greencastle, on the north-eastern shores of Inishowen.

13 David Dickson, 'Derry's Backyard: The Barony of Inishowen 1650-1800', in William Nolan, Liam Ronayne & Mairéad Dunlevy (eds), *Donegal: History and Society* (Geography Publications, Templeogue 1995), p. 413; J.B. Leslie, *Derry Clergy and Parishes* (Enniskillen 1937), p.161. Note that Tohill offers different information, suggesting that one brother was called Dominic, not Daniel, and putting the date when he was rector as 1630. On balance, the other sources appear more authoritative (J.J. Tohill, *Donegal: An Exploration* (Donegal Democrat, Ballyshannon 1995 (1976)) p. 75).

14 Tohill 1995, p. 75.

15 Dickson 1995, p. 413.

16 Barkley, *Blackmouth and Dissenter* (White River Press, Belfast 1991), pp. 18-20.

17 The Bishop of Derry, Ezekiel Hopkins, possibly hoped to use Toland and other Irish-speaking theology students to convert and 'civilize' the natives (Doherty, p. 151). He attended Redcastle school in Co. Donegal, between Muff and Moville (Grid Ref.: C5534). Hopkins was succeeded by William King, who continued this policy (John Laird, 'Ulster Philosophers', in *Proc. Rep. Belfast Nat. Hist. & Phil. Soc.* (1921-2), p.12). King was later to be an opponent of Toland's, attacking the ideas expressed in *Christianity not Mysterious*: 'As to Toland's concern, there is a great difference to be made between a man that differs from others in the manner and method of worshipping God, and another that denys any God at all, that has no principles of Morality, nor owns any obligations on him besides his present interest, that holds falshood, perjury, murder, etc. to have no evil in them besides the opinion of the world nay that denys there is any Such thing in nature as virtu or vice. 'Tis to these principles that we owe all the mischiefs and villanys that have disturbed the world, and they never were received or countenanced in any commonwealth, but the destruction of it followed, now this I take to be avowed by Toland's case.' (Letter to Robert Molesworth, 29 Sept. 1720. [King Papers, Trinity College, Dublin]; quoted in Caroline Robbins, *The Eighteenth-Century Commonwealthman: Studies in the Transmission, Development and Circumstance of English Liberal Thought from the Restoration of Charles II until the War with the Thirteen Colonies* (Harvard University Press 1959), pp. 144-5). Ironically, Toland was to attempt to gain employment from King towards the end of his life, but King's refusal is a perceptive analysis of Toland's unemployability at the time: 'I wou'd not refuse even his assistance, if it might be useful, but I am assured his intermeddling will be mischievous and it will be thought as suffi-

cient answer to all he offereth, that he is the author ...' (King, same letter as above, as quoted in Robert E. Sullivan, *John Toland and the Deist Controversy* (Harvard University Press 1982), pp. 38-9.)

18 Benjamin Furly (1693), letter introducing Toland to John Locke, as quoted in Heinemann (1949), p. 348: 'I find him a freespirited ingenious man; that quitted the Papacy in James's time when all men of no principles were looking towards it; and having now cast off the yoak of Spiritual Authority, that great bugbear, and bane of ingenuity, he could never be persuaded to bow his neck to that yoak again, by whomsoever claymed; this has rendered it somewhat difficult to him, to find a way of subsistence in the world ...'

19 H.F. Nicholl, 'John Toland: Religion without Mystery', in *Hermathena* 100 (1965), p.57.

20 John Hunt, 'John Toland', in *Contemporary Review*, 8 (1868), p. 178.

21 Episcopalian equivocation is well illustrated by the Siege of Derry. The then Bishop of Derry, Ezekiel Hopkins, hesitated in closing the gates, and was preempted by the actions of the Apprentice Boys.

22 Most commentators call that monarch William III, but this is true for England only. He is more correctly known in Scotland as William II. (Similarly, thousands of Scottish postboxes have been incorrectly embossed with EIIR: Elizabeth I was Queen of England only.)

23 Although the term 'Ascendancy' began to be used only in the 1780s to describe the Protestant ruling class of Ireland, I am using it retrospectively here to refer to the hegemonic class that controlled Ireland from 1691 until the Act of Union in 1800. See W.J. Mc Cormack, *Ascendancy and Tradition in Anglo-Irish Literary History from 1789 to 1939* (Clarendon Press, Oxford 1985).

24 Bardon, pp. 165-8.

25 J.G. Simms, 'John Toland (1670-1722), a Donegal Heretic', in *Irish Historical Studies*, 16 (1969), p. 305.

26 Robert Rees Evans, *Pantheisticon: The Career of John Toland* (Peter Lang, New York 1991), p. 3.

27 Alan Harrison suggests that Toland might have returned to Ireland between 1710 and 1722, but this is by no means certain. (Alan Harrison, 'John Toland (1670-1722) and Celtic Studies', in Cyril J. Byrne, Margaret Harry and Pádraig Ó Siadhail (eds), *Celtic Languages and Celtic Peoples: Proc. 2nd North American Congress of Celtic Studies* (1992), pp. 564-5.)

28 Tom Clyde (ed.), *Ancestral Voices: the Selected Prose of John Hewitt* (Blackstaff Press, Belfast 1987), p. 71.

29 Caroline Robbins, *The Eighteenth-Century Commonwealthman* (Harvard University Press 1959), p. 114.

30 *An Inquiry Concerning Virtue* later became part of Shaftesbury's *Characteristicks*.

31 Ian McBride, 'William Drennan and the Dissenting Tradition', in David Dickson, Dáire Keogh & Kevin Whelan (eds), *The United Irishmen: Republicanism, Radicalism and Rebellion* (Lilliput Press, Dublin 1993), p. 56.

32 William Molyneux, *Correspondence of Locke* 6 (1697), p. 132 (as quoted in Daniel, p. 146).

33 Elaine McFarland, *Ireland and Scotland in the Age of Revolution: Planting the Green Bough* (Edinburgh University Press 1994), p. 5 and Appendix I. This recent study of educational, theological and intellectual links between Scots and Irish Presbyterians (Scoto-Hiberni) suggests that 25 per cent of Edinburgh MD. gradu-

ates between 1740 and 1800 were Irish, as were 17 per cent of matriculating students at the University of Glasgow.

34 A.T.Q. Stewart, *A Deeper Silence: The Hidden Roots of the United Irish Movement* (Faber and Faber, London 1993), pp. 76-8.

35 See Stewart, *passim*, and the *Fortnight Supplements* on 'Free Thought in Ireland' (1991) and 'Francis Hutcheson' (1992), both published in Belfast.

36 Robbins, p. 169.

37 Terry Eagleton, *Heathcliff and the Great Hunger* (Verso, London 1995), p. 121.

38 Francis Hutcheson, *An Inquiry Concerning the Original of our Ideas of Virtue or Moral Good* (1725), as quoted in Eagleton, p. 121.

39 Stewart, pp. 103-4.

40 See Stewart, pp. 109-12, and David Berman, 'The Irish Counter-Enlightenment', in Richard Kearney (ed.), *The Irish Mind: Exploring Intellectual Traditions* (Wolfhound Press, Dublin 1985), p. 121.

41 Elisha Smith, Letter to Thomas Hearne (1706), as quoted in Daniel, p .71, n.33.

42 This copy of *Pantheisticon* was later donated by Belfast First to the library at the Queen's University of Belfast, where it remains.

43 An excellent introduction to these Reading Societies can be found in J.R.R. Adams, *The Printed Word and the Common Man: Popular Culture in Ulster 1700-1900* (Institute of Irish Studies, Belfast 1987).

44 Stewart, pp. 121-4.

45 Stewart, pp. 124-5.

46 *Catalogue of Books belonging to Alexander Stewart Esq. of Newtownards.* Public Records of Northern Ireland, D654/S1/2 and D654/S1/3. The Toland volume is his *Collection* (1726). (Presumably the copy of Harrington's *Oceana* is Toland's edition.)

47 William Bruce was also buried in that grave. The Latin epitaph was written by Thomas Drennan.

48 For more detail on the Stewarts see Ian McBride, 'Presbyterians in the Penal Era', *Bullán*, 1(2) (1994), pp. 73-86.

49 Stewart, pp. 159-62.

50 The original use of the term 'Orange lodge' referred to a Masonic lodge in Belfast in 1783, some twelve years before the 1795 foundation of the Orange Order.

51 Stewart, p. 176.

52 Stewart, pp. 173-4.

53 Margaret Candee Jacob, *The Radical Enlightenment: Pantheists, Freemasons and Republicans* (George Allen and Unwin, London 1981), pp. 267-72.

54 Daniel, p. 218.

55 Eagleton, p. 123.

56 The quotations are, respectively, from Daniel, p. 76; Evans, p. 144; Kenneth Craven, *Jonathan Swift and the Millennium of Madness: The Information Age in Swift's 'A Tale of a Tub'* (1992), pp. 4-5; and F.H. Heinemann, 'John Toland and the Age of Enlightenment', in *Review of English Studies* 20 (1944), p. 131.

57 Berman, p. 120.

58 Daniel, pp. 7, 147.

59 J. Pocock (ed.), *The Political Works of James Harrington* (Cambridge 1977), p. 159.

60 See section 3, chapter 5 of *Christianity not Mysterious*; and part II of *Nazarenus, Or Jewish, Gentile, and Mahometan Christianity*.

61 Silvia Berti, 'At the Roots of Unbelief', in *Journal of the History of Ideas*, 56 (1995), p. 573.

62 Doherty, p. 151.

63 See pp. 8-9. The full title is *Reasons Most humbly offer'd to the Honourable House of Commons, Why The Bill sent down to them From the Most Honourable House of Lords, Entitul'd, An Act for the better Securing the Dependency of the Kingdom of Ireland upon the Crown of Great-Britain, Shou'd not Pass into a Law*.

64 *Ibid.*, p. 14.

65 Robbins, p. 127.

66 Toland, *Reasons* ..., p. 23.

67 *Oxford English Dictionary*, 2nd Ed., Vol. XI.

68 William Walwyn, *The English Soldier's Standard, to repair to for Wisdom and Understanding, in these doleful, back-sliding Times: to be read by every honest officer to his soldiers and by the soldiers to one another* (1649) (as quoted in H.N. Brailsford, *The Levellers and the English Revolution*, ed. Christopher Hill (Spokesman, Nottingham 1961 (1983)), p. 499).

69 Pierre Des Maizeaux, 'Memoir of Toland', in *Collection of Several Pieces* (1726).

70 The full title is *Limitations for the Next Foreign Successor, Or A New Saxon Race. Debated in a Conference betwixt two Gentlemen. Sent in a Letter to a Member of Parliament*, pp. 27-8 (as quoted in Evans, pp. 83-6).

71 Jonathan Swift, *An Argument against Abolishing Christianity* (1708), p. 37. Slurs cast on Toland's origins may explain why Toland actually used the Franciscans in Prague to verify his (Catholic) origins; see Harrison, pp. 561-3. (Incidentally, a recent study of Swift's *Tale of a Tub* (1704) suggests that 'Toland is Swift's major satiric victim and foil in the Tale'. Craven suggests that Swift satirized Toland's *Christianity not Mysterious*, his edition of Harrington's *Oceana*, his *Life of Milton*, and his unauthorized publication of Shrewsbury's *An Inquiry Concerning Virtue* (Craven, p. 5).)

72 Few English people would regard themselves as British first and English second. It is noticeable that Afro-Caribbean persons living in England tend to regard themselves as Black British rather than Black English, as if Englishness were not an available identity; the 'rivers of blood' speech of Enoch Powell in 1968 effectively closed off that pathway. For a provocative discussion of Englishness and Britishness see Peter Berresford Ellis, 'Do "The British" Really Exist?', in *Celts and Saxons: The Struggle for Britain AD 410-937* (Constable, London 1993), pp. 215-51.

73 Jim Smyth, 'Anglo-Irish Unionist Discourse, c.1656-1707: From Harrington to Fletcher', in *Bullán*, 2(1) (1995), p. 21.

74 See Roy Foster, 'The Ascendancy Mind', in *Modern Ireland 1600-1972* (Penguin, London 1988), pp. 167-94. The reader is also urged to consult Joep Leerssen's two magisterial surveys, *Mere Irish and Fíor-Ghael: Studies in the Idea of Irish Nationality, its Development and Literary Expression prior to the Nineteenth Century*, and *Remembrance and Imagination: Patterns in the Historical and Literary Representation of Ireland in the Nineteenth Century* (both Cork University Press/Field Day 1996).

75 Linda Colley, *Britons: Forging the Nation 1707-1837* (Vintage, London 1996 (1992)), p. 387.

76 John Toland (ed.), *The Oceana of James Harrington* (1700), pp. ii-iv.

77 Reference given by Toland: *Apud Baron. ad annum 1159 & apud alios complures, praecipuè verò apud Usserium nostrum in Epistolar. Hibernicar. sylloge; & ex autro-*

grapho apud Rymerum, tom. 1. pag. 15.

78 *Nazarenus* (London 1718), Letter 2, pp. 2, 16-17, 35-6, and 41-3. Note that 'Albanian Scots' refers to those Scots who spoke Gaelic – Alba being the Gaelic for Scotland – and not to the fellow countrymen of Enver Hoxha.

79 As quoted in Richard Kearney, *Postnationalist Ireland: Politics, Culture, Philosophy* (Routledge, London 1997), p. 25.

80 I am indebted to Thomas Bartlett's excellent essay on Wolfe Tone for much of the detail on Tone in this paragraph (Thomas Bartlett, 'The Burden of the Present: Theobald Wolfe Tone, Republican and Separatist', in David Dickson, Dáire Keogh & Kevin Whelan (eds), *The United Irishmen: Republicanism, Radicalism and Rebellion* (Lilliput Press, Dublin 1993), pp. 1-15).

81 J.G.A. Pocock (ed.), 'The Commonwealth of Oceana' and 'A System of Politics' by James Harrington (Cambridge University Press 1992), pp. xi-xii.

82 *Ibid.*, p. xi.

83 *Ibid.*, p. xv.

84 Holmes, p. 86. (Samuel Barber, Presbyterian minister of Rathfriland and founder of a United Irish society there, interpreted the French Revolution in the same light. See McBride (1993), p. 55.)

85 Marianne Elliott, *Wolfe Tone: Prophet of Irish Independence* (Yale University Press, 1989), p. 175

86 *Christianity not Mysterious*, p. 9 in the present edition.

87 'A Memorial for the Earl of Oxford, 1711', in *Collection*, Vol. 2, p. 230.

88 Daniel, p. 30.

89 *Appeal to Honest People*, p. 38.

90 Toland, *Apology*, p. 116 in the present volume.

91 Anonymous, 1697, as quoted in Hunt, p. 184.

92 A full discussion of the Standing Army controversy can be found in Lois G. Schwoerer, *'No Standing Armies!': The Antiarmy Ideology in Seventeenth-Century England* (Johns Hopkins University Press, Baltimore 1974).

93 Evans, pp. 44-9.

94 Smyth, p. 20.

95 R. F. Foster, *Paddy & Mr Punch: Connections in Irish and English History* (Penguin, London 1993), p. 78.

96 *The Destiny of Rome* (1718), pp. 4-5,7.

97 Bartlett, p. 7.

98 H.B. Butler & C.R.L. Fletcher, *Historical Portraits 1600-1700* (Clarendon Press, Oxford 1911).

99 Geoffrey Cantor, as reported in Craven, p. 23.

100 Seamus Heaney, 'Frontiers of Writing' in both *Bullán*, 1:1-15 (1994) and *The Redress of Poetry* (Faber & Faber, London1995).

101 Had the 1925 Boundary Commission been ratified, the new border would have bisected the Grianán of Aileach, making its appropriateness as a symbol of division and unity even more potent.

102 It is deeply ironic that Henry VIII was awarded the title 'Defender of the Faith' for his loyalty to Rome!

103 *History of the Druids*, p. 53.

TOLAND ON FAITH AND REASON

Desmond M. Clarke

John Toland's polemical style and his penchant for controversy were noted by an anonymous commentator after his death: 'Dabbling in controversy was his delight, in which he was rude, positive, and always in the wrong.'[1] This gives the impression of Toland as a maverick whose views were unrepresentative even of the more revolutionary thinkers of the seventeeth century. However, style aside, Toland's philosophical critiques were not as odd as many of his contemporaries claimed; in fact, the intensity of the hostility he provoked suggests that he had identified a central weakness in the positions he criticized and that it was easier for those he challenged to classify him as crank, as a kind of Giordano Bruno from Donegal, than to acknowledge and answer the objections he raised. Nowhere is Toland's ability to identify the raw nerve more obvious than in his discussion of the role of reason in religious belief in *Christianity not Mysterious*.

The Preface summarizes one of the central issues in philosophy of religion: 'I hope to make it appear, that the Use of Reason is not so dangerous in Religion as it is commonly represented, and that too by such as mightily extol it when it seems to favour 'em, yet vouchsafe it not a hearing when it makes against them, but oppose its own Authority to it self.'[2] Apart from the suggestion at the end of this quotation that religious believers rely on rational argument when it helps their cause, and use reason to argue against reason when it doesn't, Toland is claiming to defend Christian belief by explaining that Christianity is not incompatible with reason because it does not require Christians to believe in so-called mysteries. This raises a much larger issue than anyone in this period might have anticipated, about the range of arguments or considerations that are properly classified as rational. Before saying something about that, it is useful to situate *Christianity not Mysterious* within an established tradition of inquiry in the seventeenth century.

Pierre Bayle, one of the most acute and authoritative reporters on current debates towards the end of the seventeenth century, points out in his *Dictionary* that Catholic and Protestant Christians, despite their other differences, agree on the transcendence of religious mysteries:

> The Roman Catholicks and Protestants fight it out upon abundance of articles of religion, but they perfectly agree on this point, that the mysteries of the Gospel transcend reason. ... If some doctrines are above reason, they are out of its reach; if they are out of its reach, it can't attain to them; if it can't attain to them, it can't comprehend them; if it can't comprehend them, it can't find any idea or principle that can afford solutions; and consequently, its objections will remain unanswered or, which is the same thing, will be answered by some distinction as obscure as the thesis itself which is attacked. The conclusion from this is, that the mysteries of the Gospel ... neither can nor ought to be submitted to the rules of natural reason.[3]

The apparent unanimity of Christian opinion is qualified by Bayle's acknowledgement that Roman Catholics and some Protestant churches differed in their understanding of how mysteries transcend the faith.[4] The key element in this difference of opinion was whether they would accept mysteries that seemed to conflict with reason, or whether they were willing to believe only those mysteries that were in some sense beyond their comprehension.

The distinction between ways in which religious mysteries might transcend reason may be illustrated by two books published in the same year, 1641, by representatives of two traditions with which Toland was familiar. In the 'Objections and Replies' included in the first edition of the *Meditations*, René Descartes raised the question whether we can believe in God if we have no concept or idea of God.

> If one has no idea, i.e. no perception which corresponds to the meaning of the word 'God', it is no use saying that one believes that God exists. One might as well say that one believes that *nothing* exists, thus remaining in the abyss of impiety and the depths of ignorance.[5]

Descartes made this claim in a context in which he argued that he did have an idea or concept that was adequate to support his proof of

God's existence. Whatever about his claim about the adequacy of his concept of God, he argued that it is not possible to distinguish belief in God, as distinct from belief in something else, by merely attaching the term 'God' to the former; in order for a belief to have a specific content, the believer must be equipped with some concept or idea of what they believe in.

However, Descartes also argued that the reality of God cannot be limited by our impoverished human concepts and that God may well be able to do many things that we cannot understand:

> For my part, I know that my intellect is finite and God's power is infinite, and so I set no limits to it; I consider only what I am capable of perceiving, and what not, and I take great pains that my judgment should accord with my perception. And so I boldly assert that God can do everything which I perceive to be possible, but I am not so bold as to assert the converse, namely that he cannot do what conflicts with my conception of things – I merely say that it involves a contradiction.[6]

Thus, for Descartes, our finite intellect is not the measure of what is possible for God; in particular, God may do things the descriptions of which, from the perspective of our concepts or our logic, are inconsistent. If that were the case, we would have to acknowledge the inconsistency and it would not be possible for us to believe what, from our point of view, is inconsistent. By combining both points suggested by Descartes, we get an apparently paradoxical result: while acknowledging the limits of human understanding and the inappropriateness of limiting God's reality or power to our concepts, it is also true that in order to believe something one must have a concept which is at least adequate to support the belief in question.

While Descartes published a relatively orthodox version of the Catholic position on God's transcendence, the respective roles of faith and reason in religious belief were also discussed in the same year by Moise Amyraut, a Calvinist theologian, in *The Elevation of Faith and the Depression of Reason*.[7] Amyraut describes the tension between faith and reason by analogy with the arms of a simple balance, asking whether if one is depressed the other must automatically be elevated. If that analogy were appropriate one would have to accept that, in matters of religion, 'one must elevate one's faith and depress one's reason'. Amyraut, however, does not accept the analogy with the balance and tries instead to explain how faith and reason are compatible. To do this he suggests that there are three ways in which religious beliefs may be related to reason:

a) a particular belief might be such that, at least in principle, it can be discovered by reason;
b) a belief may not be discoverable by reason but, once revealed, it is not inconsistent with reason (here Amyraut suggested, as an example, the doctrine of the Trinity);
c) a belief apparently proposed by faith may be incompatible with reason (Amyraut gave the Catholic doctrine of transubstantiation as an example of this kind).

In considering these possibilities, Amyraut proposed a standard Calvinist account of the relationship between faith and reason and argued that Christianity requires us to believe only what falls within (a) or (b) above. Under no circumstances does our faith require us to believe what is irrational or what is inconsistent with reason.

Evidently, all these claims presuppose an account of what is meant by 'reason' or 'rational'. The background to these distinctions is the way in which we interpret the written and traditional sources on which religious faith is based. Amyraut argues that it is more likely that we misunderstand the text of the Bible than that God would commmand us to believe what is irrational. Given the hermeneutic difficulties associated with biblical criticism, what is 'rational' provides a minimum threshold for what is credible.

Even the second option mentioned above is not very clear in Amyraut's discussion, because he defines belief as the state of being 'persuaded of the truth of something, either by reason which proves it, or by its own evidence which shines in it'.[8] This raises a question about what kind of evidence could persuade us of the truth of something if what is proposed for belief is beyond our comprehension. In the case of the Trinity, Amyraut claimed that the concept transcends human intelligence – in fact, he argued that scholastic philosophers had compromised their faith by explaining their religious belief in terms that made it no longer a mystery. The problem, then, is to give content to a belief when what we are invited to believe so transcends our comprehension that we cannot even express it in concepts that are intelligible to us.

These two texts from 1641 – one written within the Catholic tradition and the other a reflection of standard Calvinist thinking –

agree in claiming that we cannot be expected to believe something that is inconsistent with reason, and that in order to believe anything we must first of all have some conception of what is involved so that we can give a specific content to our belief.

None of these questions was esoteric or particularly revolutionary in seventeenth-century discussions. The issues involved were constantly and publicly discussed in a wide-ranging series of publications in most European languages. When *Christianity not Mysterious* is read in this context, it emerges as a sharply worded, polemical examination of the same concerns, with the addition of empiricist claims from Locke's theory of knowledge. As in the discussion of Amyraut, Toland distinguishes between mysteries that are against reason and those that are above reason, and he divides his discussion equally between the two. By 'contrary to reason' he means 'what is evidently repugnant to clear and distinct Ideas, or to our common Notions' (p. 3). This suggests that there are some truths that are so certain that anything inconsistent with them cannot be true. However he also defines reason as 'that Faculty every one has of judging of his Ideas according to their Agreement or Disagreement' (p. 48), and this suggests a weaker condition, that the beliefs we accept must be at least internally consistent.

Toland also argues that there is no benefit in making a distinction between what is inconsistent with reason and what merely appears to be inconsistent with reason, and then accepting that we may be required by divine revelation to believe what appears to be irrational. Toland's answer to this objection is remarkably similar to Descartes's: if we relax the criterion of what is credible to admit propositions that at least appear to be irrational, then there is no limit to what we may be invited or required to believe. 'If we once admit this Principle, I know not what we can deny that is told us in the Name of the Lord' (p. 33).

However, in contrast with Descartes, Toland seems to establish reason not only as a criterion of what *we* can believe but also as a criterion of what is possible for God. 'When we say then, *that nothing is impossible with God* ... we mean whatever is possible in i tself' (p. 40). And what is possible in itself is determined, apparently, by what we conceive as possible relative to the concepts and common notions with which we usually think.

297

The other class of mysteries, namely those that are allegedly above reason, may include some beliefs that are made obscure only by the artificially erudite language used by those who claim a monopoly in their interpretation. Here Toland reflects a common complaint of the seventeenth century, that school philosophy had degenerated into what he called the 'gibberish of your divinity schools', and that such mysteries were an academic invention. Apart from beliefs that have been artificially rendered mysterious, Toland argues that it is not possible for us to believe in mysteries that are genuinely beyond our comprehension. This is not a question of the adequacy or otherwise of our concepts to a full comprehension of the reality in question, for Toland adopts Locke's thesis that we do not understand fully the nature of anything, and that human knowledge is limited to identifying the observable qualities of things (p. 58). An inadequate concept is enough to provide some understanding. But our concept cannot be so inadequate that we know nothing at all of what we are invited to believe, so that all we can say is that we believe in a *Blictri* (pp. 81-2). This is equivalent to Descartes's point, that believing in a *Blictri* is the same as believing in nothing as long as we know as little about the former as the latter.

The polemical tone of Toland's essay is more evident when he comments on the possible motivation of those who take doctrines that are perfectly intelligible to the educated reader and turn them, needlessly, into mysteries. Anticipating developments in the nineteenth and twentieth centuries, Toland linked knowledge and power and focused especially on the power of the priesthood, in any religious tradition, if priests claim a special insight into arcane knowledge that is not available to others. Toland's proposed laicization or democratization of beliefs was part of a wider theory of the true church that he defended – that the original church of the first century was a community of believers which lacked the hierarchical structures and similar historical accretions inherited from the Roman Empire. It was also consistent with Toland's understanding of how we should read or interpret a text such as the Bible. 'Nor is there any different Rule to be follow'd in the Interpretation of *Scripture* from what is common to all other Books' (p. 44). Borrowing from the Calvinist hermeneutic, Toland argued that each reader has to confront a text by assuming that the text is intelligible, that it can be interpreted in such a way that it makes sense, and that the only other assistance available in its interpretation is our knowledge of languages, of the historical context in which the text was written, and of the logic of coherence that guides our interpretation.

I suggested above that the discussion of the role of faith and reason in the seventeenth and early eighteenth centuries was not in any way special to Toland, and that most of the concepts or distinctions used in his essay were already available in the religious traditions with which he was familiar. However, it is also true that this way of characterizing the ongoing debates of the seventeenth century may give the impression that they were primarily philosophical discussions, best conducted in reflections on theory of knowledge, about the relative scope of two different, overlapping means of accessing the truth, viz. faith and reason. In fact, the philosophical positions sketched above were set out in a polemical context in which strongly held religious beliefs were subjected to apparently hostile criticism, and the strength of the participants' reactions is best explained by the implications for their religious beliefs rather than the merits or otherwise of some purely speculative position in philosophy. For example, Amyraut wrote a book which, from the title, might appear to be about faith and reason; in fact, most of the book was designed to argue that the Catholic doctrine of transubstantiation should be rejected because it was irrational.

The sense in which this doctrine was irrational was explained by an anonymous Calvinist critic of the Cartesian position, in a tract entitled *Physical Reflections on Transubstantiation.*[9] The author argues that the irrationality of the doctrine does not derive from the claim that one body can be transformed into another. Whether this is possible or not is a question for physics, and our knowledge of physics is too imperfect a criterion for what is credible by faith. The Calvinist argument against transubstantiation depends, he argues, not on its alleged conflict with physics, but on the fact that it implies a logical contradiction that undermines the most basic axioms of reason:

The axioms on which I rely to show that transubstantiation is a dogma which implies a contradiction are not the simple principles of physics, but the axioms of eternal truth which one cannot doubt without quenching the light of reason completely. For exam-

ple, when I say that a round and flat host cannot be the body of a man, which is neither round nor flat, and when I emphasize all those other contradictions which were
mentioned above, I rely on this axiom: that a thing cannot both be and not be at the
same time.[10]

This anonymous text accurately summarizes one strand of Amyraut's
argument. There are some objects of knowledge that fall naturally
within the scope of human reason and these constitute a negative
criterion of what the Scriptures invite us to believe, in this sense:
whatever mysteries are revealed, they cannot include beliefs that are
irrational. Therefore, if a particular interpretation of the Scriptures
results in an irrational belief, it is more likely that we are misinter-
pretating the texts than that God is demanding our assent to what is
irrational. There are miminal rational standards which any proposed
interpetation of the Scriptures must satisfy.

There was a second strand to Amyraut's argument, which relied
on the claim that the evidence of our senses is to be believed unless
either reason or faith provides a good reason for overruling that evidence. In the case of the eucharistic liturgy, our senses seem to indicate that we are presented with bread and wine and that they do not
undergo any substantial change during the course of the liturgy. This
evidence could be set aside if reason persuaded us otherwise. But
those who defend transubstantiation claim that this mystery transcends reason, and therefore reason could not provide the relevant
overriding evidence. We have to rely, then, on our reading of the
Scriptures. But the Scriptures often have to be interpreted metaphor-
ically rather than literally, so that we are not invited to believe, for
example, that God is literally a shepherd. Hence, failing any counter-
vailing evidence either from reason or the Scriptures, we should trust
our senses and not accept the doctrine of transubstantiation.[11]

Toland claims in the preface to *Christianity Not Mysterious* that he
had been 'educated, from my Cradle, in the grossest Superstition and
Idolatry' (p. 7). Given his exposure to Calvinist hermeneutics in his
studies in Holland, and the extent to which his critique of religious
mysteries reflects the dominant Calvinist position of the seventeenth
century, it is plausible to read his book as falling within an established
pattern of criticism at that time. The novelty of his approach comes
from the influence of Locke's empiricism, and the greater confidence

in the powers of perception than was claimed, for example, by either Descartes or the anonymous critic of Rohault quoted above. But these are relatively minor, local differences within a much wider critical agenda. The wider question concerns a theory of interpretation. The Scriptures present us with texts written in an earlier age in languages that we no longer speak. Toland did much work on apocryphal texts in an effort to exclude false scriptures from the official canon of genuine scripture. But even if the genuine books of the Bible have been identified, there remains a fundamental question about how to interpret what we are invited by its authors to believe and, in attempting to interpret the texts, about how to recognize different styles of writing, whether metaphorical or literal; what role should be given to our day-to-day knowledge of the world around us and of the scientific theories of our day; at the deepest level, to what extent must we observe the laws of logic – or logic as we know it – and to what extent must the content of what is allegedly revealed by God be expressed in terms or concepts that are accessible to human reason?

Toland's *Christianity not Mysterious* was immediately notorious for the sharpness with which it expressed his objections to the established churches of the time, thereby challenging their claim to possess an arcane, salvific knowledge that was not available to ordinary mortals. Today's readers will hardly be surprised at the questions he raised – or at the reactions of those he criticized. I have argued that Toland's critique falls squarely within a tradition of inquiry that was well established by the middle of the seventeenth century and that, historically, he was not an uninformed maverick who delighted merely in asking questions for the sake of generating controversy. The questions raised by Toland, in the language and within the general background assumptions that were typical of the period, remain with us in the late twentieth century. It remains an open question for us, even today, whether we should trust our senses and our reason when we are invited to believe any doctrine or theory, including religious or theological doctrines. Of course the way in which we discuss these issues has changed significantly since Toland's day. We realize that there is no single logic that is either innate or presupposed by all theoretical initiatives. Nor are we confident about identifying socalled 'common notions', if that term includes some kind of absolute knowledge claim with which all possible theories or doctrines have to agree. Finally, we have learned to recognize that what is 'rational' cannot be established a priori, and that what counts as rational is partly a function of what theories, scientific or otherwise, we have found to work (in the relevant senses). All these post-Kantian insights widen and deepen the scope for questioning the acceptability of different religious doctrines. Yet despite the progress made and the greater conceptual tolerance created, Toland's questions remain to be articulated in the language of each generation. If we are invited to believe something, whether its source is religious or otherwise, do we not need an account of the limits of what is humanly credible? In particular, how is it possible to believe what is allegedly beyond our conceptual capacities, and what would it mean to believe what is logically incoherent?

NOTES

1   'Some memoirs of the life and writings of Mr Toland', in P. Des Maizeaux (ed.) A Collection of several pieces of Mr Toland (London 1726), vol. I, p. cx.

2   See page 6 in the present edition. All further page citations for Christianity not Mysterious are given in the text.

3   Pierre Bayle, An Historical and Critical Dictionary by Monsieur Bayle, trans. into English, with many editions and corrections, made by the author himself, that are not in the French editions, 4 vols (London 1710), vol. I, p. lvi.

4   'It seems that the Papists and Lutherans ought more strongly to insist upon this principle than the Calvinists; for the doctrine of the real presence has a more particular occasion for it.' Bayle, Dictionary, vol. I, p. lviii.

5   The Philosophical Writings of Descartes, trans. J. Cottingham, R. Stoohoff and D. Murdoch, vol. II (Cambridge University Press 1984), p. 273.

6   Descartes to More, 5 February 1649, in The Philosophical Writings of Descartes, Vol. III (Cambridge University Press 1991), p. 363.

7   Moise Amyraut, De l'elévation de la foy et de l'abaissement de la raison en la créance des mystères de la Religion (Saumur 1641).

8   Ibid., p. 59.

9   Reflexions physiques sur la transubstantiation, & sur ce que Mr Rohault en a ecrit dans ses Entretiens (La Rochelle 1675).

10 Ibid. pp. 33-4.

11 Amyraut, Apologie pour ceux de la religion, sur les sujets d'aversion que plusieurs pensent avoir contre leurs personnes & leur creance (Saumur 1647), pp. 265-76.

TOLAND'S SEMANTIC PANTHEISM

Stephen H. Daniel

Despite John Toland's prior academic association with Presbyterian and Remonstrant centres of learning in Scotland and Holland, most discussions of *Christianity not Mysterious* approach the text as if it were part of an English theological debate. That is understandable, considering how the participants in British religious disputes at the end of the seventeenth century were generally familiar with the doctrinal claims of their Protestant adversaries. But as is indicated by the amazing inclination of those disputants to misinterpret one another, their use of identical or similar terms masks profound differences in mentality epitomized by the contrast between Anglican and non-Anglican schools of thought.

That contrast is nowhere more evident than in the idea that there are two Tolands: one, the champion of civil theology who seeks to dissolve religious and civil disputes by appealing to a Lockean vocabulary; the other, the heterodox proponent of the materialist and esoteric doctrines of the hermetic tradition.[1] Whether these two aspects of his thought can be reconciled depends, I suggest, on noting how Toland's studies at Glasgow, Edinburgh, and Amsterdam immersed him in ontological doctrines promoted by Henry More (1614-87), Joseph Raphson (1648-1712), and seventeenth-century followers of the Renaissance logician Peter Ramus. By determining how Ramist principles in particular qualify the Scholastic, Cartesian, or Lockean terminology used by Toland, we are in a better position to understand how his doctrines differ fundamentally from those of English writers with whom he is usually linked.

The path from Toland to the Ramists is circuitous. It is based on circumstantial evidence made all the more tenuous by three centuries of scholarly association of Toland with Locke. Complicating matters further is the fact that some of the authors to whom Toland was exposed in Scotland and Holland propose syntheses of Ramist, Neoplatonic and hermetic themes that are not always consistent. Indeed, because these authors adopt the same terminology as that found in Locke and others who assume an alternative mentality, they are sometimes misinterpreted by Toland even when he agrees with them.

For the study of *Christianity not Mysterious*, however, it is not crucial to differentiate those ideas as much as it is to note how one Ramist presupposition in particular expands on an early Stoic claim often invoked in hermetic tracts – namely, that intelligibility depends on a material, rhetorical communication (or *logos*) that is expressed as 'the Book of Nature'.[2] In the Cambridge Platonist version of this doctrine, the divine *Logos* or Word is a substantial emanation from God. But Cambridge Platonism does not explain what it means to talk about an 'emanation', because it does not provide a semantics that justifies claims in Platonic-Aristotelian metaphysics.

The solution to this difficulty comes from one of the Cambridge Platonists himself. Henry More's distinctly un-Platonic solution to this difficulty – the equation of God and space – depends on a radical reunderstanding of the presuppositions of meaning. Such a reunderstanding underlies the millenarian, mystical writings of Newton and fellow mathematician Joseph Raphson.[3] It also provides Toland with an idea that can hardly be called a mere extension of hermeticism or a variation of Neoplatonic thought. Instead, it requires a critique of the discursive space in which distinctions (including metaphysical ones) are made. And though Toland assumes that More and Raphson (whom Toland mistakenly calls Ralphson) think of space or God in terms of the same Platonic-Aristotelian metaphysics of substance to which Descartes and Locke are indebted, he uses their analyses to reinstate the Ramist sensitivity to the space of discourse and the primacy of communicability in ontology.

Through the end of the seventeenth century, Presbyterian theologians in Scotland, Holland, and Cambridge encouraged their students to read Ramist authors (e.g., William Ames and Alexander Richardson). As in the seventeenth century at Trinity College, Dublin, the Ramist education of Puritan divines continued to fashion curricula well into the eighteenth century at Harvard and Yale.[4] The Dutch Remonstrant Seminary at Amsterdam – where Toland went to study with More's friends Philip van Limborch and Jean le Clerc – was famous for its Ramist ties.[5]

But to see how More's ideas would have meant something quite different for Cambridge scholars and Scottish, Irish, and Dutch students of Ramist ways of thinking – vis-à-vis Scholastics, Cartesians, or Lockeans – we have to turn to Raphson or Jonathan Edwards. They open up the possibility for a new understanding not only of More (and perhaps Newton) but also of Toland. Once we take into account this intellectual environment – as opposed to what he encountered at Oxford in 1693 – we can begin to understand how his reading of hermetic texts and interpretation of references to pre-Socratics, Cabalists and Spinoza by Raphson, More and Theophilus Gale could have been affected by Ramist principles. We can also begin to understand why More and especially Raphson (who may have been schooled in Ireland) attract the attention of Berkeley.[6]

When Toland adopts both the vocabulary and presuppositions of the Cartesian-Lockean mentality to criticize those other thinkers – as in his Letters to Serena (1704) – he misinterprets them. But even then, his half-hearted criticisms draw attention to the shaky foundations on which they are based. He thus invites a shift away from the un-self-critical presuppositions of substantialist metaphysics to the semantic ontology that informs Christianity not Mysterious. In doing so, he retrieves the fundamentally Ramist insight that the infinite and unavoidable space of discourse is the rhetorical context in terms of which all beliefs are evaluated for meaning.

For More and Raphson, this seemingly methodological constraint is an ontological doctrine. For Toland, it becomes a semantic principle with only indirect theological import. So when Toland first mentions pantheism in Socinianism Truly Stated (1705), he merely hints at its metaphysical connotations. Though his subsequent references to pantheism (e.g., in the 1709 Origines judaicae and the 1720 Pantheisticon) identify God with the universe, he rejects the view that this entails atheism.[7]

How Toland's pantheism avoids the charge of atheism is clear from approaching it in terms of the work of More and Raphson. Despite the oft-repeated claim that Toland coined the word 'pantheist', it seems more likely that he picked up the term from Raphson who had referred to 'pantheos' and 'pantheismus' in *De Spatio Reali seu Ente Infinito* (1697).[8] In his *Letters to Serena*, Toland had criticized Raphson's endorsement of pantheism because the characterization of space as abstract extension or 'extension in general' appears to identify God with empty (i.e. incorporeal) space. That, Toland notes, is like saying that God is 'a new kind of nothing endowed with the propertys of a being', which (he cautions) borders on atheism.[9]

But not long after the publication of *Serena*, Toland refers to himself (in *Socinianism*) as a pantheist. This turnabout is to be explained, I suspect, by noting that Toland, following Raphson, recognized that *pantheism* can mean two things. First, it can refer to a belief that God is nothing more than the totality of extended, material nature. Raphson refers to proponents of such a belief as 'panhylists' because they believe that there is nothing superior to matter, and he agrees that they are appropriately called atheists.[10] Such theorists had been the targets of Toland's critical remarks in *Serena*.

In contrast to these atheistic panhylists are those who Raphson calls 'pantheists': they believe in 'a certain universal substance, material as well as intelligent, that fashions all things that exist out of its own essence'.[11] This second, more appropriate way to understand Toland's pantheism portrays God as an omnipresent space or 'immaterial extension'. As More suggests, this means that the divine semantic space, in terms of which material and immaterial distinctions are first made intelligible, should not be confused with material body. God is 'antecedent to all matter, forasmuch as no matter nor any being else can be conceived to be but in this. In this are all things necessarily apprehended *to live and move and have their being*'.[12] All determinate things, whether they are bodily or spiritual, depend on this 'extended substance' for their identity and existence. Because its identity consists in being the matrix for discernment and intellection, it is eminently accessible to any speaker or thinker – and, as Toland argues, can hardly be considered mysterious.

Like Spinoza, More and Edwards, when Raphson and Toland use the Cartesian-Lockean vocabulary of substance, they can be misinterpreted (and sometimes even are by one another) as implying that pantheism is yet another metaphysical doctrine. But instead of referring to a particular doctrine about the relation of God and the world, these thinkers are concerned with the discursive space in terms of which any thing is intelligible. Pantheism for these thinkers cannot be contrasted with any other -ism, because it inscribes the domain in terms of which all existence and thought (including that of God or nature) is aboriginally meaningful. As More puts it, 'This distinct space cannot but be something, and yet not corporeal, because neither impenetrable nor tangible; it must of necessity be a substance incorporeal necessarily and eternally existing of itself: which the clearer idea of a Being absolutely perfect will more punctually inform us to be the self-subsisting God.'[13] Edwards makes the point even more explicitly:

Space is this necessary, eternal, infinite and omnipresent being. We find that we can with ease conceive how all other beings should not be. We can remove them out of our minds, and place some other in the room of them; but space is the very thing we can never remove and conceive of its not being. ... But I had as good speak plain: I have already said as much as that space is God.[14]

God is the space in which intelligible distinctions are made. To think that that space itself can be the object of predication is to attribute to the discursive matrix of intelligibility characteristics that are purely derivative. In opposition to such a move, pantheism retains the hermetic sensitivity to the sensual immediacy and efficacy of signs and language and resists the temptation to assume that the distinction between word and thing or idea is simply a given.

Though the pantheism of the late seventeenth and eighteenth centuries – like deconstruction and post-structuralism – thus seems to be a form of materialism or linguistic idealism, it in fact reveals how such latter -isms presuppose domains of discursive exchange that cannot themselves be called material or immaterial. Even to refer to these domains as divine (as More and Raphson do) can be misleading insofar as such references imply that the distinction of divine and created is already intelligible.

That is why in *Christianity not Mysterious* Toland steadfastly refuses to subordinate 'right reason' to either divine revelation or the 'natural' pronouncements of self-interested human beings.[15] Both the supernatural and the natural must rely for their intelligibility on a discourse that is neither divinely inspired nor a human creation, for even to make that claim would entail appealing uncritically to some prior meta-language. Instead, both forms of expression must depend on a vocabulary and grammar that are identified as such only in derivative terms.

To speak, therefore, about this discursive space already invokes a syntax that precludes knowing anything about its essence. Likewise, any attempt to understand the essence of God, the Lockean 'real essence' of material bodies, or the internal constitution of the soul must inevitably fail, because to understand them would mean interpreting them in the derivative terms of what is useful and necessary (pp. 61-4). To know the real essences of God, bodies, or the soul would assume another network of meanings in terms of which such essences are intelligible. This, in turn, would raise the question of how the semantic network that depicts real essences is itself intelligible; and that network would be intelligible in terms of yet another network, and so on.

Toland's alternative to this regress is to argue that, because our knowledge of meaningful things is limited to what we find useful and necessary, we know only the 'nominal essences' of things (61-2). Our shared, communicable experience with others forms the context for what we can legitimately claim to know. These 'common notions' comprise the discursive domain of intelligible experience and provide the basis for what we can legitimately claim to comprehend (34-5, 81). Since comprehending a thing means knowing 'its chief properties and their several uses' (59), comprehension entails discerning how the thing is consistent with our common notions (60).[16]

Common notions are not mere commonplaces that provide practical guidance or aid rhetorical presentations. Rather, they define the structure of 'reason in general' (22). They do not reveal any natural order or *logos* of things, nor do they express the inner operations of the soul. They simply mark out objective, communally regulated guides for interpreting thought and action by indicating how ideas agree or disagree. They thus provide a means to differentiate and relate discernible things (including individual minds).

Apart from the discursive context of 'common sense' by which meanings (e.g., of what a 'self' is) are specified, there is no way to identify a self or, more importantly, to determine how an idea could be self-evident. For an idea to be *self*-evident, it must be evident to some intelligible and identifiable self. And since the self or mind is defined by sense impressions (29), self-evident ideas are meaningful only insofar as they are expressions differentiated extensionally in the space of discourse. That is why self-evident truths are not limited to a few axioms or maxims, but are 'indefinite' in number (23) – and why what is self-evident to one person might not be self-evident to another (30). Insofar as an idea is incorporated (or 'comprehended') into the complex of ideas that define the self, it is *self*-authorizing. That is why 'He that comprehends a thing, is as sure of it as if he were himself the Author' (37). To comprehend a thing means to know how it relates to the other ideas that comprise the self, and that means suspending the belief that the self somehow transcends its ideas.

As in his subsequent writings, however, in *Christianity not Mysterious* Toland contrasts the self or mind with the active principle of knowledge, the soul.[17] The soul cannot be discerned or discursively identified because it is the expression of discernment itself. It is the figural, rhetorical possibility of the radical disruption and realignment of meanings that threatens the stability of common sense.[18] Accordingly, it can be reflexively alluded to only through the derivative identification of the self (23). It is, as Berkeley later observes, the subjective principle that speaks or *subsists*, not an object that *exists* distinct from the expressions that designate it as an intelligible entity.[19]

The experiences that form the mind are the unintelligible 'revelations' that identify the self. The mind cannot refuse to recognize what is presented to it or to be unconscious of its own operations because, properly speaking, there is no self to which revelations are originally made. Even after its formation, the self continues to be modified by revelations (experiences) that become self-evident only after they are recognized as intelligible (i.e. relatable to the self). In this way, so-called 'mysteries' are really revelations that subsequently become either intelligible claims or self-evident truths.

Since the discursive space of expression itself cannot be objectified other than in the derivative terms of substantialist metaphysics, it is not surprising that references to it as a book or a language are typically dismissed as mere metaphors. Consistent with the Ramist emphasis on the centrality of communication, though, Toland is more sensitive to the hermeneutic complexities of such images. He points out that 'to comprehend the sense' of the New Testament, we have to know the grammar of the language in which it is written (87). Likewise, to comprehend experience or nature in general, we must consider it as much a text in need of interpretation as the Bible.[20] This does not mean that we treat nature and Scripture *as if* they are texts. It means, instead, that we acknowledge their ineluctably textual character.

This pointed way of expressing the semantic nature of pantheism suggests that there is something wrong-headed about thinking of the Ramist principles that underlie Toland's position as rhetorical rather than ontological. For if the means for distinguishing rhetoric from ontology are themselves functions of an *Ur*-text that human history inscribes, then Toland's confidence in the soundness of right reason appears justified. To critics who claim that human reason is flawed due to its fallen condition, Toland replies that we have to rely on what we comprehend as long as our experience of meaning is mediated by self-evident ideas. The only alternative to such a view (as Edwards points out) is to imagine a 'new sense of things' in which meaning is no longer tied to the self and each thing is known in terms of its inherent significance for everything else.[21]

However, rather than subsuming the self in the regenerate mentality of the saint, Toland affirms the right of the self to a place in divine, discursive space by highlighting the rhetorical legacy of Stoic legal theory in Ramism. In terms of that theory, there must first be a hearing to determine whether a thing has standing before any judgment about the agreement or disagreement of ideas can be made. If no hearing is granted, the thing is unintelligible and incomprehensible. If it receives a hearing, it becomes a *matter* before the court of reason and can be comprehended.[22] So when Toland remarks, 'I know no Difference between not hearing a thing at all, and not comprehending it when you do' (67), he draws attention to a common Ramist theme – namely, that comprehension presupposes the placement of a topic in a network of intelligible relations.[23]

By associating Toland with Ramism, I do not mean to suggest that Toland is a Ramist, any more than that Spinoza, More, Raphson, Newton, or Berkeley are Ramists. I intend merely to indicate how the Ramist rhetorical presuppositions of intelligibility qualify attempts to counteract the substantialist ontology and representationalist epistemology of Cartesian-Lockean thought. Because these responses are so heavily conditioned by the vocabulary and syntax of the mentality they try to undercut, they are easy prey for critics who interpret their divine semantics as atheistic materialism. Indeed, as their comments about one another sometimes show, they can be misled by the enticements of philosophic discourse as easily as their critics. That, of course, only makes all the more forcefully Toland's claim about the pervasiveness of discourse.

NOTES

1   Cf. Robert E. Sullivan, *John Toland and the Deist Controversy* (Harvard University Press, Cambridge 1982), pp. 115-22; and Stephen H. Daniel, *John Toland: His Methods, Manners and Mind* (McGill-Queen's University Press, Montreal 1984), p. 222.

2   See Stephen H. Daniel, *The Philosophy of Jonathan Edwards: A Study in Divine Semiotics* (Indiana University Press, Bloomington 1994), pp. 32-4, 41-2, 73-96.

3   See Brian P. Copenhaver, 'Jewish Theologies of Space in the Scientific Revolution: Henry More, Joseph Raphson, Isaac Newton, and their Predecessors', *Annals of Science* 37 (1980), pp. 520-46; Richard H. Popkin, *The Third Force in Seventeenth-Century Thought* (E.J. Brill, Leiden 1992), p. 91; and Philip C. Almond, 'Henry More and the Apocalypse', *Journal of the History of Ideas* 54 (1993), pp. 189-200.

4   See William Samuel Howell, *Logic and Rhetoric in England, 1500-1700* (Russell and Russell, New York 1961), pp. 237-8; and E.J. Furlong, 'The Study of Logic in Trinity College, Dublin', *Hermathena* 60 (1942), p. 39.

5   See Rosalie L. Colie, *Light and Enlightenment: A Study of the Cambridge Platonists and the Dutch Armenians* (Cambridge University Press, Cambridge 1957), pp. 27-51.

6   See George Berkeley, *Philosophical Commentaries* 298, 827, in *Philosophical Works*, M.R. Ayers (ed.) (Charles E. Tuttle Co., Rutland, Vt. 1992), pp. 278, 331, and *A Treatise concerning the Principles of Human Knowledge*, sec. 117, in *Philosophical Works*, pp. 113-14. Cf. A.A. Luce, Berkeley and Malebranche: *A Study of the Origins of Berkeley's Thought* (Clarendon Press, Oxford 1934), p. 49; and David J. Thomas and Judith M. Smith, 'Joseph Raphson, F.R.S.', *Notes and Records of the Royal Society of London* 44 (1990), p. 161.

7   See Daniel 1984, p. 224; and Sullivan 1982, p. 182. Cf. David Berman, 'Disclaimers as Offence Mechanisms in Charles Blount and John Toland', in *Atheism from the Reformation to the Enlightenment*, ed. Michael Hunter and David Wooton (Clarendon Press, Oxford 1992), p. 272.

8   Raphson's work was attached to the second edition of his *Analysis Aequationum Universalis* (1690), for which he is better known today because of the Newton-Raphson method for approximating the roots of a mathematical equation. Another of Raphson's friends, Pierre Des Maizeaux, was Toland's acquaintance and biographer.

9   Toland, *Letters to Serena* (Bernard Lintot, London 1704), p. 219. Cf. Sullivan 1982, pp. 179-85.

10 Joseph Raphson, *De Spatio Reali seu Ente Infinito* (John Taylor, London 1697), pp. 8, 21. Cf. Copenhaver, 'Jewish Theologies', p. 534.

11 Cf. Henry More, *Divine Dialogues* (James Flesher, London 1668), p. 125; and Copenhaver, 'Jewish Theologies', p. 536.

12 More, *Divine Dialogues*, 106-7. Cf. Wallace E. Anderson (ed.), *Scientific and Philosophical Writings* by Jonathan Edwards (Yale University Press, New Haven 1980), 57n-58n; and Copenhaver, 'Jewish Theologies', pp. 520-1. The italicized phrase is the oft-cited remark from *Acts of the Apostles* 17:28.

13 Henry More, *An Appendix to the Foregoing Antidote against Atheism* (William Morden, London 1662), p. 165. Cf. Anderson (ed.), 1980, p. 61.

14 Jonathan Edwards, 'Of Being' [c. 1721], in Anderson (ed.), *Scientific and Philosophical Writings*, p. 203. Cf. More, *Divine Dialogues*, p. 125. See also Daniel, *Philosophy of Edwards*, p. 87.

15 See *Christianity not Mysterious*, sec. 2 ch. 4. Subsequent pag references to CNM are included parenthetically in the text.

16 See Daniel 1984, pp. 57-8, 84-7, 222; and Joel C. Weinsheimer, *Eighteenth-Century Hermeneutics: Philosophy of Interpretation in England from Locke to Burke* (Yale University Press, New Haven 1993), pp. 58-9.

17 See Daniel 1984, pp. 76, 190-1.

18 See Stephen H. Daniel, 'The Subversive Philosophy of John Toland', in *Irish Writing: Exile and Subversion*, ed. Paul Hyland and Neil Sammells (Macmillan, London 1991), pp. 4-7.

19 Cf. Berkeley, *Principles of Human Knowledge*, secs. 89-90, 146, in *Philosophical Works*, pp. 104-5, 123.

20 Cf. Weinsheimer, *Eighteenth-Century Hermeneutics*, 51-8, 63-8.

21 Cf. Daniel, *Philosophy of Edwards*, 58, 130-3.

22 On the Stoic legal character of this mentality, see Stephen H. Daniel, 'Vico's Historicism and the Ontology of Arguments', *Journal of the History of Philosophy* 33 (1995), pp. 441-3; and Stephen H. Daniel, 'The Semiotic Ontology of Jonathan Edwards', *The Modern Schoolman* 71 (1994), pp. 289-304.

23 Cf. Craig Walton, 'Ramus and Socrates', *Proceedings of the American Philosophical Society* 114 (1970), pp. 123-6.

'PERPETUAL FLUX':
NEWTON, TOLAND, SCIENCE
AND THE STATUS QUO

Philip McGuinness

'I am said to have the greatest Man in the World against me.'
John Toland, *Letters to Serena*, p. 182

I

Two of the greatest scientists of the seventeenth century were Robert Boyle (1627-91) and Isaac Newton (1642-1727).[1] Every schoolgirl has heard of Boyle's Law and the story of Newton and the apple. But dig deeper into the science and society in which these two men were embedded, and one is allowed not only a fascinating insight into the use and abuse of science by ideologues, but also a glimpse into how the particular social situation of a scientist can affect his scientific-philosophical conclusions. In the 1640s Boyle was influenced by hermeticism, alchemy and natural magic at a time when many adherents of radical groups such as the Quakers, Seekers, Diggers, Ranters and Levellers believed that all matter is alive and moving (hylozoism). The revolutionary threat from the Levellers and the Diggers was a real one in Civil War England, and such ideas would doubtless be a threat to Boyle's interests if they gained wider circulation. Sibley suggests that Boyle propounded instead a corpuscular theory of inert, dead matter in order to help in undermining these radical groups.[2]

Sixty years later and this scenario of conflicting interest between the scientist's speculations and societal conservatism is replayed with Newton inheriting Boyle's mantle and Toland as an able stand-in for the English radicals. Born in the year of Galileo's death, Newton later codified the observations of that great Italian into his three Laws of Motion and brilliantly explained Kepler's Laws via his Law of Universal Gravitation in the *Principia* in 1687, a triumph of mathematical physics.[3] Among myriad other achievements, Newton was the first to show conclusively that white light is a combination of colours. In his *Opticks* (1704), he described a series of experiments with light using prisms, lenses and a straight edge which were easily reproducible by the interested reader. This ease of reproducibility played no small part in disseminating a knowledge of and respect for science among educated people in the eighteenth century.

The influence of the *Principia* and the *Opticks* has been gigantic. A. Rupert Hall – an authority on Newton's publications and unpublished manuscripts for fifty years – has described this influence:

That *Principia* and *Opticks* together shaped the future of astronomy, chemistry, mechanics, physics, and physiology requires no emphasis here. The same books also moulded for some generations the thinking of philosophers, theologians and poets as no specialist work concerned with the physical sciences have done since.[4]

The *Principia* was written in mathematical Latin. Few read it directly; it was popularized by university lecturers such as Newton's friend David Gregory (1661-1708) at Edinburgh and by the Boyle lectures (see below).[5] By contrast, the *Opticks* was written in English and was 'a gadgeteer's delight'.[6] At the back of the *Opticks* was a collection of 'Queries' wherein Newton gave full vent – in the first edition – to his philosophical conjectures on the nature of phenomena. This rendered the *Opticks* a curious yet compelling *mélange* of easily replicated experiments and occasionally wild speculation.

The triumph of Newton was complete in both science and society. Already Lucasian Professor of Mathematics at the age of twenty-seven (a post later held by Paul Dirac (1902-84) and Stephen Hawking), he became an MP in the aftermath of the Williamite settlement in 1689. Cleric and radical alike embraced his scientific achievements with enthusiasm. By the late 1680s the *Principia* was being taught at universities. Indeed, it is extremely likely that

Toland studied the book at Edinburgh under David Gregory.[7] At the same time, the Newtonian system was being appropriated by the new post-1688 English ruling class. In Robert Boyle's view, the accession of James II had threatened to unify the papists with atheists and sectaries and destroy the Reformation in England.[8] The stability of Newton's cosmos could also be applied to Williamite civil society and yield a stable and harmonious order which kept the privileged at the apex of power. After the success of the Glorious Revolution of 1688 the Catholic menace receded, but there was still a threat to social stability from the religious and political radicals.

On the death of Boyle in 1691, a series of annual lectures was provided for in his will, their purpose being to advance the Christian religion 'against notorious Infidels, namely, Atheists, Theists, Pagans, Jews, and Mahometans'.[9] The early lecturers became known as the Newtonians. Margaret Jacob describes the 'Boyle lectures' as 'the most influential and widely read lectures ever delivered in the eighteenth century'.[10] In a later work she describes the ideological function of Newton's science as follows:

The cosmic order and design explicated in the *Principia* became [...] a natural model for a Christian society, providentially sanctioned, reasonably tolerant of diverse religious beliefs provided they did not threaten the stability of the polity (hence the exclusion of Catholics [...]), yet in need of no further political reform beyond that embodied in the Revolution Settlement.[11]

It is instructive to examine the tortuous history of two separate extracts from *Opticks* (II and III below) because they illustrate the complex interweaving of religion, politics and science in Williamite England.

II

With the lapsing of the Licensing Act in 1695, John Toland was preparing to publish *Christianity not Mysterious*.[12] Outrage greeted Toland's literary bombshell. In the eyes of the Newtonians, such a book evidenced the continuing rise in atheistical tendencies. Friends of the eminent scientist were urged to 'keep Sir Isaac Newton at work, that we may have ... his thoughts about God'.[13] However, Toland hadn't finished upsetting the cosily-stacked Newtonian-Anglican applecart. In 1696 he had unearthed a copy of Giordano Bruno's *Lo Spaccio de la Bestia Trifontane*, known in English as *The Expulsion of the Triumphant Beast*.[14] This book – Bruno's most scathing attack on the Roman Church – had a huge influence on Toland. In it Bruno states that God is the source of all change in matter which is in constant motion.[15] *Spaccio* may have cost Bruno (1548-1600)[16] his life: it was the only book mentioned in the sentence of death by *auto-da-fé* handed down by the Cardinal-Inquisitor.[17] And no wonder! Many took the *bestia* to be the Pope himself. Toland disagreed, being convinced that Bruno was referring to religious systems:

... either paganism, or Judaism, or Christianity; he [Bruno] attacks and ridicules them and rejects them all equally without ceremony or exception.[18]

The signature of Bruno's ideas on motion and matter is evident throughout Toland's *Letters to Serena* (1704), especially in the fifth letter, entitled 'Motion essential to Matter'. For example:

All the parts of the Universe are in this constant Motion of destroying and begetting, of begetting and destroying; and the greater Systems are acknowledg'd to have their ceaseless Movements as well as the smallest Particles, the very central Globes of the Vortexes turning about their own Axis; and every Particle in the Vortex gravitating towards the Centre.[19]

In *Serena*, matter is one, motion is inherent in matter, and no void exists. Toland's matter is the source of life itself, whereas Newtonian matter is 'sluggish, inactive, brute and stupid'.[20] Toland fully accepted Newton's *physics*, and professed his respect for Newton by calling him 'that deservedly admir'd Author, who has seen the farthest of all Men living into the actual State of Matter'.[21] In fact Toland was one of the first writers to bring word of Newton's science into France.[22] However, he argued that Newton's *interpretation* of his own laws was not the only possible interpretation.[23]

The acceptance of Newton's physics in *Letters to Serena* by the most notorious freethinker of the time appears to have had the effect of making Newton somewhat suspect to orthodox Anglicans. The first edition of *Opticks* in 1704 had only sixteen Queries; Newton added seven more between 1704 and the 1706 Latin version. However, there is in existence an early draft of the twenty-third Query which differs significantly from the published version. Thus Newton wrote and rewrote this Query between the publication of *Serena* and the Latin edition of the *Opticks* in 1706.[24] Here he tried to grapple with the significance of Toland's hylozoism. The draft version of the twenty-third query states:

… it seems to have been an ancient opinion that matter depends upon a Deity for its laws of motion as well as for its existence. These are passive laws and to affirm that there are no others is to speak against experience. … all matter duly formed is attended with signes of life.[25]

This text does not appear in the final version of Query 23.

Why did Newton not publish this draft version? To state publicly that 'all matter duly formed is attended with signes of life' would have aligned Newton with Toland and the heretic Bruno. One suspects that Newton may have become a prisoner of his own ideology, trapped in the cul-de-sac of orthodoxy.

III

Rupert Hall discusses another example of self-censorship by Isaac Newton after *Letters to Serena* was published.[26] In Query 28 of *Optice* – the 1706 version of *Opticks*, translated into Latin by Samuel Clarke – Newton originally stated:

Is not universal space the sensorium ['place of sensation'] of a Being Incorporeal, Living and Intelligent, because he sees and discerns, in the inmost and most Thorough Manner, the Very Things themselves, and comprehends them as being entirely and immediately Present within Himself … [27]

However, after page 315 was printed either Newton or Clarke realized that to admit that universal space was the place of God's knowledge was to flirt with heresy. A 'cancel sheet' was inserted and the new text read:

... does it not appear from Phenomena that there is a Being incorporeal, living, intelligent, omnipresent, who in infinite Space, as it were in his Sensory, sees the things themselves intimately, and thoroughly perceives them, and comprehends them wholly by their immediate presence to himself ...[28]

Although Newton's new God is omnipresent, no longer are things 'present within Himself'; rather, 'presence to himself' implies a God somewhat above and beyond matter.

Unfortunately for Newton, an original copy of the 1706 *Optice* was read by his arch-rival Leibniz, who was greatly disturbed by the pantheistic sympathies expressed in Query 28.[29] (Leibniz and Toland had debated passionately about religion, philosophy and politics when Toland had stayed in Hanover. While not agreeing with him, Leibniz appreciated Toland's pantheistic views.[30]) Leibniz and Newton had also clashed in the past, ostensibly about science, but in reality about the Protestant Succession to the English crown: Leibniz stating that their arguments reflected not 'a quarrel between Mr Newton and me, but between Germany and England'.[31] Leibniz translated *sensorium* as meaning 'the organ of sensation' and he protested to Newton via Clarke that Newton was attributing organs to God! Clarke, in reply, denied this, unaware that Leibniz had seen the original *Optice* text. In the 1717 edition of *Opticks*, Newton disclaimed the idea of God having organs, saying that

... we are not to consider the World as the Body of God, or the several Parts thereof, as the Parts of God. He is an uniform Being, devoid of Organs, Members and Parts, and they are his Creatures subordinate to him, and subservient to his Will ...[32]

Newton was here attempting to distance his speculations from pantheism. On another occasion he stated:

Indeed however we cast about we find almost no other reason for atheism than this notion of bodies having, as it were, a complete, absolute and independent reality in themselves.[33]

This quotation suggests that Newton – like many others – believed that pantheism was identical to atheism.

IV

What the above two examples suggest is that Newton was publicly distancing himself from the idea of God being at the heart of all matter. It is not clear if Newton *privately* accepted this distancing. Newton's friend David Gregory suggested that this might not have been the case. He stated in 1705 that

His doubt was whether he should put the last Quaere [Query 31] thus. *What the space that is empty of body is filled with.* The plain truth is, he believes God to be omnipresent in the literal sense; ... God must be sensible of every thing, being intimately present with every thing: for he supposes that as God is present in space where there is no body, he is present in space where a body is also present.[34]

Newton may have felt it politic to distance himself from the free-thinkers. It was not in Newton's interest to draw the suspicions of the orthodox clergy upon himself. He was extremely anti-Catholic, but he also denied the trinitarian doctrines of the Anglican Church.[35] Although a deeply religious man, Newton had become convinced by the 1670s that scripture and Christianity had been deliberately corrupted in the fourth and fifth centuries, a claim that Toland strongly propounds in *Christianity not Mysterious*.[36] Newton was not as hostile to the freethinkers as were the Newtonians. He was involved with a Dutch literary journal published by associates of Toland and he might well have felt at home in the coffee-house milieu that had sprung up in late-seventeenth-century London.[37] David Kubrin has admirably summarized the unique confluence of the political and the personal in Newton, which may help us to understand his reluctance to be fully public with his thoughts:

Newton ... at least at one level of his consciousness, agreed with Toland that nature was alive, sensate, infused with self-energy (identified with God), and, in fact, pervaded by the literally omnipresent God. But with the association between the concept of nature of Toland and the radical political and social ideology of the republicans and freethinkers, it was at all costs imperative for Newton to avoid being linked with Toland's ideas. It was this fear, I think, that accounts for Newton's marked reluctance to publish his real thoughts. His specific personality and his paranoic fears of attacks on his ideas were clearly responsible for Newton's sensitivity, but the specific social and political environment in which he lived ... certainly provided the context that enabled this sensitivity to lead Newton to hide some of his most important ideas.[38]

Let us return to the philosophical and spiritual implications of Newton's estrangement from a pantheistic God. If God is made more remote from matter one is then faced with a need to explain how God can effect action in the universe. Newton's solution – like many scientists before him – was to invoke the *ether*. The notion of the ether originated in Ancient Greece as the divine rarefied kind of air – the fifth element (*quintessence*) – surrounding the Earth. Aristotle (384-322 BC) held that the ether was incorruptible, unlike the other four elements (Earth, Air, Fire, Water).[39] However, Newton realized that any such medium would cause the planets to drag and eventually slow down and this had not been observed. At the same time, he refused to accept the idea that any action could take place at a distance without a medium of some kind. No such problem faced the pantheist: the ether was philosophically superfluous. If God was everywhere, there was no need for this extra medium permeating the cosmos.

In 1887, the ether hypothesis was finally disproved by Albert Michelson and Edward Morley.[40] Building on this result and on the work of the Irishman George Fitzgerald and the Dutchman Hendrik Lorentz, Albert Einstein proposed his Special Theory of Relativity in 1905.[41] One wonders if it would have taken so long to disprove the ether hypothesis had pantheistic ideas been taken more seriously by Newton and the Newtonians.

V

Why were the Newtonians so opposed to Toland, pantheism, and the freethinkers? Throughout his writings, one finds a consistency in Toland's declamations. If he concluded some truth about the natural world then he sought analogies in the turmoil of human behaviour. Toland was feared by the Newtonians because he believed that if the universe was in 'perpetual flux', then so was the political world:

All things are in a perpetual Flux, nothing permanent or in every Regard the same for one Moment. But none of them is so visibly subject to such Variations, as Kingdoms, States, and (in a word) all sorts of *Governments*.[42]

Like Hegel, Toland believed passionately that *das Wahre is das Ganze* (the true is the whole).

We tend to think today of scientists as disinterested pursuers of truth, and the right of scientists to investigate nature is not seriously questioned. In the late seventeenth and early eighteenth centuries, however, science had not the pre-eminence it possesses today. The Stuart-Williamite transition had been a traumatic one for conservatives, and many non-scientists believed that science itself was responsible for the growth of religious and philosophical heterodoxy, described then in the blanket term of 'atheism'. Scientists were forced to respond to this pressure by fiercely attacking 'atheism' and accepting the political and economic status quo.[43] Some prominent scientists (for example Boyle and, arguably, Newton) were even fervent believers in miracles.[44] Margaret Jacob has pointed out that 'freethinker' conjures up the French word *libertin*, and Anglican clergy were not slow to denounce dissolute lifestyles, the implication being that freethinkers lived in the coffee-houses and possessed questionable morals. Perhaps it was a case of free love against free trade, since Newtonians argued strongly for self-interest in a cosmically ordered market economy poised to take full advantage of England's coming primacy on the high seas and in North America.[45]

Toland had unambiguously thrown down the gauntlet to the Williamite ruling class in *Letters to Serena*. Pantheism led inevitably to political democracy: if the universe needed no Grand Architect controlling from above, England needed no king. The republican genie of the Levellers, which had been brutally confined in the 1640s by Cromwell, was now well and truly out of the bottle. The counterattack was quick in coming. Samuel Clarke gave the 1704-5 Boyle lectures and denounced Toland, Hobbes and Spinoza as atheists. Clarke argued from Newton's philosophical arguments presented in his *Opticks* that nature can only be explained by observation from experiments, i.e. from reasoning by induction, whereas Toland was deducing the nature of matter from his own principles. The fact that many of Newton's speculations in the Queries were not based solidly on evidence in the *Opticks* seems to have been lost on Clarke. (Scientists tend to use both approaches today: a theory may suggest certain experiments to be carried out in order to test the limits of that theory; results from such experiments may then cause the theory to be modified which in turn signposts new experiments, and so on.)

321

By allying Newton's achievements so closely with the Anglican establishment, the Newtonians arguably stifled the growth of science. Rupert Hall has succinctly summarized this suffocation:

> Newton carefully distinguished the affirmations in the text of *Opticks* which he believed to be well-founded and virtually unimpugnable from the speculative content of the Queries. His successors obliterated this distinction at their own risk, and in so far as they alleged that Newtonian substantive science depended upon the deeper 'truths' of these Queries, they betrayed Newton's own methodological principles. In proclaiming that their own writings flourished upon the assurance of the truth of concepts that Newton had labelled as merely conjectural, they renounced in advance the possibility of developing experimental sciences like chemistry and physiology along truly independent lines, starting from analysis of, and thought about, their respective phenomena. ... In the long run the attempts of the Newtonians to reduce all systematic scientific inquiry to the discovery of theories of atoms and forces, for all the sanction given to their example by Newton himself, had to be abandoned.[46]

The Newtonian scientific paradigm lasted from 1687 until the work of Max Planck, Albert Einstein and others in the early years of this century.[47] One could argue that a body of work that lasted for over two hundred years must be treated with huge respect and, indeed, Newton's scientific achievements were gargantuan, but the hijacking of Newton's speculations in the Queries by the conservatives led to the imposition of a rigid scientific orthodoxy which also took God out of everyday life for many.

It is also worth noting that, by refusing to accept the pantheistic musings of Toland and others, both Church and State could not adapt philosophically to the great eighteenth-century social swarm of change that was brought to a head in the French Revolution. In his *Reflections on the Revolution in France*, Edmund Burke wrote that 'a state without the means of some change is without the means of its conservation'. Eighteenth-century science had removed God from the universe, seeing the cosmos as being like a clockwork model which, once wound up, had no further need of God. This God, outside of the universe, was one that many could not relate to, or even believe in. The growth of unbelief during the Age of Reason was to threaten the stability of societies, especially where the monarch was absolute and regarded as divine, as in France. As Albert Camus put it, 'if God is denied, the king must die'.[48]

Scientists sometimes like to portray themselves as single-minded pursuers of knowledge, and innocents abroad when it comes to poltiics. The public tends to view scientists as socially withdrawn: nerds in white coats pursuing obscure, if not dangerous, research. Both stereotypes neglect the fact that the vast majority of scientists are either civil servants or employees of multinationals, at the beck and call of governments and business. This century of technological advance and total warfare has seen many scientists deeply involved in both harmful and beneficial social movements: for every Josef Mengele, there has been a Joseph Rotblat.[49] The skirmish between Newton and Toland outlined in this essay suggests that political pressure on scientists is not a modern phenomenon, but goes back hundred of years. Perhaps such pressure is as old as the concept of 'scientist' itself.

NOTES

A shorter version of this essay appeared in *History Ireland* (winter 1994).

1 Born in Lismore Castle, Co. Cork, Boyle is remembered for being the first person to confirm Galileo's conjecture that a feather and a piece of lead would fall at the same rate in a vacuum. In 1662 he showed that if the pressure on a volume of air is doubled, then the volume halves: this is Boyle's Law. His book *The Sceptical Chemist* (1661) transformed chemistry, separating it from medicine.

2 D. Sibley, *Geographies of Exclusion: Society and Difference in the West* (Routledge, London 1995), pp. 161-2. See also James Jacob & Margaret Jacob, 'The Anglican Origins of Modern Science: The Metaphysical Foundations of the Whig Constitution', *Isis*, 71(257) (1980): 251-67 , p. 255.

3 Galileo Galilei (1564-1642) was born in Pisa. His scientific achievements were manifold. He was the first to notice that the time of swing of a pendulum was independent of the amplitude of the swing. Galileo was the first to observe the heavens with a telescope. He noticed that the moon had mountains and showed that the Sun rotated on its axis every twenty-seven days. These 'flaws' on sun and moon destroyed forever the philosophic notion of the perfection of the heavens. Galileo's observations firmly established the heliocentric view of the solar system propounded by the Polish astronomer Nicolas Copernicus (1473-1543). In 1632 he published *Dialogue on the Two Chief World Systems*, which consisted of a conversation between a Copernican and a supporter of the views of Ptolemy (*fl.* AD 127-151), who saw the Sun and planets as circling the Earth. The victory by the

Copernican in this dialogue caused Galileo to be hauled in front of the Inquisition, where he was forced to renounce his views in favour of the Ptolemaic world-view. Legend has it that while doing so Galileo muttered under his breath 'Eppur si muove' ('And yet it moves'), referring to the motion of the Earth round the Sun.

An apprentice to Tycho Brahe (1546-1601) at Prague, Kepler (1571-1630) inherited his data on the orbit of Mars after Brahe's death. He deduced that planetary orbits are elliptical with the Sun at one focus. Thus the many-centuried sacredness of circular orbits was destroyed and the idea of celestial spheres had to be dismantled. Galileo had sent Kepler one of his telescopes, and by investigating how light was refracted through the lenses Kepler founded the science of modern optics. His tables of planetary orbits were the first important use to which logarithms – invented by the Scotsman John Napier (1550-1617) – were put.

4   A. Rupert Hall, *All Was Light: An Introduction to Newton's Opticks* (Clarendon Press, Oxford 1993), p. 235.

5   David Gregory came from a distinguished family of Scottish mathematicians. He was made professor of mathematics at the University of Edinburgh just before the publication of Newton's *Principia* in 1687. He claimed to be the first person to lecture publicly on Newton's theories. Gregory later disagreed with Newton's ideas of chromatic aberration, believing that a combination of two kinds of glass would eliminate any unwanted spectrum. He was proven to be correct fifty years later.

6   I. Bernard Cohen, *Franklin & Newton: An Inquiry into Speculative Newtonian Experimental Science* (American Philosophical Society, Philadelphia 1956), p. 121.

7   Margaret Jacob, 'John Toland and the Newtonian Ideology' in *Journal of the Warburg and Courtauld Institutes*, 32 (1969): 307-31, p. 310.

8   Jacob and Jacob, p. 261.

9   E. Budgell (1737), *Memoirs of the Lives and Characters of the Illustrious Family of the Boyles*, as quoted in Margaret Jacob, 'Newtonianism and the Origins of the Enlightenment: A Reassessment', *Eighteenth-Century Studies*, 11 (1977-8):1-25, p. 8.

10   Jacob 1977-8, p. 10.

11   Margaret Jacob, *The Radical Enlightenment: Pantheists, Freemasons and Republicans* (George Allen & Unwin, London 1981), p. 91.

12   From 1663 to 1695, under the Licensing Act, books were 'licensed' by the lord chancellor, the Archbishop of Canterbury and the secretaries of state, depending on subject. A book that was permitted to be published had the word 'Licensed' printed opposite the title-page. By 1695 the Licensing Act had become discredited and was allowed to lapse. After 1695 the press flourished and the works of many radical and satirical voices, such as Toland and Daniel Defoe, became widely available. (See David Ogg, *England in the Reigns of James II and William III*, Clarendon Press, Oxford 1995, pp. 510-23.)

13   Letter from Archibald Pitcairne to David Gregory, as reported by Jacob (1981), p. 91, n.6.

14   F.H. Heinemann, 'John Toland and the Age of Enlightenment' in *Review of English Studies*, 20(78): 125-46 (1944), p. 140. According to Jacob (1969, pp. 313-15), Toland purchased *Spaccio* in 1698. Heinemann quotes from a letter Toland wrote in which he states that he found it in 1696. Heinemann suggests

that Bruno's *Spaccio* might have influenced Toland while he was writing *Christianity not Mysterious*.

15 Arthur Imerti (trans.), *The Expulsion of the Triumphant Beast* (1964), pp. 126-37, as reported in Jacob (1969), p. 316.

16 Giordano Bruno was a disciple of Nicholas of Cusa (1401-64). Nicholas believed that the Earth turned on its axis and moved round the Sun, that space was infinite and that stars were other suns. Bruno also lost no opportunity to promote his views on the infiniteness of space and the inhabitability of other worlds. Both derived their view of nature from intuition rather than experiment.

17 Ramon G. Mendoza, *The Acentric Universe: Giordano Bruno's Prelude to Contemporary Cosmology* (Element Books, Dorset 1995), p. 137.

18 '… soit la religion paienne, soit la judaique, soit la chrétienne; il les attaque, les tourne en ridicule, et les rejette également sans aucune cérémonie et sans exception', in 'Lettre de Mr Toland, sur le *Spaccio della bestia trionfante*', in *Nova Bibliotheca Lubecensis*, Vol. VII; as quoted in Heinemann (1944), pp. 140-1. I am grateful to John Lewis for the translation.

19 John Toland, *Letters to Serena* (London 1704), p. 188.

20 Jacob (1969), p. 320.

21 Toland (1704), p. 202.

22 Jacob (1981), p. 99.

23 Toland (1704), p. 183.

24 With the addition of eight new Queries after the original sixteen in the 1717 English second edition of *Opticks*, the twenty-third Query became the thirty-first Query in later editions.

25 Cambridge MSS., British Museum, MS. Add. 3970, fols. 619r; as quoted in Jacob (1969), pp. 323-4.

26 This example may be evidence of censorship by Samuel Clarke, Newtonian apostle and Boyle lecturer. Clarke translated the *Opticks* into Latin (1706) and although the front page of *Optice* states that all changes were made on the author's authority, it is possible that Newton was actually unaware of this change.

27 Isaac Newton, *Optice* (1706), p. 315; as translated by Hall, pp. 136-7.

28 This text was used in the second English edition of *Opticks* in 1717, translated by either Newton or Clarke.

29 Gottfried Wilhelm Leibniz (1646-1716): philosopher, mathematician and diplomat. The first person to recognize the Law of Conservation of (Mechanical) Energy, he also served the rulers (Electors) of Hanover for forty years. A rationalist-idealist, he tried to reconcile Descartes' mechanistic philosophy of nature with the Christian faith, believing in a dynamic rather than mechanistic universe. He proposed the basic building-block of nature as the *monad*, a term he borrowed from Giordano Bruno. The *monad* was a simple, living entity, with God being the Principal Monad. (This brief life of Leibniz is culled from Mendoza, *op.cit.*, pp. 260-1.) Newton had clashed with Leibniz in the 1680s over their rival claims to be the originator of the calculus (both actually discovered it independently; however, Leibniz's notation is used today worldwide). It is likely that both watched each other's pronouncements with interest after that controversy. Daniel (p. 195) suggests that Clarke's attack on Toland (discussed below) was Newton's means of getting at Leibniz and continuing the feud.

30 At Robert Harley's request Toland had travelled in July 1701 to Hanover, where he presented the Act of Settlement – guaranteeing the Hanoverian succession in

England – to the Electress Sophia (mother of George I). While there he became intimate with Sophie Charlotte, Queen of Prussia and daughter of the Electress Sophia. Toland dedicated his 1704 book to her: 'Serena' was actually Queen Sophie Charlotte. Moreover, he presented Sophie with his treasured copy of *Spaccio*. Toland's behaviour towards Leibniz regarding Bruno's works is puzzling: while he encouraged Leibniz to read Bruno, Toland avoided showing *Spaccio* to him (Jacob 1969, pp. 314-15, and Daniel, p. 10). (Queen Sophie Charlotte is referred to as Sophia Charlotte by many historians; I have used the former to clearly distinguish her from her mother. Further information on both may be found in A.W. Ward, *The Electress Sophia and the Hanoverian Succession* (Longmans & Co., London 1909).)

31   Steven Shapin, 'Social Uses of Science', in G.S. Rousseau & Roy Porter (eds), *The Ferment of Knowledge: Studies in the Historiography of Eighteenth-Century Science* (Cambridge University Press 1980), p. 96.

32   Isaac Newton, *Opticks*, 2nd Edition (1717 (1704)), Query 31, p. 346; as quoted in Hall, p. 138.

33   Isaac Newton, 'De Gravitatione et aequipondo fluidorum', in A. Rupert Hall & Marie Boas Hall (eds), *Unpublished Scientific Papers of Isaac Newton* (Cambridge University Press 1962), p. 144.

34   David Gregory, as quoted in Hall, p. 151.

35   David Kubrin, 'Newton's Inside Out! Magic, Class Struggle, and the Rise of Mechanism in the West', in Harry Woolf (ed.), *The Analytic Spirit: Essays in the History of Science in Honor of Henry Guerlac* (Cornell University Press, Ithaca, New York 1981), p. 116.

36   *Christianity not Mysterious*,sec. III, ch. 5. For a discussion of Newton's ideas on the corruption of Scripture, see D. Gjertsen, 'Introduction', in John Fauvel, Raymond Flood, Michael Shortland & Robin Wilson (eds), *Let Newton Be: A New Perspective on his Life and Works* (Oxford University Press, 1988).

37   Jacob (1981), p. 99; Hall, p. 235.

38   Kubrin, p. 116.

39   Aristotle accepted Empedocles' four elements but suggested that a fifth element existed, which he called the ether. Aristotle believed that the heavier an object was the faster it fell, reasonable at the time since Earth was at the centre of the known universe, Water covered the earth, Air was above the water, and the stars and Sun represented Fire. This belief in differential rates of fall of objects held until Galileo and Boyle showed that, by removing the effect of air resistance, all objects fell with the same acceleration.

40   Albert Michelson (1852-1931) spent much of his life trying to measure the speed of light. He constructed an interferometer which could split light beams into two directions. He realized that if the ether existed, then one of these half-beams should travel faster than the other. When recombined, the beams should then interfere with each other. No such interference was found in 1887 when he and Morley (1838-1928) tried. In 1907 Michelson won the Nobel Prize in Physics for this negative result.

41   George Fitzgerald (1851-1901) was born in Dublin and attended Trinity College, where he later became professor of natural philosophy. He is best known for his explanation in 1895 of the failure of the Michelson-Morley experiment to detect the ether. Fitzgerald suggested that the length of an object contracts in the direction in which it is travelling. Fitzgerald's length-contraction was the first indica-

tion that the velocity of light might be an ultimate limit to the speed of any moving body.

Hendrik Lorentz (1853-1928), a student and professor at Leyden University
in Holland (one of Toland's old academic haunts), elaborated on Fitzgerald's
work and showed that as an object speeds up, its mass enlarges, so that at the
speed of light its mass becomes infinite.

Einstein's Special Theory of Relativity said that all motion is relative to some
frame of reference, and that the velocity of light was a fundamental limit to the
speed of an object.

42 John Toland, *The Destiny of Rome* (London 1718), p. 7.
43 Michael Hunter, 'Science and Heterodoxy: An Early Modern Problem
    Reconsidered', in David Lindberg and Robert Westman (eds), *Reappraisals of the
    Scientific Revolution* (Cambridge University Press 1990), pp. 453-6.
44 P. Harrison, 'Newtonian Science, Miracles, and the Laws of Nature' in *Journal of
    the History of Ideas*, 56(4) (1995), pp. 531-3.
45 Jacob (1977-8), pp. 11-12.
46 Hall, p. 191.
47 Max Planck's fame rests upon his proposal in 1900 that energy is not infinitely
    subdivisible; rather, it exists in bundles or quanta of energy.
48 Albert Camus, *The Rebel* (Penguin, Harmondsworth, 1981 (1951)), p. 84.
49 Joseph Rotblat shared the 1995 Nobel Peace Prize with the Pugwash Conference
    on Science and World Affairs, of which he is president. That organization brings
    together scientists and politicians from East and West to discuss arms control and
    disarmament. Rotblat worked on the Manhattan Project at Los Alamos, where
    the atomic bomb was developed. When he realized that the target of the bomb
    was the Soviet Union and not Germany, he left the project. With Bertrand
    Russell, Albert Einstein and Linus Pauling, he laid the foundations of the
    Pugwash Conferences.

BIBLIOGRAPHY OF THE WORKS
OF JOHN TOLAND

It is difficult to ascertain when John Toland actually wrote much of what is listed below. Daniel (p.16) states: 'To depend heavily on the dates of publication [in analysing the development of Toland's thought] would be as unhelpful as to ignore them totally.' Nevertheless, providing both a list of published works and the full titles of these works by Toland in chronological order of publication is still helpful to those who are new to Toland, because it gives the newcomer a feel for the catholic tastes of this scholar and – as many of his works had a political impact in their time – helps us to form a clearer picture of the political and intellectual issues contemporary with Toland. Information on pseudonyms employed by Toland comes from Carabelli's book and from Daniel (p. 69, n.28).

Some scholars disagree about the authorship of some of the works listed below: Evans, Sullivan and Carabelli regard *Limitations* ... (1701) as written by Toland, for example, whereas Daniel excludes it from his Toland bibliography. From the quoted fragments in Evans (pp. 80-6), I sense the stylish pen of Toland behind it, so I have included it here. I am extremely grateful to Rhoda Rappaport for sending me an advance copy of her paper discussing the authorship of *Two Essays* ... (1695). She points out that Sullivan (1982) gives *Two Essays* an 'enthusiastic acceptance' as being authored by Toland. Professor Rappaport sifts through the evidence for Toland's authorship and concludes that 'Carabelli's conjecture [that Toland was the author] was based on feeble evidence'.

SOURCES

Carabelli, Giancarlo. 1975. *Tolandiana: Materiali Bibliografici per lo Studio dell'Opera e della Fortuna di John Toland (1670-1722)*.

Catalogue Général des livres imprimés de la Bibliothèque Nationale. Paris, 1964.

Catalogus Librorum Impressorum qui in Bibliotheca Collegii Sacrosanctae et individuae Trinitatis, Reginae Elizabethae, juxta Dublin., adservantur. Vol. 8. [TCD] Dublin, 1885.

Daniel, Stephen. 1981. *John Toland: His Methods, Manners and Mind.*

Evans, Robert Rees. 1991. *Pantheisticon: The Career of John Toland.*

Sullivan, Robert E. 1982. *John Toland and the Deist Controversy.*

Rappaport, Rhoda. 1997. 'Questions of Evidence: An Anonymous Tract Attributed to John Toland', in *Journal of the History of Ideas* (April 1997).

TOLAND'S WORKS

1692

Letter from Toland to Jean LeClerc on Daniel Williams's *Gospel Truth Stated and Vindicated.*

1695

Two Essays Sent in a Letter from Oxford to a Nobleman in London. The First concerning some Errors about the Creation, General Flood, and the Peopling of the World. In Two Parts. The Second concerning the Rise, Progress, and Destruction of Fables and Romances. [Pseudonym: 'L.P.']

1696

Christianity not Mysterious: or, a Treatise Shewing that there is nothing in the Gospel Contrary to Reason, Nor above it: And that no Christian Doctrine can be properly call'd a Mystery.

Davanzati, Bernardo. 1588. *A Discourse upon Coins.* [Trans., with a preface, by Toland.]

1697

An Apology for Mr. Toland, in a Letter from Himself to a Member of the House of Commons in Ireland [Septemb. 3. 1697], written the day before his Book was resolv'd to be burnt by the Committee of Religion, to which is prefix'd a Narrative containing the Occasion of the said Letter.

A Defence of Mr. Toland in a Letter to Himself.

A Lady's Religion. In a Letter to the Honourable my Lady Howard. By a Divine of the Church of England. With a prefatory Epistle to the same Lady, by a lay-Gentleman. [Pseudonym: 'Adeisadaemon' (meaning 'The Unsuperstitious Man' {Daniel, p. 111, n.37}).]

LeClerc, Jean. *A Treatise of the Causes of Incredulity. Wherein are examin'd the general Motives and Occasions which dispose Unbelievers to reject the Christian Religion. With Two Letters, containing a direct Proof of the Truth of Christianity.* [Trans., with a preface, by Toland.]

1698

A Letter to a Member of Parliament, shewing that a Restraint on the Press is inconsistent with the Protestant Religion, and dangerous to the Liberties of the Nation.

The Life of John Milton, Containing, Besides the History of His Works, Several Extraordinary Characters of Men and Books, Sects, Parties, and Opinions. In A Complete Collection of the Historical, Political, and Miscellaneous Works of John Milton. Both English and Latin. With som Papers never before Publish'd. Vol.1.

The Militia Reform'd; Or An Easy Scheme Of Furnishing England with a Constant Land-Force, capable to prevent or to subdue any Forein Power; and to maintain perpetual Quiet at Home, without endangering the Publick Liberty.

1699

Amyntor; Or A Defence of Milton's Life Containing I: A general Apology for all Writings of that kind; II: A Catalogue of Books attributed in the Primitive Times to Jesus Christ, his Apostles, and other eminent Persons, with several important Remarks and Observations relating to the Canon of Scripture; III: A Complete History of the Book Entitl'd Icon Basilike, proving Dr. Gauden, and not King Charles the First, to be the author of it: With an Answer to all the Facts alledg'd by Mr. Wagstaf to the contrary; and to the Exceptions made against my Lord Anglesey's Memorandum, Dr. Walker's Book, or Mrs. Gauden's Narrative, which last Piece is now the first Time publish'd at large.

Memoirs Of Denzil, Lord Holles, Baron of Ifield in Sussex, from the Year 1641 to 1648.

Memoirs of Lieutenant General Ludlow, The Third and Last Part. With A Collection of Original Papers, serving to confirm and illustrate many important Passages of this and the preceding Volumes. To which is, added, A Table to the whole Work.

Earl of Shaftesbury. *An Inquiry Concerning Virtue in Two Discourses.* [Published by Toland without Shaftesbury's permission; later republished in Vol. II of Shaftesbury's *Characteristicks* in 1711.]

1700

Clito: A Poem on the Force of Eloquence. [Pseudonym: 'Adeisadaemon' – see *A Lady's Religion*, 1697.]

The Life of James Harrington. In The Oceana of James Harrington, And His Other Works; Som whereof are now first publish'd from his own Manuscripts. The whole Collected, Methodiz'd, and Review'd, With An Exact Account of his Life Prefix'd, by John Toland.

1701

Anglia Libera: Or The Limitation and Succession of the Crown of England explain'd and asserted; As grounded On His Majesty's Speech; the Proceedings in Parliament; The Desires of the People; The Safety of our Religion; The Nature of our Constitution; The Balance of Europe; And The Rights of all Mankind.

The Art of Governing By Partys: Particularly, In Religion, in Politics, in Parlament, on the Bench, and in the Ministry; with the ill Effects of Partys on the People in general, the King in particular, and all our foren Affairs; as well as on our Credit and Trade, in Peace or War, &c.

Propositions for uniting the two East-India Companies: In A Letter To A Man of Quality, who desir'd the Opinion of a Gentleman not concern'd in either Company.

Limitations for the Next Foreign Successor, Or A New Saxon Race. Debated in a Conference betwixt two Gentlemen. Sent in a Letter to a Member of Parliament.

1702

Christianity not Mysterious.....with An Apology for him, in Relation to the Parliament of Ireland's ordering this Book to be Burnt.

I: Reasons for Addressing His Majesty to invite into England their Highnesses, the Electress Dowager and the Electoral Prince of Hanover. And Likewise, II: Reasons for Attainting and abjuring the pretended Prince of Wales, and all others pretending any Claim, Right, or Title from the late King James and Queen Mary. With Arguments for making a vigorous War against France.

Vindicius Liberius: Or Mr. Toland's Defence of himself, Against the late Lower House of Convocation, and Others; Wherein (Besides his Letters to the Prolocutor) Certain Passages of the Book, Intitul'd, Christianity not Mysterious, are Explain'd, and others Corrected: With A Full and clear Account of the Authors Principles relating to Church and State; And a Justification of the Whigs and Commonwealthsmen, against the Misrepresentations of all their Opposers.

1704

Boissat, Pierre de. *The Fables of Aesop With the Moral Reflections Of Monsieur Baudoin. To which is prefix'd by another Hand; The true Life of Aesop, by the most Learned and Noble Critick Monsieur de Meziriac, proving by unquestionable Authorities, that Aesop was an ingenious, eloquent and comely Person, a Courtier and Philosopher; contrary to the fabulous Relation of the Monk Plaundes, who makes him Stupid, Stammering, a Buffoon, and monstrously Deform'd.* [Trans., with a preface, by Toland.]

Letters To Serena, Containing: I: The Origin and Force of Prejudices; II: The History of the Soul's Immortality among the Heathens; III: The Origin of Idolatry, and Reasons of Heathenism; as also IV: A Letter to a Gentleman in Holland, showing Spinosa's System of Philosophy to be without any Principle or Foundation; V: Motion essential to Matter, in Answer to some Remarks by a Noble Friend on the 'Confutation of Spinosa'. To all which is Prefix'd: VI: A Preface, being a Letter to a Gentleman in London, sent together with the foregoing Dissertations and declaring the several Occasions of writing them.

1705

An Account Of The Courts of Prussia and Hanover; Sent to a Minister of State in Holland. In which are contain'd the Characters of the Elector of Hanover, now King of England; The Electoral Prince, Duke of Cambridge, and others of that Illustrious Family.

A Defence of her Majesty's Administration; particularly against the notorious forgeries and calumnies, with which his grace the Duke of Marlborough, and the Right Honourable Mr. Secretary Harley are scandalously defamed and aspersed in a late scurrilous Invective, entituled, 'A Letter to the author of the Memorial of the State of England'.

The Memorial of the State of England, In Vindication of the Queen, The Church, And The Administration; Design'd To rectify the mutual Mistakes of Protestants, And to unite their Affections in Defence of our Religion and Liberty.

The Ordnances, Statutes, And Privileges Of The Royal Academy, Erected by his Majesty the King of Prussia, in his Capital City of Berlin. [Trans. by Toland.]

Socianism truly Stated, Being An Example of fair Dealing in all Theological Controversys. To which is prefixt, Indifference in Disputes: Recommended by a Pantheist to an Orthodox Friend.

Some Plain Observations Recommended to the Consideration of every Honest English-Man; Especially to the Electors of Parliament-Members.

1707

The Declaration Lately Publish'd, In Favour of his Protestant Subjects, By The Elector Palatine; And notify'd to her Majesty. To which is prefix'd, An Impartial Account of the Causes of those Innovations and grievances about religion, which are now so happily redress'd by his Electoral Highness.

Schiner, Matthew Cardinal. *A Phillipick Oration to Incite the English against the French; But especially To prevent the treating of a Peace with them too soon after they are beaten: Offer'd to the Privy-Council Of England, In the Year of Christ, 1514. By an uncertain Author Who was not for pareing the Nails, but quite plucking out the Claws of the French.* [Trans. by Toland.]

1709

Adeisadaemon, Sive Titus Livius A Superstitione vindicatus. In qua Dissertatione probatur, Livium Historicum in Sacris, Prodigiis & Ostentis Romanorum enarrandis, haudquaquam fuisse credulum aut superstitiosum; ipsamque Superstitionem non minus Reipublicae (si non magis) exitiosam esse quam purum putum Athiesmum. Annexae sunt ejustem Origines Judaicae. [See *A Lady's Religion*, 1697.]

Origines Judicae, sive Strabonis de Moyse et religione judaica historia breviter illustrata. [See above.]

1710

The Jacobitism, Perjury, And Popery Of High-Church Priests.

The Judgement Of K. James the First, And King Charles the First, Against Non-Resistance, Discover'd by their own Letters, and now offer'd to the Consideration of Dr. Sacherevell and his Party.

Reflections on Dr. Sacheverells Sermon Preach'd at St. Paul's, Nov.5, 1709: In A Letter From An English-Man To An Hollander, Lately Published in French in Holland, and translat'd into English, to let the world know how Dr. Sacheverell's Case is represented Abroad.

1711

The Description Of Epsom, With The Humors and Politicks of the Place: In A Letter To Eudoxa. There is added a Translation of Four Letters out of Pliny. [Pseudonym: 'Britto-Batavus'.]

High-Church Display'd: Being A Compleat History Of The Affair Of Dr. Sacheverel, In its Origin, Progress, and Consequences. In several Letters to an English Gentlemen at the Court of Hanover. With an alphabetical Index, by which at one View any Particular in the Doctor's History and Tryal may be found.

1712

Cicero Illustratus, Dissertatio Philologico-Critica: Sive Consilium de toto edendo Cicerone, alia planè methodo quom hactenus unquam factum. [See also 1726.]

Her Majesty's Reasons For Creating the Electoral Prince of Hanover A Peer of this Realm: Or, The Preamble to His Patent As Duke of Cambridge. In Latin and English, With Remarks upon the same.

Sophia Charlotte of Prussia. *A Letter Against Popery: Particularly, against admitting the Authority of Fathers or Councils in Controversies of Religion; By Sophia Charlotte The late Queen of Prussia. Being An answer to a Letter written to her Majesty by Father Vota, an Italian Jesuit, Confessor to King Augustus. There is prefixt by the Publisher, a Letter containing the occasion of the Queen's writing, and an apology for the Church of England.* [Dedicatory letter by Toland – pseudonym: 'J. Londat'.]

1713

An Appeal To Honest People Against Wicked Priests: Or, The very Heathen Laity's

Declarations for Civil Disobedience and Liberty of Conscience, contrary to the Rebellious and Persecuting Principles of some of the Old Christian Clergy; With an Application to the Corrupt Part of the Priests of this present Time, publish'd on Occasion of Dr. Sacheverell's last Sermon. [Pseudonym: 'Hierophilus']

Dunkirk Or Dover, Or, The Queen's Honour, The Nation's Safety, The Liberties of Europe, And The Peace of the World, All at Stake till that Fort and Port be totally demolish'd by the French.

1714

The Art of Restoring; Or, The Piety and Probity Of General Monk In bringing about The Last Restoration, Evidenc'd from his own Authentic Letters: With a Just Account of Sir Roger [Harley], who runs the Parallel as far as he can. In a Letter To A Minister of State, at the Court of Vienna.

Cicero, Quintus Tullius. *The Art of Canvassing At Elections, Perfect in all Respects; And Highly necessary to be understood by the Electors, no less than by the Candidates: Written Near two thousand years ago, for the use of the greatest Scholar, and most consummate States-man then in the world; And now Publish'd in the English tongue, against the ensuing Election of Parliament.* [Trans., with a preface, by Toland.]

The Funeral Elogy And Character Of her Royal Highness, the late Princess Sophia: With the Explication of her Consecration Medal, Written Originally in Latine: translated into English and further illustrated by Mr. Toland, Who has Added the Character of the King, the Prince, and the Princess.

The Grand Mystery Laid Open: Namely, By dividing of the Protestants to weaken the Hanover Succession, and by defeating the Succession to extirpate the Protestant Religion. To which is added, The Sacredness of Parliamentary Securities: Against those, Who wou'd indirectly this Year, or more directly the next (if they live so long) attack the Publick Funds.

Monk, George. *A Collection Of Letters Written by His Excellency General George Monk, Afterwards Duke of Albemarle, Relating to the restoration of the Royal Family. With An Introduction, proving by incontestable Evidence, that Monk had projected that Restoration in Scotland; against the Cavils of those who wou'd rob him of the Merit of this Action.* [Edited, with an introduction, by Toland.]

The Reasons and Necessity Of The Duke of Cambridge's Coming To, and Residing In Great Britain, Argu'd from the present Posture of Affairs. To which is Prefix'd the Preamble to the Duke of Cambridge's Patent.

Reasons For Naturalizing The Jews In Great Britain and Ireland, On the same foot with all other Nations. Containing also, A Defence of the Jews Against All vulgar Prejudices in all Countries.

1717

The State Anatomy Of Great Britain, Containing A Particular account of its several Interests and Parties, their bent and genius; and what each of them, with all the rest of Europe, may hope or fear from the Reign and Family of King George. Being A Memorial sent by an intimate friend to a Foreign Minister, lately nominated to come for the Court of England. [Pseudonym: 'Patricola.']

The Second Part Of The State Anatom, &c., Containing A short Vindication of the former Part, against the Misrepresentations of the Ignorant or the Malicious, especially relating to our Ministers of state and to Foreigners; with some Reflections on the design'd Clamor against the Army, and on the Suedish Conspiracy. Also, Letters to his Grace, the late Archbishop of Canterbury, and to the Dissenting Ministers of all denominations, in the year 1705-6, about a General Toleration, with some of their Answers to the Author: Who Now offers to Publick Consideration, what was then transacted for Private Satisfaction; together with a Letter from their High-Mightinesses the States-General of the United Provinces, on the same Subject.

1718

The Destiny Of Rome: Or, The Probability of the Speedy and Final Destruction of the Pope. Concluded Partly, from natural Reasons, and political Observations; and partly, on Occasion of the famous Prophesy of St. Malachy, Archbishop of Armagh, in the XIIth Century: Which Curious Piece, Containing Emblematical Characters of all the Popes, from his own Time to the utter Extirpation of them, is not only here entirely publish'd; but likewise set in a much clearer Light, than has hitherto been done. In a Letter to a Divine of the Church of England, From a Divine of the Church of the First-born. [Pseudonym: 'X.Z.']

Nazarenus: Or Jewish, Gentile, and Mahometan Christianity. Containing I: The history of the antient History of Barnabas, and the modern Gospel of the Mahometans, attributed to the same Apostle: this last Gospel being now first made known among Christians. Also II: The Original Plan of Christianity occasionally explain'd in the history of the Nazarens, whereby diverse Controversies about this divine (but highly perverted) institutio may be happily terminated. With III: The relation of an Irish Manuscript of the Four Gospels, as likewise a Summary of the antient Irish Christianity and the reality of the Keldees (an order of Lay-religious) against the two last Bishops of Worcester. {Note 1: Inside *Nazarenus* this section is called *Letter II: An Account Of An Irish Manuscript Of The Four Gospels; With A Summary of the ancient Irish Christianity, before the Papal Corruptions and Usurpations: And The reality of the Keldees (an order of Lay Religious) against the two last Bishops of Worcester*} {Note 2: In the 1818 edition, the above title in Note 1 is added to: ... .*before the Papal Corruptions and Usurpations of the Church of Rome had enslaved both their Mind and Body.*} *Appendix containing:* I: Two Problems, historical, political, and theological, concerning the Jewish Nation and Religion. II: A further account of the Mahometan Gospel of Barnabas, by M. de la Monnoye of the French Academy. III: Queries fit to be sent to any curious and intelligent Christians, residing or travelling in Mahometan Countries; with proper directions and cautions in order to procure satisfactory answers. [Pseudonym of Toland's French version: 'Pantheus'.]

1720

Pantheisticon: Sive Formula Celebrandae Sodalitatis Socraticae, In Tres Particulas Divisa, Quae Pantheistarum sive Sodalium, Continent: I: Mores et Axiomata: II: Numen et Philosophiam: III: Libertatem, et non fallentem Legem, Neque fallendam. Praemittur De antiquis et Novis Eruditorum Sodalitatibus, Ut et de Universo infinito et aeterno,

Diatriba. Subjicitur De duplici Pantheistarum Philosophia sequenda, Ac de Viri optimi et ornatissimi idea, Dissertatiuncula. – *Cosmopoli.* [Pseudonym: 'Janus Junius Eoganesius' (Toland signs himself 'Philogathus' in a letter to Barnum Goode commenting on his pseudonym in the *Pantheisticon*).]

Reasons Most humbly offer'd to the Honourable House of Commons, Why The Bill sent down to them From the Most Honourable House of Lords, Entitul'd, An Act for the better Securing the Dependency of the Kingdom of Ireland upon the Crown of Great-Britain, Shou'd not Pass into a Law.

A Short Essay Upon Lying, Or A Defence of a Reverend Dignitary, who suffers under the Persecution of Mr. Toland, for a Lapsus Calami.

Tetradymus. Containing I: 'Hodegus'; or the Pillar of Cloud and Fire, that Guided the Israelites in the Wilderness, not Miraculous, but, as faithfully related in Exodus, a thing equally practis'd by other nations, and in those places not onely useful but necessary; II: 'Clidophorous'; or of the Exoteric and Esoteric Philosophy, that is, of the External and Internal Doctrine of the antients: the one open and public, accomodated to popular Prejudices and the establish'd Religions; the other private and secret, wherein, to the few capable and discrete, was taught the real Truth script of all disguises; III: 'Hypatia': or the history of a most beautiful, most virtuous, most learned and every way accomplish'd Lady; who was torn to pieces by the Clergy of Alexandria, to gratify the pride, emulation, and cruelty of their archbishop Cyril, commonly but undeservedly stil'd Saint Cyril. IV: 'Mangoneutes': being a defence of Nazarenus, address'd to the right reverend John, lord Bishop of London; against his Lordship's Chaplain Dr. Mangey, his Dedicator Mr. Patterson, and (who ought to have been nam'd first) the Reverend Dr. Brett, once belonging to his Lordship's Church.

1721

Shaftesbury, 3rd Earl of. *Letters From The Right Honourable The Late Earl of Shaftesbury To Robert Molesworth, Esq.; Now the Lord Viscount of that Name. With Two Letters written by the late Sir John Cropley. To which is prefix'd A large Introduction by the Editor.* [Toland published these without Molesworth's permission, Shaftesbury having died in 1713; pseudonym: 'Z.Z.']

1726

A Collection Of Several Pieces Of Mr. John Toland, Now first publish'd from his Original Manuscripts: With Some Memoirs of his Life and Writings.

Vol.1: I: Some Memoirs Of The Life And Writings Of Mr. John Toland: In A Letter To S*** B*** L***. II: An Elegy On the Late ingenious Mr. Toland. III: A Specimen Of The Critical History Of The Celtic Religion And Learning: Containing An Account of the Druids, or the Priests and Judges; of the Vaids, or the Diviners and Physicians; and of the Bards, or the Poets and Heralds of the antient Gauls, Britons, Irish and Scots. With The History of Arabis the Hyperborean, Priest of the Sun. In Three Letters To The Right Honourable The Lord Viscount Molesworth. Mr. Tate's Questions About The Druids And Other Brittish Antiquities, With Mr. Jones's Answer To Them. A Specimen Of The Armorican Language. IV: Cicero Illustratus [see 1712]. *V: Conjectura Verosimilis, De Prima Typographiae Inventione. Viro nobilissimo, tam antiqu, prosapi, quom multiplici doctrina spectabili, Hugoni*

Wrottesleio Armigero, Hospicii Lincolniensis Socio Dignissimo, S.P.D. Joannes Tolandus. VI: De Genere, Loco, Et Tempore Mortis Jordani Bruni Nolani. Viro Illustrissimo Baroni Hohendorfio, S.P.D. Joannes Tolandus. VII: An Account Of Jordano Bruno's Book Of the infinite Universe and innumerable Worlds: In five Dialogues: Written by himself in a Dedication of the said Book to the Lord Castelnau, Ambassador from the French King to Queen Elizabeth. Translated from the Original Italian, printed in the Year 1514. VIII: A Catalogue Of Books Mention'd by the Fathers and other ancient Writers, as truly or falsely ascrib'd to Jesus Christ, his Apostles, and other eminent Persons; or of such Books as do immediately concern the same: some of which Pieces are still extant entire, most of which shall be markt in their places; tho the fragments only of the greatest part remain, and but the bare Titles of oth-ers. To A Person Of Quality In Holland IX: The Secret History Of The South-Sea Scheme [not by J.T., but the MS had been corrected with his own hand]. *X: The Scheme, or Practical Model, Of A National Bank; to be commenc'd and erected by political Art alone, going, not upon visionary Calculations, or private, mercenary, and temporary Views: but upon such stated rules and easy methods, truly natural, public, and perpetual, as cannot fail effecting it; yet without any stock in Cash, Subscriptions of mony, or collateral Security in Lands. Written by a Gentleman, who died in the Year 1708. To The Right Honourable ***.*

Vol.2: *I: A Letter Concerning The Roman Education. II: The Fabulous death Of Atilius Regulus: Or, A dissertation proving the receiv'd History of the tragical Death of Marcus Atilius Regulus the Roman Consul, to be a Fable. III: Some Letters Of Pliny Translated into English to Mr. ***. IV: A New Description Of Epsom, With The Humours and Politicks of the Place: in a Letter to Eudoxa. V: The Primitive Constitution Of The Christian Church, With an Account of the principal Controversies about Church-Government, which at present divide the Christian World. VI: A Project Of A Journal Intended to be published weekly. VII:Two Memorials for the Earl of ***. VIII: A Memorial presented to a Minister of State. IX: A Memorial concerning England in 1714. X: Physic without Physicians: In a Letter to B*** G***, Esq. XI: Fifty Two Letters to Various Persons. XII: An Appendix, Containing Some Pieces Found Among Mr.Toland's Papers: 1: Of The Immateriality Of The Soul, And Its Distinction From The Body: by Mr. Benjamin Bayly, M.A. 2: Critical Remarks Upon Mr. Toland's Book, Entitled Nazarenus. 3: Annotatiuncolae Subitaneae ad Librum De Christianismo Mysteriis carente: Conscriptae 8 Augusti 1701.* [Edited by Pierre Des Maizeaux.]

1751

Pantheisticon: or, the Form of Celebrating the Socratic Society. [Anonymous translation.]

EXPLANATION OF SOME OF TOLAND'S PSEUDONYMS

Adeisadaemon: 'The Unsuperstitious Man.'

Britto-Batavus: 'The Briton living in Holland.' Batavia is an ancient name for the area around the mouth of the Rhine. In 1619 the Dutch founded Batavia in Java, now better known as Jakarta. With the arrival of a French revolutionary army in 1795 into the United Provinces of the Netherlands (as the Dutch Republic was then known), the Batavian Republic was set up.

Janus Junius Eoganesius: 'Janus Junius' is supposedly the name given to Toland when he was christened a Catholic in Inishowen. Alan Harrison suggests that it is far more likely to have been 'Seán Eoin'. In his usage of Janus Junius, Toland may be representing himself as a trickster: Janus being the two-faced God, with Junius referring to Junius Brutus, the reputed founder of the Roman Republic. 'Eoganesius' in all likelihood refers to Inishowen which in Irish is 'Inis Eoghain'. Thus Toland may be calling himself 'the two-faced classical republican from Inishowen'.

J. Londat: 'Londat' is an anagram of 'Toland'.

Patricola: 'The lay-priest' or 'hedge-priest'. Toland may be regarding himself as head of a pantheist sect. Alternatively, he may be making an oblique reference to the workings of the Penal Laws in Ireland: priests were typically forced to say mass in the open. Many districts of Ireland have a 'mass rock' as a local landmark.

NOTES ON CONTRIBUTORS

DAVID BERMAN is a Professor of Philosophy at Trinity College, Dublin.

DESMOND M. CLARKE is an Associate Professor of Philosophy at University College Cork.

STEPHEN H. DANIEL is a Professor of Philosophy at Texas A&M University.

ALAN HARRISON is a Lecturer in Modern Irish at University College Dublin.

RICHARD KEARNEY is a Professor of Philosophy at University College Dublin.

PHILIP MCGUINNESS is a writer and a research student at the Department of Pure and Applied Physics, Queen's University, Belfast.